P9-DGY-367

DIEFENBAKER'S WORLD
A POPULIST IN FOREIGN AFFAIRS

Diefenbaker's World

A POPULIST IN FOREIGN AFFAIRS

H. BASIL ROBINSON

UNIVERSITY OF TORONTO PRESS
TORONTO BUFFALO LONDON

© University of Toronto Press 1989
Toronto   Buffalo   London
Printed in Canada

ISBN 0-8020-2678-8

Printed on acid-free paper

Canadian Cataloguing in Publication Data

Robinson, H. Basil (Henry Basil), 1919–
  Diefenbaker's world

Bibliography: p.
Includes index.
ISBN 0-8020-2678-8

1. Diefenbaker, John G., 1895-1979. 2. Canada –
Foreign relations – 1945-   . I. Title.

FC615.R6 1989   327.71   C88-094700-4
F1034.2.R6 1989

This book has been published with the help of
the Canada Council and the Ontario Arts Council
under their block grant programs.

Dedicated to my family
and to the memory of our friend
John W. Holmes

Contents

Preface

When John George Diefenbaker became Canada's thirteenth prime minister in June 1957, it was the first time he had been in government office. Since his election to the House of Commons in 1940, his reputation as an opposition member of parliament had been built largely on his powers of criticism and on a compelling speaking style. He had not been required to deal with the ambiguities and the difficult choices that have to be faced by those who are elected to govern. Now that he was in power, what was to be expected of him?

The election had brought him into office as the leader of a minority government. Elated as he was with the results, he was determined to build on his public support so that, when circumstances favoured the holding of another election, he could be returned to power with a clear majority in the House of Commons. It was obvious that, in the meantime, Canadian foreign policy would be conducted in accordance with his domestic political strategy.

During the summer of 1957 the new government and the civil service were getting to know each other. Some people had expected Diefenbaker to make substantial changes in the senior levels of the service. Partly because of an instinctive caution in personnel matters and partly because the senior civil servants quickly made themselves useful to their ministers, he resisted the temptation to move in that direction. It was no secret, however, that he was uneasy about the Department of External Affairs, evidently because some of its leading figures had long-standing professional and personal associations with L.B. Pearson, now the leader of the Liberal opposition, and other members of previous Liberal governments. Although Diefenbaker was known to some members of the department through his travels abroad, he was regarded as something of a puzzle. His opinions on foreign affairs were always expressed in emphatic language that attracted press attention, but it was far from clear what they would really add up to when policy matters had to be decided.

It was during this time of transition and adaptation that I was assigned to the Prime Minister's Office by the Department of External Affairs, in August 1957. I had been in the department for twelve years, having entered in 1945 with the first wave of diplomat recruits from the armed forces at the end of the war. Of those twelve years, I had spent two (from 1946 to 1948) at Oxford University; I had had a total of five years at the department's headquarters in the East Block of the Parliament Buildings in Ottawa; and five years abroad, three in London at Canada House and two at the Canadian embassy in Paris. My wife Elizabeth Gooderham and I were married in Ottawa in 1950. She had joined External Affairs in 1948 on graduating from Queen's University after a wartime spell in the RCAF. By 1956, when we were posted back to Ottawa from Paris, our family had grown to include Katharine and David, both born in London, and Brigitte Ann, in Paris. In August 1957, three weeks before I reported to the PMO, our fourth child, Geoff, was born.

My appointment was arranged between R.B. Bryce, the secretary to the cabinet, and Jules Léger, then the undersecretary of state for external affairs, the most senior official in the department. (By the term 'official' I mean what is now often referred to as 'bureaucrat,' a career member of the civil service, thus not, like politicians, exposed to the vicissitudes of elections every few years.) According to a memo from Bryce to Léger, the appointment was to be 'for several months ... to assist the Prime Minister in completing the organization of his Office and the liaison between it and the Department.' In performing these functions, I was to report directly to and receive instructions from the prime minister. He had already attended his first meeting of Commonwealth prime ministers and, having not yet appointed a minister for external affairs, was becoming more involved than he wanted to be in the day-to-day conduct of the government's business in international matters. He was persuaded of the need to have someone nearby to organize the flow of information and advice from External Affairs, to help with visiting celebrities and foreign diplomats, and to provide everyday support. That, in summary, was to be my job.

I remember being quite shocked at the prospect. I had never met the new prime minister and had no idea what he would be like to work for. It happened that, in the position I was leaving – head of the Middle East Division of the department – I had been closely involved in providing advice and support for Pearson who, as secretary of state for external affairs in the St Laurent government, had directed Canadian policy in the Suez crisis late in 1956. At that time, I had felt no sympathy for Diefenbaker's contention that Canada had let down its British and French allies, and I shared the general regret at the departure of Pearson as the department's minister. So I thought it ironic and perhaps a little hazardous to be entering Diefenbaker's service. I did not, however, think of objecting. Like most others in the civil service at that time, I welcomed the opportunity to demonstrate that we could serve a Progressive Conservative government as well as we had the Liberals.

It had been made clear to me before the assignment began that this was one of those brave experiments which could be said to have served its purpose if, after a short time, the prime minister did not like the way it was turning out. It was stipulated, too, that the new position would not be given any special title 'unless experience showed that one was necessary.'

In view of all this, I was not suffering from over-confidence when I made my introductory call on the prime minister. I had wondered if he would want to talk about the Suez crisis and its aftermath. Fortunately he did not. He asked me about my early years in Vancouver, my education, wartime service, and in some detail about my family. Though obviously pressed for time, he was very courteous and generally made me feel more at ease than I had expected. I remember, however, being struck by the penetrating force of his eyes, as if he were directing them to read me. He did not get into foreign policy subjects and reserved until later his thoughts on the service he expected from the department. The only guidance he gave me was to use my own judgment in bringing 'stuff' to him.

With some trepidation I began the new job in the last week of August. On the first few occasions I accompanied Jules Léger to his periodic sessions with the prime minister. One problem about these sessions was that Diefenbaker always seemed to have something else more urgent on his mind. That was why Léger had concluded that the system might work better if someone were continually available at the prime minister's call to provide a channel of information and advice from External Affairs and a ready means of getting his requirements complied with. He wanted speech material and briefing for the daily question period in parliament. When he was away from Ottawa, he wanted to be kept fully up to date on international developments and to be given advice on what might be said publicly about them. The shareholders of Bell Telephone benefited accordingly. While access was never a problem, the time available was frequently short and, in the first few weeks, it was exceptional to have an uninterrupted quarter of an hour. Priority items might use up the available time, with the result that his reactions and decisions were often delayed and the agenda for the next meeting grew longer. Often he spent the whole session telling wonderful political stories. Meanwhile, the foreign diplomats were impatiently waiting their turn to pay calls on him, and their claims on his time were not easy to divert as long as he was acting as his own minister of external affairs.

I had hardly been launched on my new functions when signs began to appear that the prime minister was agonizing over the appointment of a secretary of state for external affairs. What precipitated things was his concern that unless he made an appointment by the time the UN General Assembly opened in mid-September, he might have to take time to attend the Assembly himself. His mind was canvassing the possibilities and, from his unguarded comments, it was quite clear that he was searching for a candidate who would, as it were, be 'worthy' of taking over from Pearson. Of the 'inside' possibilities, Roland Michener was 'too close to Pearson,' and Donald Fleming and Davie Fulton were in effect disqualified because they had opposed Diefenbaker for the party leadership and might still have aspirations. When it was necessary to give someone an explanation for their exclusion from the list, he would say that Fleming was needed in Finance and Fulton had the makings of a great minister of justice. I was startled by the candour with which he spoke on these and other current matters. Only later did I realize that he had a habit of testing the discretion of those around him.

There was a general feeling of relief tinged with surprise when the appointment of Dr Sidney Smith, president of the University of Toronto, as secretary of state for external affairs was announced on 13 September. Among more momentous things, this raised the question whether a full-time liaison officer from External Affairs was any longer needed in the Prime Minister's Office. A memorandum of 16 September from Bryce recorded Diefenbaker's agreement that I should carry on in his office for the next two months while the new minister would be busy at the United Nations and in seeking a seat in parliament at a by-election. I was to be 'appointed to the staff of the Secretary of State for External Affairs ... and should expect to carry on with Mr. Smith after the next several months ... when he settles down to full-time activity in Ottawa.' The assumption was that the prime minister's needs would probably diminish and could be served from the minister's office.

I suppose in hindsight that the flaws in this arrangement should have been foreseen. In condensed form, they were simply that the prime minister's needs did not diminish; in fact, they increased as he became more involved with international issues and as he grew accustomed to the material he was receiving from the Department of External Affairs. And Sidney Smith's needs and difficulties in taking hold were far greater than had been anticipated. From his point of view I am sure it was not a satisfactory arrangement. From my standpoint, the uncomfortable experience of the following year bore out the impossibility of serving two masters. One might add that the saying applies with particular force when one of them happens to be prime minister.

After just over a year, the minister's need for increased full-time staff support at last became apparent to the department and, late in 1958, the position I had been occupying was divided into two. Ross Campbell, a friend and colleague from External Affairs, became special assistant to the minister and I returned to full-time service with the prime minister. I remained with him until after the federal election of June 1962, when I went to Washington as no. 2 in the Canadian embassy. Thus, for the last ten months of Diefenbaker's term of office as prime minister, which ended in April 1963, my viewpoint was somewhat distanced but equally instructive, since the job of representing him and his government in Washington at that time had its own excitement and trials.

In writing this memoir, my point of departure has been that John Diefenbaker is a controversial and complex figure, and that, in forming their judgments about him, historians, students, and others should have as much first-hand evidence as possible. I confess to a certain sympathy with him, but I have not set out to prove or disprove a particular thesis. My aim is to contribute to an understanding of him by examining his attitudes and role in international affairs during his years as prime minister.

I had some difficulty in deciding how the book might best be organized. Should it be divided according to a number of major themes (the Commonwealth, nuclear weapons policy, US-Canadian relations, etc.) or on a chronological basis? I chose to stick as closely as possible to the order in which things happened. Not only did I find the material easier to organize in that way, but I could count on the flow of international events to supply context within which Diefenbaker's reactions and decisions on particular matters could be more readily understood and judged. I have not attempted to stray from international into domestic affairs, although I have tried to call attention briefly to major domestic happenings when they seemed to have some bearing on the way in which international problems were handled.

I should emphasize that this account does not pretend to be an all-embracing history of Diefenbaker's decisions and activities in the foreign policy field. I have concentrated on the major issues in which I was in some way involved, but there are numerous subjects and events which, because of limitations on space, have had to be omitted. Among these are some of his travels, notably to Mexico, Ireland, Northern Ireland, and Japan, in all of which he and his constantly supportive wife Olive made many friends for Canada and refreshed themselves for trials to come. Inevitably, too, it has not been possible to include more than a few of the most important of the visits to Ottawa of Commonwealth and foreign VIPs. Apart from these omissions, many important but more specialized subjects – in the economic and legal fields, for example – are not dealt with, in part because I had little or no role in shaping them or presenting them to the prime minister.

Many people who observed or took some direct part in the Diefenbaker years will find episodes omitted, individuals unmentioned, and tales inadequately told in this account. To them I can only say that one has to stop somewhere and that this is essentially one man's perspective and, thus, necessarily partial and subjective.

Acknowledgments

In preparing this book, I have drawn on notes and memos written at the time, on correspondence with family and friends, on a personal diary which I kept for most of the Diefenbaker period, and on my own impressions and recollections. In the diary, Mr Diefenbaker shares the daily space with my young family and their doings. I have quoted from it more freely in Part Five because at that stage the daily entries were somewhat more detailed, and also because it seemed the only way to capture the pace and the atmosphere of the frantic pre-election months in the spring of 1962.

I have consulted many people. It has been especially helpful to talk with politicians and others who took a prominent part in the events described. I am particularly indebted to Howard Green, Davie Fulton, and Douglas Harkness who were generous in answering questions and who gave me permission to examine their confidential papers. Bill Hamilton gave me shrewd reflections on personalities and proceedings. Through Paul Martin and Jack Pickersgill I saw the picture from the Liberal point of view. R.B. Bryce, secretary to the cabinet throughout the period, and Bunny Pound, Mr Diefenbaker's private secretary, read drafts of the manuscript and gave me valuable comments which I have done my best to reflect.

Several other friends and colleagues have read all or some chapters. Those on whom I repeatedly imposed in this or other ways are John Holmes, Arthur Blanchette, Ralph Collins, Jack Granatstein, Norman Hillmer, Davie Fulton, Ross Campbell, and most often and most heavily, John Hilliker, head of the historical section of the Department of External Affairs. Jim McCardle, Geoffrey Pearson, I. Norman Smith, Peyton Lyon, and Don Page commented helpfully on individual chapters. John English and Alex Inglis were encouraging at crucial times. My wife Elizabeth, who had to read successive drafts of everything, was encouraging throughout. The same goes for our sons David and Geoffrey, who gave candid advice without making me feel that it was desperately needed.

Conversations with three American friends, Louise and Willis Armstrong and Rufus Smith, helped me greatly by supplying the indispensable perspective of the US embassy in Ottawa and the State Department in Washington. Other Canadian friends with whom I had particularly helpful discussions or correspondence include Jim Barker, Bill Barton, Yvon Beaulne, Allan Blakeney, Dacre Cole, R.I.K. Davidson, Bev Dewar, Orme Dier, Jean Fournier, Sidney Freifeld, Douglas Fullerton, David Golden, Gowan Guest, George Ignatieff, Douglas LePan, Mary Macdonald, Ross Martin, Jack McCordick, Russ McKinney, Arthur Menzies, Frank Miller, Frances and Herb Moran, Geoff Murray, Jim Nutt, Sydney Pierce, Peter Roberts, Charles Ritchie, Ed Ritchie, Ben Rogers, Arnold Smith, John Starnes, Gerry Stoner, and Bruce Williams, all of them actors on one or another part of the stage between 1957 and 1963.

With regard to documentary sources, I wish to thank the various institutions listed in the bibliography. I am also indebted to a number of people for making it possible for me to examine papers of special interest. These are Mrs N.A. Robertson, Madame Jules Léger, Madame Marcel Cadieux, Professor R.H. Roy, Mrs Mary Louise (Connell) Hose, and Colonel R.L. Raymont. I am also very grateful to the Reverend Livingston T. Merchant Jr for authorizing me to include certain quotations and citations from his father's papers.

Absorbing information is one thing; it is quite another to put it all together in a book. In this regard I wish to mention in particular Roberta M. Styran, whose discerning advice at an early stage helped me to shape an unwieldy mass of material, and Rosemary Shipton, who gave me sensitive and skilful guidance in preparing the book for publication. I have also been most fortunate from the outset in having first-rate secretarial assistance from Louise Arnold. I take this opportunity to thank the Department of External Affairs for allowing me office space and facilities during the research and writing of this book. Finally, I acknowledge with appreciation the financial assistance received from the Explorations Program of the Canada Council and the Research Grants Program of the Social Sciences and Humanities Research Council. Grants from these agencies made it very much easier to meet the expenses involved in undertaking this work.

Abbreviations

DEA	Department of External Affairs
DHist, DND	Directorate of History, Department of National Defence
EEC	European Economic Community
EFTA	European Free Trade Area (or Association)
GATT	General Agreement on Tariffs and Trade
HBR Papers	Author's Papers
HBR Diary	Author's Diary
ICBM	Intercontinental ballistic missile
IRBM	Intermediate range ballistic missile
NA	National Archives of Canada
NATO	North Atlantic Treaty Organization
NORAD	North American Air Defence Command
OAS	Organization of American States
OECD	Organization for Economic Cooperation and Development
POF	Presidential Office Files, J.F. Kennedy Library
RCAF	Royal Canadian Air Force
SAC	(US) Strategic Air Command
SACEUR	Supreme Allied Commander Europe
SACLANT	Supreme Allied Commander Atlantic
SSEA	Secretary of State for External Affairs
UAR	United Arab Republic
UN	United Nations
UNOGIL	United Nations Observer Group in Lebanon
USAF	United States Air Force
USSEA	Undersecretary of State for External Affairs

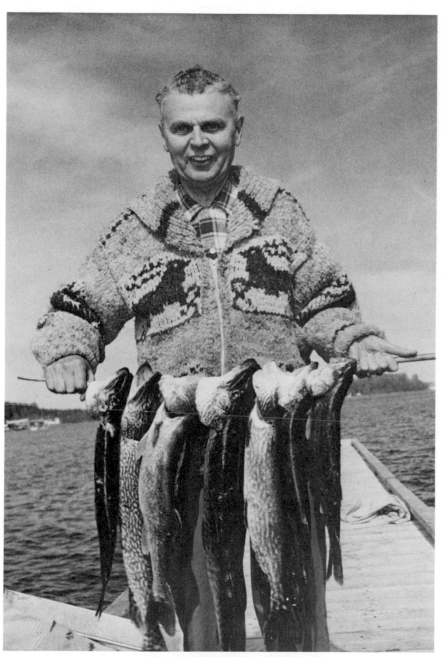

In his element, at Lac La Ronge,
Saskatchewan, July 1957

A cordial moment. The Diefenbakers with L.B. Pearson
at Government House, Ottawa, 14 January 1958, the night before Pearson
became leader of the Liberal party

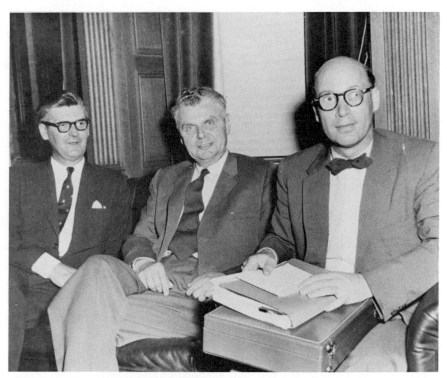

With Jules Léger (left), undersecretary of state for external affairs,
and R.B. Bryce, secretary to the cabinet,
soon after taking office in June 1957

Sidney Smith, soon after taking over as
secretary of state for external affairs, 1957

Norman A. Robertson, as high commissioner
in London, 1955

With Prime Minister Macmillan at Oxford University

With President de Gaulle, Governor General and Madame Vanier,
and Mrs Diefenbaker, Ottawa, April 1960

With Chancellor Adenauer and Sidney Smith
at the NATO Summit Meeting, Paris, 1957

The Diefenbakers with President Ayub Khan
of Pakistan, November 1958

With Prime Minister Nehru in New Delhi,
November 1958

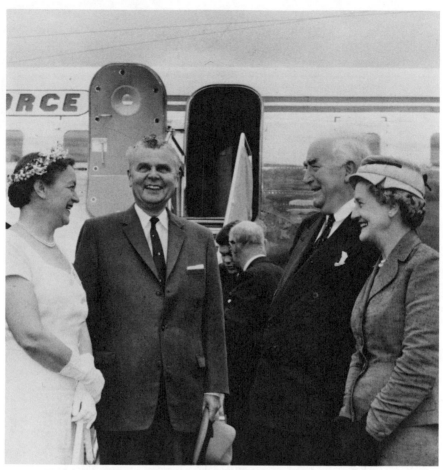

The Diefenbakers met by Prime Minister and Dame Pattie Menzies,
Canberra, December 1958

Canada's 'Explorer' in orbit

'Get lots of practise, there are some tigers to ride when you get home!'

'Mr. Diefenbaker – I presume?'

'Any comments, gentlemen?'

With Governor General Vincent Massey and Howard C. Green at Green's
swearing-in as secretary of state for external affairs

Celebrating his induction into the Kainai chieftainship
as Chief Many Spotted Horses at Beebe Flats, Alberta,
June 1960, with Mrs James Gladstone

With President and Mrs Kennedy, Governor General Vanier,
and Mrs Diefenbaker, Ottawa, May 1961

Diefenbaker with the author at a press conference,
Singapore, November 1958

PART ONE

First Encounters

JUNE 1957 TO
MARCH 1958

1

Settling In

In 1957 the Second World War seemed well behind, yet it still placed its imprint on world politics. Wartime leaders held political office in many countries, not least in the United States where Dwight D. Eisenhower was in his second presidential term. In Britain, after the humiliating adventure of Suez, Harold Macmillan had taken over from Anthony Eden. In France, General Charles de Gaulle had yet to stage his second coming. Western Europe was struggling towards unity – or something like it.

Josef Stalin had died, but in Eastern Europe Soviet power held complete sway. Although the Cold War still personified the climate of East-West relations, the United States and the USSR, leading powers of NATO and the Warsaw Pact, had at least begun to talk. And disarmament diplomacy was being conducted more by negotiation than by megaphone.

But the bomb had become the badge of national power. Britain and France, their colonies graduating to political independence from the leavings of empire, were bidding to preserve great-power status by the possession of nuclear weapons.

China stood apart, in uneasy alliance with the Soviet Union but still excluded from the United Nations and formally unrecognized by most Western governments, including Canada and the United States. In the 'underdeveloped' world, newly independent governments were facing massive problems of health, poverty, and hunger. The United Nations, having failed the test of ensuring collective security, stood with its specialized agencies as a source of progress in international social, economic, and legal affairs as well as in the process of 'decolonization.' The Commonwealth was moving with the times; every meeting of its prime ministers welcomed new members to the table.

International affairs had long been among the fields of special interest to Canada's new prime minister, John Diefenbaker. Since his election to the House of Commons in 1940, he had been a prominent participant in foreign affairs

3

debates, and for a time had served as the Progressive Conservative party's official external affairs critic. He had attended joint conferences with Commonwealth and US parliamentarians, and could claim to have been present as an unofficial observer at the birth of the United Nations at San Francisco in 1945.

Like most political leaders of the time, Diefenbaker's thinking on East-West issues had been shaped by the Cold War. His fear of Soviet power and of the potential spread of communist influence in Europe and the non-aligned regions of the world was coupled with an emotional commitment to 'freedom,' as exemplified by the Western democratic nations. He was thus a ready supporter of Canadian partnership in the NATO alliance, and he had no hesitation in welcoming US political and military leadership of the free world so long as the American leaders did not take Canadian support for granted.

In the 1957 election campaign in Canada he had seen and heard enough to confirm his belief that, notwithstanding Lester Pearson's acclaimed performance at the United Nations, a sizeable number of pro-British and pro-Israeli voters had been uneasy over the Canadian stand in the recent Suez crisis. Diefenbaker had an almost religious devotion to the Crown and to the relationship with the United Kingdom. He could be counted on to move to repair relations between Ottawa and London.

He could also be relied on to maintain, and to try to enhance, Canada's standing in the Commonwealth. If he had a vision in international affairs, it fell within the Commonwealth framework. This relationship not only provided a wider setting for the bonds linking Canada with the United Kingdom and the Crown, but it was an essential counterweight to US influence. It could, Diefenbaker thought, be developed as a commercial association to benefit its members, and as an instrument through which economic and technical aid could be channelled to new members in need. He was, of course, not alone in seeing the Commonwealth as a bridge to the newly independent nations of Asia and Africa, which might help them progress along the constitutional path already followed by Canada, Australia, and New Zealand. The establishment of personal links with individual Commonwealth heads would be among his primary aims. He regarded these leaders, in some cases rather optimistically, as potential allies in a world-wide struggle between communism and freedom. On a different plane, as a politician with his roots in the western prairies, he was on the lookout for new markets for Canadian agricultural exports.

Diefenbaker's view of the bilateral relationship with the United States was based on considerable exposure to American audiences and politicians over many years. While he was by no means consistently anti-American, he had always been a vigorous opponent of US restrictive trade practices and surplus disposal legislation. A politician with his combative temperament and power of oratory

4

had no difficulty in making the United States appear as the source of unfair pressures on Canada and Canadians. As he came into office, however, the forging of a harmonious relationship with the president of the United States would be of paramount importance (although, unlike Prime Minister Mulroney twenty-seven years later, he would not be tempted to profess it with such openness). He already admired Eisenhower, a man of his generation who had achieved supreme success both as a military leader and as a politician, and who still had two-and-a-half years to serve in the White House. John F. Kennedy and the problems over Cuba and nuclear cooperation were not yet on the horizon.

As for the United Nations, Diefenbaker paid it rhetorical tribute from time to time, but he shared the general disillusionment with the organization at the end of its first decade. Partly this was because of the Soviet veto and the breakdown of the collective security system conceived at San Francisco. The United Nations, moreover, had been the main scene of Pearson's achievements, and it was not surprising that Diefenbaker would tread warily there after he came into office. Nevertheless, he appreciated the considerable degree of public support which existed in Canada for the United Nations as a potential instrument for peaceful solutions to world problems. On many matters within its wide orbit, Diefen-baker's background as a lawyer and civil rights advocate could be expected to guarantee his abiding interest and support – as in the jurisdiction of the International Court of Justice, the law of the sea, outer space, human rights, and concern for persecuted minorities.

Broad issues such as disarmament and aid to the underdeveloped nations were related in his mind to one or other of his principal themes or interests. For example, he saw disarmament in the context of the Cold War and the propaganda contest with the USSR. And when he looked at Canada's responsibilities in foreign aid, he saw them in a Commonwealth focus and, given his prairie base, as providing yet further opportunities for the distribution of Canadian agricultural produce.

Finally, it must be said that there is little or no sign that Diefenbaker's view of the world in 1957 took account of issues or directions of special interest to French Canadians in the evolution of Canadian foreign policy. Not that the governments of Mackenzie King or Louis St Laurent had done much in that direction. But objectives such as the strengthening of links with France or the case for lending assistance to newly emerging francophone countries had no appeal for Diefenbaker at that time. In fairness to the prime minister, it should be added that in External Affairs there was little movement towards these objectives as early as 1957, although, largely as a result of the combined efforts of Marcel Cadieux, then the department's legal adviser, and Howard Green, foreign minister from 1959 to 1963, the Diefenbaker government later took the first modest steps towards Canadian diplomatic representation and economic assistance in francophone Africa.

As he crossed the sobering border from opposition into government, Diefenbaker would encounter a whole array of new influences: events in a world stirring with danger, change, and opportunity; relations with his counterparts in other governments; the views of his colleagues in cabinet; and the flow of advice from the civil service, notably from the Department of External Affairs. Quick as he was to absorb a brief, he was bound to feel the weight of these new pressures, augmented as they were by the demands of parliament and the press.

He was sixty-one years of age. There were gaps in his training for office. He had no more experience in management than may be acquired in a relatively small law office. His experience with the bureaucracy was limited to occasional (and to him seldom satisfactory) contacts in the search for information of value to an opposition member. His habits of thought were more those of the critic than the creator of policy. His reading diet – largely of history, political biography, and the law – had never included confidential reports and analyses from official sources abroad. Nor had he had regular access to the flavour and flow of departmental advice and outlook on the external world. His knowledge of the processes whereby cabinet decisions are reached was naturally indirect. He could not look back on occasions of shared confidence or crisis with colleagues in government on either the national or the international stage. He was an outsider, not yet on the network.

John Diefenbaker was to suffer from these handicaps, especially in the external affairs aspects of the prime ministerial task. He was keenly aware that his immediate predecessor, Louis St Laurent, had served a term as foreign minister. And he did not need, or want, to be reminded of Pearson's legendary reputation as an international statesman. His respect for Pearson's accomplishments was seldom expressed, but it was there, not far below the surface. It was obscured by the corroding envy that he never could control in his attitude towards Pearson.

Diefenbaker knew from the outset that Pearson's standing and experience in international affairs would leave him little room for manoeuvre in that area of policy. Where St Laurent before him and Pearson later would tap into familiar and trusted sources of advice and assistance in the Department of External Affairs, Diefenbaker was familiar with few such contacts. It was clear that while he had been impressed with the reputation of the department, in general he felt uneasy with its style and approach and at first was reluctant to rely on it for advice and support. In his scale of priorities, however, he gave a high place to international relations, and he understood that the department would be important to his own and his government's success in this field.

In the first months after he took office in June 1957, Diefenbaker had a concentrated exposure to the foreign affairs issues of the day. In late June he flew to London for the Commonwealth prime ministers' meeting, which had been scheduled many months before. At the end of July he met with the US secretary of state, John Foster Dulles, in Ottawa. Early in September he made his first major speech on Canada-US relations, at Dartmouth College, New Hampshire. On 23 September he was in New York addressing the UN General Assembly. By the end of October he had held his first meetings with President Eisenhower and Prime Minister Macmillan. In December he attended the NATO winter meeting in Paris, which was elevated in that year for the first time to the head-of-government level.

This heavy flow of engagements had a number of advantages for Diefenbaker. First in his mind was the political benefit of being seen to be active in world affairs. No one expected miracles of him in these early months, but he took advantage of the various engagements to indicate the attitude his government would take towards its international responsibilities.

In pursuing these purposes, Diefenbaker set out to reassure Canadians generally that they could count on him to continue Canada's active participation in traditional friendships, associations, and alliances. Those who feared that he might be less than enthusiastic about the United Nations were told that the United Nations was 'the cornerstone' of Canadian foreign policy. Those who were worried, as he certainly was, about Soviet intentions and capabilities were assured of Canada's belief in NATO as the guardian of Western security and freedom. Those who deplored Canada's part in the Suez crisis of the previous winter took courage from his determination to repair and strengthen the British connection. Those who wondered how he would deal with the United States found in his meetings with Eisenhower and Dulles, and in his Dartmouth College speech, a suitable blend of goodwill and vigilance.

The Department of External Affairs, meanwhile, had been undergoing its own inner turmoil. In the last week of June 1957 the shock of Pearson's departure had to be absorbed in an effort to prepare for the incoming administration. Pearson himself contributed to the emotional transition. At farewell occasions in his honour he offered predictable but nonetheless moving reminders of the public servant's responsibility to serve the government of the day. These occasions stick in the memory. They had something of a valedictory ring about them, a final nostalgic tutorial before what both teacher and student knew would be a difficult examination with an unpredictable set of questions.

In the weeks and months that followed, the department was put to a test of a kind it had not met before. Jules Léger, the undersecretary, a wise and perceptive

7

man, was frankly puzzled. He told a friend returning from service in an embassy abroad that he could not understand 'how this man's mind works.' Clearly the habits and style of communication which had served the experienced needs of King, St Laurent, and Pearson would have to be modified. But how? And what policy problems would arise? The new prime minister's opinions had not been thoroughly analysed. In the election campaign he had warned that Canada was becoming increasingly dependent on the United States in economic affairs. He had been critical of the Liberal party's Suez policy. He was known to have been a long-standing friend of Israel. His devotion to the Commonwealth was at least rhetorically established, but would it survive the transition from the old Commonwealth to the new multiracial association? Where would he stand on issues before the United Nations, on China's representation in the organization, for instance, or on disarmament? Support for NATO seemed assured, but would Diefenbaker's outspoken anti-communism make it more difficult for Canada to play some useful political role in relations between East and West? As for France and Latin America, or, for that matter, most of Asia, there was nothing to go on.

Diefenbaker's style of operation was even less well known. What was his conception of the prime minister's role in foreign affairs? How would that role be related to the responsibilities of the secretary of state for external affairs? How would external affairs items be dealt with in cabinet? What use would be made of cabinet committees? What special requirements would the department be called on to fulfil? How would foreign policy issues be handled in his office? Was there substance to the many rumours that Diefenbaker did not trust the department, and, if there was, what should be done about it?

In recent years the department had known the kind of experienced leadership which made it unnecessary to provide detailed background information or to justify the absence of black and white in the design of recommendations. With the sudden change in management, assumptions about policy that could safely have been made before might be worth nothing in the new environment. Every piece of advice must be tested.

Did it give enough, or too much, background? Were all the factors brought into play before the possible courses of action, since called options, were deployed? Would the meaning be clear to the new prime minister and minister, or would the form of presentation raise more questions than it answered? Not least important, did the advice contain allusions to the past or other references which might irritate the incoming administration? Too ready an assumption, for example, that the UN Emergency Force in the Middle East, a creature of Pearson's diplomacy, would be automatically extended by the new government might be unwise. As for the chill pervading official relations with Britain and France since the Suez crisis, no special genius was required to forecast a warming trend. It was not what the Liberals had done in office but what the Progressive Conservatives had said in opposition that must now be taken into account.

2

Meeting the Family:
Commonwealth PMs

The conference of Commonwealth prime ministers was to begin in London on 26 June, only five days after Diefenbaker had been sworn in. It could hardly have been better timed to mark his arrival on the Commonwealth scene.

The principal reasons for scheduling the meeting in mid-1957 had been the desire of the new British government of Harold Macmillan to reassert Commonwealth harmony in the wake of the Suez crisis, and for Macmillan himself to establish personal relations with his Commonwealth counterparts. Diefenbaker was as determined as Macmillan to promote these objectives. Before leaving for London, he had told his cabinet colleagues that the improvement of Commonwealth relations would be the most important topic on the agenda.[1] He went on to say that he was convinced it was in the best interests of the Commonwealth to assure its non-white people of 'reasonable advancement and equal opportunities.' He mentioned that prime ministers Nehru and St Laurent had 'achieved a high degree of understanding' and said there was no reason to believe that this close relationship would not continue after the change of administration in Canada.

Diefenbaker also referred in cabinet to his intention to stress Commonwealth economic and trade ties, and said he might take the opportunity of a Dominion Day speech in London to extend an invitation for a Commonwealth trade and economic conference in Ottawa. This was a clear echo of election campaign promises, a signal that he was serious in hoping to revitalize trade among Commonwealth members. Reservations were expressed, however, especially by the minister of finance, Donald Fleming. Others questioned the role of a Commonwealth trade conference in relation to negotiations then taking place for a European Free Trade Area which would include the United Kingdom. Thus, Diefenbaker's ideas on trade strategy were being challenged, but he left for London by no means discouraged from an initiative aimed at expanding Commonwealth trade.

On arrival in London, Diefenbaker found himself the focus of attention in the media and among his counterparts, all of whom were eager to size up the conqueror of St Laurent, his well-regarded predecessor. Diefenbaker relished the occasion. At last he was where he had aimed to be – calling with his wife on the Queen at Buckingham Palace; meeting with the British prime minister at 10 Downing St; visiting his favourite hero, Sir Winston Churchill; making the acquaintance of his partners in what was to him the most exclusive political fraternity of them all. It was the kind of moment which brought forth one of his rhetorical standbys, 'They said it couldn't be done.'

He had done it. He was there, seized by the exhilaration of his first hours on the mainstage. He set himself to play his role, rehearsing his lines, meticulous in his appearance, conscious of the figure he was cutting, demanding deference due, savouring the fruits of victory long-denied. At the same time, he was not over-confident of the part he would play in the conference: 'I'll do my best, but I am quite disturbed that I have had no time to prepare by reading. There is a vast volume of briefs, all marked Top Secret. Cabinet making is a trying job and took all my time.'[2]

Diefenbaker was right in regarding the meeting as primarily a bracer for the Commonwealth, but the proceedings also underlined another truth about these affairs: that Commonwealth diplomacy is as much outward- as inward-looking, as much concerned with the state of the world as the state of the Commonwealth. For him it was an introduction to the global scene, to the interplay of widely differing perspectives on East-West and North-South relations in their broadest compass. He could not have had a more instructive seminar at the outset of his apprenticeship in power.[3]

In a discussion on relations with the Soviet Union, Diefenbaker was characteristically sceptical that any fundamental changes in Soviet policy had occurred, despite what might appear to be a softer Soviet line on disarmament. The only realistic policy towards the Soviet Union, he said, was the maintenance of an effective system of defence, however much the concept of neutralism might appear to further the cause of peace. He said that any agreement on the suspension of nuclear testing should be accompanied by some measure of conventional disarmament and by an effective system of inspection. He offered all or part of Canada's territory for aerial inspection as part of a disarmament agreement, subject to Soviet willingness to cooperate. Mutual inspection from the air was a favourite theme with Diefenbaker, reflecting his deep suspicion of Soviet motives. He found it a practical way to show Canada's readiness to help in the disarmament process, but in a manner that would put propaganda pressure on the Soviet authorities who were not likely to welcome aerial inspections of sensitive northern defence installations.

On Middle East topics, Diefenbaker's position was awaited with great interest, especially in External Affairs where, in view of Progressive Conservative criticism of the Liberal party's policy in the Suez crisis, the new government's intentions had been the subject of much speculation. Whatever inner reservations he might have felt, Diefenbaker in effect followed the department's advice on one important aspect – the future of the UN Emergency Force in the Middle East. He gave assurance to his colleagues that Canada would continue to support the force for as long as it would reasonably be needed – perhaps, he estimated, some six to nine months.

On other major items, Diefenbaker gave brief but significant indications of his thinking. He inquired whether the recognition of Communist China would weaken anti-communist forces in Asia, a question which drew opposite responses from prime ministers Menzies of Australia (yes) and Nehru of India (in effect, no). He spoke in general support of the United Nations, with warnings about the ill effects of the veto in the Security Council and of bloc voting in the General Assembly. He inquired of the British why they had recently reduced their forces in Europe, and was told for economic reasons.

In the discussion on Britain's economic links with Europe and the Commonwealth, Diefenbaker expressed a broad sympathy for the movement towards integration in Europe but he requested and obtained British assurances that closer British association would not be at the price of Canadian trade interests. Conscious of the views of Menzies of Australia and others who either opposed or saw no benefit in an early Commonwealth trade conference, Diefenbaker did not attempt to gain general agreement to the principle of holding such a conference in Canada. The final statement of the meeting did record, however, that he had extended an invitation to Commonwealth finance ministers to meet in Canada in September, following the meetings of the International Monetary Fund and the International Bank in Washington. He had to content himself with private indications that the ministers would in fact talk about Commonwealth trade.

A clue to his preoccupation with the expansion of Commonwealth trade might have been detected in his remarks on sterling balances and investment flows. Here Diefenbaker made a point of describing the threat which American investment posed to Canada's economic independence. This interpretation came as a shock to the other prime ministers, for whom an injection of American capital would have been welcome. Diefenbaker, however, was simply reflecting his current belief that with an expansion of Commonwealth trade it would be possible for Canada to lessen its dependence on the United States and in that way to guard against surrendering control of its economic affairs.

Except for the question of Commonwealth trade, the London meeting presented no difficulties for Diefenbaker. On his return he made a full report to his colleagues in cabinet.[4] Characteristically, he spoke at length about his interview with the Queen, with whom he had discussed plans for the royal visit to Canada and the United States later in the year. Commenting on the prime ministers' meeting itself, he dwelt on the multiracial nature of the Commonwealth, as reflected in the presence for the first time of Dr Kwame Nkrumah of Ghana, and in the imminent induction of Malaya into Commonwealth membership. Diefenbaker remarked on the way in which the Commonwealth was changing in its multiracial composition. In retrospect, the fact that he singled out this point seems striking. Neither St Laurent nor Pearson would have remarked on it in 1957.

It is worth emphasizing that governments and leaders who come into power with no previous experience in office, or after lengthy periods in opposition must overcome severe handicaps. This applies in varying degree across the whole range of prime ministerial responsibility but is especially acute in foreign affairs, where personal trust among leaders, combined with common experience with policy issues, is often influential in getting things done and in preventing or modifying unwanted outcomes.

Diefenbaker had neither experience nor personal links, and he lacked a natural talent for team play. In his efforts to encourage Commonwealth trade, he had to rely heavily on his powers of persuasion. It was not a popular cause, but his determination was impressive. Doubtless too there was a general desire around the table to find a means of accommodating an important new colleague. In his account to the cabinet, Diefenbaker went out of his way to acknowledge the assistance and support of Macmillan. It was clear, Diefenbaker said, that the United Kingdom would have to become a member of the European Free Trade Area; otherwise, Germany might become the dominant economic force in Europe and displace Britain from many of her foreign markets. He repeated that the British prime minister had given assurances, however, that the position of Commonwealth agricultural products in the United Kingdom would not be prejudiced by the EFTA. Diefenbaker was satisfied for the moment.

On the subjects of interest to him, Diefenbaker had said enough at the meeting to warn his Commonwealth colleagues that he could not be taken for granted as an orthodox partner. Macmillan was quick to identify Diefenbaker as a colleague who, though 'a fine man – sincere and determined,' was 'still the victim of his election oratory,' one who had formed a 'rather misleading' picture of 'what can and cannot be done with the Commonwealth today.'[5] No doubt he was too diplomatic a chairman, and too sensitive a political colleague, to offer direct advice.

Prime Minister Robert Menzies of Australia did not suffer from the same constraints. With what Macmillan describes as his 'usual directness,' Menzies spoke of the 'great and expert preparation' which would be needed for an economic conference, and warned of the dangers of failure. Whatever Diefenbaker thought of this advice (he and Menzies would not be comfortable partners), he later impressed on the cabinet the importance of making a success of the finance ministers' meeting and of preparing for a full-scale Commonwealth trade conference to be held in Canada in the following year.

On the day after his return to Ottawa, Diefenbaker told a press conference that the government intended to achieve a 15 per cent diversion of trade from the United States to the United Kingdom.[6] It was a remark made apparently on the spur of the moment in reply to a question. He had not said as much to the meeting of prime ministers or to the British government. Nor was it the result of a cabinet decision. Most likely it was a political impulse, a need he sensed at that moment to show that, with the experience of the London meeting behind him, he was still planning to deliver closer and more profitable relations with Britain and to achieve greater economic independence from the United States. It was an incautious move and, before long, the British government made him pay for it when they responded by proposing a free-trade agreement which Canada could not accept. Diefenbaker never publicly admitted that his 15 per cent diversion remark had been a mistake. It did, however, provide a painful lesson on the constraints of office, not least in international affairs.

3

Meeting the Neighbours

Although in the first weeks of his administration Diefenbaker seemed to be taking all the fresh challenges in his stride, the appearance was not altogether reliable. No system has yet been devised to provide realistic training for prime ministers and ministers before they assume office. The circumstances in which Diefenbaker committed his government, on 1 August 1957, to the approval of what became known as NORAD – the North American Air Defence Command – provide an example of the perils of inexperience. They also portray him in an uncharacteristic stance, for while he tended in private to react intuitively to new developments, he was not normally quick in reaching important decisions.

A VISITOR FROM WASHINGTON

John Foster Dulles, President Eisenhower's secretary of state, spent the last weekend of July 1957 on a private visit to Canada. For part of that time he was in Ottawa, where the United States ambassador, Livingston T. (Livie) Merchant, had orchestrated a program of informal conversations with the prime minister and some of his senior ministers.[1] Merchant told John Holmes, then acting undersecretary in External Affairs, that the exchanges on economic questions had been of particular value 'because they had been quite frank on both sides.' Diefenbaker had spoken of Canadian feeling against US policies for the disposal of surplus wheat. In later years, Merchant recalled that finance minister Donald Fleming and justice minister Davie Fulton, 'by far the strongest ministers' in the new Diefenbaker cabinet, were anxious to prove that the new government was going to be 'extremely tough' with the United States. Fleming said that the government proposed 'to shift a substantial proportion of Canada's export and import business from the United States to the United Kingdom,' to which Dulles replied that that was Canada's business and that the Canadian government should

15

'tell us when you have made up your minds.' 'It was just like sticking a pin into them,' Merchant continued. 'The conversation was rather limping thereafter.'[2]

A good part of the meeting was devoted to developments in the disarmament field. Diefenbaker was concerned, as he always would be, with putting disarmament in terms which the Canadian voter would be most likely to understand and support. He and Dulles discussed ways of associating Canada publicly with the offer Eisenhower had put forward for zones of aerial inspection reciprocally agreed between the United States and the USSR. Dulles thought that the wording Diefenbaker preferred would appear to divide Canada from the United States, and the question was left open. Dulles also brought up policy towards China. Diefenbaker assured Dulles that while he did not necessarily rule out the eventual recognition of Communist China, he thought it would be mistaken at this stage because it would discourage anti-communist forces in Asia. In this comment he was giving his view at the time he came into office. Privately, as became evident later, he was sensitive to the arguments in favour of Communist China's admission to the UN. Finally, on a note that gratified Diefenbaker, Dulles made a point of saying that President Eisenhower would be happy to have the prime minister visit Washington for an official visit.

On Dulles's departure he gave a statement to the press, emphasizing the value and informality of the talks, and, incidentally, obliging the prime minister by recalling that they had first met at the UN conference in San Francisco in 1945. Diefenbaker had attended that conference as an observer, very much on the fringe of the action, but he never ceased to claim a certain kudos for having been there and having met the architects and early builders of the United Nations.

As Merchant had doubtless hoped, the visit provided Dulles with an early exposure to the attitudes and preoccupations of the leading members of the new Canadian government. Henceforth, in reporting on Canadian developments, Merchant could feel assured of Dulles's awareness of the principal personalities and political tendencies in Canada. Later Merchant was to say, candidly, that the Progressive Conservative government had 'entered office with a lack of experience and a fundamental irresponsibility which comes from too long a disconnection with responsibility in government.'[3]

Although Diefenbaker, and especially Fleming and Fulton, had clearly made their mark in their first encounter with Dulles, the prime minister himself had not formed a warm impression of the secretary of state. He told me later that he did not altogether 'trust' Dulles. By questioning the statement Diefenbaker had wanted to issue on the offer of Canadian territory for aerial inspection, Dulles had nettled the prime minister. It was the kind of situation which would provoke Diefenbaker many times in the future – a tendency, as he saw it, for American officials to expect Canada's unquestioning acquiescence in a course of action favoured by the United States. I think, too, that Dulles had not shown as genuine an appreciation as Diefenbaker thought was warranted of the political significance in Canada of the various economic issues Diefenbaker and his ministers had raised.

Here was an early manifestation of Diefenbaker's attitude towards Americans. It was subtler than the meaning one normally gives to the term 'anti-Americanism.' It had more to do with 'anti-establishmentism,' a habit of mind which was deep-rooted in Diefenbaker and which he did not direct exclusively at Americans. But there was a certain 'caste' of American, highly educated, professionally secure, and socially well-connected, whose attitude and style he thought betrayed an insensitivity or indifference to the interests of others, including, of course, Canadians. On this score, whether Dulles realized it or not, he had not made Diefenbaker more comfortable. Perhaps the same was true the other way around. The problem would recur many times in the next six years, although for nearly half of that time the conciliatory genius of President Eisenhower, and Diefenbaker's affectionate regard for the president, combined to ease the normal strains in Canadian-American relations.

NORAD: STUMBLE AND RECOVERY

In the week before Dulles was to visit Ottawa, General George Pearkes, the minister of national defence, had obtained the prime minister's approval of the agreement which had been worked out between the Canadian and US defence authorities on the integration of air defence forces in North America. Although neither Diefenbaker nor Dulles was familiar with the details of the agreement, they had taken the opportunity of Dulles's visit to review it.

The air defence forces of the United States and Canada had cooperated closely for many years, but under the new plan they would be placed within a system of joint operational control and under an integrated headquarters responsible to the Chiefs of Staff of the two countries.[4] It sounded, and indeed it was, logical enough, being justified on the principle that for purposes of air defence and protection of the US strategic deterrent, the two countries and the NATO alliance as a whole could be better served if the air defence forces of the United States and Canada operated as one. A recommendation to this effect from a joint US-Canada military study group had been under consideration by the two governments in the months before the Canadian election on 10 June 1957. The Liberal government, sizing up the political sensitivity of the subject but not questioning the substance of the recommendation, set it aside for post-election decision. It was one of the first subjects requiring action by the Progressive Conservatives when they took over the government.

17

The immediate problem lay in the anxiety of the government's military advisers, and particularly the chairman of the Chiefs of Staff, General Charles Foulkes, to obtain the earliest possible decision on the air defence plan from the new government. Foulkes felt responsible for having caused his counterparts in Washington to obtain the approval of the US secretary of defence some three months previously.[5] Diefenbaker had first heard of the proposal from Pearkes in late June 1957, when they were together on their way to London for the Commonwealth prime ministers' meeting. Diefenbaker and Pearkes were friends and political comrades of long standing, and it happened that Pearkes and Foulkes had a similarly solid relationship based on their service together during the Second World War. No other minister was involved in the decision-making sequence at that time, since the prime minister had not yet appointed a minister of external affairs and was himself carrying that portfolio. Parliament was not in session, and the press had not got wind of the proposal.

When Diefenbaker and Pearkes returned from London, word soon reached Foulkes that the prime minister had given his 'tentative approval' to the air defence recommendations. How fully Diefenbaker understood what was proposed is not clear. He had been in office for only two weeks and he had not received any detailed explanation. However, given his concern about Soviet military capabilities and his trust in Pearkes, it is not surprising that he should have been receptive to a proposal for improving the quality of continental air defence. The Liberal government, he was told, had been on the point of approving the plan, which was merely an extension of long-standing cooperation between the RCAF and the USAF, and which had been designed as the best conceivable method of enabling quick joint response to possible bomber attack on North America.

The normal channel for getting the proposal formally approved would have been through the Cabinet Defence Committee. That committee, however, had not been formed and the prime minister made it known that he was not yet willing to establish it. After discussion with R.B. Bryce, the secretary to the cabinet, on how to proceed, Foulkes equipped Pearkes on 22 July with a draft memorandum addressed to the cabinet. Pearkes saw no reason to wait. On 24 July he took the proposal straight to the prime minister, who gave his agreement immediately, without inviting the views of either Bryce or Léger, both of whom might have tendered useful advice. Foulkes himself was astounded that the decision had been made with so little discussion. Considering, however, that Dulles was soon to be in Ottawa, it is likely that Diefenbaker wanted to be in a position to give the news personally to Dulles, even though it was not to be made public until the following week when a joint statement by the defence ministers would be issued.

Before the change of government, External Affairs had argued strongly in the Chiefs of Staff Committee that the establishment of NORAD should be used to remind the United States of the need for adequate political consultation between the two governments on matters which might lead to the alerting of the air defence system.[6] Pearson, external affairs minister at the time, made the same argument. at a meeting of the Cabinet Defence Committee in February.[7] The point about political consultation had been included in the proposal which had been awaiting decision by the Liberal cabinet. Significantly, it did not appear in the version submitted by Foulkes to Pearkes for his discussion with Diefenbaker.[8] Had the prime minister's attention been drawn to that issue, it would have helped him to appreciate the political advantage of using the air defence agreement to obtain a formal undertaking on consultation from the United States. Meanwhile, at External Affairs, the responsible officials had no knowledge that the proposal was being submitted to the prime minister.[9]

In his memoirs, Diefenbaker makes the point that if the Department of External Affairs had any useful suggestions to make before the NORAD agreement was taken or announced, it was the department's clear duty to put them forward.[10] The fact is that, despite their ignorance of Pearkes's direct approach to the prime minister, the External Affairs officials responsible for continental defence matters did put forward the department's view before the announcement of 1 August. For the Dulles visit on 27 July they provided Diefenbaker with a briefing paper on the main issues in Canada-US defence.[11] That paper noted that the channel between the Department of External Affairs and the State Department was the proper one for the conclusion of all formal intergovernmental agreements on defence matters. It also stated that recommendations on joint air defence from military advisers on both sides of the border were to be expected, and that the decision on these matters would involve control of security forces in Canada by a foreign commander in peacetime.

These points indicated concern in External Affairs about the way in which the air defence proposal should be handled. Markings on the paper indicate that at least part of it was read by Diefenbaker, but by the time it could have reached him – probably on 26 July as part of a comprehensive briefing book for the Dulles visit – he had already approved the document put before him by Pearkes. At the time the prime minister may have thought that diplomatic formalities could come later or he may have been otherwise unconvinced by the case for a formal agreement between the two governments. Whatever the explanation, it is strange that he failed to realize that issues of policy broader than military cooperation alone would have to be addressed immediately, and that, if this were not taken care of, the Liberal opposition, so recently in office, would be well placed to ask awkward questions. He might have spared himself at least some of the political embarrassment that soon descended on him. NORAD might have started life somewhat later, but its birth would have been less painful.

External Affairs' first certain knowledge of what was afoot came, to its embarrassment, from ambassador Livingston Merchant on 31 July in the conversation he had with John Holmes. Merchant had come to discuss the arrangements for a joint press release on the air defence agreement to be made the following day and also the question of informing NATO. After seeing Merchant, Holmes sought confirmation from Bryce that the air defence decision had in fact been taken. Bryce confirmed to Holmes that the prime minister and the minister of national defence had reached the decision in consultation, and that they had decided it would not be necessary to discuss the item in cabinet before informing the United States of Canadian agreement.[12]

In External Affairs, officials were indignant at the tactics used by General Foulkes but, more seriously, they were concerned about the consequences. Diefenbaker and Pearkes had been led to make an important international decision without giving consideration to the non-military implications. The prime minister would have to be advised on a variety of difficult questions from the opposition parties, the press, and other governments. Holmes wrote on 2 August to National Defence requesting information on the document which the prime minister had approved. He took occasion to reiterate that 'there should be some written governmental agreement [with the United States] which would be completed through diplomatic channels.'

The correspondence between August and October shows how far apart the two departments were in their approach.[13] Responding to Holmes's inquiry, Foulkes wrote scathingly of an agreement such as that proposed in the letter. Not only would it cause unacceptable delays, he said, but also it was unnecessary. The minister of national defence had authority to set up military commands. And by requiring an exchange of notes between the two governments, Canada would question the authority of the US secretary of defence to set up a joint command with Canada. He was 'unaware of any advantage' in setting up a military command by means of an intergovernmental agreement. If, however, the Department of External Affairs wished 'to draw up with the State Department' any written agreement, the Department of National Defence would not object.

Pearson now entered the debate with a new line of criticism which questioned the link between NORAD and NATO. This and other issues involved in the NORAD arrangement would clearly cause problems when parliament met in October.

It was at this stage that I began work in the prime minister's office. From the notes I have of my early calls on Diefenbaker, he was not at first seriously discomfited by press criticism of the NORAD decision. However, by mid-October, when he was preparing for a conversation in Washington with President Eisenhower, it was clear that Pearson's criticisms had touched a political nerve. Diefenbaker was especially concerned to ensure the government's political control of major military decisions. The president proved sympathetic. He agreed that the NORAD command must consult both the prime minister and the president or their representatives before or during action that might lead to the use of NORAD's operational forces. Diefenbaker reported in these terms to the cabinet on his return, adding that the minister of national defence would communicate with the US authorities on the terms of a joint statement confirming civilian control over the initiation of operations under NORAD.[14]

The prime minister's exchange with the president had given impetus and final authority to measures which were already in train behind the scenes. Pearkes withdrew National Defence's objection to the negotiation of the proposed agreement.[15] Work on the military terms of reference for the NORAD commanders had been in progress at NORAD headquarters at Colorado Springs. Once these terms were ready, they would require the approval of both governments. For security reasons, they would not be made public but they would be covered by the broad umbrella of the intergovernmental agreement which itself would find expression in an exchange of diplomatic notes. It had taken three months to get acceptance within the government for such an agreement.

After the new session of parliament began in late October, the opposition parties (Liberal and CCF) both saw NORAD as an issue on which the government could be faulted. The prime minister and Pearkes tried, with only partial success, to explain how NORAD had come into being, how civilian control of major military decisions would be protected under the new arrangement, how the chain of authority would work in a crisis, and what NORAD's relationship to NATO would be. Some of Pearson's questions seemed to Diefenbaker to be based on information that must have come from 'only one source' – by which he obviously meant someone in External Affairs. When Bryce informed him that Pearson's questions could have been based on documents formerly available to him as secretary of state for external affairs, his suspicions on this score seemed to die down, although they were never entirely dissolved. I had many frank talks with the prime minister about this, and in spite of his readiness to believe the worst of Pearson and of some people in External Affairs, I never heard any evidence from him or from other sources that his suspicions were founded in fact.

Meanwhile, in drafting the text of the intergovernmental agreement, External Affairs concentrated on ensuring political control of the decision-making process governing NORAD's operations. Bound up with this was the provision for prior consultation between governments on any decision or crisis which might involve the operational use of the air-defence forces. The governmental agreement had also to take account of the relationship between NORAD and NATO, for this was an issue still embarrassing to the Canadian government. Clearly NORAD was in line with NATO's basic purpose, but should it be left as a bilateral arrangement between the two North American members of the NATO alliance, or established as a full-scale command reporting directly to NATO's political and military headquarters in Paris?

Under pressure from Pearson and others, the prime minister developed his own ideas. Quite unexpectedly, in the preparation of his policy statement to the NATO heads of government meeting in Paris in December, he decided to describe the relationship between NORAD and NATO in a manner that linked the two more closely than had previously been contemplated by either his military or diplomatic advisers. On the night before the NATO meeting opened, Foulkes was instructed to clear Diefenbaker's line of argument with the Americans. This Foulkes accomplished, on the evening of 15 December, in a lengthy telephone call with his US counterpart, General Nathan S. Twining.[16] Whether at that time Foulkes obtained Twining's agreement to the exact wording of the passage in question, I do not know. But in his speech the prime minister described NORAD as 'an integral part of our NATO military structure in the Canada-USA region' which 'will report to the Standing Group of [NATO] and the NATO Council in a manner similar to that followed by other NATO military commands.'

It was not at all clear what these words were intended to mean. They could be interpreted as placing NORAD on the same footing as the two major NATO commands, SACEUR and SACLANT. But the words 'similar to' allowed room for a different interpretation. Another question was the meaning of the term 'report to.' Did he simply mean 'inform' or something closer to accountability? Diefenbaker was not above being deliberately ambiguous, and it seems quite likely that he was aiming to work both sides of the equation, using fuzzy language as a bridge between opposing aims. A few days later, perhaps because he had come to realize that too close a link with NATO would be more trouble than it was worth, Diefenbaker pulled back a small step when he was reporting on the meeting to the House of Commons: 'These integrated forces are an integral part of the NATO military structure in the Canada-United States Region ... anything we have done has been reported to the [NATO] Standing Group and that course will be followed in the future. The NATO Council will have full reports on everything we do, similar to the practice followed in all other NATO military commands.[17] In other words, he put the emphasis now on keeping NATO informed of what NORAD did, rather than on its 'reporting to' the NATO authorities.

It was a fine distinction perhaps, but Diefenbaker's political sense told him to mark out a position which, while blocking Pearson's angle of fire, would not make it impossible to cooperate with the American military authorities. For the Pentagon could be relied on to resist any language which might imply that other members of the alliance had a right to interfere in plans for the air defence of North America.

The prime minister now thought that he and his colleagues had done enough to neutralize the NORAD issue and, at least in the short run, he was right. The 1958 election came and went, triumphantly for him, and he was not seriously embarrassed by the NORAD affair in the campaign. The negotiation with the Americans produced no surprises, the officials on both sides being thoroughly aware by this time of each other's obsessions. With some inevitable delay because of the election, it was early May before the new cabinet considered the text of the final NORAD documents as they had emerged from the negotiations. The intergovernmental notes were duly exchanged on 12 May.[18] By that date, too, agreement had been reached separately on the secret terms of reference by which the NORAD commanders would operate. The prime minister and his colleagues were finally satisfied that the several references to NATO in the Canadian Note were together a sufficient reflection of the kind of NATO connection to which Diefenbaker and Pearkes had committed themselves. The two governments had also agreed on the increased 'importance of the fullest possible consultation ... on all matters affecting the joint defence of North America, and that defence cooperation between them can be worked out on a satisfactory basis only if such consultation is regularly and consistently undertaken.' Four years later, the events leading to the Cuban missile crisis demonstrated the fragility of such worthy intentions and such carefully crafted language.

Diefenbaker never doubted the soundness of the decision on NORAD but he was annoyed about the criticism he had let himself in for. What especially got under his skin was the charge that he had authorized an important military commitment to the United States without asking and receiving answers to a number of searching questions as to how the new arrangement would work, how it would relate to Canada's other defence obligations, and how the Canadian government's political control could be ensured. After the controversy erupted, his tactics were designed above all to blunt the political effect of Pearson's charges. In this he was fairly successful. The affair did not endure as a major political issue. It did, however, leave an early mark of confusion on the new government's record in the defence aspect of foreign policy. Psychologically it was not a comfortable point of departure for the more explosive issues the prime minister would face in the following years in North American defence affairs. Before long, too, it became evident that Canada's obligations as a partner in NORAD would require the acquisition of weapons systems which could not function at peak efficiency without nuclear ammunition. The controversy over the birth of NORAD would soon be overshadowed.

4

Meeting the Allies

Conferences of prime ministers were routine in the Commonwealth by 1957, but heads of NATO governments had never before met as a group. On taking office, therefore, Diefenbaker had no reason to expect that, in his calendar for 1957, he would have to make room for a week's stay in Paris in company with his counterparts from other NATO countries.

When Diefenbaker and Macmillan met at the Commonwealth prime ministers' meeting in London in June 1957, they had agreed that the British prime minister would visit Ottawa as soon as possible. The first opportunity arose in October when Macmillan was invited on short notice to visit Washington for talks with President Eisenhower and Secretary of State Dulles. Diefenbaker immediately welcomed Macmillan's offer to come to Ottawa after the meetings in Washington.

The first Soviet *Sputnik*, launched into orbit on 4 October, along with the recent test in August of a Soviet intercontinental missile, had given dramatic proof of Soviet technological achievement. Public reaction in the United States had shown signs of alarm at this new evidence of Soviet power, and Eisenhower and Dulles were feeling the need for a display of Anglo-American solidarity and leadership.

Nothing could have suited Macmillan better. His highest immediate aim was to restore Britain's relationship with Washington which had been ruptured by the Suez crisis in 1956. Eisenhower and Macmillan had begun the work of restoration in Bermuda in March. Now they met to consolidate it in circumstances of high challenge, which reminded them both of the spirit of their wartime collaboration. On 25 October they issued a statement of principles which they called the Declaration of Common Purpose.[1] Dulles, its chief architect, described it in a press briefing as a statement of transcendent importance for the free world. That was the mood of the time in Washington.

The declaration was designed to serve a number of purposes. For the United States it reflected the conviction of Eisenhower and Dulles that they must strive not only to forge a stronger sense of unity and cooperation among friendly nations, but also to educate the allies of the United States, especially those in NATO, about the full implications of defence cooperation in the nuclear age. Macmillan shared these views. He treasured the role of primary partner. And as his own account testifies, he took satisfaction from Eisenhower's assurance that the administration would ask Congress to amend the Atomic Energy (McMahon) Act in such a way as to permit British scientists access to information previously withheld under US legislation.[2] This was, as Macmillan described it, 'the great prize,' and it was no wonder that he was in high spirits when he arrived in Ottawa in the late evening of 25 October. He had, after all, done a good deal to revive the Anglo-American special relationship as well as to add credibility to Britain's claim to a continuing major role in world affairs.

Compared to the Washington meeting, the Macmillan visit to Ottawa was brief and hardly momentous. Before Macmillan arrived, however, Diefenbaker took pains to ensure that the visit would be put to profitable use. He arranged for the British visitors to attend a meeting of the cabinet where Macmillan and Selwyn Lloyd, the foreign secretary, entered into the spirit of the occasion. They gratified Diefenbaker and his colleagues by acknowledging the support the Progressive Conservative party had given Britain at the time of Suez.[3]

Macmillan's talk to the cabinet revolved around the Washington declaration, with emphasis on the need for much closer cooperation among nations of the free world in the face of Soviet military and scientific strength, and for a better coordinated response to Soviet propaganda and economic activities in the non-aligned world. The *Sputnik*, Macmillan said, had been a blow but it had helped to restore a spirit of cooperation. President Eisenhower was a man you could cooperate with; Dulles had previously been in sharp disagreement with some British policies but on this occasion his attitude had been much more positive. Even on the Middle East, he seemed to have modified his views and was now willing to admit some past misjudgment. Generally, Macmillan told Diefenbaker, the mood was one of interdependence – not in terms of exclusive Anglo-American bilateralism but as a basis for cooperation among wider groups of friendly nations.

Diefenbaker applauded the efforts made by Macmillan and Eisenhower to generate a revived sense of cooperation among the Western and other friendly nations. In the presence of his cabinet colleagues he paid flattering tributes to Macmillan's statesmanship. Privately, too, Diefenbaker spoke in the most admiring terms of both Macmillan and Eisenhower. He had recently met Eisenhower in Washington and had immediately felt comfortable with him. In an interlude during the visit, he remarked how fortunate it was that two men 'of such outstanding spiritual quality' as Macmillan and Eisenhower were in their positions of leadership.

Visits by British ministers to Ottawa would not always be so harmonious. The day would come when there would be a hint of reluctance in London to make Ottawa an automatic pit-stop on visits to Washington. But on this day such a thought would not have seemed conceivable. For Macmillan the Ottawa visit completed a highly successful expedition to North America. The visit had been a political success for Diefenbaker, too, for he was so eager to be seen as the agent for the restoration of Anglo-Canadian harmony. I remember wishing that the prime minister were a shade less deferential to his distinguished guest.

During this visit, one small episode personified Diefenbaker's tendency to disregard diplomatic convention. Among the points discussed in Washington by Eisenhower and Macmillan was the idea that heads of government should attend the next meeting of NATO ministers scheduled for Paris in mid-December. When Diefenbaker heard privately from Macmillan that a NATO summit was in the cards, it was too good a story to withhold. He immediately made it public and said he would lead the Canadian delegation.

The appearance of this item on the news wire before the meeting had been confirmed caused a small agitation. The US embassy made the point that President Eisenhower would not formally declare his intention to attend the NATO meeting unless in response to an invitation from the NATO Council. The Department of External Affairs was concerned because the premature release might seem part of an effort to stampede other heads of government into undertaking to attend before they had had a chance to consider whether there was much profit in a NATO summit meeting on such short notice. The British visitors bravely strove to ignore the faux pas.

In the weeks from the end of October to the opening of the Paris meeting in mid-December, the prime minister's chief preoccupation was with the domestic scene. Parliament was in session. Cabinet meetings were frequent. Every policy problem was new and more complex than it had seemed from the perspective of parliamentary opposition. If Diefenbaker had felt inclined to establish a system of cabinet committees, that might have relieved him of at least some of the operational burdens he faced. But he was doing it his own way. He was leading a minority government, preparing the ground for another election, and consolidating his authority. Some of his cabinet colleagues less than a year before had opposed him for the leadership of the party. He was now assessing them, their talents, and above all their loyalty. He was hesitant about delegating authority on major issues unless he was comfortable with the political consequences that might flow from decisions taken without his participation. He was also extremely concerned to do justice to his role in the House of Commons, preparing himself assiduously for the daily question period and for major debates. He travelled extensively, to test the political barometer in different regions. When in Ottawa he seemed incessantly in conference or on the phone. His offices, whether in the East Block or the Centre Block of the Parliament Buildings, were alive with visitors waiting to make their mark or to hear good or less good news from the Chief. He was at the centre of his universe. It was as though nothing important could happen without his word or nod of assent.

The Washington declaration prompted consideration of the political and military measures which NATO governments might take, and discuss at the summit meeting, in their search for a higher level of solidarity and for means of improving the political reputation of the Western nations in the developing world. Even before the idea of a summit meeting was advanced during the Macmillan visit to Washington, the US administration had been preoccupied with the immensely complicated issues involved in organizing, with its 'community' of allies in various regions of the world, a system of collective defence capable of providing security against Soviet military strength. The essential problem was that allied and friendly nations should know more than they did know about atomic weapons and their capabilities. They had to have sufficient knowledge to feel sure that atomic weapons were capable of protecting them, and they had to be confident that these weapons would be used to protect them and that atomic power would not be misused through premature or reckless employment of the weapons.[4]

The implications for Canada took the form of proposals for the stockpiling in Europe of US tactical atomic weapons for NATO's 'Shield' forces, and the installation in certain European countries, yet to be determined, of intermediate-range ballistic missiles (IRBMs). Of these two proposals, the first had direct implications for Canada, since Canadian forces, both land and air, formed part of the Shield forces in Europe. The IRBM proposal would not directly affect Canadian territory, although it was clearly of great significance in broad strategic and political terms. The details of these proposals were not received until a week or so before the Paris meeting, but enough was known of their substance to permit them to be considered by the different departments concerned and to be assigned to the Panel on the Economic Aspects of Defence, chaired by R.B. Bryce.[5]

In the Department of External Affairs, a policy debate was shaping up as work began on the briefing papers for the prime minister and his delegation to the summit. While there was no disposition to question the importance of responding to the call for unity from Eisenhower and Macmillan, there were obvious risks and disadvantages in what was known about the US military proposals. For

27

example, if IRBMs or even tactical nuclear weapons were placed in Western Europe, the Soviet Union might find new political and military reasons to tighten its grip on its Eastern European satellites. In both Ottawa and at the United Nations, the Polish government had argued that the stationing of intermediate-range missiles in Europe would make it more difficult for Poland to pursue a policy even mildly independent of Moscow. Moreover, there was concern that the introduction into Europe of nuclear weapons would make it more difficult to counter Soviet propaganda about NATO in the non-aligned world.

In a memorandum to Jules Léger, John Holmes warned that Canada should see NATO in relation to its other international responsibilities: 'We must try to remember, even with all the emotions of December in Paris, that NATO is only one of several associations which is important to us ... Our concern to keep our links with our Commonwealth associates and to hold the affection of Asians and Africans in the United Nations is not just a sentimental frill. It is a thoroughly hard-boiled effort to prevent the Russians from turning our flanks and exposing NATO as a Maginot Line ... We must maintain enough flexibility in our diplomacy to associate when necessary with non-NATO countries in the United Nations and elsewhere, to pursue policies with which other NATO countries do not agree, and even to support non-NATO countries in disputes with NATO countries. The NATO association implies an obligation to seek agreement with other members and to oppose them with special reluctance, but it does not involve any more than that.'[6] Léger, though a firm believer in NATO, took a somewhat different view. After hearing General Norstad, the supreme allied commander in Europe (SACEUR), address a meeting of the Cabinet Defence Committee in November, Léger said how struck he had been by the assumption underlying Norstad's talk that NATO planning was 'inspired by the anticipation of war.' He remarked how his hopes for NATO had been disappointed. He would have liked the alliance to serve as the interpreter and messenger of all that was good in Western civilization rather than have it regarded as nothing but a military alliance with no appeal to the non-aligned world. His conclusion was that, important as the prospective military changes were, NATO countries had severe problems of a non-military character which should not be left unattended.[7]

Despite the misgivings of some of its most senior and respected officials, there was an underlying recognition in External Affairs that the government would want to respond in as positive a way as possible to the call for unity from Eisenhower and Macmillan. Within the department there was little, if any, disposition to question openly the judgment of the military authorities in both the United States and Canada that the deployment of nuclear weapons in Europe was necessary as a counter to possible Soviet military probes. Those who were anxious about the wisdom of introducing nuclear weapons into continental Europe, as Ambassador George Kennan was in his Reith Lectures that autumn in England, found only modest public echo in Canada.

Yet there was one critical source of apprehension recognized by both civilian and military advisers. It was the problem of how to reconcile the efficient operational use of nuclear weapons with a satisfactory system for ensuring political control of their use. Because a decision to use tactical nuclear weapons 'could cause a local conflict to spread into general nuclear warfare ... the maximum degree of political control would seem desirable.'[8] This put the issue rather mildly. And the fact that political control would be the more difficult to exercise in the case of smaller tactical weapons, which in time would be assigned for use by Canadian forces in Europe, brought the problem into particularly sharp relief.

Despite the difficulty of the issue of political control, a decision on the US proposals was urgent. Bryce's panel recommended that the government should accept the proposal for the stockpiling of atomic weapons in Western Europe and that Canadian forces should, if necessary, be armed with defensive nuclear weapons.[9] No recommendation was forthcoming on the proposal to provide IRBMs to NATO countries in Europe, on the ground that this was primarily a matter for the European countries, along with the United States, to determine. The panel's recommendation was submitted for joint signature by the ministers of national defence and external affairs. It did not, however, become a formal cabinet document, although it was among the papers discussed informally by the prime minister with other ministers concerned. The final decision was left for solution in the wording of the prime minister's policy statement to the Paris meeting.

On 5 December, a few days before the various recommendations and briefing papers could be assembled – the final texts of the US proposals did not reach Ottawa until 6 December – the prime minister asked for papers he could read in preparation for the meeting. As this was the first time he had inquired, my initial reaction was to encourage his interest. Being unable to give him the briefing material in its finished form, I gave him what papers were available, a mistake I came to regret almost immediately. He made it plain the following day that he was dissatisfied and Bryce also let me know that the External Affairs contribution was inadequate.

It became clear that what the prime minister really wanted was not a bundle of policy papers but notes for the main speech he would be making at the Paris meeting. A lifetime of opposition politics had taught him to use speeches as the vehicle for formulating policy. A draft was ready, but incomplete, on 12 December. As the text stood when the delegation left Ottawa, it was lacking in one important particular – a passage on the American nuclear proposals which had been left for the prime minister to decide. From comments he made during the flight to Paris, I know that there remained genuine doubts in his mind on what position to take.

I think because he felt inadequately prepared, Diefenbaker's mood on arriving in Paris was decidedly pessimistic. He was tired from the trip but seemed also cynical about the meeting. Press reports were casting doubt on its likely success. Eisenhower's health might not stand up. Dulles was said to be wondering if the summit had not received too much ballyhoo. A private conversation with Macmillan failed to reverse Diefenbaker's estimate that nothing significant would come of the whole affair. Even Saturday night at the Folies Bergères failed to raise his spirits. He slept through most of the performance. What a contrast with the Macmillan visit to Ottawa when Diefenbaker had welcomed the NATO summit.

He was to speak in the afternoon of the first day. As usual before an important speech he was extremely nervous. In the morning he held a meeting of ministers and advisers in which Foulkes spoke in a knowledgeable and balanced way on the American nuclear proposals. None of the ministers was enthusiastic about placing atomic weapons in Europe. Even Pearkes, although supporting tactical nuclear stockpiles in Europe, was privately discouraging of too open an endorsement by Canada of the US proposals.[10]

The eventual section on the military proposals took the form of a cautious compromise. The decision to stockpile atomic weapons, the prime minister said, followed logically the decision taken in 1954 to organize NATO forces in Europe on the understanding that they would be able to use atomic weapons to repel attacks. This made it clear that the Liberal government had originally been a party to this process, and that the present government was simply acquiescing in the consequences of that collective decision taken three years before. As for IRBMs, the prime minister's statement was even more cautious. The IRBM proposal had serious financial and political implications which 'the NATO countries concerned' (ie, not Canada) would wish to consider very carefully. The statement supported the idea of postponing decisions on the IRBM proposal until it could be further studied at a future meeting of defence ministers early in 1958.

A broader issue was the balance to be struck on relations with the USSR. The speech draft spoke of keeping the door open to negotiations on disarmament and other major problems. It mentioned the benefits of an increase in contacts with the Soviet authorities through a mutual exchange of information and visits. It foresaw the possibility of a summit meeting at a later date. Diefenbaker accepted a substantial part of these 'liberal' ideas, choosing to omit only the specific reference to a summit meeting, which he knew would be unwelcome at that moment to Eisenhower and Dulles. The statement, not unnaturally, bore the marks of conflicting currents of policy advice. But on the whole, with its emphasis

on disarmament, on limiting NATO commitments, on balancing the political with
the military purposes of the alliance, and on contacts and readiness to negotiate
with the USSR, it placed Canada close to two of its traditional partners in NATO
– Norway and Denmark – without antagonizing the major NATO governments.
By chance, Diefenbaker had met with the Norwegian foreign minister, Halvard
Lange, immediately before the final drafting session on the Canadian statement.
Lange's presentation of the Norwegian position, with its misgivings about the
changes proposed in NATO's nuclear policy, echoed the thoughts which had been
expressed in recent weeks by Léger and Holmes in Ottawa, Escott Reid from
New York, and Norman Robertson from Washington. Even Diefenbaker, who
had approached the meeting uneasily in the knowledge of Lange's friendly links
with Pearson, told me that he had been 'very much struck with Lange's presentation of the issues.' He had not been sufficiently impressed to make changes
of substance in his speech, but the emphasis and tone he chose – especially on
relations with the Soviet Union – were more conciliatory than usual. It was the
first time he had been struck by the arguments against the deployment of nuclear
weapons in Europe. The episode also revealed another side of his character: a
tendency to accept from impressive foreign leaders advice or points of view
which he had not taken seriously at home.

The final public statements consisted of two documents. The first was a declaration, a restatement of the principles and objectives of the alliance. The idea
for this had originated in Ottawa, as part of the effort to generate a greater sense
of unity in NATO. A Canadian text was circulated and, after being fertilized and
shaped by numerous others, finally emerged in worthy and forgettable prose.
Associated with it was the meeting's final communiqué, setting out a number
of significant agreements in principle, to guide the work of NATO in the following
year. At the close of the last day, the heads of government and foreign ministers
left it to their senior advisers and the NATO Secretariat to complete the final
wording of the communiqué – a task which kept Bryce and Léger, and their
counterparts, around the table until the early hours of the morning.

The declaration contained one new paragraph proposed by Diefenbaker, drawing attention to the growing desire for freedom in the areas under 'international
Communist rule.' He had been prompted to introduce a passage along these
lines by a group of representatives of peoples behind the Iron Curtain who had
called on him in Paris. That meeting had made him forty-five minutes late for
lunch at the British embassy, where he was one of the senior guests of honour.
His British hosts, including Macmillan, were not amused. But it would be highly
beneficial, on returning home, to be able to point to the paragraph he had caused
his partners to approve in their common declaration.

This incident highlighted a theme which Diefenbaker had brought with him into office and which he never surrendered – a concern for those ethnic communities in Canada of Eastern European origin and a sympathy with their virulent anti-Soviet feeling. Some of his sharpest conflicts with the Department of External Affairs arose in this area of policy. As he made plain in his memoirs, he could never understand the department's resistance to his campaign of rhetoric against Soviet policy towards the 'captive nations.'[11] In its turn the department thought that, inspiring though the prime minister's anti-Soviet speeches were in the ethnic communities in Canada, they could have no useful impact on Soviet policy and might even be used against the people they were designed to encourage within the Soviet empire. The department also considered that Diefenbaker's obsession with Soviet colonialism might impair the possibilities of dialogue between the Canadian and Soviet governments. The extent to which this would become a bone of contention with External Affairs had not, however, become evident at the Paris meeting. Or perhaps at that time we were blind to its emergence.

The Diefenbakers took time for a brief stopover in London, where under the benevolent eye of Macmillan, the prime minister became a member of the United Kingdom Privy Council. He had scheduled his return to Ottawa in time to report to the House on the last day before adjournment. He based his speech on the declaration and communiqué approved by the NATO meeting, adding points of emphasis which he wanted especially to have on the record. On East-West relations he spoke in somewhat tougher anti-Soviet terms than he had used in Paris. This was closer to his instinctive voice. But he was careful to leave the door open for genuine negotiations on disarmament with the Soviet Union. His references to the major military decisions taken by the meeting were brief. He made clear his view that the alliance had no choice but to have nuclear weapons available in Europe in case of need. The weapons would, however, be provided to SACEUR, and negotiations with the nations concerned would be 'on a bilateral basis.' In other words, the decisions taken were alliance decisions in principle but there was no obligation on individual member countries to have missiles or nuclear ammunition on their territories.[12]

In assessing the role played by the Canadian delegation to this meeting, one must remember that this was the first NATO conference for the prime minister and his three ministerial colleagues. It was also the first time such a large Canadian team under his leadership, and including a sizeable cluster of senior officials, had functioned together as a unit in a conference setting away from Canada. For reasons no one in Ottawa could have controlled, the ministers had had only a few days of serious preparation, and to a man they were almost entirely without background in the meeting's agenda. The meeting itself had been hastily planned and the proceedings were so dominated by the search for consensus on the declaration and communiqué that the opportunities for serious debate on the central issues were notably limited. It was not therefore an occasion in which newcomers were likely to shine, and it must be said that Canada was not, to anything like the degree it had been in the past, a central player in the conference diplomacy.

For the prime minister himself, this was not a matter of concern. Deep down he knew his limitations. He was not sufficiently knowledgeable to take a major part in the discussions. He had for a time been privately cynical about the whole enterprise. Gradually, and once his main speech was behind him, his mood improved and he became more engaged in the proceedings. Although he played no more than a supporting role in a large production, the experience was educative and in the end enjoyable. Before the meeting, NATO had been a club he had joined but never visited and whose rules and procedures he would encounter for the first time. The agenda had posed dilemmas more familiar to his political opponents than to him and his colleagues. Now he could put faces to names, knew more about the dilemmas, and could bring first-hand experience to bear on these issues in the future. By the time he met the House, his grasp of subject matter was stronger as he spoke of the achievements of the conference.

Only on the nuclear issue could a note of uncertainty be detected, although little was said of it at the time. By giving cautious support to one of the US proposals on NATO nuclear strategy, he had implicitly accepted a nuclear commitment for Canadian air and land forces in Europe. But his statements at the Paris meeting and in the House of Commons showed what a delicate balance he felt must be maintained between defence preparedness and the continuing search for progress on disarmament. The peace movement in Canada was not yet a major political force, but anxiety about disarmament prospects, and especially nuclear weapons testing, was beginning to make itself felt in the press and in parliament.

This is not to say that Diefenbaker was personally undergoing a conversion or even that at that stage he was beginning seriously to doubt the necessity of becoming involved in nuclear commitments. It was simply that with some prompting from External Affairs, his political sense was telling him that nuclear weapons issues would have to be handled with care. He had found a domestic rationale to match the anxieties of those in External Affairs who were concerned about the international political consequences of US nuclear proposals. The nuclear dilemma which took root so early in his years in office would never disappear, and would, in the end, prove too much for his powers of decision.

5

Assembling the Team

The first weeks under the new prime minister had left a mixed reaction in the Department of External Affairs. Some of those who had direct dealings with him, including John Holmes, then the senior assistant undersecretary, found him considerate, attentive, and quick to absorb the broad lines of an issue. Many in External Affairs, however, thought he had shown a lack of confidence in the department on a number of events clearly within its responsibility. The visit of Dulles had been one example. Another was the agreement with the United States on air defence announced on 1 August. Yet another was the apparent reluctance of the prime minister to involve the department in external affairs issues before the cabinet. The fact that officials had been instructed not to speak to the press, and that the prime minister had not used the department's advice in the few public statements he made on international questions, added to the apprehension and the challenge. All this was furrowing the earnest departmental brow, but it was not worrying the prime minister one bit. He often chuckled about it.

In the first weeks after he became prime minister, he was determined to take the measure of the department, to seek ways of getting it under control – his control. Diefenbaker could not hope to match the Liberals in their comfortable command of the bureaucracy, but he wanted to arrange matters so that the department's competence – which he made clear had yet to be demonstrated to him – could be harnessed to his purposes. It would not do to hand such a prize to an ambitious political rival. To whom, if anyone, among his parliamentary colleagues could he entrust the department when the time came?

The fact that Diefenbaker waited three months before appointing his first secretary of state for external affairs was also partly attributable to his curiosity about the department and its people. The uneasy prejudice he felt against Pearson

34

certainly coloured his expectations of the people he would find in External Affairs. He wanted to gain some insight into what he liked to call the 'Personalities,' to the way they thought and operated, before turning them over to a minister. He wanted to prepare himself to assert control of the department no matter who became its minister. At that time the most senior External Affairs officials occupied offices on the second floor of the East Block, down the corridor from where the prime minister himself worked when parliament was not in session. So long as he could get a rise out of someone, he called these officials 'those babies down the hall.'

Diefenbaker possessed some preconceptions about diplomats and diplomatic style. He thought that diplomats paid too much attention to formality and protocol, that they often failed to understand and take into account political realities, that they were theoretical rather than practical in their approach to international dealings, and that they were too ready to see the other side's point of view. He was particularly suspicious of senior members of the Department of External Affairs who were long-time colleagues and friends of L.B. Pearson. A fierce partisan himself, Diefenbaker could not imagine that Pearson and the Liberals would not benefit from these old relationships. He liked people to be practical, definite, and decisive, to know which side they were on. He wanted officials to understand politics but to keep themselves behind the curtain, available, knowledgeable, up to date, loyal, and discreet and on no account to get their names in the *Globe and Mail*. Face to face he expected, indeed demanded, frankness, the full story, warnings of difficulties ahead, advice that would help him deal with the political problem.

The prime minister was fortunate to inherit in R.B. (Bob) Bryce, the secretary to the cabinet, a man who could 'handle' the bureaucracy and, at the same time, be his principal adviser on nearly everything. From the outset, Diefenbaker took to Bryce, admired the extraordinary range of his knowledge of government affairs, liked his straightforward style and his shrewd appreciation of political realities. Throughout the Diefenbaker years, Bob Bryce was a Herculean figure.

Foreign affairs to Diefenbaker were first and always a domestic political challenge. If he could see the domestic benefit in what was proposed, he would give the advice a serious look. But if the question were put to him as something that was good for purely international reasons, it had two strikes against it from the start. He often said that External Affairs had been insulated from real-life political pressures and that its members operated in a political vacuum. He had some justification for feeling as he did. It was quite possible in the External Affairs of the late 1940s and 1950s to have the impression that domestic politics was extraneous to the real job.

Not for Diefenbaker, however, was the crusading search for ways of saving the world, nor the cautious avoidance of undiplomatic oratory. The regard or acclaim of non-Canadian opinion was and would always be secondary; foreign policy was fascinating, and it was special, but it was not so special that it justified abandoning his normal political tactics. A bi-partisan foreign policy for Canada was not an aim he was likely to pursue, much as he might profess to believe in it. Pearsonian statesmanship was all very well, but would it help to win the next election?

Among the numerous claimants on his time while he was acting as foreign minister were the heads of diplomatic missions in Ottawa. To the normal ambassador, and most ambassadors are exceedingly normal in this respect, a meeting with a prime minister newly in power is one of the ultimate professional challenges. Prime ministers are supposed to understand this. They are supposed to cooperate in shaping the ambassador's discerning appraisal of the prime minister's probable policy line on the great issues of the day, especially those affecting the interests of the government the ambassador has the honour to represent.

To John Diefenbaker, the value of playing this game was by no means evident. 'Why don't they relax?' he would say, with a look half cynically amused and half impatient. I soon learned that routine courtesy calls by ambassadors were 'a hell of a long way down [his] list of worries.' How often I was to hear those words!

At that stage in my own career, I was under the impression that ambassadors were significant and, whenever possible, ought to have their own way. They had replaced generals, whom I had glimpsed during the war in Europe, as figures of authority. The fact that the undersecretary, the chief of protocol, and other senior departmental officials were also anxious to accommodate the curiosity of the ambassadors may have moved me to embrace the cause more conscientiously than was warranted. The prime minister made it unmistakably clear that I had my priorities wrong.

It was about that time that I came to appreciate the delicacy of my role. The department might expect its liaison officer to convey information or advice, and to report the prime minister's reactions or instructions. But the prime minister expected service and support too. I was to work for him and not for the department or the foreign diplomats.

SIDNEY SMITH ARRIVES

If there was one thing Diefenbaker relished, it was to spring a surprise on the press. The appointment of Dr Sidney E. Smith, president of the University of

Toronto, as secretary of state for external affairs on 14 September 1957 qualified as a genuine surprise. Dr Smith – on arrival in External Affairs he asked to be known as Mr Smith – had an established reputation as a university administrator, and it was assumed that his qualities of mind, his wide interests, and his outgoing personality would compensate for his relative lack of experience in international affairs.

The prime minister had correctly assumed that political and public reaction would be favourable. The response was also good in the Department of External Affairs, although this was a long way from being Diefenbaker's leading criterion for the appointment. For several days before the announcement he enjoyed making teasing remarks about the shock that was about to hit the department. In fact the Smith appointment seemed to make everybody happy, except perhaps those who had themselves aspired to the post; and media reaction allowed no serious objections to surface.

Diefenbaker had engineered and produced a coup. His delight in it was somewhat diluted when Smith, on the day of his swearing-in, confessed he had seen nothing wrong with Canadian policy in the Suez crisis and was quickly corrected by the prime minister. This was the first indication that Smith might be less than a natural politician. It might be a sign that his personal views were such as to place him in the mainstream of previous Canadian foreign policy thinking as personified by Pearson. But the evidence was tenuous and the incident did not seriously diminish the prime minister's understandable satisfaction in the appointment.

Although Sidney Smith was far from well informed on international questions, he was warmly welcomed by the department and it was generally assumed that he would 'grow' without serious difficulty into the minister's role. This proved to be too optimistic an assumption. The fact is that for a number of reasons, not all of his own making, Smith had much more difficulty in mastering the new role than he, the department, or, I believe, the prime minister himself anticipated. Smith was a friendly, approachable, and popular minister but his tenure of the portfolio was one of disappointed hopes. Only in the last months before his much lamented passing in March 1959 did he begin to do justice to the expectations aroused by his appointment.

Perhaps Smith's biggest handicap was that he did not possess a close relationship with the prime minister. They were friendly but did not know each other well and had not previously worked together. The division of labour between them was not formally planned or even informally agreed. Smith was away so much in the first few weeks, winning a seat and moving house, that the day-to-day work he would have taken on gravitated to the prime minister or to another acting minister, with the result that he was deprived of the opportunity to settle in to his enormously demanding job. It was not Diefenbaker's habit to arrange regular meetings with individual ministers, and Smith was diffident about asking for the prime minister's time. Both of them were working at full stretch, and although Diefenbaker was by no means indifferent to the minister's difficulties, the fact was that the minister was left to fend for himself, with whatever help the department could give him.

On the first day he showed a streak of independence. Why had Canada not recognized Communist China, he asked, addressing a group of startled departmental officials who were left to wonder whether the government might embark on a new policy towards China, and whether the new minister might have other initiatives up his sleeve. But what had seemed refreshing at first blush was soon submerged by reality. There was a mass of unfamiliar subjects to tackle. There were policies in place or in the making, not only on China but on a hundred other issues. There was a full agenda of a new session of the UN General Assembly, and important meetings about to take place with the United States in the economic and defence fields. In these and all the other policy areas, the bulk of international activity was conducted among foreign ministers and their ministries. This had been the territory that Pearson had dominated, always subject to the consultation he was careful to undertake with Prime Minister St Laurent when new or important points of policy arose. This was now Smith's territory, and it remained to be seen how he would put his stamp on it, and how his role would mesh with that of the prime minister.

DIEFENBAKER'S CONTINUING NEEDS

While Sidney Smith was settling in, the prime minister made it clear that he wished to be kept fully informed on international developments. Although the formal channel to the prime minister on important policy matters was the minister, it was out of the question to expect that all the necessary information and advice could be channelled through him, especially during the early months when he was frequently obliged to be away from Ottawa. Even when the minister was in Ottawa, the prime minister insisted on being provided with a direct and continuous flow of telegrams, memoranda, and speech material in order to be equipped to deal with questions that might arise in parliament, in cabinet, or in his encounters with foreign diplomats, the press, and in public appearances.

The prime minister was also the recipient of a considerable flow of special messages from his counterparts in other governments. Macmillan in particular was clearly determined to do his part in building up a friendly relationship. His messages, marked confidential and personal, phrased in elegantly informal language, reassuring and understanding in tone, were perfectly tailored to appeal to Diefenbaker and to attract his approval of their content. The British high commissioner, Sir Saville (Joe) Garner, made effective use of the access created by his instructions to deliver and facilitate this correspondence. Later, Eisenhower occasionally wrote informally. Diefenbaker treated such letters with special care, regarding them as messages directed to him personally by friends who did not intend them to be passed around through official channels. At times he took such correspondence to his residence at 24 Sussex Drive in Ottawa, and I suppose that this is the source of at least some of the stories that have circulated about secret papers being found under his mattress or elsewhere in the house.

The unfortunate fact was, however, that frequently the foreign representatives in Ottawa were aware of what had been written while their Canadian counterparts were not. This gave rise to much concern in the Department of External Affairs in the first year or so of Diefenbaker's term of office. Because these letters often contained information of an official rather than personal character, I was commissioned to field or locate as many as I could on the assumption that most if not all of them would require some staff work. As time went on, the prime minister came to recognize that a considerable body of official business was transacted by high-level exchanges of correspondence, and, except for entirely personal exchanges, it became the normal procedure to have such material circulated to ministers or officials responsible for dealing with the subject matter. This device did not always avoid difficulties. Diefenbaker was not amused to be approached about a diplomatic message which he thought was known only to himself. His conversion would be gradual and grudging, influenced over the years more by his observation of Macmillan's trust in his private secretaries and their links with the British Foreign Office than by any other factor.

Among the hazards and burdens of serving John Diefenbaker, one of the most trying was his way of approaching speaking engagements. He would accept them in principle many months in advance. You knew they were on the list and often that something on external affairs might be required. But to guess what he would want was a lot more difficult, and to prescribe subject matter without checking with him in advance was generally hard on the digestion of everyone concerned. You had to wait until he had focused on the problem and hope that there would be enough time to respond with something he would accept.

It was clear to me from the outset that material for speeches would be a high priority and that Diefenbaker's requirements would not be easy to satisfy. To some extent, this was because he was put off by the style in which the material was presented. Long years of serving St Laurent and Pearson had not been the ideal preparation for meeting the needs of Diefenbaker. The positions he had taken previously on foreign policy issues had, with the exception of the Suez crisis, not differed much in substance from those of the Liberal government. But the elaboration of his views, now that he was in power, proved to be an arduous trial both for him and his advisers. He was not comfortable with a carefully crafted departmental speech draft of the kind that Pearson, with a combination of deft infusions and ruthless surgery, would quickly make his own. Diefenbaker often made fun, privately as well as publicly, of diplomatic language. Double talk, typical Pearsonian flannel-mouthing, he would explode, enjoying whatever traces of shock one might have failed to conceal. (It was one of the ironies of the Diefenbaker style that a man so given to obfuscation in his public rhetoric should not have been more attracted to the language of old-fashioned public diplomacy.)

The External Affairs part in the preparation of Diefenbaker's early speeches on foreign policy was complicated by another factor: his habit of inviting contributions from a variety of sources. Not surprisingly there were plenty of volunteers, especially in the early months. A draft sent forward by External Affairs would find itself in competition with offerings from members of the Parliamentary Press Gallery, occasional academics, staff members, or candidates for employment in Diefenbaker's office, and from his friends or political supporters around the country.

Small wonder that Diefenbaker, with his habit of personally coordinating and editing his speeches, put his own time and energies under heavy pressure on this account; or that the Department of External Affairs had a struggle to adapt itself to the new prime minister's methods. The normal practice had been to make important speech texts available in advance to Canadian offices abroad as well as to the Ottawa Press Gallery and the wire services. Diefenbaker had no objection in principle to this procedure but frequently he made it impossible to carry out. Almost invariably the final product was arrived at by a sort of quilting process, the pieces assembled and stitched together only at the last minute and in a design that no one else could have predicted, and only the right honourable craftsman himself could have achieved.

And if this had not been enough of a worry for a department accustomed to knowing what was going to be said before the words were uttered, Diefenbaker had another habit, a disturbing tendency to doctor his text as he went along. The written word was always subject to change, whether in the order of paragraphs, by the deletion of sentences, or the introduction of new passages sometimes qualifying or offsetting points made elsewhere in the text. The performer in him rebelled against the discipline of a cut and dried script. His chosen means of communicating was the spoken word, and no matter how carefully a policy statement had been written, or how many drafts it had been through, or whether it had been released as an advance text to the media, he treated it as having no legitimate status until he had delivered it.

TAKING THE PULSE

Diefenbaker's overriding thought as 1958 opened was to plan for the election. Foreign policy would probably not provide a campaign issue. By the time, however, that the Liberal party chose Pearson as its new leader in January, Diefenbaker had already taken steps to block off openings that Pearson, with his experience in international affairs, might have exploited. The prime minister had played a well-publicized if not influential role in the international meetings he had attended – the conference of Commonwealth prime ministers, the UN General Assembly, and the NATO summit. He had been quick to enter into correspondence with the Soviet leaders when they showed an interest in summit diplomacy. In his speech at Dartmouth College in September, he had expressed the misgivings widely felt in Canada about the advancing tide of American economic influence. He had headed off Pearson's attempt to portray the NORAD agreement as a surrender of Canadian sovereignty. He had established himself in the public mind as having new, if untried, ideas on subjects such as Commonwealth trade and the disposal of agricultural surpluses. He could not be as experienced or knowledgeable as St Laurent or Pearson, but in his own way he had emerged as a leader more responsive than they to the mood of the time in Canada.

The normal process of education in office, learning on the job, was also having its effect. Diefenbaker had now had six months of regular exposure to the everyday traffic by which national governments communicate and to the process by which they try to cope with international problems as they arise. He was now accustomed, if not without complaint, to the shaded language of the diplomats. He had begun to absorb what was important to other governments and, in particular, to other leaders with responsibilities comparable to his own, although he was not easily influenced by the priorities of others – unless he could see a link with his own political objectives. In his outlook on the world, he would never be far from home.

After six months in the service of the Diefenbaker government, the Department of External Affairs remained psychologically uncomfortable. Sidney Smith's difficulties had not been eased by the NATO experience. The sheer volume, range, and complexity of the subject matter, and of the new style of life and work, had exposed the minister's inexperience and taxed his powers of concentration. The openness of his mind did not seem to be matched by a capacity to put his own imprint on new information or advice. Smith's instincts – generous, humanitar-

41

ian, and conciliatory – were apparently not complemented in his new setting by the necessary powers of persuasion and advocacy. He was not at home in cabinet meetings; in fact he seemed to dread them. He had shown himself, moreover, to be ill at ease in parliamentary debate, with a compulsion to speak off the cuff when pitfalls could have been avoided by sticking to an available text.

Nevertheless, at the turn of the year, it was natural to hope that as the minister's familiarity with the foreign policy issues and his experience in parliament grew, so might his influence in the government and with the prime minister. If things went well, some thought there was a chance that the department at home and the foreign service abroad might be able to recapture in some degree the sense of purpose that had distinguished them under St Laurent and Pearson. Was that too much to hope?

Those who gave Smith the benefit of the doubt argued that, despite his inexperience and other limitations, his instincts and outlook on the world were more enlightened than Diefenbaker's and deserved every support the department could furnish. It was true that Smith was open to new ideas and approaches and anxious to chart an independent foreign policy. While he was far from unrealistic about the problems involved in co-existence with the communist powers, he was more interested than Diefenbaker in exploring the feasibility of new political solutions to East-West problems. He was concerned about nuclear weapons before it became a hot political topic. He remained personally attracted to the idea of recognizing Communist China and of having the Peking regime replace the Nationalist Chinese government in the United Nations.

These signs were promising, but they would have no chance of influencing government policy unless Smith could establish with Diefenbaker a solid working partnership. This never happened. Partly the problem was a matter of personality and wavelength. Smith was awed by Diefenbaker, reluctant to bother him, afraid to provoke his disapproval. Diefenbaker was not a natural co-operator or consulter. Their contacts, apart from cabinet meetings, were sporadic and fitful, and not sufficiently thorough to shape the foundation of a coherent foreign policy. Smith, entirely loyal, soldiered on, gradually mastering the day-to-day affairs of the department. But he was impeded by Diefenbaker's disinclination to delegate initiative, and by the increasing tendency towards top-level correspondence and high-level meetings between heads of government. It was not so much that Diefenbaker deliberately set out to snatch the spotlight from Smith but that he found him slow in coming to the point and diffident in presenting his case. Too often Smith was in the position of having to accommodate himself to something the prime minister had already done or said he would do.

In these difficult circumstances the department was still feeling its way towards an understanding of what the prime minister, as distinct from the minister, wanted of it. Diefenbaker's often critical judgments were not aimed so much at individuals as at what reached him in the form of advice. He would have liked to receive a clear-cut submission on every issue, without so many conditions and so much balancing of pros and cons. He had noted, for example, that on the major strategic issues confronting the NATO meeting, External Affairs opinion had been divided and lacking in focus. He remarked on the excessive time and resources devoted to the preparation of sophisticated briefing essays as compared with the effort put into the drafting of effective speech material.

Yet while he was frequently hard to please, his appetite for comment on the international news gave the Department of External Affairs a special entrée to his attention which it grasped quickly and did not relinquish as long as he was in office. The news of the day frequently reached him first through the wire services, but the department was able to satisfy his need for a regular flow of analysis and comment, based on reports from Canadian diplomatic offices abroad and assessments composed in the department, supplemented where necessary by recommendations for action or possible comment. On occasion, the prime minister found the External Affairs style 'academic,' one of his favourite labels for unduly high-minded advice. By early 1958, however, his desire to receive such material regularly was firmly established. For the department, this had the important related advantage of providing regular access to him at times when his reaction or decisions were urgently required.

Diefenbaker's own thoughts were elsewhere. He was poised to choose the moment for the election. On 21 January he and Pearson had their first parliamentary passage at arms since Pearson, a short time before, had become leader of the Liberal party. I was in the House of Commons on that afternoon when Pearson took the extraordinary course of moving an amendment which, in effect, called on the government to hand over the reins to the Liberals. When he took his seat, his face already betraying his doubts as to what he had done, the stage was set for Diefenbaker. His performance was devastating. The episode had at least three tangible consequences. It brought on an early election, because Diefenbaker knew better than to forego the advantage he had won. It determined the momentum with which the election campaign would begin. And it gave Diefenbaker an even greater confidence than he had had before in his capacity to defeat the Liberals under Pearson.

The calling of the election for 31 March 1958 meant that, for a few weeks, the prime minister had time for only the most urgent international matters. And the fact that foreign policy did not become a major issue in the election campaign at least gave Sidney Smith a relief from the pressure he had been under since his appointment in September.

THE PEOPLE'S CHOICE

Diefenbaker exuded confidence during his brief ricochets with Ottawa during the campaign, but even he was surprised by the vote of confidence he received – 208 out of the 265 seats in the House of Commons, the biggest majority up to that time in Canadian history.

My first opportunity to visit him came two days after the election. He dealt quickly with some decisions that had been held for his return and then began reminiscing about the campaign. The results in Quebec, he began, had vindicated his judgment. Some people had advised him to go into Quebec and buy their support with promises. He had rejected this advice. If he had shown himself too anxious for their support, they would have reacted the wrong way. It would have been the same thing in Toronto. If he had gone there and said, 'I love you people, I just love you,' what would they have done? Well, they would have had their hands on their holsters in a second. People don't like that kind of approach and Quebeckers, he said, were no different in this respect from anyone else. The result, he went on, was 'sobering.' It would never be repeated. There would never be as big a majority for any one man again. I said that personally I had been sorry to see both M.J. Coldwell and Stanley Knowles of the CCF lose their seats in the election. Yes, he was sorry about them too, but they had made the mistake of attacking him personally and that was unwise in this election.

Thus inflated by his triumph but badly needing rest and time to ponder plans for the future, he went off to Bermuda for a break. Before he left we were only a little surprised to learn that Sidney Smith was to be reappointed as secretary of state for external affairs. On 5 April, I wrote in my diary: 'he now feels himself in the saddle with a long clear road ahead. He has a chance to show what stuff he is made of and I just hope he does well.'

PART TWO

Distant Summits

APRIL 1958 TO
JUNE 1959

6

Surveying the World Scene

In the year following the 1958 election, Diefenbaker never relaxed the pace of his own involvement in international affairs. He maintained his keen interest in the prospects for an East-West summit meeting; presided over visits to Ottawa by a series of foreign leaders including Prime Minister Macmillan and President Eisenhower; and took a personal hand in dealing with dangerous crises in the Middle East and Berlin. In the late months of 1958, he undertook a seven-week tour of Western Europe and the Asian and Pacific parts of the Commonwealth.

In the shadow of the more conspicuous events, there was almost no end to the diplomatic exertions being undertaken around the world, most of them demanding or at least inviting some form of Canadian participation. It had already become clear that under Diefenbaker and Sidney Smith, Canada would be hardly less involved than under their predecessors in, for example, discussions on disarmament, efforts to bring stability to Indochina, the search for ways to bring China into the mainstream of world affairs, and the increasingly difficult and expensive problem of bringing needed assistance to newly independent countries.

But of all the international issues facing the new government, none more consistently preoccupied Diefenbaker than the continental relationship. Although he was anxious to get off on the right foot with Eisenhower, he was also conscious of the nationalistic mood his government had helped to create in Canadian opinion, particularly in economic matters.

Perhaps most intractable, although not yet as visibly troublesome, was the cluster of problems stemming from cooperation with the United States in air defence. The NORAD issue was on the way to being settled after an untidy start, but now that the machinery for integrated planning and control was in place, there arose the daunting question of the equipment it would need. The cancellation of the Avro Arrow project and the opening rounds in the long and painful battle over nuclear armaments took their place on the agenda of government business during this period. External Affairs was a minor player in the Arrow affair, but soon it would become heavily involved in nuclear weapons policy, if only because that issue was to become the principal sore point in the political relationship between Ottawa and Washington.

These were the chief international issues facing Canada in the first year of the second Diefenbaker administration. Then, in March 1959, just as he was growing in confidence as foreign minister, Sidney Smith died suddenly of heart failure. Diefenbaker, shocked and saddened, and needing time to decide on the replacement, acted as interim foreign minister until he appointed Howard Green in June. With that decision he unknowingly set the stage for a radical change of emphasis in his government's foreign policy.

THE VIEW ACROSS THE ATLANTIC

Like other Western heads of government, Diefenbaker had been engaged since the turn of the year in correspondence with the Soviet leaders, Bulganin and Khrushchev. He was keenly aware of the propaganda ingredients of these exchanges and particularly of the idea of a summit meeting, which was being advanced by the Soviet government. Having discussed this idea in Paris with both Eisenhower and Macmillan, he knew that while Macmillan was in principle favourable, Eisenhower was reluctant. Diefenbaker was anxious not to embarrass Eisenhower by coming out too strongly for a summit meeting, but he could not resist getting into the action. Already, before the election, he had publicly suggested that if a decision were taken to hold a summit meeting, it might take place in Canada, a suggestion which landed an easy headline or two but which evoked no reaction from governments likely to participate, or indeed from anywhere else.

Underlying all this, as so often with Diefenbaker, was a collision of impulses. Politically he recognized that concepts such as NATO solidarity and nuclear deterrence must be balanced by a proclaimed readiness to seek peaceful solutions to East-West problems. Yet his deep suspicion of Soviet motives, strong doubts that the Soviet leaders could ever be brought to make real concessions, concern for the plight of minorities within the Soviet perimeter, fear of the impact of Soviet economic strategy in the developing world, and conviction that strength alone would deter Soviet expansionism – all these ideas he embraced as ardently as John Foster Dulles, the leading Cold War advocate of the 1950s.

These opposite tendencies produced a chronic tug-of-war in his thinking on global policy. Now the hard-shelled side would be uppermost, now the soft, and in determining which had the upper hand, one became accustomed to observing the influences to which he had recently been subjected. It was not a particularly good recipe for exerting influence on other governments, nor did it bring the best out of the Department of External Affairs, where many of the officials sensed that the prime minister was more interested in scoring political points than in getting at the real problems. I felt as frustrated as most, but, being in the buffer zone between the prime minister and the minister, I was perhaps more resigned than most to the necessity of doing the best we could with the current management.

By the middle of May the agitation for an early summit meeting had receded. The exchanges between Western governments and Moscow had confirmed what might have been anticipated – that a meeting without extensive preparation risked being fruitless. Preoccupied with the new parliamentary session, Diefenbaker's attention was diverted from the summit, but it was never far from his mind and he looked forward to Macmillan's visit in June, and to Eisenhower's in July, to keep abreast of their assessments of the prospects and the value of direct contacts with the Soviet leadership.

Diefenbaker attached importance to the practice that visits by British prime ministers to Washington should be extended to include Ottawa. Macmillan usually preferred to have met with the president before coming to Ottawa, and Diefenbaker also seemed to prefer this order of proceeding. Macmillan, an accomplished exponent of international events, was in the habit of revealing in Ottawa just enough of what had transpired in Washington to leave Diefenbaker with a sense of knowing what was really going on in the world.

By the time Macmillan reached Ottawa in the second week of June, the return to power of General de Gaulle in France was already fascinating Diefenbaker. How should other Western governments respond so as to influence France to stay in the Western alliance? Macmillan said he had found in Washington a great anxiety to help de Gaulle. He agreed with the American approach. Every effort must be made to persuade de Gaulle to assist in making Europe cohesive, but de Gaulle was 'sensitive, mystical and vain,' and it would be important not to 'run after him.' Diefenbaker wondered about de Gaulle's attitude towards a summit meeting. Macmillan thought it might be better to have a 'tiresome' summit including de Gaulle than run the risk of having him take France into isolation from its Western allies.[1]

Diefenbaker wondered whether there was anything helpful the Canadian government could do to influence de Gaulle favourably towards the West generally and NATO in particular. De Gaulle, he said, 'must realize there would be no survival for France if France broke her alliances.' One could see, as the conversation progressed, that Diefenbaker was working up enthusiasm for a meeting with de Gaulle. After Macmillan's visit, Diefenbaker approved a message of congratulation to de Gaulle and invited him to visit Canada whenever circumstances permitted. De Gaulle responded warmly, saying that he hoped he would be able to visit Canada soon. Diefenbaker was struck by the tone of de Gaulle's reply and, when later in the summer he was planning a tour of some Western European capitals, he told me that a meeting with de Gaulle was a very high priority.

SHAPING THE LINK WITH WASHINGTON

Diefenbaker's concern about the state of Canada's relations with the United States was fully matched in the US embassy in Ottawa. Since the Diefenbaker government had taken office, Ambassador Livingston Merchant had made a number of speeches discreetly but plainly challenging what he evidently took to be disturbing trends in Canadian policy.

The ambassador went to Washington in May to help lay the groundwork for Eisenhower's visit to Ottawa in July. On 16 May he appeared before the Senate Foreign Relations Committee and gave a considered statement of his views on Canadian-American relations. Asked about anti-Americanism in Canada, he preferred to talk of 'a very powerful Canadianism' which had been aggravated by the electoral atmosphere prevailing in Canada over the previous year. Canadians were highly sensitive to anything the United States or its representatives might do to infringe on Canadian sovereignty or to overlook economic interests that Canadians regarded as vital. Diefenbaker had 'persistently advocated vigorous remedies and strong approaches to the United States' in finding solutions to economic problems. He could be expected to continue to protest 'eloquently and with vigor' what he considered as protectionist actions by the United States, while at the same time yielding to protectionist pressure groups in Canada by imposing restrictions on certain categories of imports. The words were carefully chosen and the tone was reasonable, but the ambassador's meaning and anxiety were unmistakeable. It is interesting to note that from the US standpoint, defence had not yet emerged as a source of difficulty in Canadian-American relations. The United States, Merchant said, 'certainly ... could not look for more effective cooperation than exists in our common defence efforts,' words which seem incongruous in the light of the turmoil which was brewing and would soon erupt over defence costs and nuclear cooperation.

I happened to be taking papers to the prime minister at his residence on Sussex Drive just as he finished reading reports of the ambassador's testimony. His first reaction was typically ambiguous – impressed by Merchant's analysis yet betraying a certain resentment at the implication that the present government of Canada was itself partly to blame for the change of climate in Canadian-American relations. Later, during Eisenhower's meeting with the Canadian cabinet in

Ottawa, Diefenbaker would embarrass Merchant by praising the ambassador's testimony to the Senate Committee.

At the end of May I was asked to obtain the prime minister's response to a memorandum informing him of the progress of preparations for the president's visit. Diefenbaker was taken aback by a suggestion in the memorandum that for health reasons the president might not be prepared to discuss in detail any of the important bilateral issues, but he agreed without hesitation that the president's health and convenience must be the prime consideration.[2]

By a strange turn of fate, an illness then kept me at home for several weeks in June and July and prevents me from offering a live commentary on the president's visit.[3] Watching the Eisenhower visit unfold, however, and keeping in touch with events by telephone, I could see the interplay of familiar tendencies and influences.

Diefenbaker's preference was that talks between him and Eisenhower should be as informal and private as possible. Other ministers would bring forward their special subjects in the various formal meetings, but what Diefenbaker wanted was to reinforce the personal links that had developed promisingly in his earlier meetings with the president in Ottawa and Paris. He insisted on plenty of time alone with Eisenhower. They spent part of it fishing in a small rowboat at Harrington Lake, the PM's summer house north of Ottawa, and part on an automobile tour of the surrounding area. I saw no record of their exchanges but clearly the prime minister's main purpose was served. His personal relationship with Eisenhower was strengthened and, although Eisenhower spoke strongly on bilateral economic issues in his speech to parliament, Diefenbaker knew he could always have access to the White House in case of need.

As for the more specific results of the visit, Diefenbaker attached particular importance to an understanding designed to avoid the imposition of US restrictions on trade between Canada and Communist China. Eisenhower and Dulles took the position that US foreign-assets control regulations should not operate to the disadvantage of Canadian companies, but, as Dulles told Canadian ministers, the US government did not want to open the door to subsidiaries of US companies around the world. This was good enough for Diefenbaker, especially after he had seen the indignant reaction of the president and Dulles to a remark made (half in jest) by Sidney Smith to the effect that Canada ought to recognize the Chinese communist regime. On hearing this Eisenhower pounded his fist on the desk and shouted that the day Canada recognized the Peking regime he would kick the United Nations out of the United States. The point was not pursued.

Not all the exchanges were as stormy, but neither were the other meetings, especially those on economic issues, all sweetness and light. The arguments made in parliament by the president on surplus agricultural policies, trade differences, and US investment in Canada were refined and reflected in Dulles's meetings with Canadian ministers and officials. The problems of nuclear co-operation had not ripened enough to be laid before the American leaders, but at least the occasion was taken to direct their attention to some of the problems that would soon confront the two governments.

CRISIS IN THE MIDDLE EAST

The first major international crisis of the Diefenbaker years came to a head only three days after Eisenhower and Dulles had completed their visit to Ottawa. A sudden uprising in Iraq on 14 July not only unseated the generally pro-Western regime in Baghdad but set off heavy political currents throughout the Middle East. Within twenty-four hours, US marines were landing in Lebanon in response to President Chamoun's urgent appeal to Washington. Two days later, on the 17th, British troops occupied the airport at Amman, the capital of Jordan, King Hussein having managed to convince the United Kingdom government that he too was deserving of immediate military support.

Two points are essential to an understanding of the crisis.[4] First, the United Kingdom and the United States had given certain guarantees that they would intervene if they were asked to do so by Chamoun in the event of a threat to the 'independence and integrity' of his regime. Second, although the crisis had entered spontaneously into its final stage, the United Nations had been working to defuse it for the past several weeks. Canada had agreed to participate in a new peacekeeping operation (UNOGIL) in Lebanon.[5]

In the weeks before the United States and the United Kingdom decided to intervene with military force, Diefenbaker's great concern had been to satisfy himself that they were cooperating closely. He had castigated the Liberal government in the Suez crisis of 1956 for not doing more to prevent the collapse of allied unity.[6] He was anxious not to allow the roles to be reversed.

The crisis lasted at full pitch for three weeks. Events at the United Nations, in which Sidney Smith played a persevering part, paved the way for the eventual withdrawal of American and British forces. All in all, the Canadian government's performance resembled that of its predecessor in 1956 – close consultation with its allies, an active conciliatory role at the United Nations, and a continuing readiness to accept peacekeeping responsibilities. True, not all Diefenbaker's ministers favoured the connection with the United Nations – perhaps it smacked too much of Suez and of the Pearson days. But Diefenbaker himself was pragmatic about it. He could see that to refuse a call from the United Nations would be far worse politically than to be blamed for following in Pearson's tracks.

The intensity of the crisis had some positive side effects. It brought the prime minister and Sidney Smith to work more effectively together than at any previous time. Yet Diefenbaker was still suspicious of External Affairs, a distrust that this time had its origin in two opposing views of how Western interests could best be served in the Middle East. Departmental officials – not all, but most – thought that an Arab regime which needed Western forces to sustain it would not survive for long, and that Canada should use its influence to encourage the use of the United Nations as a means of restoring stability in that area. For the prime minister, these factors were secondary. From his point of view it was far more important to retain the goodwill of Eisenhower and Macmillan than to agitate at the United Nations against the fulfilment of an Anglo-American commitment. He shared their lack of confidence in the capacity of the United Nations to prevent the overthrow of 'moderate' (ie, pro-Western) regimes in the Arab world.

There was also the Nasser factor. Diefenbaker had singled out Nasser as the arch-villain of the Suez crisis and as a co-conspirator with the USSR for control of the Middle East. The root of the problem in Lebanon, Jordan, and Iraq, as he saw it, was the political influence of Nasser. The idea that the United Arab Republic and Nasser's leadership were political forces with which the Western governments would be wise to come to terms was not a natural winner with Diefenbaker. Later his ideas would undergo some modification, but not now, in the face of the measures which his illustrious friends in Washington and London thought necessary in this emergency.

Another by-product of the crisis was a rare instance of harmony between Diefenbaker and Pearson. Diefenbaker was extremely conscious of Pearson's experience at the time of Suez – so much so that on 21 July, at a critical stage, he consulted Pearson on the government's course of action. The Diefenbaker-Pearson decade would not produce many such examples of practical cooperation. At the time it seemed a propitious omen.

7

World Tour: Europe

During his first administration from June 1957 to March 1958, Diefenbaker had been too much preoccupied with domestic affairs to devote more than the minimum necessary time to international travel. But soon after his government returned to office with a decisive majority, he felt free to plan for visits abroad. Various possibilities existed – a visit to the Queen at Balmoral, Scotland, might have been combined with stops in London, Brussels (for the international exposition), and Paris (at the invitation of de Gaulle). These were tentatively planned for late August, but after much dithering he decided to combine visits to the main Western European capitals with an extensive tour of the Asian and Pacific Commonwealth, to take place later in the year.

The tour was not to be all business. He saw it as a celebration of his political success as well as an appropriate mission to undertake. He wanted to gain the kind of education in international affairs which could only be obtained by first-hand observation and by personal meetings. And a trip to many foreign capitals with wire service journalists aboard was sure to pay publicity dividends in Canada.

Prime Minister St Laurent had undertaken a similar journey three years before, and Diefenbaker, with typical political caution, had his staff use the St Laurent tour as a model. He asked for details of the St Laurent itinerary, the engagements undertaken in each country visited, the methods of transportation, the costs of the trip, and the passenger list. He was especially careful to avoid being criticized for the size of his entourage. St Laurent having taken two members of his immediate family, there could be no objection to the inclusion of Diefenbaker's brother Elmer and, of course, Mrs Diefenbaker. Similar parallels were used throughout the planning process. The total cost of official gifts should not exceed the $8000 which had been spent by St Laurent, a limit which had awkward consequences, especially towards the end of the journey.

Six weeks before departure, beset by the problems of asserting the External Affairs role in the planning and conduct of the tour, I told the department in a memorandum that the atmosphere in the prime minister's office was like that of a family preparing for a tourist excursion around the world. I remarked on Diefenbaker's tendency to minimize the advice he would need from External Affairs, and expressed the fear that he did not fully appreciate the hard test in foreign affairs that he would be undergoing. I knew from frequent meetings with colleagues in the department that every stop along the route would have its own agenda of prickly issues. I feared that, without thorough preparation, the prime minister would not make the most of this first opportunity for a concentrated exposure to foreign policy problems. Despite the various international occasions he had experienced in his first year in office, there was still an ad hoc character to much of his participation in the process of reaching decisions in matters relating to external affairs.

It was not surprising that he should have decided to limit his visits to member countries of NATO and the Commonwealth. He was temperamentally a vigorous partisan in the Cold War. He felt it proper to seek solidarity with confirmed or potential allies. One of his problems with the Department of External Affairs was its habit of talking about flexibility and open-mindedness. These were qualities which, to him, betrayed a tendency to underestimate the importance of gathering allies for a long-term struggle against the spreading poison of communism, especially the Soviet brand.

Notwithstanding his desire to keep to a NATO and Commonwealth orbit, Diefenbaker accepted two significant additions to the original program. Having previously undertaken to address the Pilgrims Society in New York en route to his first major stop in London, he agreed, without much enthusiasm, that a meeting with the secretary-general of the United Nations, Dag Hammarskjöld, might be of benefit at the outset of the tour. Pressure had been building up, too, from a handful of other countries which would have welcomed a visit by Diefenbaker at that time. For example, a visit to Indochina, where Canadians were serving with the International Control Commissions, was discussed. Diefenbaker was, however, adamant that apart from the normal courtesies at refuelling stops such as Beirut or Tehran, the tour should not be extended beyond Western Europe and the Commonwealth countries of Asia. Only in the case of Indonesia was the pressure so insistent and the likelihood of offence so strong that an exception was made. Even then Diefenbaker would agree only to the briefest staging stop at Djakarta.

There being no shortcuts to knowledge of major international issues, the prime minister's briefing books for each stage of the expedition were considerable in girth and complexity. They contained background memoranda and talking points on each country to be visited, together with personality sketches on the hosts. Still another volume contained notes for the prime minister's use at press conferences. At the request of the RCAF, a 'dry run' was taken over every step of the tour a month in advance of the real thing. In this way, any number of potential administrative disasters were averted. Before the tour began, too, I wrote in advance to some of our ambassadors along the route: 'The Prime Minister is an early riser and is generally in particularly good form early in the morning. That is the time when we ... try to get decisions from him and this becomes less easy as the day wears on ... It is a cast-iron rule that he likes to go to bed as early as possible and from all points of view this is desirable since if he tires he tends to be difficult.' I also suggested in a letter to Canberra 'it would be wise to leave him as much time as possible for shirt sleeves and feet up. He and Mrs. Diefenbaker are very jealous of their time together and she tends to be quite militant about rest and relaxation time for him.'

Diefenbaker's quizzical view of diplomats and their preoccupations might have been reinforced if he had seen a telegram sent by Pierre Dupuy, the ambassador to France, some two weeks before the prime minister would be in Paris. In planning an appropriate dinner party for the occasion, the ambassador, who had only recently been appointed to Paris after serving for some years in Rome, wrote as follows to the department:

Prime Minister's Visit: Tablecloths

There is only one lace tablecloth at this mission which can be used at important functions such as the forthcoming visit of the Prime Minister. This tablecloth cannot rpt not in any event be utilized in the case of functions attended by more than fourteen guests.
2. I understand there are five such tablecloths available in Rome. My recollection is that two of them are actually too narrow for the dining table there. They are of venetian lace and greyish brown (bis) in colour. I would suggest that these two tablecloths be transferred to this mission where they will serve a useful purpose. If you agree with this suggestion, I should very much appreciate your issuing appropriate instructions to Rome in order that the transfer may be effected in time for the Prime Minister's visit (Nov. 5). Our mission in Rome should be asked to send at the same time the yellow satin lining which goes with the two tablecloths mentioned above.

The reader will be relieved to know that the necessary instructions were sent for the transfer of the tablecloths and the yellow satin lining, and that both were in place for the ambassador's dinner. The department knew a priority when it saw one. The best comment – that it was a case of Arsenic and Old Lace – came from Jules Léger many years later.

Writing to Canadian representatives along the route, I included another advisory point, this one to be shared with the host governments: 'the Prime Minister is a little bit harder of hearing than he will admit. He likes to have the person to whom he is speaking on the right side (this is obviously not always possible) and he prefers as small groups as possible. He does not wear a hearing aid, except in the House of Commons. If you could give the tip-off to people to speak clearly and directly to him in conversation, it would help the Prime Minister and, of course, it would improve the discussion.'

The prime minister's journey took place against a background of change in world affairs. Britain's endeavour to forge new economic links with Western Europe, de Gaulle's proposal for a three-power (US, UK, and France) directorate for the Western world in and beyond NATO, movement in the Moscow hierarchy and intriguing signs of flexibility in East-West relations, continuing tensions in the Middle East, new leadership in Pakistan with corresponding uncertainties in Indo-Pakistani relations, the growing force of neutralism in Commonwealth affairs, the looming presence of Communist China and its dispute with Formosa (Taiwan), most recently over the offshore islands of Quemoy and Matsu – these were the elements of the diplomatic climate in which Diefenbaker embarked on his voyage. Most of these had implications for Canada's foreign policy.

As he prepared to leave on a journey that would take him to several Commonwealth countries, the prime minister absorbed a good deal of reflected glory from the success of the Commonwealth trade and economic conference at Montreal in September. He admired and freely acknowledged the leading role played by Donald Fleming in organizing and chairing the conference, but, as he had sown the seed at the 1957 prime ministers' meeting in London, he felt justified in taking some personal credit. A somewhat ambitious agenda had permitted discussion of every problem of concern to Commonwealth (and 'colonial') delegations in the field of trade, finance, and development aid. Diefenbaker was especially gratified that the United Kingdom had used the conference to announce the removal of restrictions against the import of dollar commodities of interest to Canadian producers. Nothing pleased him so much as bringing good news to the agricultural industry. Other items of importance to Canada included a progress report on the United Kingdom's pending negotiations regarding the establishment of a European Free Trade Area (consisting of most Western European countries outside the European Economic Community), a Commonwealth Scholarship program initiated by Canada, and an increase from $35 to $50 million in Canada's annual contribution to the Colombo Plan over the following three years. Diefenbaker was to make good use of the achievements of the Montreal conference during his tour.[1]

On the domestic front, the horizon was not as clear as he would have liked as he prepared to leave. Economic conditions were worsening and there was a threat of increasing winter unemployment and of a national rail strike. That he was prepared to contemplate an absence from Canada of just over seven weeks was a sign of Diefenbaker's self-confidence and of the trust he placed in Howard Green, who was to serve as acting prime minister, and other leading ministers.

The tour began on 28 October with a cheerful send-off from Ottawa. Diplomats from the countries to be visited made the customary trek to the airport, and several ministers and their wives came to see the Diefenbakers off and pay homage to the Chief. Diefenbaker himself seemed quite relaxed at the outset. He surmised, correctly, that with the St Laurent world tour still not lost to the public memory, the Liberal opposition was in no position to criticize his absence.

THE UNITED NATIONS

The decision to meet with the secretary-general of the United Nations, Dag Hammarskjöld, proved a wise one. It was their first substantial talk, and Diefenbaker was nervous about it. He knew how closely Pearson had worked with Hammarskjöld in earlier years, particularly during the Suez crisis and its aftermath. Hammarskjöld, quiet, composed, and friendly, soon put Diefenbaker at his ease. It was as though this was the important item of the secretary-general's day. The conversation itself, like most conversations of this character, took the form of a 'tour d'horizon.'[2] It gave rise to no surprises with one exception – a remark made by Diefenbaker himself on the issue of Communist China's place in the world and its claim to representation in the United Nations.

China had been a subject of recurring concern to Diefenbaker ever since he became prime minister. The Chinese Nationalist (Formosa) ambassador in Ottawa had extracted from the prime minister in the late summer of 1957 the assurance that Canada's policy of not recognizing the Peking regime was unchanged.[3] Eisenhower and Dulles had taken care to underline how displeased the United States would be if Canada were to alter its policy either on recognition or on China's representation in the United Nations. Diefenbaker was also on the receiving end of advice (via Howard Green) from the pro-Chiang Kai-shek Chinese community in Vancouver. He could therefore not ignore the strength of the pressure for maintaining the status quo. At the same time he was never comfortable with a situation in which a government controlling something like one-quarter of the world's population had no voice in the United Nations and no official contact with Canada. His uneasiness had been stimulated more than a year before when he heard Nehru argue before the Commonwealth prime ministers that it made no sense to exclude China from the world community. The fact that Britain itself had diplomatic representation in Peking, which enabled Macmillan to speak with some degree of first-hand familiarity on relations with China, heightened Diefenbaker's sense of awkwardness on the China issue.

In New York, Diefenbaker went further than he had gone in any previous official conversation in expressing his concern on these issues. In asking Hammarskjöld for his views on recognizing Peking, the prime minister led off by saying that he had for a long time been opposed to recognition but that he was 'more and more coming to the very definite opinion that you can't continue to have six hundred million people in a corral.' What stand did the secretary-general think Canada should take, 'detached as we are,' Diefenbaker inquired.

Hammarskjöld had not been expecting this question. His face showed a faint tremor of surprise and he avoided answering directly. The Western world would sooner or later have to accept Communist China, he said; there was no prospect of its de-communization. As the issue of recognizing Peking came to be 'a stronger negative influence' in international affairs, it increasingly became a question of face for the United States. As for the effect which recognition of Peking would have in Southeast Asia, the majority of Asian governments would be relieved if the recognition of Peking became more widespread. He had been told in 1955 by the president of Burma, Dr Ba U, drawing from the latter's discussion with Chou-en-lai, that the Peoples' Republic of China was extremely sensitive to being regarded and treated as a pariah, and that Burma would sleep more soundly the moment Peking was admitted to the United Nations. This Hammarskjöld thought to be a significant illustration coming from an Asian leader friendly to the West. Diefenbaker said he was impressed by this argument and added that he had noticed a pronounced change in Canadian public opinion in favour of some move forward on China.

A strange aftermath to this conversation took place later the same evening as we flew to London. I had prepared a summary of the conversation with Hammarskjöld. The prime minister did not have time to look at it before leaving New York but told me he was anxious to see it in view of the remarks he had made about China. He said he did not want it to include anything of 'political' significance, adding that he often found it useful to take a position in order to draw out the other side. Somewhere between New York and Goose Bay, I heard that the prime minister was agitated over the reports that would be made about his meetings on the tour, and in particular about his remarks to the secretary-general on China. It was obvious that his misgivings about the reliability of the Department of External Affairs had come to the surface again. I went to the

59

back of the plane, where the prime minister and Mrs Diefenbaker were sitting, and told him I had heard of his concern and assured him that reports on his meetings would not be sent to Ottawa without his approval. I showed him how I had drafted the China section of the report and how it could be changed if he wished. This immediately caused him to throw aside some papers, fix me with a very severe eye, and say: 'I'll tell you frankly. What I am worried about is that Pearson is going to find out what is in these reports 24 hours after they reach Ottawa.' I said that I simply did not believe this sort of thing was going on, but he went on at length in the same vein. When we got to London, the telegram was dispatched in slightly revised form to Ottawa and New York. I also sent a personal letter to Norman Robertson, who had taken over as under-secretary in October after Jules Léger went to Paris as Canada's representative on the NATO Council. Part of it read: 'The immediate problem is that in view of the Prime Minister's instructions, it will be difficult if not impossible to keep the Department informed on what the Prime Minister actually says in his conversations ... In the longer run, the problem is, of course, worrying since it illustrates the depth of the suspicion with which the Department is regarded. Without giving examples, the Prime Minister said that there had been three recent instances in which Mr. Pearson had received information which could not have come from any other source than the Department. This struck me as a pretty wild assertion and I told the Prime Minister that I could not believe that his suspicions were well founded. He keeps on insisting that they are, however, which is more to the point.' Diefenbaker never referred again to the incident, and while I was anxious at the time that reporting would be a constant problem, it did not in fact turn out that way.[4]

THE UNITED KINGDOM

Travelling to London with John Diefenbaker, one always felt caught up in the aura of a pilgrimage. A dimension of the man had survived from childhood – a sense of excited wonder – and it emerged afresh whenever he revisited the sacred places, Buckingham Palace, Windsor Castle, No. 10 Downing Street, and the Mansion House in the City of London. On this journey the pilgrimage went beyond the traditional pattern. It included a long weekend (31 October – 2 November) devoted to visiting Edinburgh and the home of his mother's family, the Bannermans, at Kildonan in Scotland. Here, with much volunteer help from local citizens, he was shown the house where his grandfather was believed to have lived as a boy. It was the only house still standing in the area, he reported to his mother, in sending her four photos on his return to Ottawa.[5] The interlude in Scotland delighted him, his brother, and Mrs Diefenbaker, but it gave them only a fleeting break from the inevitably relentless pace of official engagements facing them on their tour.

At the time of his visit, Britain, though not fully recovered from the self-inflicted wound of Suez, was striving to sustain its role as a world power. In Prime Minister Macmillan the country had a leader of energy, experience, and sagacity. Already, in less than two years since succeeding Anthony Eden, he had repaired Britain's vital bridge to Washington, become a force in East-West relations and the affairs of the Middle East, and given impetus to an historic change in Britain's relationship with continental Europe. Nor had Macmillan ignored the Commonwealth, having chaired the meeting of prime ministers in June 1957 and, early in 1958, travelled almost the same path as that which Diefenbaker would shortly follow. All this could not, however, obscure the fact that Britain's relationship with Canada had been seriously affected by the parting of ways over Suez in 1956. No matter how much the two governments might now wish to restore the spirit of the old family partnership, the post-Suez mentality would make reconciliation more difficult, even if Britain, under Macmillan, were not determined to forge stronger links with Europe. Between Canada and Britain, things would not be the same again.

One might not have drawn such a gloomy conclusion from seeing the two prime ministers together. This would be their fifth meeting. From the outset, in June 1957, Macmillan had made a deep impression on Diefenbaker, who trusted him implicitly and greatly prized the relationship. Now again, at this early stage of Diefenbaker's adventure, Macmillan wove his spell, sharing with avuncular generosity the treasure of his vast experience and his comprehension of the issues confronting Britain in Europe, the Middle East, and Asia. In a series of talks, ranging from official to entirely private and informal, Macmillan gave Diefenbaker exactly the tuning-up he needed, as much for his tour of the Asian and Pacific Commonwealth as for that in the capitals of Western Europe.

It happens with remarkable frequency, when national leaders meet, that the agenda planned months earlier for them by their officials is upset or distorted by unexpected events. So it was on this occasion owing to a recent diplomatic initiative by General de Gaulle, typically sweeping in its range and awkward in its implications for all but France. In letters addressed personally to Eisenhower and Macmillan, de Gaulle had put forward an idea which, if it were carried through, would give France, in company with the United States and Britain, a special place in the strategic management of the free world.[6] As such it would challenge one of the basic principles of NATO – that of equal status – on which the alliance had been established. Although de Gaulle's message had not been addressed to governments of other NATO countries, it was a prime subject of speculation in the alliance by the time Diefenbaker met with Macmillan.

Diefenbaker's reaction to what he knew of de Gaulle's initiative was quite predictable. It was among the first items of foreign policy he took up with Macmillan and it was no surprise that he should have expressed vigorous objections to any plan that might result in a two-tiered structure for NATO along the lines apparently contemplated by de Gaulle. Indeed, for Diefenbaker, the issue raised by de Gaulle's letters to Washington and London was in a sense a political gift. It handed him a worthy cause to champion not only in London but in Paris, Bonn, and Rome, where otherwise his visits might have seemed lacking in specific purpose.

In their informal meeting on 31 October, at which no one else was present, Macmillan explained to Diefenbaker that as de Gaulle's letter had been a personal message, there had been an inevitable delay in making it available to other governments.[7] The contents, Macmillan said, did not amount to concrete proposals and he did not fully understand what de Gaulle had in mind. Macmillan thought that the general must have been aware that his ideas would arouse misgivings in many NATO governments. French prestige was, however, a factor and the best course was to try to smooth things over by putting emphasis on the need for improved consultation in NATO.

When the subject arose in a later, official meeting on 3 November, Macmillan's tone had changed.[8] He now showed greater concern at the potential effects of de Gaulle's letter. There was a risk of serious effects on the attitude of several NATO nations towards the alliance. More pointedly for Britain, he now feared that there might be a connection between de Gaulle's initiative on NATO and the state of the negotiations then taking place with the French over the European Free Trade Area.[9] There were indications that de Gaulle might use the contents of his letter as a bargaining counter. The French foreign minister, Couve de Murville, would be in London soon, and Macmillan wondered if the French government might offer to take a less rigid position on the EFTA negotiations if Britain would make some concession regarding France's status in the Western alliance. He did not think de Gaulle would insist on institutional reforms within NATO, but that he might emphasize France's global interests and commitments with a view to securing some preferential role for France in the affairs of the Free World. Diefenbaker replied that in talking to de Gaulle he would have to take a strong stand against any attempt by France to achieve a reorganization of NATO. Public opinion in Canada would be highly unfavourable to any such outcome, particularly in view of the reduction in the French military contribution to NATO forces in Europe and the fact that Canada had kept all its NATO undertakings. This brought from Macmillan a renewed assurance that Britain would oppose any idea of a political directorate. He went on to ask Diefenbaker to probe de Gaulle's intentions as to a possible link with the EFTA negotiations.

Diefenbaker readily agreed, and undertook to inform Macmillan in time for the British government's talks with the French foreign minister later in the week. Reports on the progress of the negotiations were to influence Diefenbaker's conversations in Paris, Bonn, and Rome.

Among the several other topics discussed in London, most drew the focus away from Europe. Macmillan reviewed the current scene in the Middle East, confessed uncertainty about Pakistan (where Ayub Khan, a military leader whose political views were not known, had recently assumed presidential powers), and speculated that the Communist Chinese were not impatient for an early settlement of the dispute with Formosa over the offshore islands of Quemoy and Matsu.

Diefenbaker, who had earlier wondered if he should proceed with his visit to Pakistan, agreed to inform Macmillan of any points of interest on the situation there. He also stressed the value of Commonwealth trade as a means of reducing the dangers inherent in communist economic relationships with non-aligned countries. A related initiative which the Canadian government would like to see pursued was the idea of a world food bank. He had raised this before in NATO. He said he knew there were many difficulties of implementation, but insisted that there was merit in the idea of using food surpluses to raise living standards in deprived areas of the developing world. Macmillan's reaction could not be said to be eager. With infinite courtesy he said how helpful it would be if the Canadian authorities could leave a detailed memorandum for study by the British ministries concerned. This Diefenbaker agreed to do.

Before departing for Paris early on 5 November, the prime minister had two more major engagements. At lunch on 4 November he discussed with the Queen her forthcoming visit to Canada. In the evening, he was to address a large meeting of the Commonwealth and Empire Industries Association in the Albert Hall in London. This occasion, arranged and encouraged by George Drew and publicized enthusiastically by Lord Beaverbrook's *Daily Express*, was something of a political nightmare. At a moment when Macmillan was struggling to keep alive Britain's negotiations for a European Free Trade Area, the prime minister of Canada, serenaded by the anti-Europe organs of the British press, was to address an organization dedicated to the expansion of British trade with the Commonwealth. The irony was not lost on Diefenbaker – nor doubtless on Macmillan, who did the brave and decent thing by attending and addressing the meeting – but of course there was no turning back.

As almost always happened before a major speech, a condition not far short of panic prevailed. Numerous contributions in the form of drafts had been forthcoming – from departments in Ottawa, from the high commissioner's office in London, from members of the prime minister's staff, and freelance volunteers and well-wishers. Having taken part in efforts during the weekend to weave these disparate offerings into an acceptable whole, I was not surprised to find, on his return from Scotland, that the prime minister wanted to do further work himself on the draft. Unfortunately, his schedule of engagements was so crowded, and his anxiety about the speech so mounting, that on the afternoon of the meeting he developed a high fever which threatened to keep him from going. There was bedside consultation on the last draft of his address. Despite all the travail, he rose as usual to the oratorical occasion. Most of the audience, delighted with his faith in the Commonwealth and in the prospects and benefits of expanded Commonwealth trade, gave him enthusiastic applause. Not everyone agreed. The *Economist* in its next issue called it 'a really rather dreadful speech.' Fortunately this stern verdict did not catch up with his caravan until we had reached Ceylon, where the most exacting parts of the journey lay behind.

FRANCE

On 5 November the Diefenbaker party arrived in Paris. My diary reads: 'We got out of London with fair success and the flight to Paris was straightforward. He read an arrival statement in execrable French, at the close of which he veered over to me with his boys-will-be-boys wink and said "don't give me any more damn words like *équilibre*," a reference to the one word in his text which he really fumbled.' It was a brief visit – less than twenty-four hours – but despite the awkward start, it turned out to be one of the most successful and enlightening of the entire tour. It was clear that the prime minister was looking forward to meeting de Gaulle. It struck me at the time, too, that short, concentrated meetings often brought the best out of Diefenbaker, who did not have a well-stocked larder of diplomatic talk or great reserves of patience with protocol and social formality. The result on this occasion was an absorbing exchange with de Gaulle, largely on the latter's view of France's place in the world, with particular reference to Anglo-American dominance of NATO and the wider Western alliance.

The meeting took place in the general's elegant office in the Hotel Matignon, the official residence of the prime minister.[10] There was a smallish table, and de Gaulle and Diefenbaker sat opposite one another, not more than five feet apart. In my diary I wrote of de Gaulle: 'The old fellow sits like a giant eagle, blinking his enigmatic eyes slowly and turning his head from side to side as if surveying some great global battlefield.' Invited by de Gaulle to begin the conversation, Diefenbaker said that, while there were not many problems between Canada and France, one question particularly concerned him, arising from the general's recent letters to Eisenhower and Macmillan. If these letters were designed merely to improve consultation in the alliance, as he expected, he could only agree. But if the general had in mind a triumvirate which could take decisions without consultation with other members, an interpretation he did not think the general intended, then Canada could not accept such a thing. It would be impossible to sell in Canada, and, by turning NATO into a virtual military alliance, it would have a bad effect in the uncommitted world.

These opening comments were made in a conciliatory vein but sometimes with angular phrasing with which the excellent French interpreter did his courteous best. De Gaulle, looking at first rather stiff, responded quietly as a learned professor feeling it necessary to supply broad background before dealing with a narrowly based question. Recalling NATO's beginnings in the late 1940s, the general said that while it had been logical then to take measures to meet an immediate danger, the situation had changed. The direct threat of Soviet military aggression was less, and, while it was still important for the Western powers to maintain NATO, there were new dangers in North Africa, the Middle East, and the Far East which were beyond NATO's compass. These dangers were being dealt with, as NATO's affairs were too, by political decisions dominated by the United States and by military strategy whose 'preparation and execution' was Anglo-American. In his opinion we had to face the reality that the West was experiencing 'a sort of integration' under American domination. He was not, he said with some emphasis, suspicious of American leadership, nor did he fail to understand American power or responsibility. It was just that the methods which had been developed did not correspond to the requirements of the world as it now was, nor indeed to France's situation. Now that neither the United States nor the USSR intended deliberately to make war, a new modus vivendi was needed between East and West in, for example, the Middle East and the Far East. Issues of this kind, and disarmament too, were not being successfully dealt with as problems of US-Soviet relations. Without dismantling the NATO alliance, a greater 'souplesse' was called for in diplomatic relations between East and West. France, he said, and perhaps other countries, could serve this cause. Moreover, France's revival since 1947 was a demonstration of French unity and conscience, and the solutions he could foresee in North Africa would reinforce France's position and qualify it to play a useful role in East-West relations without threatening the breaking up of NATO.

The general paused for a brief moment before resuming. It was as though he was expecting a reaction, but he quickly resumed before the prime minister could jump in. For the reasons given, the general said, France was putting the question: Should the present working of the Western alliance be maintained or should it be altered? Answering the question, he recalled that the United States and the United Kingdom had landed forces in the Middle East the previous summer with no advance consultation, and after Dulles and Macmillan had said they had no thought of such military action. France had large interests in that area. Other countries might have suffered from US action over Quemoy and Matsu – another crisis on which there had been no consultation and from which a war might possibly have emerged. This situation could not go on. This was why he had written as he had to Eisenhower and Macmillan.

The prime minister was equal to the occasion. He began by saying that he had no objection to what de Gaulle had said so far as the matter of consultation was concerned. He wished to make it clear beyond doubt, however, that Canada could not accept decisions 'given out by one, two or three powers' without consultation. Diefenbaker was speaking with considerable force and de Gaulle, coughing and rubbing his fingers across his throat, became visibly attentive. When the prime minister paused and inquired how the general intended to proceed with his ideas, de Gaulle resumed his argument. He asked rhetorically whether it was true that Canada was obliged to accept decisions of the great powers regarding the Middle East, the Far East, and disarmament. France was not prepared to do so. His aim was to have some conversations to see how a new system might be organized. He had no detailed programme to put forward to Eisenhower and Macmillan; the important thing was to have talks. NATO as presently constituted caused problems for France. To have its forces integrated with others was not good, psychologically, for the French people. It detracted from a feeling of obligation for their own defence. And (military) integration was unsatisfactory for another reason. It limited the French government's use of its forces outside the NATO area – for example, in North Africa, where France had major burdens and interests and at the same time defended Western interests.

The prime minister said that he could not comment on, although he fully appreciated, de Gaulle's observations on the psychology of the French people. He warned against any change in NATO's geographical area of responsibility. 'You would find,' he said, 'that smaller powers could not see their way clear' to accepting such a change. In fact, an extension of NATO's area might well lead to the breakdown of the whole NATO concept and perhaps lead to the dissolution of the alliance. It might also call in question Canada's military contribution in Europe which, in present circumstances, there was no thought of removing. He hoped that the matter of reorganizing NATO would not be brought before the NATO Council.

General de Gaulle, after observing that France as a 'coming atomic power' was naturally concerned about its political and strategic responsibilities, summed up the current situation by saying that he believed the American and British leaders had not refused to join in talks. Diefenbaker again warned against bringing the matter before the NATO Council, and de Gaulle agreed that it would be inadvisable to raise it at the NATO meeting in December. Diefenbaker received de Gaulle's permission to convey a message to this effect to Chancellor Adenauer in Bonn and to Prime Minister Fanfani of Italy. Both leaders were said to have been nettled at not having been on the general's short mailing list.

De Gaulle then asked the prime minister for his views on the Common Market and free trade area negotiations. Diefenbaker replied that Canada was glad to see Europe strengthened economically and politically, but hoped that the process would not involve a protective tariff barrier. He would be especially concerned if Canada's agricultural products were denied access to the Common Market, since they amounted to a large proportion of Canada's exports to Europe and Britain. A genuine expansion of trade, however, could not but be beneficial to NATO and the free world generally.

It is a long cultural leap from Paris to the Canadian prairies. Yet, at least for this short span of time, these two extraordinary men somehow hit it off. Their spirited discussion of the morning brought them to a superb lunch in the best of humour. The general displayed a mischievous benevolence, and the warmth and informality of the occasion was enhanced by the unassuming presence of Madame de Gaulle.

On taking leave of de Gaulle, the prime minister instructed me to get a message immediately to Macmillan's staff. The message was that Diefenbaker had detected no link in the general's thinking between his proposals on NATO and his attitude towards the EFTA negotiations. I telephoned this message, and some comments on the Paris visit, in suitably cryptic language to Macmillan's private secretary in London. A splendid dinner took place that evening at the Canadian ambassador's residence. Twenty-four people were seated around a table adorned by a magnificent lace tablecloth. No one mentioned that it had just arrived in Paris from Rome.

While in Paris, Diefenbaker also saw the secretary-general of NATO, Paul-Henri Spaak, and the supreme allied commander, Europe (SACEUR), General Lauris Norstad. The prime minister emphasized to them that a 'directoire' (he was getting more bilingual by now) was unacceptable to Canada. Spaak and Norstad differed in their assessment of de Gaulle's intentions, Norstad being much more convinced than Spaak that de Gaulle would realize his proposal could not materialize. Much of the remaining time was devoted to an explanation by Norstad of NATO military strategy. Diefenbaker was impressed and asked if he might have it in writing.

It was a fact of life with Diefenbaker that he was frequently more receptive to 'occasional' briefings of this kind than to the same advice available from sources within the Canadian official family. General Norstad's exposé, though lucidly given, was not in substance different from the advice which the senior

Canadian military leaders would have welcomed regular opportunities to provide. Distant, or at least different, voices were often more successful than familiar ones in catching Diefenbaker's attention.

Between Paris and the next major stop, Bonn, Diefenbaker visited the Canadian air division at Gros Tenquin, France. My diary entry reads, in part: 'You have to hand it to the services. When they organize a thing nothing is left to chance, and the way they organized the spontaneous cheering of the children, all carrying flags, was a credit to them. The D's were very touched by it all ... I spent the afternoon organizing the papers for Bonn and recording what had happened in Paris.'

FEDERAL REPUBLIC OF GERMANY

In Bonn, the prime minister's engagements were so scheduled that he had at least three opportunities for private conversation with Chancellor Konrad Adenauer before his main official meeting on the late afternoon of the first day. Apart from the fact that he was fatigued by that time, he had used up a good part of his best ammunition, including the highlights of his talks with Macmillan and de Gaulle, in these private exchanges with Adenauer.

Adenauer would soon complete his tenth year in the office of chancellor. At eighty-two, he was old even as elder statesmen went in the postwar era, but in his presence one felt little sense of his age. The Diefenbakers had met and liked him at the NATO summit meeting in Paris a year before. The prime minister respected him as one who had been in the business of national leadership long enough to have formed clear and definite views on the important issues. And what Adenauer thought, especially on NATO matters and relations with Moscow, was very close to Diefenbaker's own instincts. The omens for a harmonious meeting were therefore good.

It happened that Professor Hallstein, chairman of the European Economic Commission, who was in the midst of the negotiations for a European Free Trade Area, was in Bonn that day. Adenauer invited Hallstein to report to them both. In this way, Diefenbaker was able to take part in an exceptionally interesting review of the difficulties underlying the negotiations and the prospects of a settlement of the crisis then threatening. In general, there was agreement among Hallstein, Adenauer, and the German officials present that while the technical difficulties in the negotiations were soluble, the political difficulties were fundamental, and that France under de Gaulle was the central question mark.

Diefenbaker then asked Adenauer to discuss what the reaction should be to de Gaulle's recent initiative. He replied that in the past year, big changes had taken place on the world scene. The Soviet Union was worried about inner tensions and also about its relations with China. The West had serious problems too, in Iceland, Cyprus, and in the Middle East, where a succession of bad mistakes had been made, including the Anglo-French move at Suez two years before. In Western Europe, it was a blessing that de Gaulle had taken over, and he hoped that the general would put an end to internal divisions in France which might have led to civil war. He emphasized the importance of continued American leadership. Without the United States, Europe, including Britain, would be lost to the USSR. With tributes to the steadfastness of Secretary of State Dulles, the chancellor hoped for a continuing commitment to NATO by the United States, and for an early decision by NATO members to extend NATO beyond 1967 when it would be up for renewal.

The prime minister agreed wholeheartedly with the chancellor on the importance of NATO unity, observing enigmatically that members sometimes acted without regard to the interests of their allies. Consultation was vital. He sensed no weakening in Canada towards NATO and called the chancellor's attention to recent developments in the organization of North American air defence which he said was a part of the NATO system. He reassured the chancellor, who had expressed concern about possible changes in US foreign policies as a result of Democratic party gains in the mid-term election, that he had seen absolutely no sign of any change in the views of the American people on world issues. He ended his remarks by agreeing with Adenauer that the Western nations were all greatly dependent on the United States and must make every effort to prevent it from slipping back into semi-isolationism.

This meeting was instructive for the prime minister, as were his more private and informal exchanges with Adenauer, whom he found well-informed, wise, and excellent company. Diefenbaker was particularly struck by Adenauer's penchant for thinking in terms of what the world would be like in ten or fifteen years.

LAST LEG IN EUROPE

Talks with Prime Minister Fanfani and an audience with Pope John XXIII were the principal events in Rome. Fanfani was much preoccupied with cabinet business, and full-scale discussions were not possible, although Italian hospitality did much to ease the situation. The papal audience was brief, but the Diefenbakers were much impressed by the Pope. The occasion would have been perfect if someone had not forgotten to alert the Vatican photographer. 'Diefenbaker Regrets No Photo with Pope,' was the *Globe and Mail*'s headline the next day.

The Western European part of the world tour was now over. For two weeks, in London, Paris, Bonn, and Rome, Canada's prime minister had had a rotating front-row seat from which to observe the action and an unusual opportunity between scenes, as it were, to hear at first hand what the principal actors thought about the events they were living through. It was an experience of great interest and value to Diefenbaker, whose understanding and attitude often hinged on the personalities he associated with events. As he left Europe, he could legitimately feel that he had achieved one of the prime objectives of his journey: to ensure cordial personal relations with his counterparts in the major allied governments. He had confirmed to them Canada's belief in the continuing need for the NATO alliance and its readiness to maintain air and ground forces in Europe. On de Gaulle's ideas on the organization of the Western alliance, he had not shrunk from expressing his misgivings directly to the general and he could claim some credit for preventing de Gaulle's proposals from reaching the formal agenda of the NATO Council, where they might have had a disruptive effect. In the European economic field, he was not as effective. The truth was that he was not fully prepared for what he found in the Western European governments he visited, for the intensity of their preoccupation with the problems and the opportunities inherent in their economic relationships. No one could say, however, that he had not seized every chance to express concern at the effect that new economic arrangements in Europe might have on Canadian exports, especially agricultural exports, to European markets. Now he was about to undergo a completely different experience, a passage to and through parts of Asia, where his exposure to the leaders and the problems of Commonwealth countries might be expected to widen his perspective on world affairs.

8

World Tour: Asia and the Pacific

With the exception of Australia and New Zealand, the countries Diefenbaker would visit in the second part of his tour were entirely new to him.[1] In planning to visit Asia, he was influenced by a number of motives in addition to a healthy curiosity about places and civilizations he had never seen. The framework of his thought was the Commonwealth and the role which it and its members could play in world affairs. He had met and been impressed by the leaders of the non-white nations, especially India's Nehru, at the 1957 prime ministers' meeting in London. He reckoned then that if he was to continue to be a credible advocate of the Commonwealth, he would have to have first-hand experience of the problems, and personal acquaintance with the leaders, of the non-white Commonwealth countries in Asia. He was persuaded that economic offensives directed from Moscow and Peking were gathering momentum and threatening the freedom and independence of developing nations. It concerned him that the benefits of Commonwealth membership were not more influential with these nations. He wanted to try out his ideas on the possibilities for much expanded trade among Commonwealth countries, a cause which had received a degree of encouragement from the Trade and Economic Conference in Montreal in September.

Closely connected in his mind with the prospects for expanded Commonwealth trade was the Canadian role in development aid through the Colombo Plan. At the time of his tour, Canada's annual contribution had been increased by $15 million to a new total of $50 million for the next three years. Diefenbaker was interested in knowing how this money was spent, whether the recipients saw it as a benefit of Commonwealth membership, and not least whether some or all of them might be prevailed on to accept Canadian wheat as part of their annual allocations. The program of Commonwealth scholarships, set in motion by the Montreal conference, gave the Canadian aid effort a further dimension in which Diefenbaker had developed a personal interest.

PAKISTAN

Diefenbaker arrived in Karachi, then the capital of Pakistan, on 13 November. Since early October, when General Mirza Khan had taken power in a military coup, the country had been in political and constitutional turmoil. General Mirza's rule lasted only a month. General Ayub Khan, a former commander-in-chief of the Pakistan army, took over the presidency from Mirza a few days before Diefenbaker's visit, and Canada's prime minister was thus his first official guest. Martial law was still in effect in Karachi.

In the External Affairs briefing note, Ayub Khan was described as 'a relatively able commander-in-chief, and a man of moderate views,' but what his capacity or inclinations would be in domestic or foreign affairs was of course unknown when Diefenbaker met with him. Heavy-set, broad-faced, wearing a Sandhurst moustache and an unmistakable air of command, Ayub Khan was an impressive figure. He was also straightforward and friendly, and seemed to welcome the opportunity to explain to the Canadian prime minister the reasons for his decision to assume supreme power. Ayub's uncompromising anti-communist sentiments helped further to attract Diefenbaker's regard. Effectively tutored by the Canadian high commissioner, Herb Moran, the prime minister quickly became persuaded of the sincerity of Ayub Khan's motives and also of his desire to rebuild Pakistan's constitution along democratic lines. Thereafter Diefenbaker's regard for Ayub never wavered.

Ayub Khan's listing of Pakistan's economic problems and needs drew from Diefenbaker a response that he was to employ throughout his Asian tour. The Canadian government wished to aid Pakistan but it was obliged to take account of its economic limitations as well as the state of public opinion. Canada was facing a serious problem in disposing of its surpluses of food products. The question was complicated by the fact that the United States disposed of its surpluses on terms much more favourable to recipient countries. Canada's readiness to provide other forms of aid would depend to a large extent on the willingness of recipient countries to increase the proportion of agricultural products under Canadian aid programs.

In Diefenbaker's international dealings there was, as this account shows, a tendency to assume that his domestic priorities would carry greater weight than in fact they could with the leaders of other nations. The truth – as politely pointed out by a senior adviser to President Ayub – was that Pakistan could obtain American wheat over and above the normal US aid program. If it chose to take Canadian wheat, the total amount of Canada's aid funds available for other economic purposes would be reduced. To imagine that some abstract benefit of the Commonwealth relationship would persuade the Pakistanis otherwise was to underestimate seriously both their negotiating talents and the scale of their national needs.

On a visit to the Warsak hydro project near Peshawar, Diefenbaker had his first glimpse of the Canadian aid program in action. It made a strong impression on him to see Canadians and Pakistanis working together, and to meet with the Canadian community. The visit to Warsak did not, however, entirely offset his personal doubts about the value of Canada's contribution to the Colombo Plan. He encountered at least one important Pakistani who appeared unaware of the scale of the Canadian aid effort. This combined with his failure to persuade his Asian hosts to accept more agricultural content in Canada's regular aid programs, rankled with him and was reflected in his subsequent attitude in aid matters.

The prime minister encountered in Pakistan a degree of disillusion with the Commonwealth much greater than he had anticipated. He had been warned of this, but thought that the department's advice was unduly cynical and pessimistic. The limitations of the Commonwealth's appeal became clearly apparent, however, in his meeting with Ayub Khan. After talking of Pakistan's dispute with India over Kashmir, Ayub Khan said that the prime minister would understand that 'the Commonwealth does not mean all that much to us unless it helps in solving our basic problems; unless it does that, it is a very defective organization.' Commonwealth countries should say to Nehru, regarding Kashmir: 'You are playing with fire.' Diefenbaker had, of course, no intention of taking sides between Pakistan and India. He avoided doing so in his meeting with the president and also in a press conference. Asked whether Canada would offer its good offices to solve the Kashmir problem, he replied smoothly: 'Well now, my friend, sometimes volunteering is considered presumption.' Within the Commonwealth, direct consultations between the parties to such problems were the best approach to a solution.

The program in Pakistan – it would be the same in India – was designed to display as many different facets of society as possible, and the result for the Diefenbakers was varied and fascinating. The prime minister would have enjoyed it even more had he not taken so literally the advice of his medical adviser to avoid fresh milk, eat local food sparingly, and take no local water under any conditions. As a result, he merely toyed with the food served at the inevitable banquets. Thus abstaining, he became weaker and gaunter until at one stage he was genuinely ill and unable to fulfil an afternoon's engagements. Characteristically, however, he recovered in time for the major occasions. In one ceremony of exceptional dignity and pageantry, he received an honorary degree from the University of Punjab at Lahore, an occasion to which he rose with eloquence.

His own comment was that he had 'wowed them.' The same day, on a different wavelength, his brother Elmer, attending another colourful reception, remarked to a Pakistani army officer that it was 'just like the Shriners back home.'

The Diefenbakers ended their visit to Pakistan by driving through the Khyber Pass, an expedition the prime minister, as a devotee of Rudyard Kipling, had always wanted to make. The first stage of his Asian tour was behind him. At the farewell ceremony in Peshawar it was a noticeably different John Diefenbaker from the man who only five days before had arrived edgy and apprehensive in Karachi. He had worried a great deal about his speeches, and he had suffered from his dietary restraint. But he could look back on a generally successful visit in which he had struck a chord of friendship with Pakistan's charismatic new leader. Ayub Khan had accepted many of his views, and there had been a warm public response to the Canadian prime minister which got his political juices flowing. As he prepared for departure, he was jaunty again, the chuckle had returned, and those piercing eyes were alight with enjoyment and anticipation. It was a fortunate circumstance that Pakistan had been the first stop on the Asian part of the tour. He had come through – even enjoyed – his first exposure to an Asian nation and its leader. The experience and insights he had gained in his talks with Ayub Khan and other Pakistanis, and in his private discussions with Moran, had done much to rekindle his confidence. It also helped to shape his approach to the discussions he was to have with his counterparts in New Delhi and Colombo, the next two ports of call.

INDIA

For the prime minister, the week in India, which began on 18 November, was the most demanding of the tour. It included meetings with Prime Minister Nehru, speeches to the Indian parliament and at the University of Delhi, a press conference, and the usual pattern of calls and social functions. None of this was avoidable if he was to receive the treatment and the honours which the Indian authorities wished to confer, and which he wished to receive, but it made for a hectic few days.

In his memoirs Diefenbaker relates in some detail his main conversation with Nehru.[2] It was a broader-ranging discussion than he had had with Ayub Khan. Nehru, in long black coat, white trousers, and familiar white cap, was friendly and attentive, clearly attaching importance to the occasion. Diefenbaker was placed beside his host, on a sofa before a beautiful low table bearing a vase of flowers, silver cigarette boxes, and the ever-present offerings of tea.

The obvious first topic was the change of regime in Pakistan, on which Diefenbaker might have been expected to offer interesting impressions. Nehru opened, however, with a disparaging reference to Ayub Khan ('whom no one has accused of too much intelligence') and then made a joking inquiry as to what we would think in Canada if Vincent Massey (then governor general) had been removed in the same way as Ayub Khan had got rid of Mirza Khan. He wondered if Ayub had been put up to it, probably by the army.

Perhaps because he was thrown off balance by these comments, Diefenbaker was muted in his reply. He spoke of Ayub's good intentions, adding that on the basis of his talks in Pakistan, the coup in early October had been popular in the sense that people generally felt the need for change. To this Nehru signified a reluctant assent, but with a troubled frown he went on to draw pessimistic conclusions about Pakistan's chances of economic recovery and, by implication, about the outlook for Indo-Pakistani relations.

It was not a theme that Diefenbaker was enjoying and he soon steered the conversation onto safer ground, inviting Nehru's views on current Soviet intentions, relations between Moscow and Peking, and other questions concerning China. Nehru was reassuring about Khrushchev's intentions towards the West ('he does not want big trouble'), but agreed with Diefenbaker that Khrushchev felt 'a certain apprehension' about longer-term trends in Communist China's policy. Referring to the current tension between Peking and Formosa over the offshore islands, Quemoy and Matsu, Nehru thought Peking would not press the matter. Otherwise they would be under pressure to do something about Formosa itself. Peking had no intention of precipitating a war with the United States. In the course of his remarks, Nehru paid a graceful tribute to Chester Ronning, Canada's high commissioner in New Delhi, by drawing him into the conversation as an acknowledged expert in Chinese affairs.

Some of Nehru's critical references to US policy on China led Diefenbaker to explain Canada's position. Here he was clearly conveying a political message to Nehru. He was sure that the Americans would welcome some solution of the China problem. As for Canadian opinion, he said it was now stronger than at any time in favour of the recognition of Peking. The administration in Washington, however, would strongly resent Canada's taking a stand against the United States either on the offshore islands or by advocating recognition of the Peking regime. Still somewhat provoked by Nehru's criticism of the United States, Diefenbaker chose the moment to express approval of US policies towards Canada. He had, he assured Nehru, been critical in the past, but his experience since coming into office had been that the Americans were going out of their way to remove causes of unnecessary friction.

Diefenbaker was interested in exploring Nehru's thinking on the attitude of the non-aligned world towards communism. The opportunity came while Nehru was reviewing the political situation in the Middle East. Nehru described the

United Arab Republic under Nasser as the most stable government in the Middle East and attributed Nasser's 'enormous prestige' to the fact that he had come to represent Arab nationalism. Diefenbaker asked whether Nasser would really be able to keep communism out of the UAR. Nehru replied that a government could be favourable to communism, and thus communism could exert an influence, but Arab nationalists would turn against a communist country if they thought it was interfering. A communist system could not be imposed if the conditions were not right. I do not believe that Diefenbaker came away fully reassured. What he had gained, however, not only from Nehru but also from Fanfani and Adenauer earlier, was an affirmation of the strength of Arab nationalism and neutrality and a new perspective on the influential role which Nasser was playing in world affairs.

Sandwiched between more formal engagements was a day of tiger-hunting with the Maharao of Kotah in the state of Rajasthan. The prime minister had been apprehensive about the impact of this activity on his image back home, but when the time came he surrendered happily enough to the excitement. The hunt was based on two small launches on a narrow and slow-moving river. The Maharao, who had 350 tigers to his credit since he shot his first at the age of eleven (he was now forty-nine), sat in the more river-worthy of the launches with the prime minister and Chester Ronning, each of them pith-helmeted and alert, with guns resting in their laps. Diefenbaker sported a loud check shirt which he discarded as the weather and the excitement got warmer. Great tension built up as the beaters swept through the undergrowth on the bank of the river, crying out loudly, banging pots, and doing everything possible to flush the tiger out into an open space where the hunters could have a clear shot. Once it seemed that the animal would break cover, and all hands had their guns or cameras cocked. But the tiger confounded the experts and, after a fruitless search for another tiger further up river, we returned in darkness to the Maharao's splendidly appointed palace. The tiger had won the day. Was the prime minister privately relieved or disappointed? Opinions were divided. After dinner we were entertained with moving pictures of past tiger hunts in which the animals had been less successful.

CEYLON

In Ceylon (Sri Lanka), public interest in Diefenbaker's visit was warm and the hospitality even warmer. The prime minister fulfilled nervously his ambition to ride on an elephant. Elmer Diefenbaker found himself referred to on a printed program as the son of the prime minister and his wife, with much resultant mirth and good humour.

In Diefenbaker's official meetings with Prime Minister Solomon Bandaranaike, however, things did not go so smoothly. Bandaranaike had the manner of a professor combined with the mind and rhetoric of a politician. One thought of the left wing of the Labour party in Britain as his alternate habitat. Diefenbaker's preoccupation with the threat of communist economic penetration, and his faith in the Commonwealth as a vehicle for the expansion of trade, met with a chilly response. When Diefenbaker asked if Bandaranaike did not agree that by setting up at the Montreal conference a committee of experts to consider the problem of commodity surpluses, the Commonwealth had taken a useful initiative, the Ceylonese prime minister looked unimpressed. He examined the propeller-like fans rotating in the ceiling above him, blew a cloud of pipe smoke in that direction, and said in a flat tone, 'not really.' Commodity prices must be stabilized on a basis wider than the Commonwealth, encompassing *all* countries that were prospective buyers and sellers. Soviet and Chinese competition would not prove a serious menace. Returning to the Commonwealth, he said with a glint of mischief that efforts had been made, notably by Lord Beaverbrook, to make the Commonwealth into a self-sufficient economic unit. This was not realistic. Nor would economic aid such as that provided through the Colombo Plan, valuable as it was, be enough to solve Ceylon's problems. They required more fundamental economic measures. Economic improvement was the best hope of preserving the essence of democracy in Asia.

For Diefenbaker this was a disconcerting conversation. The emphasis he had placed on the promise of economic cooperation through the Commonwealth and on the danger of communist economic strategy had been directly challenged. At the same time he was told by Ceylon's governor general, Sir Oliver Goonetillike, of the effective work of Soviet diplomats in Ceylon. Nik Cavell, the Canadian high commissioner, said too that in comparison with the communist nations, the West's message was not really getting across. This was exactly what Diefenbaker had feared, and he reacted to it, in his only major public speech in Ceylon, by underlining the purity of Canada's motives in contributing through the Colombo Plan. It sounded a little off-key, but it was his way of warning his audience of parliamentarians against the insidious purposes of communists, both foreign and Ceylonese, in their midst. For good measure he added a warm testimonial to the United States, just as he had done in New Delhi. The effect of this on the audience was one of puzzlement, but Diefenbaker was quite unrepentant. Whenever on this journey he sensed a coolness towards the United States, he felt it was his duty to speak in support of Canada's neighbour and ally, if only as an act of solidarity with his esteemed friend, the president. Three years later he might not have offered quite as solid support to Eisenhower's successor.

Closest to his heart were the interests of Canada's western farmers. At his press conference in Ceylon, he again expressed the hope ('if not the expectation') that countries receiving increased Colombo Plan aid from Canada would take a substantial part of that increase in the form of wheat turned into flour. These statements sounded peculiar alongside his equally emphatic agreement that aid was best when given without strings attached. I knew from reports reaching us from Ottawa that the officials there were hoping that the prime minister could be prevailed on not to press the case for recipient countries taking a bigger proportion of aid in the form of foodstuffs. In a letter on this subject to the department sent from Canberra on 3 December, I wrote, resignedly, 'I have been waiting for a free moment to let you know that the Prime Minister has deliberately taken this position in Karachi, New Delhi, Colombo, Kuala Lumpur and Canberra, both in public and private.' In other words, the prime minister knew what he wanted to do and all arguments to the contrary had been fruitless. I think they just annoyed him.

SOUTHEAST ASIA

The prime minister found his visits to Malaya and Singapore, from 27 November to 2 December, much less taxing than those to India and Ceylon. The change of atmosphere owed much to the Malayan prime minister, Tunku Abdul Rahman ('the Tunku'), whose warm and approachable manner made Diefenbaker feel immediately at home. In Kuala Lumpur there was little if any sign in government circles of the spirit of determined neutralism which Diefenbaker had struggled to understand and respond to in New Delhi and Colombo.

One of Diefenbaker's special interests was to explore how the Malayans viewed the China problem. The Tunku was not afraid to declare his political differences with the Peking regime or his support for the United States in the stand it had taken over the islands of Quemoy and Matsu. Malaya could not look favourably on any territorial expansion by Peking. He spoke at length about the difficulties of preventing the infiltration of terrorists and Chinese Communist agents through Singapore.

At a press conference on 28 November, Diefenbaker skated around attempts to get him to discuss neutralism and the dangers of communism in Southeast Asia. He described Canada's position on aid to the region, stated that participation in joint defence arrangements was beyond Canada's resources, and explained the Canadian government's policy on recognition of the Peking regime:

There has been a great deal of speculation on the subject. The stand taken by Canada has been consistently followed since the Korean episode. We realize that China is a nation of 600 million people, that it cannot be ignored. We have had a long and friendly

78

relationship with the Chinese people in the past and Canadian association with religious, educational, commercial, diplomatic and other activities would indicate and emphasize that relationship. We hope that the friendly spirit will be restored. We are prepared to trade with continental China excepting in those products which in our opinion are strategic. But the question of formal recognition is one for which we have not made a final consideration.

We feel that recognition would be interpreted in many parts of the world among those who have taken a strong stand as against Communism and its dangers, as recognition of Communism ... We do not intend to take any course which will weaken the opposition to Communism anywhere or be so interpreted as constituting on the part of Canada a weakening in our stand.

Hammarskjöld's judgment – that the majority of Asian governments would be relieved if the recognition of Peking became more widespread – was thus not shared by two of the four Asian governments he had consulted (Pakistan and Malaya). It was hardly a reliable basis for disagreement with Hammarskjöld's view, nor was it very surprising. With Ayub Khan and the Tunku you knew where you stood, firmly against communism. Diefenbaker was allowing his anti-communist sentiments to prevail, even though reason kept reminding him of the arguments for bringing Peking into the world community.[3] He continually said during the tour how unfortunate it was that the Liberal government had not recognized Peking sooner, since the longer recognition was delayed, the more anomalous the position became. This would remain as one of the persistent dilemmas of foreign policy in the Diefenbaker years.

A feature of these visits was the frequency with which gifts were exchanged. By the time the Diefenbaker caravan had reached Kuala Lumpur, the store of Eskimo carvings, maple syrup, and other Canadian wonders was running dangerously low. One of my painful memories is of a day when, in steamy tropical heat, a small hooked rug portraying a Quebec snow scene was presented by the Diefenbakers in exchange for an exquisitely crafted silver tea service.

Less painful because more amusing was the prime minister's presentation of a silver-framed photograph to his Malayan counterpart. The appropriate inscription had been made by Diefenbaker beforehand. The photograph was then reinserted in the frame, which was held in its blue Birks container until the moment for presentation. When the moment came, after another embarrassing wave of gifts from the hosts, and in the presence of the entire Malayan cabinet, Canada's prime minister made a ceremonious extraction of the frame and displayed it proudly for all to see. It took him a few seconds to realize what the laughter was about. The frame contained a blank white mat; the photograph had been placed with his face to the back of the frame. It flashed across my mind that someone might be shot for this, but instead he quickly joined in the merriment and won friends in the process.

Next it was Singapore, at that time still a British colony and the site of Britain's largest overseas military base. Diefenbaker's visit came at a time of great political uncertainty and also in an atmosphere of anxiety over internal security matters. He made excellent use of his meetings which, however, did not reassure him as to the prospects for stability either in Singapore or in the Southeast Asian region. On the question of aid under the Colombo Plan, Diefenbaker said he was in doubt about the best policy towards potential recipients which were not 'on our side.' The British officials replied that it would be a mistake to stop helping marginal recipients. The West should try to do everything possible in the neutral countries despite the 'blackmailing value' of a neutral position. I reflected on the efforts made in the past, in Ottawa, to persuade the prime minister to include non-Commonwealth countries in our aid programs. We had gone halfway around the world to get the same message taken seriously. Whether it would be acted on, only time would tell.

The prime minister had resisted recommendations from External Affairs that he accept the Indonesian government's invitation to pay a brief visit to Djakarta. A compromise in the form of a two-hour refuelling stop was eventually reached. Much to the credit of the planners, both Indonesian and Canadian, the visit turned out to be a considerable success in spite of President Sukarno's apparently genuine absence through illness.

To brief the prime minister, Russ McKinney, first secretary at the embassy, joined the Canadian party at Singapore and it was arranged that his briefing would be given en route to Djakarta. The prime minister slept soundly through most of the flight but somehow a few minutes were found just before arrival. McKinney did his job superbly. He was aided by the prime minister's capacity to absorb enough in a short time to get through an engagement for which he had done little if any previous homework. Typically, he threw a scare into McKinney just as the aircraft was circling the Djakarta airport. Pointing below, he said the place was full of communists, and pretended that he would not leave the airport as provided in the program. Of course, he relented, but ...

A brief discussion with Prime Minister Djuanda on economic matters led Diefenbaker to express his belief that for underdeveloped nations, a liberal policy on foreign investment would be in their best interests. Canada's experience with US capital was that it was 'not as avaricious as it was made out to be in other parts of the world.' Otherwise Canada would not have survived as an independent state, and he had no worries whatsoever about Canadian survival even with an extremely liberal policy towards foreign investment. It was language he would not have used before a Canadian audience.

AUSTRALIA AND NEW ZEALAND

The Diefenbakers and their entourage reached Canberra on 3 December. He was to be the prime object of Australian hospitality for six days, roughly balanced among Canberra, Melbourne, and Sydney. He was tired after the exertions of some five weeks' travel in Europe and Asia, but he was also relaxed. He had the advantage of having first met with leaders of several nations of importance to Australia, and his impressions were awaited with evident interest by the Australian government and press.

There was, too, an unspoken factor of which Diefenbaker, and doubtless Robert Menzies, were conscious. After the 1957 meeting of Commonwealth prime ministers in London, Menzies had made what one British newspaper thought was a disparaging public reference to Diefenbaker. Menzies had sought later in Ottawa to repair the damage by saying that he had been misrepresented. Diefenbaker kept his feelings to himself but the incident lay not quite forgotten in the undergrowth of their relationship. This visit, however, was the first to Australia by a Canadian prime minister in office, and Menzies and his wife, Dame Pattie, certainly went out of their way to be hospitable, even to the extent of deciding, just before the Diefenbakers' arrival in Australia, to spend the weekend with them informally in Sydney. This late change of plan may have generated – it certainly fanned – a press rumour that one of the purposes of Diefenbaker's visit to Australia was to approach Menzies about his becoming governor general of Canada. A less likely appointment would have been hard to imagine, but it was the first question Diefenbaker faced at the press conference he gave after arriving in Canberra. He dealt with it effectively enough, saying it was based on conjecture and concealing the incredulity he must have felt at the thought of paying court to Menzies at Rideau Hall, the governor general's residence in Ottawa.

Diefenbaker reported in his official meetings with Menzies that Asian governments were learning about communism primarily from the Soviet and Chinese economic offensives. They were by and large aware of the problem presented by the dumping of goods but found it hard to combat this tactic, and their task was made more difficult by the impression of progress which they received from observation of Communist China. Strangely enough, recognition of the Peking regime was not discussed in the official talks, although it may well have come up in private conversation. Diefenbaker's opinion had been evolving since his sympathetic reaction to Hammarskjöld's pro-recognition view at the end of October. He was now firmly of the view that 'the Dulles concept was right': recognition would be regarded as 'the acceptance of a welcome to communism' and would be so viewed in the countries of Southeast Asia.

A prime minister of Canada visiting Australia must be in his best oratorical form. Fortunately Diefenbaker, fatigued as he was, found Australian audiences responsive. He had nothing like the trouble he had experienced in Asia in finding appropriate themes and language. Here he could revert to homespun jokes with a better hope of their being understood. And he could speak spontaneously about the common heritage of Australians and Canadians and about the mystical virtues of the Commonwealth. It must be said, however, that Diefenbaker and Menzies, though both staunch Commonwealth loyalists, were anything but soulmates. Neither excelled at listening to the other, though both were accomplished raconteurs. Diefenbaker felt uncomfortable in the presence of Menzies' polished wit and jovial sophistication. Menzies may have seen Diefenbaker as a late-coming rival for senior status in the Commonwealth.

On arriving in New Zealand, Diefenbaker experienced the same feelings of nostalgia as he had in Australia. He had a particularly warm place in his heart for New Zealanders. From seeing him in their company, I think he felt generally more at home than with most of the people he knew in British or even Australian public life. He especially liked Prime Minister Walter Nash, whose independence of mind and devotion to the Commonwealth he admired so much that he forgave him for being a socialist. Nothing pleased Diefenbaker more than to fall in with Nash's proposal that their official meeting should be entirely private. It was the first time on the tour that such a meeting took place without high commissioners or other advisers present.

In New Zealand, the prime minister was scheduled to spend just under a week, the second half of which was to be rest and relaxation, much needed by one and all. As it happened, word came from Canada just as his formal program ended that his mother had fallen ill, and he was obliged to cancel the recreational part of the visit and head for home three or four days ahead of schedule.

In the Department of External Affairs, the end of the tour brought a wave of relief. Nothing serious had gone wrong. The prime minister had come through it to his satisfaction. Press coverage had been extensive and mostly favourable. Important lessons had been learned about his habits, priorities, and attitudes. There was hope that the experience would make it easier to advise and support him in policy matters.

From my personal point of view, the tour had its difficult moments, especially in the matter of speeches. In a post mortem, I wrote later: 'Mr. Diefenbaker went from major speech to major speech rather than from one official conversation to another, and I sometimes had the feeling that he could not understand why so much trouble had been gone to in telling him what to say to other prime ministers when what he really needed was some meat to put into his speeches.'[4]

What we had was sound enough but in his view lacking in news value – the ultimate stigma. Fortunately we had valuable help from the staff in our various offices along the way – and not only on the content of the speeches. I was a natural target for the prime minister's impatience over the speech material, being submerged in drafts contributed from Ottawa and from each Canadian post and having only the most general indication from the prime minister of what he would like to say on each of the numerous speaking occasions. In Pakistan, where he reached a peak of irritation, Herb Moran came to my defence without my knowledge. Later Diefenbaker told me what Moran had said, and after that he was more understanding, if seldom satisfied. More generally, however, the tour had been a turning point in my relationship with the prime minister. On the way home he told me that he wished me to continue to assist him, and I felt that at least for the time being I had a measure of his confidence.

9

No Rest for the Leader

On returning to Ottawa I found that I was to be released from my responsibility to Sidney Smith and would be working full time as special assistant to the prime minister. I had been serving the two masters for more than a year and, although the prospect ahead was far from restful, I took some encouragement from the fact that as a result of the rigours of a seven-week global trip, I had a pretty good idea of the prime minister's needs and moods. When I called on Sidney Smith to take leave of him, he made the moment more poignant by remarking that hard as he knew I had tried to help him, I had seemed so often to be 'at the other end of the hall' – at the prime minister's end of the corridor. Ross Campbell then became special assistant to Sidney Smith and, in partnership, we did our best for the next three-and-a-half years to coordinate the department's links with the prime minister and the secretary of state for external affairs.

The world tour had broadened the prime minister's knowledge and further sharpened his interest in the major foreign and defence policy issues. He had become accustomed to the several services he received from the Department of External Affairs. He was still a regular consumer of the telegraphic reports from Canadian offices abroad, and was insistent on seeing any major policy analysis, recommendations, or instructions emanating from the department. He required briefings before cabinet meetings on foreign policy subjects and before the daily question period in the House of Commons. A large proportion of his public speeches, whether in the House or elsewhere, contained foreign policy material. And there were frequent high-level visits by foreign leaders which involved Diefenbaker whether he liked it or not. There was therefore no shortage of liaison work between the Prime Minister's Office and the Department of External Affairs.

THE DEFENCE OUTLOOK

The prime minister's most agonizing policy problem in the first year after his election victory in March 1958 concerned the Avro Arrow interceptor aircraft which had been under development at A.V. Roe of Canada near Toronto. The project had first been examined by the Diefenbaker cabinet in October 1957, and, with some hesitation, development had been continued for a further year. The issue was basically economic. Because of cost increases, the Arrow was consuming an undue proportion of the defence budget. RCAF requirements were less than had been anticipated and there appeared to be no prospect of generating export sales of sufficient volume to justify continued development. Pearkes, the minister of national defence, recommended cancellation, and his cabinet colleagues agreed that this was the only course that made sense. But that made the decision no easier. Some 25,000 jobs in the Toronto area were at stake. What made things worse was that, as Minister of Finance Donald Fleming put it, 'with the growing cost and complexity of weapons and weapons-systems, Canada would never again be able to develop an important weapon of her own. New developments in Canada's defence effort must be even more closely intermixed with the United States than heretofore.'[1] A distasteful truth to face for a government feeding on nationalism.

The government took two bites at the Avro bullet. On 23 September 1958, it announced that 'it would not be advisable at this time to put the CF-105 [Arrow] into production.[2] In the same announcement, the government made it known that it had decided to introduce the Bomarc guided missile into the Canadian air-defence system. Strangely, as has been pointed out by expert critics, the adoption of the Bomarc was not justified on the basis that it was a cheaper weapon designed to perform the same (anti-bomber) role, although this was clearly the case. Instead, the language of the press release implied that the progress made by the Soviet Union in the development of intercontinental ballistic missiles (ICBMs) was somehow responsible for the decisions that had been taken. In fact, the Bomarc would be of no more use than the Arrow in defending against an ICBM.

The final decision on the development (as distinct from the production) of the Arrow was held over until after the New Year. The prime minister carried the worry with him around the world – he always hoped that postponements might beget miracles – but the inevitable could not be stemmed. After a long series of cabinet discussions, he announced to the House of Commons on 20 February 1959 that the development of the Arrow was being terminated.[3] At the same time, as if to offset the impact of what he was saying, he made further important statements. The full potential of these defensive weapons, he said, was achieved only when they were armed with nuclear weapons. Canada was examining with the United States government questions connected with the acquisition of nuclear warheads for the 'Bomarc and other defensive weapons for use by the Canadian forces in Canada, and the storage of warheads in Canada. Problems connected with the arming of the Canadian Army brigade in Europe with short range nuclear weapons for NATO's defence are also being studied.'

Further studies were being made of the 'various alternatives' to the CF-100, which the Arrow had been intended to replace but which was 'still an effective weapon in the defence of North America against the present bomber threat.' And the US and Canadian governments were proceeding towards the establishment of production-sharing arrangements. Finally, at the urging of External Affairs, Canada's opposition to the spread of nuclear weapons 'at the independent disposal of national governments' and its devotion to the cause of disarmament were, albeit briefly, reaffirmed.

This necessarily short summary is included here as a point of reference for later discussion of defence and disarmament problems. Together with the government's acquiescence in the decision of the NATO summit in December 1957 to establish nuclear stockpiles for the use of NATO forces in Europe, the press release of 23 September 1958 and the prime minister's statement of 20 February 1959 might not unreasonably have been taken to mean that the Diefenbaker government was firmly committing itself to the acquisition of nuclear weapons for Canadian forces both in Europe and Canada. Personally, I had no reason to doubt that the Department of National Defence, led by a minister who had ready access to, and at that time the full confidence of the prime minister, would succeed in securing the government's agreement to the acquisition of nuclear weapons. R.B. Bryce, the secretary to the cabinet, was in support and was trying to help the prime minister to articulate his solution to the problem .

While the voices against nuclear commitment, at least from 1957 to early 1959, had little influence with the prime minister, there were early signs of some of the problems that lay ahead. In April 1958, when Pearkes brought to the Cabinet Defence Committee a proposal concerning the deployment of nuclear weapons at Goose Bay for the use of the US Strategic Air Command (SAC), Sidney Smith reminded the committee of the political difficulties that had arisen in the United Kingdom over nuclear cooperation. Diefenbaker reacted nervously, observing that it would be unfortunate if public opinion in Canada became divided on the nuclear question. He told his ministers that it would be necessary to have Pearson's agreement to any arrangements for the use of nuclear weapons for SAC in Canada.[4] A spirited discussion took place, but the proposal was held over for further consideration, as it would be many times in the future, to the frustration of the defence authorities in both Ottawa and Washington.

BERLIN—SOVIET PRESSURES

While the prime minister was touring the world, the Soviet government launched an attempt to terminate the occupation responsibilities of the Four Powers in Berlin, to transfer at least some duties to the East German authorities, and to give West Berlin the status of a demilitarized free city. The rights of the three Western powers, and the obligations of the Soviet Union to respect them, had been set out in agreements dating from the end of the war in Europe and the Berlin blockade in 1948. The Western powers were determined to maintain their rights of access to the Western part of the city and to resist Soviet efforts to force them to recognize the East German regime. The Soviet government had declared that it would turn over its responsibilities in Berlin to the East Germans on 27 May 1959.

As a member of NATO and with armed forces stationed in Europe, Canada was inevitably caught up in the tension which built up over the Berlin issue during the winter of 1958–9. It was the first time since the Diefenbaker government had come to office that a serious East-West crisis had been precipitated. The Western governments consulted furiously on the response they should give to the Soviet proposals. There were those in the alliance who insisted on a tough line and others who saw in the situation the possibility of progress through negotiation. In the Department of External Affairs, a group of officials led by the undersecretary, Norman Robertson, were engaged in policy planning reminiscent of the Pearson years. They were casting around for moves that might generate impetus for East-West negotiations on Berlin and the wider questions of Germany's future and European security. Robertson was interested in the idea of accepting Germany as a 'divided country,' both parts of which might be admitted to the United Nations. The climate in NATO would not have stood for that but Robertson encouraged other ideas, designed to inject a dose of flexibility into the traditional Four-Power stance on Germany and Berlin. The ideas took the form of 'lines of inquiry,' for discussion with officials of allied governments. They included possible ways of increasing Western contacts with East Germany, the question whether Germany might be reunified by some process other than elections, and possible new approaches to schemes for partial disengagement of Soviet and Western troops in Europe.[5]

Sidney Smith took a strong personal interest in these ideas. In a handwritten letter to the prime minister, he wrote that 'we have recently been seeking for a role for Canada in the Berlin situation – a role that could be helpful and constructive ... Herewith is a memorandum into which we have put much thought.' The prime minister's reaction was less enthusiastic. I reported to the minister on 26 January that while the prime minister did not object to bilateral talks with some of our allies, he thought 'there was a danger that ... other governments might infer that the direction of thought implied [in the lines of inquiry] had become, or were on the point of becoming, Canadian policy.' He obviously did not want to subscribe to the ideas put forward in the memorandum from Smith, but nevertheless gave the department latitude to float them informally.

A few days later, Diefenbaker's suspicions surfaced again when an article by Harold Greer in the Toronto *Globe and Mail* reflected certain ideas which the prime minister remembered from his recent study of the External Affairs policy paper on the crisis.[6] The incident made him think that External Affairs was using the press to get him to endorse a policy direction with which he was not in full sympathy. That was not the case but Greer had done some clever detective work. That morning when the prime minister asked me to come to his office with a statement for the House, he really went after the department for 'unreliability.'

I had several difficult conversations with the prime minister in this period. Officials in the department wanted to know the real basis of his objections to the policy ideas they were submitting. Was he personally convinced that it would be unwise to try out ideas of this kind? Had he been persuaded, perhaps, by direct calls or messages from Eisenhower or Dulles or from George Drew in London, that there must be no breach in NATO solidarity in the current crisis? Or was it more a question of domestic political judgment in which his instincts advised him against any show of softness towards the Soviet Union?

After a lengthy conversation with him on 11 February, I sent a memorandum to Robertson in which I reported that the prime minister's skepticism of progress through negotiation sprang from personal conviction, but that he might well have been influenced by accounts he had received from Eisenhower, Macmillan, and Adenauer of their encounters with Khrushchev. It would, the prime minister had remarked, be a gross miscalculation of character if we pinned even the slimmest hope on Khrushchev's disposition to engage in a genuine compromise. Any hope he might once have had about the possibility of reaching even a small-scale agreement with the Soviet government had disappeared. The Soviet authorities believed they were in a strong position and there was no reason why they should make concessions since they were achieving their foreign policy objectives without doing so. He was afraid that efforts to wring concessions out of the Russians would result in the surrender of many of the rights and privileges in Berlin, for example, which the West now held. He discounted the proposition that Western policies might have an indirect impact on the Soviet attitude if they attracted favourable diplomatic or public attention in Eastern Europe or in influential neutral countries. He said that he had little faith in the possibility of German reunification, and he questioned whether a significant increase in contacts between East and West Germany was feasible.[7]

Prime Minister Macmillan, as alarmed as any Western leader by Khrushchev's ultimatum over access to Berlin, had recently informed Diefenbaker of his intention to visit Moscow for talks with the Soviet government. Diefenbaker's reply was drafted in External Affairs and approved on 19 February. It bore the old Canadian trademark of firmness and flexibility, but, to show Macmillan that he had had some part in the drafting, Diefenbaker added a tailpiece: 'You carry with you my sincere good wishes. I cannot overstate my certain belief that whatever its immediate tangible results may be, your visit will fill a long-felt need that Khrushchev should learn at first hand of the basic beliefs of the free nations and of their willingness to do everything short of appeasement toward the reduction of tension and the achievement of better relations between the U.S.S.R. and the Western world.'[8]

In other words, Diefenbaker was not hopeful of 'tangible results' from Macmillan's meeting with Khrushchev, but entirely trusted Macmillan to explain the Western nations' viewpoint. At this stage Diefenbaker showed no special interest in promoting new ideas which might be useful in detailed diplomatic exchanges. That was Pearsonian territory and he was apprehensive that Sidney Smith would not be able to keep control of the 'Pearsonalities.' The policy planners, meanwhile, were receiving from NATO capitals guarded replies to their 'lines of inquiry.' A summary of consultations prepared at that time refers to Canada as 'the avant-garde of the revisionists.' The planners, encouraged by Robertson, continued to urge flexibility as the desirable keynote of Western policy. They had Sidney Smith on their side but Diefenbaker remained sceptical and tended to put his faith in the collective wisdom of Macmillan, Eisenhower, de Gaulle and Adenauer. The whole episode exemplified the difference of outlook between Diefenbaker and Robertson.

Following his visit to Moscow from 21 February to 3 March, Macmillan toured the main Western capitals, first Bonn and Paris, then Washington, this time via Ottawa. He was to arrive in Ottawa on 18 March. Diefenbaker had said to me on 14 March, however, that he did not want exaggerated importance to be attached to Macmillan's visit. He regarded it as an opportunity to hear a personal report of the British prime minister's recent discussions rather than as a full-scale exchange of views on European problems. On the Canadian side, he wanted only a very small number of ministers to participate in the first of the two meetings scheduled. Since Diefenbaker did not expect to have time to prepare himself for the visit, with the help of External Affairs officials I assembled as much information as was then available, turning it over to him for weekend reading. Whether he really delved into it I do not know, for the beginning of the following week brought the sudden death from heart failure of Sidney Smith.[9]

There had been some anxiety, especially in Bonn and Paris, that during his visit to Moscow, Macmillan might prove too ready to compromise with the Soviet Union. In Ottawa these apprehensions were not widely felt. It was generally thought that, by his talks in Moscow, Macmillan had contributed to a defusing of the crisis and that he had succeeded in doing so without prejudicing Western interests. In Macmillan's account of his exchanges with the Soviet leaders, he put particular stress on Soviet withdrawal of the Berlin ultimatum due to expire on 27 May and on the readiness of the USSR to join in Four-Power negotiations among foreign ministers rather than insist on proceeding directly to a summit conference.[10]

Two points are worth mentioning to illustrate Diefenbaker's turn of mind at that time. There had been, first, some emphasis in press reports on Macmillan's alleged exchanges with Khrushchev on 'disengagement' of forces in Europe. Diefenbaker said that this was the one aspect of Macmillan's visit which had caused some public concern in North America. He was afraid that a trend towards isolationism might emerge, manifested in public pressure for the return of US and Canadian forces stationed in Europe. This observation was consistent with the doubts Diefenbaker had often expressed about the concept of disengagement. He was also concerned about means of responding to a possible Soviet move to transfer control of access to Berlin to the East German government. He asked Macmillan to convey to the US authorities the Canadian government's misgivings concerning any 'ill-considered' move, such as the placing of the US Strategic Air Command on an increased state of readiness at a time of tension, which might lead the Soviet government to conclude that the West was contemplating large-scale military action.

Agreeing with the need for caution, Macmillan mentioned an arrangement whereby a UN presence might be used to assure the right of access to Berlin, possibly associated with a symbolic presence of US, British, and French forces. Diefenbaker was intrigued by this idea, so much so that he drew attention to it in his report to the House of Commons the following day. Later he told me that he would like the department to work up a more detailed proposal on the use of the United Nations in Berlin. It was, he said, so much more promising than the vague ideas Macmillan had put forward on the thinning out or limitation of forces.

Diefenbaker also asked Macmillan if the British position on the reunification of Germany had changed. Was there now more willingness to reconsider the commitment made with Germany's entry into the Western alliance in 1955? This thought had been conveyed to Diefenbaker by George Drew, who had picked it up in conversation with R.A. Butler, Macmillan's cabinet colleague. Drew had devoted a long telegram to warning against any departure from the 1955 commitment. Macmillan's reply was that this position on reunification of Germany was now unrealistic but that the West could not admit the impossibility of reunifying Germany on satisfactory terms.

INTERIM FOREIGN MINISTER

From Sidney Smith's death on 17 March until the appointment of Howard Green on 4 June, Diefenbaker acted as his own minister of external affairs. Although Smith had been something of a disappointment both to the press and the department, Diefenbaker had not been dissatisfied with the way he was filling the post. In fact, Smith, by his readiness to move without complaint in the shadow of Diefenbaker, had fitted in well with the prime minister's conception of his own role in the management of foreign policy.

Diefenbaker's assumption of the External Affairs portfolio meant that a large volume of recommendations that would normally have been dealt with by the minister had to be referred to the prime minister. It became necessary to consult him on roughly ten times as many decisions as had been normal when Smith was in office. Although he did not attempt any uncommon policy moves, a number of significant things happened while Diefenbaker had direct charge of the department. The crisis over Berlin continued but was channelled into a conference at Geneva of the four foreign ministers (the United States, the USSR, the United Kingdom, and France), which brought the temperature down without producing agreed solutions. In Ottawa there was much emphasis on civil defence precautions, a measure of the anxiety the government felt. On 18 May General Norstad, the NATO military commander in Europe, came to Ottawa and discussed NATO's military strategy with the cabinet. The chiefs of staff had recommended that the Canadian Air Division in Europe should assume a 'strike reconnaissance' role, one which would involve the use of nuclear ammunition.[11] Norstad's presentation impressed Diefenbaker. Howard Green, not yet aware of his impending appointment as foreign minister, was also present. No one could say after Norstad's briefing that the government was not considering a nuclear commitment in Europe.[12]

Other events pointed to new directions or new emphasis in international and Canadian affairs. The death of John Foster Dulles, the US secretary of state, on 24 May seemed to Diefenbaker an event of great moment. The prime minister was not taken with Dulles personally but he admired his consistent strategy in dealing with the communist world. For all the acknowledged distinction and integrity of Christian Herter, Dulles's successor, Diefenbaker predicted that US leadership of the free nations would undergo another stage of testing by the communist powers.

In recent months there had been more clouds than sunshine in Canada-US affairs, owing largely to economic and border issues such as US import restrictions on oil, the Chicago water diversion, and the proposed passage of a Soviet ship through the St Lawrence Seaway. Then, with Dulles's passing, Diefenbaker's mood swung the other way. It was a time for solidarity. Arnold Heeney, the newly appointed ambassador in Washington,[13] supported by Norman Robertson in Ottawa, suggested that this would be a good time to put a more positive face on defence cooperation. A US decision favourable to Canada on oil import restrictions helped greatly. The prime minister approved of Heeney's suggestion and used it as the main theme of a speech he was preparing to give at Michigan State University on 7 June. In one conversation about the draft, he said that he wanted to reassure the Americans that Canada was not moving towards a policy of 'neutralism' in world affairs. The message came through clearly when he received his degree at Michigan State.

It was in April 1959 that Diefenbaker was obliged to decide whether to welcome Fidel Castro to Ottawa. Castro and a large Cuban delegation had been invited by a private group to visit Montreal and obviously hoped that an invitation to Ottawa would be forthcoming for an official welcome. Plans were at an advanced stage when Diefenbaker thought better of it. Even when Castro offered to fly to Ottawa to see the prime minister privately, Diefenbaker declined. In External, we had quite a time finding an explanation, though we were able to say that Castro had accepted in principle an invitation to come to Ottawa at an unspecified later date. The incident passed in the House of Commons without as much criticism as we had expected, but it remained an awkward beginning in Diefenbaker's relationship with Castro. For the moment, his uneasiness about the Castro regime and his unwillingness to risk offending Eisenhower had prevailed. This would not prevent the Canadian government from maintaining, in the future, an independent policy towards Cuba, one that would soon cause misunderstanding and resentment in Washington.

Among the minor tasks that Diefenbaker was obliged to carry out while he was acting as foreign minister was the approval or rejection of budgetary items over a certain spending limit. These came in the form of submissions to the Treasury Board asking Diefenbaker, as acting minister, to sign them. A request for approval to spend money on diplomats and their premises abroad was not a natural winner. Once, in this period, I presented a request for authority to cover the costs of renovations in an embassy residence abroad. About half way in the list of items was the cost of repairing chandeliers. He swept his vacuum cleaner eyes down the list and suddenly stopped. I could see we were in trouble. 'Chandeliers,' he roared, and flung the paper across the desk, unloved and, worse, unsigned. I went with it back to the department where, after deliberation, we decided to try it again, substituting the term 'light fixtures.' It turned out to be a happy choice of words. When I took it back to the prime minister he recognized the paper, glanced at the new wording, signed it with a slight smile, and returned it to me saying, 'A hundred per cent.'

On the morning after Sidney Smith's death, I had accompanied the prime minister to the Ottawa airport to meet Prime Minister Macmillan. Diefenbaker spent most of the ride reviewing the possible candidates for foreign minister. From that early stage until the middle of May, Donald Fleming was the clear favourite on Diefenbaker's list. The prime minister said he had been impressed by the capable way in which Fleming had handled the Commonwealth conference on trade and economic matters as well as other international assignments he had taken on. On 13 May, however, Diefenbaker told me that Howard Green was now the favourite, Fleming had problems in the Finance field which he would have to overcome. Davie Fulton, another likely contender, was the first good minister of justice for a long time. Green had grown in stature, had made 'a life-long study' of foreign affairs, and was comfortable in the House of Commons. The 'ambitious ones' would be disappointed, he added. I record these comments because I think that, taken together, they help to explain his choice of Green. An even more important reason, however, was that Diefenbaker felt he could work more comfortably with Green, whose judgment and loyalty he fully trusted.

It took three weeks for the prime minister to bring the Green appointment to the boil. Exactly why it took so long, I do not know, although it was Diefenbaker's habit to take soundings before making such decisions final. In External Affairs, the advance news of Green's appointment caused a stir. The anticipated emphasis on friendship with Britain, come what may, on the value of the old (white) Commonwealth, on anti-American themes, not to speak of the bitterness with which Green had attacked Canadian policy in the Suez crisis in 1956 – all these became the stuff of speculation and some anxiety. Even Norman Robertson wondered about the suitability of the appointment, despite longstanding personal acquaintance and family links in Vancouver. Would the new minister have the open-mindedness he would need to overcome his lack of experience in international affairs?

Diefenbaker may have had Robertson's doubts about Green reported to him. On the day before Green's appointment, Diefenbaker told me that the new minister would need all the department's help, and that, bearing in mind some of the things he had said in the past on foreign policy, he 'would have to change some of his ideas.' It was ironic that the prime minister, given his own attachment to the Commonwealth, singled it out as a policy area in which Green would need assistance.

PART THREE

New Directions

JUNE 1959 TO
NOVEMBER 1960

10

Teaming up with Howard Green

With the appointment of Howard Green as secretary of state for external affairs early in June 1959, the prime minister set in train a course of events quite different from what I think he had envisaged. He had chosen as his minister a man whose combination of interests and qualities ranged wider and went deeper than he had realized, and whose impact on policy proved in the end to be more than the prime minister himself could control or cope with.

At the outset the full implications were, of course, not discernible. Diefenbaker and his new minister settled in to their working relationship and pragmatically divided the foreign policy spectrum between them. The prime minister's special interests – in East-West relations, the Commonwealth, and Canadian-American affairs – left plenty of room for the minister to assert his own interests and priorities.

By the end of November 1960, Green had established himself in a number of ways. He had taken a firm hold on the department, thus assuring the prime minister that the 'Pearsonalities' would be subjected to strong, no-nonsense management. He had come to grips with a variety of international issues in which Canada was involved – the work of the international commission in Laos, peace-keeping in the Congo, the widening rift between the United States and Cuba, the outlook for Canada's relations with Latin America, and, more generally, with the developing world. Above all, however, the minister had been, to use his own word, 'inspired' by the United Nations and its work for peace, and had become a convinced and stubborn crusader against nuclear testing and proliferation and for disarmament. It was in this latter field, and in the closely related field of defence policy, that Green would come to play such a critical role in the history of the Diefenbaker government. In the first eighteen months of his appointment as foreign minister, the new directions he charted took shape and began to generate concern within the government. During this period, the stage would be set for the more serious issues confronting the prime minister in the last two years of his government's life. These issues would not only be internal between ministers and departments in Ottawa, but international, as the emphasis and effects of Green's policies caused increasing disquiet in defence circles in Washington and in NATO.

A RESOLUTE LEADER FOR EXTERNAL AFFAIRS

Howard Green, tall, white-haired, and bespectacled, was a man of dignified bearing, a ready smile, and an appealing tendency to puncture solemnity with a huge, conspiratorial wink. The first thing that became clear after his appointment was how much closer he was to the prime minister than Sidney Smith had been. Although Green had not supported Diefenbaker for the party leadership, they were old friends, whose experience and outlook on the world had much in common. They were in adjoining seats in the House of Commons and thus had frequent opportunities to talk things over and to concert tactics on questions arising in parliament or the cabinet. Their relationship was such that Green could always have immediate access to the prime minister – an advantage shared by few other ministers at that time. They had the habit of meeting periodically, often on weekends, for long talks, occasions which Green used effectively to influence Diefenbaker's thinking. A member of the prime minister's immediate staff has recalled that he respected Green because he was his own man, would answer back, and was not afraid of Diefenbaker, as so many were. Certainly, for the Department of External Affairs, Green's appointment opened up opportunities of influence which had simply not existed since Pearson's departure two years before.

A firm friendship with the prime minister was a priceless asset, but Green had other advantages over his predecessor in the External Affairs portfolio. He was accustomed to the painful knocks of political life and had no difficulty handling himself in the infighting. He had served for two years in the cabinet, earning favourable press comment and the prime minister's appreciation for his supervision of the Department of Public Works. He did not have to be hustled off, as Sidney Smith had been in his first weeks, to the United Nations. That would come only later when the General Assembly met in the fall. And as Green was already fully entrenched in the esteem of his colleagues in cabinet and in parliament, he was able readily to overcome the stresses of his inexperience with new foreign policy issues as they arose.

Not all Diefenbaker's ministers were as shrewd as Green in taking trouble to establish friendly and trusting relations with their departmental officials. The importance he attached to this is clear from letters he wrote to his mother in the weeks after he took over the job. His mother had been at first opposed to his transfer to External Affairs from Public Works but she soon relented. Green was relieved, said he was 'getting on well with my officials' and that the work was 'intensely interesting.' After attending the departmental picnic in July, his verdict was that 'the spirit seems to be excellent.' External Affairs officials and their families were 'very different from Public Works, more of the scholarship type – very friendly, perhaps not as practical as the others.' By September he was 'beginning to enjoy diplomatic functions' and 'getting educated.'

In point of fact, the spirit in the department, if that meant 'morale,' could hardly be called 'excellent' when Green took over, and as the days passed he could not have failed to notice it. The prime minister was considered by many officials to be an unfriendly critic, with little interest in asserting Canadian influence except in situations where a clear domestic political purpose would be served. A strong current of cynicism was running, in reaction to this tendency which seemed to negate the value of much that the department had become accustomed to doing. Thus a friend wrote from Paris: 'Its not that we ought to be in the front rank solving the Berlin problem or suggesting a new strategy for NATO or developing a master plan for Africa. But from our place in the second rank we might concentrate more on making the [NATO] alliance work. Our special relations with the US and with the Commonwealth are not being made to work in our favour over here, but rather to inhibit our participation and to prompt a sort of cagey timidity which baffles everyone.'[2]

While the new minister was exploring his territory and becoming acquainted with his department and the foreign diplomats, the world hardly seemed to notice. The conference of the foreign ministers of the four powers in Geneva was still sitting. The outlook in relations with the Soviet government remained uncertain. If agreements were not possible at the level of foreign ministers, would it be advisable to shift the action to a meeting at the summit? This question gave rise to differing responses. The British inclinations, reflecting Macmillan's confidence in his own ability to play a role as Eisenhower's chief of staff, was in favour of moving to the summit. The president was reluctant. In the middle of June, George Drew reported from London that Macmillan would like Diefenbaker to speak to Eisenhower with the aim of persuading the president to be more flexible. Diefenbaker took the matter to cabinet, reviewing Drew's message, including the point that neither de Gaulle nor Adenauer shared Macmillan's enthusiasm for a summit meeting. A few days before, Diefenbaker had spoken at Princeton University, advocating a continuation of negotiations. Previously he had more than once supported a meeting at the summit, and had even suggested Quebec City as a suitable location.

It might have been expected, considering Green's reputed pro-British prejudice and Diefenbaker's known interest in promoting a summit meeting, that the new minister would support an approach to Eisenhower. But Green's position went against the expectations. He told the cabinet that he thought Macmillan was unnecessarily excited, that the United States was doing its best to reach agreement, and that Canada should not use up its credit in Washington by trying to persuade the president to decide in favour of a summit meeting. He was partial to the British, the minister admitted, but Canada need not pull their chestnuts out of the fire. Diefenbaker supported Green's advice and the cabinet agreed that the prime minister should not call the president.[3] If the decision had gone the other way, it would have been hard to sell. A week later, at the opening of the St. Lawrence Seaway, Eisenhower made it profanely plain to Diefenbaker that he did not relish a summit meeting with Khrushchev. The episode had shown Green to have an independence of judgment for which he had not been given credit. It was also only the first of numerous occasions on which the minister expressed privately his understanding of the responsibilities carried by US leaders in world affairs. To label him 'anti-American' was to use a term far too broad to be apt.

Although Green's friendly and inquiring approach soon won him friends in External Affairs, it was not long before a disturbing incident arose. Diefenbaker had been reluctant to authorize the attendance of senior advisers at meetings with visiting foreign leaders. As undersecretary since the previous autumn, Norman Robertson had suffered under this treatment, but because he knew that it would embarrass Sidney Smith if an issue were made of it, he had kept his own counsel. Now, with a new minister with whom Robertson felt himself to be on good personal terms, the expectation was that he at last would automatically have his rightful place at such meetings.

It turned out otherwise in the first test case when Christian Herter, the new American secretary of state, was about to visit Ottawa. Somehow Diefenbaker's suspicions about the 'Pearsonalities' had been revived. Robertson was 'more exasperated than I've ever seen him ... At the end of the day, he had it out with Green who agreed to discuss the whole business again with the P.M. ... I think much of this is due to ignorance of procedures, but not all, and it was, or seemed, a gloomy omen.'[4] In the event, Robertson was included, but that did not resolve the difficulty of the relationship between him and the prime minister. I can think of no single situation which was more distressing in those years. Once, after approving Robertson's presence at a conference in London of Commonwealth prime ministers, Diefenbaker called an important meeting of his senior advisers and stubbornly refused to have Robertson attend. Yet Diefenbaker knew very well that in Robertson he had available a source of experienced advice which could be of immense benefit to him, and he frequently directed me to make certain that Robertson agreed personally with a course of action that was being considered on major questions of international policy. Robertson, with a minister to serve, could not thrust himself into the prime minister's orbit, even if he had been temperamentally inclined to do so (which he was not). Only occasionally, when the situation seemed to demand it, and with Green's agreement, did Robertson throw off his reserve and more or less insist on putting a case to Diefenbaker. For the most part each stayed at his own end of the corridor, acutely conscious of the other's presence, each eager to know what the other was thinking and saying, their alienation obvious and regrettable.

A partial explanation of Diefenbaker's coolness towards Robertson may lie in an incident which took place in 1945 when the Canadian delegation was preparing to attend the UN conference in San Francisco. Diefenbaker had arranged to attend the conference as an adviser to Gordon Graydon, M.P., the Conservative party's representative on the delegation. When Diefenbaker applied for a diplomatic passport for travel to the conference, Robertson, at the direction of Prime Minister Mackenzie King, signed a letter to Diefenbaker denying his application, presumably on the ground that he had not been appointed as an official member of the delegation. That explained a great deal, Robertson said when reminded of the incident in 1960. He knew that Diefenbaker was not one to forget such a thing.

REACTING TO DÉTENTE

Despite Eisenhower's earlier reluctance to take part in a four-power summit meeting as advocated by Macmillan, a series of high-level visits during 1959 – by Macmillan and Vice-President Nixon to Moscow, and by Deputy Soviet Premier Mikoyan to the United States – contributed to a significant reduction in East-West tension. Early in August, not much more than a month after he had told Diefenbaker that he would prefer to avoid a four-power summit, Eisenhower joined with Khrushchev in announcing that they would exchange visits. In the first half of the exchange the Soviet leader would tour the United States in the autumn of 1959. Plans for Khrushchev to visit de Gaulle in early 1960 contributed to the pattern of bilateral summitry.

The news of Khrushchev's visit to the United States raised immediately the question whether he should be invited to Canada. Diefenbaker kept balancing the arguments for and against high-level meetings. They made for good publicity. They were consistent with his well-advertised belief in the value of personal contacts. If he were to be involved, he would be entering an exclusive fraternity of leaders who had gone into the ring with Khrushchev. Such an occasion would, in theory at least, consummate his standing on the world stage and would match, if not surpass, anything Pearson had done publicly in relations with the Soviet government. Moreover, as he told the cabinet on 13 August, public opinion on the whole favoured the issuance of an invitation to Khrushchev. Canada was a neighbour of the USSR. The United States was not likely to object, and it might do Khrushchev good to be exposed at first hand to conditions in Canada as well as the United States.

These were powerful arguments, to which he added the reminder that Canada had already offered to be the host for a summit meeting. The trouble was that Hungarian, Ukrainian, and Baltic groups in Canada would be bitterly opposed to any gesture which might be interpreted as conciliatory towards the USSR. This touched a most sensitive political nerve in the Diefenbaker anatomy. And there would be a serious security problem, especially if the Soviet leader were to travel widely. Diefenbaker was for some days in a quandary and took it up no fewer than five times in cabinet. He was mightily relieved when he was finally informed, after soundings had been taken in Moscow, that Khrushchev would be unable in any event to accept an invitation to Canada.

As a striking prelude to Khrushchev's visit to the United States, the Soviet government announced on 13 September that its *Lunik* rocket had landed on the moon. The occasion seemed to the Department of External Affairs to warrant a message of congratulation. Diefenbaker was easily persuaded that a message should be sent but would not include 'Canadian scientists' in the list of those for whom the message spoke. He could not, he said, speak for them all. So it was duly amended and sent off. Congratulating the Soviet government was not among his favourite activities.

On the evening of 15 September, just after Khrushchev had arrived in Washington, I took papers to the prime minister at his home. He had been listening to the news and remarked what a cool reception Khrushchev had been given. Eisenhower, he said, had in a recent broadcast virtually told people not to enthuse. All through that week, Diefenbaker had plenty of time to absorb news and analysis of Khrushchev's every move and quip. It was as though he could not help admiring the performance of a feared adversary but wanted to avoid displaying his admiration. On the morning after the Soviet leader had addressed the UN General Assembly in New York, largely on disarmament, Diefenbaker phoned me at home at 7 AM inquiring what I thought of the speech. Wasn't it just another propaganda exercise? More by instinct than anything else I said I thought it would deserve a careful look: there might be something there, comments which were not warmly received. Along with John Holmes and Arthur Campbell of External Affairs, I spent the morning putting together a few paragraphs for inclusion in a speech Diefenbaker was giving that afternoon at Mont Tremblant. The general theme of our advice was that he ought neither to convey optimistic expectations nor conclude that everything Khrushchev had said could be rightly described as propaganda. A careful study of the text was the first requirement. Diefenbaker began by adopting that tack but the rest of his remarks implied that he was not convinced of it.

Incidents like this led to questions about the prime minister's capacity to play a serious role in the international game. Inevitably, in these circumstances, it was becoming harder to enlist the wholehearted assistance of the departmental officials on whom it was necessary to rely for advice on current problems and policy issues. Sometimes it seemed that the hardest part of my job was to induce the real experts to lay out their expertise. Too often their most important consumer would treat it superficially, or so they felt. Yet his demands for speech material and other forms of advice from External Affairs were mounting. I did my best to acquaint Diefenbaker with the tremendous fund of knowledge and experience that was available to him, and as he got to know people better, he frequently spoke appreciatively of their work. But the reward they would most have prized – serious treatment of their ideas – was seldom given. Decisions or statements on foreign policy problems almost invariably seemed to be based on purely domestic political factors and to be phrased accordingly. Opportunities for using Canada's influence, which were there to be exploited, were foregone.

It was becoming clear that the prime minister, now with more than two years of experience in office, had very little inclination or talent for negotiation in the substance of foreign policy. He did not appreciate the environment in which others were operating, and was not willing to give in search of compromise. He wanted to know what was going on, and to speak about it in terms that would be domestically profitable. He was not slow to recognize and oppose developments which would threaten Canadian interests, particularly when the threat came from the United States. But for those who wanted a creative, resourceful role for Canada in the world, Diefenbaker was not the answer.

The department did not find it easy to accept this fact of life. It now had, in Howard Green, however, a minister who was a missionary and who found in arms control a cause to champion. This cause was consistent with traditional Canadian idealism and responded to the rising international concern about nuclear armaments. Green might be naïve, he might be stubborn, but he was serious and hard working and he knew how to make use of his department. Disenchanted with Diefenbaker, the department was all the more likely to respond to Green, even if his field of interest appeared to be narrow. At last here was a minister who knew where he wanted to go, and whose relationship with the prime minister was solid enough to permit him to follow the trail he had marked out. As Green took hold, Diefenbaker's first reaction was one of satisfaction. Disarmament was a more 'expert' field than he was inclined to get into, but he saw it as politically useful. Without much conscious planning, the two old friends were working out a rough division of labour in international matters.

While Diefenbaker felt he could count on Green to supervise External Affairs, he kept his own hand firmly on the tiller. In this he was influenced by Harold Macmillan's way of playing the prime minister's role in foreign policy. There was no question who was in charge. In case anyone missed the point, frequent letters and telegrams from Macmillan, and less frequent but similar communications from Eisenhower and some other foreign leaders, assured Diefenbaker of a continuing position on the high ground of Canada's relationships with other countries. Those of us who were responding to his needs in international matters tried to ensure consistency between him and the ministers, but this problem acquired a new dimension as Green's determined pursuit of disarmament introduced strains into the government's conduct of defence policy. In the late months of 1959, however, the clouds of controversy over defence policy had not yet gathered.

At the end of September 1959, with the departure of Khrushchev from the United States, Diefenbaker was feeling more relaxed about the East-West outlook. He wrote to Eisenhower, who had sent him birthday greetings, to congratulate the president 'on the judicious way in which you succeeded in bringing these meetings [with Khrushchev] to such a satisfactory and promising outcome.' He also spoke at the University of Saskatchewan, assessing the Khrushchev visit with a cautious optimism from a text provided by External Affairs. A week later, however, he revealed his own views in a conversation with Eisenhower's envoy, Robert Murphy. He asked whether Khrushchev's visit had not had a narcotic effect on American opinion, in the sense that it created a current of false security.

THE 'SPIRITUAL' SIDE

To Diefenbaker, peaceful co-existence was an acceptable philosophy in a moment of détente and restrained optimism. At the same time, the Western world must not lose sight of the principles and purposes for which it stood. In the speech at Halifax he revived an idea (it became an *idée fixe*) with which he had been experimenting on and off throughout 1959: that the Western nations should issue what he called a 'Declaration of Freedom's Creed,' redefining the purpose and principles of the democratic world. He had been attracted by this idea during the Asian part of his 1958 world tour. At that time he had been struck by the extent to which Asians were suspicious of Western attitudes and Western aid. They were asking, he said, if the communist powers were justified in alleging that Western aid was politically motivated. He was quite genuinely convinced that not enough effort or ingenuity was being put into explaining the principles of Western democracy and free enterprise. The West was not getting its message across in Asia.

What exactly was he seeking to define in 'freedom's creed'? It was not a call to arms, although he was convinced as any other cold warrior of the need for defence to deter aggression. Freedom to him was a more comprehensive, less physical concept. It had to do with social, religious, and economic liberties – these were the treasures he prized in the idealistic side of his mind, and this was what he wanted for the peoples of the Commonwealth and the other newly emerging nations. He had the greatest difficulty in understanding why political leaders, such as Nehru, preferred to be uncommitted in the East-West ideological struggle. Neutralism, one of the salient realities of the 1950s, was a creed with which he could never come to terms.

The 'Declaration of Freedom's Creed' never amounted to anything internationally, although Diefenbaker used it from time to time in Canada. Sometimes, as a listener on such occasions, I thought it was nothing more than a rhetorical crutch. At other times, there could be no doubt of his sincerity or of his tenacious faith in declaratory expression as a means of generating change.

11

Two Sides of the Defence Coin

GREEN QUESTIONS THE NUCLEAR CHOICE

To understand how Howard Green's influence grew, one must first recall what was being done to implement the government's previous decisions, especially in defence policy. The milestones include the completion of the NORAD agreement in June 1958; the first announcement, in September 1958, signifying the end of the Avro Arrow project and making known the decision to bring the Bomarc missile into the Canadian air defence system; the second Arrow announcement in February 1959, cancelling that project outright but foreshadowing the purchase of a replacement; and the decision, announced in the House of Commons on 2 July, 1959, to give the Canadian air division in Europe a new offensive 'strike reconnaissance' role and to equip it for this purpose with Lockheed F-104 Star-fighter aircraft in place of its F-86s which were fast becoming obsolete.

All these decisions were public decisions and all implied, whatever the actual wording of statements, that the Canadian forces would require nuclear weapons if the systems were to operate at peak efficiency. It was not by accident that in May of the same year, the Canadian and US governments signed a critically important agreement providing for cooperation on the uses of atomic energy for mutual defence purposes.[1]

During the same period, a number of related events occurred, most of which were not publicized, or at least not intentionally. On 15 October, 1958 the cabinet authorized negotiations with the US government for the acquisition and storage of defensive nuclear weapons and warheads in Canada.[2] These matters were discussed in December by the members of the Joint US-Canada Committee on Defence, meeting in Paris during a NATO conference. As finance minister Donald Fleming has recalled, 'no final conclusion was reached on the storage of defensive nuclear weapons in Canada, but only details remained to be discussed.'[3] General

Norstad's meeting with the cabinet in May 1959 had also been an important link in the chain of the government's nuclear involvement. It had opened the door to the decision of 2 July to re-equip the Air Division in Europe with the F-104G aircraft in the strike reconnaissance role.

In mid-1959 the Canadian government was planning for negotiations on several different nuclear weapon systems. The majority related to conditions for the storage and possible use of nuclear warheads by Canadian or US forces operating in or from Canadian territory. Continental air defence was involved in three cases: the nuclear warheads for Bomarc anti-aircraft missiles to be operated by Canadian forces in Canada, for US interceptor aircraft stationed at US leased bases at Goose Bay and Harmon Field in Newfoundland, and for the use of (as yet unselected) RCAF interceptors intended to replace the CF-100s at various bases in Canada. Separate negotiations were also required in the case of anti-submarine weapons for storage and use by US and Canadian naval forces at Argentia, Newfoundland, and to establish the conditions under which permission would be given for the storage at Goose Bay of nuclear bombs for the use of the US Strategic Air Command.

Negotiations were also planned to provide nuclear warheads for the use of Canadian forces in Europe, specifically for the F-104G strike-reconnaissance aircraft to be used by the RCAF, and for short-range ground-to-ground missiles such as the Lacrosse and its replacement, the Honest John, for use by the Canadian army.

This background is reviewed in order to make the point that in its first two years, the Diefenbaker government was consciously heading in the direction of acquiring nuclear weapons for its own forces, both in Canada and in Europe, and of allowing US forces stationed at or using bases in Canada to store nuclear weapons and equipment on them. The questions for discussion with the Americans and the NATO authorities in 1958 and 1959 had mostly to do with the how and the when rather than with the whether or the why.

This is not to say that there were no complications or misgivings. An early sign of the sensitive nature of the issue had appeared as early as December 1957 when the NATO meeting in Paris took up the US proposal for atomic stockpiles for NATO, including Canadian, use in Western Europe. Diefenbaker and his ministers may not have understood the full implications of what was being proposed but they knew enough to treat it as a sensitive problem then and increasingly so as time went on. Misgivings were cautiously expressed. Their source within the government service was to be found at the most senior levels in External Affairs,[4] where Jules Léger, undersecretary until 1958, and Norman Robertson, ambassador in Washington from 1957-8 until returning as undersecretary, were both troubled by the apparent readiness with which Western gov-

107

ernments were relying on American nuclear power and its transplantation into Western Europe. Léger had worried, too, about the prevalence of military factors in world affairs. After being briefed on the latest model of small-scale nuclear weapons, he wrote in April 1958 to Robertson in Washington and Charles Ritchie in New York: 'The more I brood on this, the more depressed I become.' Robertson's objections were even more fundamental and, in the event, more influential. The planned use of nuclear weapons, he argued, raised moral issues which could not be ignored. When he was asked in the spring of 1958 to succeed Léger, he was at the same time considering a proposal to enter academic life. Appealing as the prospect of university life then seemed, one of the main reasons he decided to accept the undersecretaryship was that he might be able to have some influence on decisions about the nuclear issue.[5]

The nuclear issue was certainly on his mind, but Robertson was not a zealot and it was not his way to urge the impossible on his political masters. He knew how strong the current was against him. More importantly, in the first six months after his return, he knew that if he spoke out too vigorously, he would be putting disconcerting pressure on Sidney Smith. It was not that he deceived the minister or that the minister resisted; rather, Robertson made his views known in a way that left it to Smith to decide whether he wished to promote them. In meetings with departmental officials, the need for such delicate restraint was less apparent. Once, just before Smith's death in March 1959, Robertson was briefed by a group of officials who had visited NORAD and SAC headquarters. As the meeting wore on, he became visibly appalled and depressed by what he was hearing. A record of the discussion sums up Robertson's reaction, in words that hardly do justice to the intensity of his mood: 'Mr. Robertson said that the whole philosophy of deterrence had been developed at a time when conditions were vastly different from those existing today. It was a sad commentary on our generation to envisage the possibility of global suicide. Our minds should be turned instead to the tremendous political effort that needed to be undertaken to avoid the awesome consequences of nuclear warfare.'[6]

Robertson knew well in advance that Howard Green was to become his minister. He had no idea what Green's views would be on the nuclear issue. Perhaps with a view to staking out his ground in case the chemistry proved explosive, Robertson made sure just before Green was appointed that the prime minister would be aware of his personal views. On 1 June he asked me to give Diefenbaker a copy of an article in the British paper *The Spectator*, in which the author, Christopher Hollis, argued that the nature of war had been changed by the hydrogen bomb, and 'there is no chance that the pattern of our own national life will still survive when we emerge from it.'[7] The argument went on in favour of unilateral nuclear disarmament and the need for the Western nations to build up their strength in conventional weapons. I made a short memorandum to the prime minister, informing him that the undersecretary wanted him to know that the views in the article coincided with his own.

Diefenbaker received the memo with an anxious curiosity, but said at once that I was to tell the undersecretary that he appreciated being informed of his views. Whether he understood at that time the strong ideas that Green, as the incoming minister, would bring on the nuclear issue has been the subject of speculation. Personally I do not believe that Diefenbaker anticipated the strength of the position that Green would take, although I think he understood well the significance of the message Robertson had sent him.

It took a few weeks before the new minister asserted his position. Although he later regretted the government's decision at the end of June to re-equip the Air Division in Europe with the F-104G in the new 'strike reconnaissance' role, he did not make an issue of it at the time. And the announcement of this important decision on 2 July seemed to indicate that the government might be emerging from the hesitancy that had characterized its defence policy for almost two years. This was encouraging to the defence authorities and also to many officials in External Affairs whose endeavour to understand and pursue the government's policy in NATO and NORAD had led them into a pattern of thought quite distinct from that of Robertson. They, like their contacts in the Department of National Defence, would find the going heavier as the new minister got into his stride. The decision to equip the RCAF Air Division with the F-104G was the last occasion for cheering from the 'defence' side during the Diefenbaker period. In a letter to Norstad, Diefenbaker wrote that the general's briefing had been of distinct benefit to the making of the decision.[8]

Robertson soon discovered that the new minister might have views close to his own on nuclear matters. In a memorandum of 12 June dealing with French conditions for nuclear cooperation in NATO, Robertson had recommended a review by NATO of its nuclear policy. This would be 'of special interest to Canada since we are, as you know, on the threshold of equipping Canadian forces with nuclear weapons.'[9] The question mark inscribed by the minister opposite that sentence was the first signal of what was in store, although of course it was not displayed to public view. Robertson followed up at the end of July with a 'think-piece' entitled 'Nuclear Weapons – Some Questions of Policy.'[10] He sent it to the minister and also to Bryce, Foulkes, and others, inviting comments. An early paragraph read: Two questions must be asked – are the issues which divide East and West sufficiently great to consider settlement of them by recourse to global nuclear war which might destroy life on the planet? Can policies which entertain the possibility of a global nuclear war long continue to recommend themselves to rational human beings?'

General Foulkes, perhaps apprehending the significance of the timing as well as the substance of Robertson's paper, responded with a long and carefully argued rebuttal on August 14. Whether all or part of this correspondence reached the prime minister, I do not know. It did not go through me, nor did he ever indicate that he saw the nuclear dilemma in the same perspective as Robertson. But Robertson had served notice of his views.

I spent my annual leave that summer with my family in Vancouver. On my return, I soon became a bit player in the controversy over the Skyhawk air defence exercise which was to take place in October. United States Strategic Air Command (SAC) bombers would, as if they were Soviet long-range bombers, attempt to penetrate NORAD defences in both Canada and the United States, and this would, among other things, necessitate the closing down of civil air traffic for several hours. Planning for this operation had been under way for months, although External Affairs was not informed until well on in August. The department felt it might be ill-advised to hold a large-scale exercise of this kind immediately following the visit of Khrushchev to the United States and his meetings with President Eisenhower. The minister strongly agreed with this view and the cabinet also endorsed it, so Arnold Heeney, the ambassador in Washington, was instructed to inform the US government of Canada's refusal to consent to the holding of the exercise at the time envisaged.

This led to an extremely sharp Canadian-American dispute. The Americans objected strenuously on the grounds that Canadian officials had collaborated in the planning of the exercise, that the minister of national defence had known of it, and that its timing in relation to the Khrushchev visit had been carefully calculated and was considered suitable in the circumstances. Despite strong representations from the US ambassador, Richard Wigglesworth, Diefenbaker would not budge. Even if it were agreed that the timing of the exercise were appropriate, Canadian public opinion would not understand why it was necessary to launch an operation involving such an extraordinary measure as the suspension of all civil air traffic for several hours. On four separate occasions in ten days, he and Green went over the situation with their cabinet colleagues but never changed their position. An exchange of personal messages between the prime minister and the president led only to the cancellation of the exercise.

The Skyhawk affair led Heeney, naturally concerned about its effect on Canadian-American relations, to draw lessons which he recorded in a memorandum on 11 September. First, the joint consultative machinery had failed and, second, there had been a difference in political judgment between the top authorities in Washington and Ottawa.[11] He was right on both counts. He might have added that the interdepartmental and interministerial communications in Ottawa had been faulty, and that the episode had shown how tenacious Howard Green was going to be as external affairs minister and how much influence his judgment was likely to have with the prime minister. Heeney was justified in being concerned.

Now, and for much of the fall of 1959, Howard Green was to lead the Canadian delegation to the UN General Assembly. The experience would have a great impact on his outlook and would incline him towards the views Robertson had already put to him. He would see disarmament as the other side of the defence coin, to a degree that had not been approached before.

THE MINISTER'S INFLUENCE GROWS

From the outset it was clear that the new minister was going to enjoy his exposure to UN diplomacy. It was also plain that he would be a man of action. On the day of his opening address to the assembly in September, he startled his advisers by telling a press conference that Canada would be presenting a set of disarmament proposals to the current session. I can recall a hurriedly called meeting in the undersecretary's office where the assembled experts tried to imagine what could be done to justify the minister's undertaking.

The minister soon found an initiative to his taste. Perhaps reflecting the thoughts of his wife Donna, a scientist with a lively and informed concern for the human condition, he fastened on to a UN report on the effects of atomic radiation. It was a measure of his tenacity that within a month he had obtained cabinet approval for the Canadian delegation at the General Assembly to offer, on behalf of Canada, to conduct analysis of materials subject to atomic radiation, conditional on the readiness of other governments to cooperate. Later, Green's initiative was translated into a resolution which was approved unanimously by the General Assembly. He had seized on the growing concern in many countries about the effects of radioactive fallout. From that beginning he went on to become probably the world's leading apostle of disarmament during his term of office.

Diefenbaker had supported Green in the cabinet on the radiation initiative. He stuck with him on another issue which Green felt strongly about and which involved a controversial vote in the General Assembly – a resolution by the Afro-Asian group of nations attacking France for its nuclear bomb-testing program in the Sahara. The minister's intention to support the Afro-Asian resolution became known to the French delegation with the result that Francis Lacoste, the French ambassador in Canada, sought an urgent interview with the prime minister on the day of the vote. Diefenbaker had taken a liking to Lacoste, who was the dean of the Ottawa diplomatic corps, and would have preferred to accommodate him, the more so because objectionable references to President de Gaulle in a recent CBC commentary had been protested by the ambassador and had led to an official expression of regret from the Canadian government to de Gaulle.

After I had given him the factual background as carefully and objectively as I could, Diefenbaker became agitated, considering that Green's directions to the Canadian delegation were unduly hard on the French. He called Green by telephone in New York. The minister had recently visited Paris to meet French ministers and to preside over his first meeting of Canadian ambassadors stationed in Europe. He told the prime minister that he had told the French authorities of Canada's intentions and had received no adverse reaction. The prime minister thereupon told Lacoste that he could not intervene 'at the eleventh hour' without damaging the minister's authority. Lacoste persevered. He insisted that the French government's views had been made known to the Canadian government at various times and levels, that nothing Green had said in Paris had prepared the French for what Canada was now proposing to do, and that Canada's support for the resolution was most upsetting to France.

Some hours after seeing Lacoste, Diefenbaker was still anxious about the decision. I was called in to review the day's developments before a group of ministers with whom he had been discussing the Canadian vote. At least some of them were doubtful about voting so directly against the French, a NATO ally. It was left to one of the ministers present to call Green in New York to go over the situation. Green was canny enough not to be reachable, and thus Canada came out against the French bomb tests as Green had been determined to do all along.

Like most other UN votes, this one is not widely remembered. In retrospect, however, I think it was a landmark of some importance in Canada. For those interested in the relationship between arms control and defence policies in particular, it pointed up the implications of the appointment of Howard Green. The government had a tough and influential peacemonger as its external affairs minister, and he was just at the dawn of his new incarnation. The prime minister was being forced to think more seriously than before about the domestic impact of the positions Green was taking in arms control matters. But if there was political credit to be claimed, as in the case of the French bomb tests, the prime minister was quick to claim it.[12]

THE DIVISION HARDENS

Diefenbaker was a resilient man, and soon his energies were focused on the new parliamentary session. Instructions went out in all directions for speech material, research, and statistics. Duplication of assignments as usual was common; as much time was spent in coordinating the various requests as in preparing the material itself. In order to anticipate Pearson's strategy, the prime minister's first speech would centre on the government's defence policy. The Liberal leader and his colleagues had for some time been pressing for clarification of its position on the acquisition of nuclear weapons for Canadian forces.

The opposition's harassing tactics would have been easier to fend off if the government had been of one mind on nuclear issues. By this stage in its life, however, the deep-seated differences among ministers on nuclear weapons policy had begun to harden. Howard Green had now been in office for more than six months, and in that time the influences to which he had been exposed had strengthened both his interest in disarmament and his resistance to the further development of nuclear weapons.

With the appointment in December 1959 of General E.L.M. Burns[13] as its adviser on disarmament, the government had equipped itself to play a seasoned part in the revival of disarmament negotiations which was then occurring. In January 1960 Green himself spoke in the strongest terms to his cabinet colleagues about the importance of disarmament.[14] He emerged with an approved statement of principles to guide Burns and the Canadian disarmament delegation at the five-power talks in Washington and later in the Ten-Nation Committee.[15] More important than the actual statement was the sustained intensity which the minister displayed on disarmament issues then and throughout the remaining three years he would hold this office.

Diefenbaker, though alive to the political appeal of disarmament, was cynical about it, as he often admitted. He saw it as a motherhood cause which must always be supported. On the day of the cabinet discussion of Green's disarmament paper, he pretended that he was disappointed by the proposals Green was putting forward. No new ideas, just the same old stuff.[16] Two weeks later, sensing the political need of the moment during a foreign policy debate, he revealed to the House of Commons the list of disarmament principles that the government was giving to General Burns. The list contained no eye-openers but he delivered it as the gospel truth. In about equal parts he earned acclaim for crystallizing the government's approach to disarmament and scorn for undercutting Green, who had earlier said, on advice from Burns, that the principles should not yet be disclosed. Green was upset by the prime minister's unexpected intervention, although he later admitted that Diefenbaker had been right in making the information public. Whatever else it did, the incident gave a small tactical victory to Paul Martin, the opposition's spokesman, whose needling had driven the government from cover.

The depth of Green's commitment to disarmament took Diefenbaker somewhat by surprise. The minister did not restrict himself to the promotion of disarmament measures. He continued his obstructive tactics towards the proposals defence minister Pearkes had been sponsoring on the acquisition of nuclear weapons for Canadian forces and on provisions for the storage in Canada of nuclear weapons for the use of US forces. After six months in office, he had become the despair of General Pearkes and the senior officers in the Department of National Defence and of their conterparts in Washington. Green had returned from the United Nations early in December to find on his desk for approval a proposal for a draft agreement defining the conditions under which Canada would acquire nuclear weapons from the United States for the use of Canadian forces. To the frustration of Pearkes and of officials in a number of departments, Green took no action on the proposal before the end of the year.

In preparation for the prime minister's opening speech in the House of Commons, the proposal was put on the cabinet agenda early in January. Cabinet ministers were thus obliged to concentrate in some detail on the meaning and implications of such terms as 'custody' and 'control' which were to become central to the nuclear weapons controversy for the remaining years of the Diefenbaker period. The necessary basis for an exchange of 'atomic' information for military purposes between the United States and Canada had been laid in an agreement of May 1959. The US Atomic Energy Act, however, still governed the conditions on which nuclear weapons could actually be supplied to allied governments. Under the act, as it applied to Canada, 'custody' of the weapons would have to remain in American hands. 'Control,' however, could be shared in a joint system, generally known as 'double key' or 'two key,' under which the consent of both governments would be required before the weapon could be armed and released for use. Much of the discussion in the cabinet at that time centred on determining the precise custodial and control provisions that would be acceptable to the Canadian government and could be made public in the immediate future.

After the cabinet meeting on 12 January, the secretary to the cabinet, on instructions from the prime minister to find a settled solution in a hurry, informed External Affairs of the outcome of the discussion and asked for a suitable statement to be prepared. When the resultant draft was shown to Howard Green on the following day, the minister said that it did not reflect the substance of the cabinet's discussion.[17] He argued that the language did not ensure the extent of custody and control that Canada should insist on, if it were to acquire nuclear weapons for its forces. The prime minister recognized the advantages of Green's delaying tactics, but he had Pearkes to deal with too, let alone the US government. The cabinet met again on 15 January and a new draft was shipped off to Washington, as it was obviously necessary to obtain US comments. The American reaction, I noted, 'was quite unfavourable and we are wondering to what extent the Minister and the Prime Minister will give in.'[18]

The prime minister's statement on 18 January contained just enough to satisfy the parliamentary purpose although less than enough to clarify the government's intentions. Eventually, he said, Canadian forces might require nuclear weapons – the Bomarc anti-aircraft missile, for example – if the forces were to be kept effective. Any such weapon would be acquired from the United States; there should be no increase in the number of countries manufacturing nuclear warheads. Negotiations were proceeding with the United States so that the necessary weapons could be made available to Canada if and when they were required. But the safeguarding and security of all such weapons would be subject to Canadian approval and consent and they would not be used by the Canadian forces except as the Canadian government decided.

The statement had not resolved the conflict between the ministers of external affairs and national defence and neither could feel that he had won the day. Diefenbaker, however, was able to resume his speech on the following day, Pearson having previously spoken at great length. Aware of Pearkes's disappointment that a more positive line had not emerged on nuclear weapons policy, the prime minister spent some time praising the minister of national defence for his wisdom a year before in saying that the real threat of the foreseeable future was to be found in missiles rather than the manned bomber. This line of argument had been obligingly facilitated by a recent speech of Khrushchev. Diefenbaker used a couple of passages from the Soviet leader to prove that he and Pearkes had been right about Soviet intentions to phase out the production of manned bombers, a refrain to which he returned whenever he judged it necessary to recall and rejustify the Avro Arrow cancellation of a year before. The point did nothing to support the government's case, however, since Canada's main contributions to continental air defence – interceptor aircraft and Bomarcs and radar systems – were for use against bombers and would be of no use against long-range missiles.

It was in these early months of 1960, when the nuclear issues were coming to a head, that the prime minister began to store up political trouble which he later found uncontrollable. He had seen it coming in the course of preparing his statement of 18 January on nuclear weapons policy. But despite his realization that the issue needed to be resolved, he had settled for a compromise which had satisfied no one, except possibly Howard Green. There was a pressing need for the authority of the prime minister to be asserted. The government was stalled, and not only on the weapons needed for continental defence. It had also been having uneasy thoughts about the program for the F-104G strike aircraft for RCAF use in Europe, a commitment which was going to cost $400 million at a time when the aircraft's suitability for use in the European theatre was debatable.

So concerned were Pearkes and some of the government's advisers about defence commitments and costs that in February, Pearkes was reported to have made a quiet journey to Paris and presented to General Norstad, NATO's supreme commander in Europe, some unofficial thoughts on future levels and roles of Canadian troops, both RCAF and army, in Europe. Norstad resisted changes, no doubt on the same grounds as in May 1959 when he had encountered similar questions on his visit to Ottawa.[19] The issue was not pursued further. Bryce, however, circulated a secret paper which looked ahead five or six years to the time when NATO might not have the same raison d'être; Europe would be standing on its own feet, leaving Canada alone with the United States in a North American defence partnership. In the age of ICBM's US and Canadian troops would not be needed to buttress the 'shield' in Western Europe.[20] This paper was circulated among the most senior civil servants. Whether it was shown to the prime minister, I do not know.

At that stage the West German government was attempting to arrange for military facilities in Spain. Green, always inclined to suspect German motives, did not like the look of this. But Diefenbaker, although not without his own misgivings, saw the danger that too strong an adverse reaction in NATO countries might encourage anti-NATO tendencies in West Germany. I took this to signify that he would not want Canada to be party to any course of action, such as a reduction of forces in Europe, which might tend to weaken West Germany's attachment to the NATO alliance. A week or so afterwards, however, thinking aloud, he remarked that he was not sure about the Canadian forces in Europe. This ambivalence would be short-lived: with the collapse of the Paris summit in May and later a sharp revival of the Berlin crisis, any temptation to pull troops out of Europe soon faded. The opportunity would not arise again while Diefenbaker was in office.

During this period I was reminded of the prime minister's disregard for External Affairs advice and I often became discouraged by my inability to persuade him to take it seriously. The situation might have been easier if Diefenbaker and Howard Green had been, as it were, in a harnessed partnership. Neither of them, however, had any wish to be harnessed. Diefenbaker had his interests, his prejudices, and his political priorities. Green, too, was ploughing his own furrow, deeply in disarmament, and energetically in a wide range of other diplomatic activity which he was able to pursue without day-to-day consultation with the prime minister. From time to time the two would meet in an emergency or for a stocktaking. They seldom invited their senior advisers to participate and the outcome of their deliberations were chronically subordinate to short-term political advantage. Planning ahead, and consulting with allies, was difficult, especially on issues affected by defence commitments and disarmament tactics.

I alternated between sharing the frustrations of my friends and colleagues in the department and trying to get them to accept the realities of the situation. During the Diefenbaker period, External Affairs came face to face with the real drive of domestic politics to a degree not experienced since the last years of the Second World War. Pearson had somehow made it possible for his officials to pursue solutions to international problems without feeling directed by domestic political pressures. In advising Diefenbaker, or in carrying out his instructions, one was never in danger of forgetting the connection between Canadian foreign policy and the all-important Canadian voter.

On 1 January, 1960 I went with friends to the annual New Year's Day Levée which was held that year in the Parliament Buildings. A huge glass bowl of hot rum punch standing on a table not far from the receiving line suddenly cracked at the exact moment that the prime minister entered the room. The incident provoked much merriment and some speculation as to what its meaning might be for the government in the first year of the decade to come.

12

Personal Diplomacy

Diefenbaker put great faith in personal diplomacy, by which he meant his meetings with national leaders and other dignitaries of high significance. The years 1960 and 1961 were especially busy in this respect. They encompassed two conferences of the Commonwealth prime ministers, three visits to Washington, and one each to Mexico, Ireland, Northern Ireland, Japan, and the United Nations. Notable visitors to Ottawa in the first half of 1960 alone included Prime Minister Kishi of Japan, President Charles de Gaulle, Prime Minister Robert Menzies of Australia, and Mr. Paul-Henri Spaak, the secretary general of NATO.

Proceedings of the more important of these occasions will be discussed in later chapters. First, however, some impressions of Diefenbaker's general approach to official visits, both outgoing and incoming, may be helpful in setting the scene.

'Bilateral' meetings with foreign VIP's were newsworthy and paid political dividends at relatively little cost. Multilateral meetings – of Commonwealth leaders or at NATO or the United Nations – sometimes exposed difficult issues such as race relations in South Africa, nuclear matters, or disarmament, but the balance of publicity was generally favourable. Had it not been, Diefenbaker would not have been such a consistent advocate of high-level meetings from the start to the close of his term of office.

Official trips outside Canada were for Diefenbaker a form of release from pressure and tension. He was liberated from the regular calendar of cabinet and parliamentary sittings, and could often find more time than at home to prepare himself for meetings with his counterparts. Moreover, on foreign territory, he was invariably treated with respect and ceremony and generally made to feel appreciated, an agreeable sensation which he relished more and more as his government's critics at home became more outspoken and disrespectful.

But there was much more to it than recognition. Diefenbaker believed profoundly in the benefits of becoming acquainted with people in positions of political power. He felt a bond with them. He wanted to see and be seen by them, to size them up. No matter how much faith he had in the judgment of others, or how good their reports, he never felt entirely comfortable until he had tested the water himself. 'The more I meet with these world leaders,' he would say, 'the more I am convinced that much more can be done through personal discussion than through correspondence.' Sometimes the point would be expressed in a slightly different way: 'There is no substitute for direct dealings among those who hold their responsibilities of national leadership.'

It was easy to be cynical about the emphasis he placed on the value of personal discussion. It meant quite often that although he had time to do little preparation before a meeting with one of his counterparts, as a result of their talk he now felt quite well informed. On occasions when the Department of External Affairs, or I personally, was in his bad books, there would be a little dig to the effect that diplomats always found a complicated way of expressing simple thoughts. Only, he would add, when you came face to face with those who had the ultimate responsibility for the big decisions did you cut through the verbiage and get to the root of things. In other words, the briefing book he had been given had failed to capture the essence of the issues as seen from the loftiest heights. But – and there was always a *but* in dealing with Diefenbaker – it was at least some compensation that he had a genuine interest in the opinions and the personalities of the famous and the powerful.

One of my functions, apart from trying to satisfy his needs for briefing material and speeches, was to discover and report what had taken place during these VIP meetings. Normally I attended the main conversation as a note-taker, but there were social occasions when visitor and host were alone together and might be saying something significant to each other. Foreign offices are, I am sure, the same all over the world. They get worried when their political masters are off by themselves. I used to regard it as something of a challenge to find out what, if anything of significance, had been said, and to report it to the minister and the department. My soundings were sometimes rather unproductive. If the chemistry had worked, the answer might be, 'He's quite a fella!' followed by a pause intended to convey that the prime minister was not at all sure that he could properly pass on all the secrets that had been exchanged. He would look at you with a small fixed smile, his head held back and shaking slightly, until you either gave up or plunged back in with an exploratory question.

Persistence was not always rewarded. If the conversation in question had been heavy going (say, if the interlocutor had emphasized ideas similar to those put forward by External Affairs and with which Diefenbaker did not agree), he would often signify that there was no point in discussing the matter further. At other times, I would present him with the record of whatever meetings I had attended and ask if he had anything to add, pointing out that the account would be needed as guidance to Canadian representatives in the country or countries concerned. Occasionally, he would jib at this, but most of the time it worked. Another technique was to tell him of information that had been obtained informally from the staff of the other leader during a visit and ask him if it was accurate. This quite often dredged up additional nuggets. It also helped to make him realize that what he had said to his opposite number often found its way to trusted advisers, even though it had been conveyed in absolute confidence.

As prime minister, Diefenbaker much preferred visiting to being visited. Playing the 'diplomatic' host to foreign leaders was taxing and often tried his patience. He found the social requirements particularly fatiguing and felt the need for support from Howard Green and other ministers who would help carry the conversation. He had no easy flow of sophisticated small talk, and his deafness was more of a handicap than he would admit. Time after time he would remark on what a strain it was to spend long evenings in social chit-chat when he had so much on his mind.

His tour of the world in 1958 had left some imprint. Although he pretended to scorn the trivia of protocol, he would be furious if some detail had been overlooked or sloppily performed. He was influenced in such matters by Mrs Diefenbaker, whose demands on the protocol people were not always easy to satisfy. Her last-minute phone calls about the value and appropriateness of the official gifts being contemplated for the next visit became part of the routine. It would have been easier to cope with the gift problem if the prime minister himself had not been so sensitive to the slightest tinge of extravagance lest it lead to political embarrassment.

Entertaining was something of a problem. At first there had been a virtual prohibition on the serving of wine and spirits. The thirsts of the dignitaries who had become accustomed to a drink before lunch or dinner were sometimes left unsatisfied, although Don Longchamps, the steward at the prime minister's residence, bravely saved the day many times. On one occasion, our worst fears were overturned. Before a dinner in honour of Prime Minister Menzies, we thought it prudent to warn the Australian High Commissioner's Office in Ottawa that since wine and spirits might not be served, they might want to take steps to see that their leader was fortified for the occasion. They took the idea aboard wholeheartedly. Menzies was exceedingly jovial on arrival, and he and his high commissioner concealed their surprise when the steward appeared with a well-stocked tray of spirits. It was a merry evening.

One of Diefenbaker's stock of Winston Churchill stories involved the difference between an abstainer and a teetotaller. When Churchill learned that Diefenbaker was merely an abstainer, he nodded approvingly and said, 'Ah, in that case, you only harm yourself.' In my experience Diefenbaker did not stray from the path of abstinence except in the name of medical prudence. The guidance sent to Canadian offices on the route of his round-the-world tour had unfortunately not foreseen (*mea culpa*) that he would accept a bottle of beer when local water or milk were judged to be hazardous to health. Once, in Pakistan, on arrival at the Warsak dam project, he was offered a cup of tea and promptly replied, 'No, I'll have a beer,' thereby stunning his hosts who had been advised to remove all their beer from the premises so that not even the essence of hops would be in the air.

Another problem which we never quite overcame concerned guest lists for official functions. It was the practice in most other capital cities to include, in addition to politicians and other dignitaries, one or more senior officials (bureaucrats) who had been involved in the planning and conduct of the visit. It was, let it be said, not that the officials hankered to attend, but rather that if they had been intimately involved in preparing for the visit, they might be of some practical assistance at a social function.

The prime minister took a lot of convincing that officials were needed on such occasions. Fortunately he had a few favourites in the bureaucracy, and he loosened up slightly on some occasions. But I was frequently asked to explain why he insisted on excluding people from External Affairs, and I cannot say that I ever found a logical answer. Undoubtedly, however, he did not feel comfortable with bureaucrats generally, and he kept on worrying that senior External Affairs officials were still in touch with his *bête noire*, L.B. Pearson. He gave himself a great deal of needless stress on this score, for Pearson had deliberately cut himself off from such contacts. It was one of many ways in which Diefenbaker antagonized the civil service, which, when he came into office, wanted nothing more than to be given the opportunity to serve his government effectively.

13

Testing the Commonwealth: South Africa

The prime ministers of the Commonwealth had agreed to meet in London from 3 to 13 May 1960. They had not met since the early summer of 1957, and it was quite obvious from the traffic of consultation before the meeting that a heavy agenda would await them. One new member, Prime Minister Tunku Abdul Rahman of Malaya, would be attending, and it was planned that the conference would formally welcome Nigeria to membership as a republic on its achievement of national independence on 1 October 1960.

By far the most controversial subject on the minds of all the prime ministers was the issue of race relations in South Africa. The issue was complicated by the fact that in earlier times these meetings had made a point of avoiding discussion of each other's internal affairs. The 1960 meeting took place at a time when, because of the discriminatory racial policies of the South African government, it had become politically unrealistic for the Commonwealth prime ministers to avoid discussing the subject. Diefenbaker, while not at all reluctant to condemn South Africa's policy of apartheid, was nevertheless doubtful about the best way of approaching the problem at the London meeting.

In January 1960 the Canadian Labour Congress had said in a public brief to the Canadian government that it would 'favour' South Africa's exclusion from the councils of the Commonwealth on account of its racial policies. It was an argument that Diefenbaker might have been expected to welcome, but instead he responded as if he were being pressed to *propose* South Africa's exclusion, a step he was clearly not ready to take. That representation, he told the Congress angrily, 'will not receive the favourable consideration of this government.'[1] He went on to argue that notwithstanding his known views on racial discrimination, the essence of the Commonwealth was 'the independence of each nation'; however strongly we might disagree with the views of another Commonwealth nation, to make it 'become a pariah' was not 'what was required.' When he emerged from this meeting he was still exhilarated by the excitement of his 'blow-up,' as he called it. I sensed he worried he had gone too far and cast doubt on the genuineness of his opposition to apartheid.

It was following this episode that he adopted for public use the distinction between a willingness to *discuss* South African policy at the Commonwealth prime ministers' meeting and a refusal to *propose* South Africa's exclusion from the Commonwealth. Diefenbaker's thinking on the tactics to follow was already being shaped along these lines, although it is easier to say this in retrospect than it was at the time.

The development of a clear-cut position on South Africa's place in the Commonwealth was complicated by both external and internal factors. It could be assumed that Britain, Australia, and probably New Zealand would be inclined to look for a solution which, while enabling them to register a condemnation of South Africa's racial policies, would nevertheless permit the continuing membership of South Africa in the Commonwealth. The newer, non-white members could not be expected to be nearly as tolerant of South Africa and it was clear to Diefenbaker that he would not have an easy ride. He watched with some apprehension as Macmillan, visiting South Africa in February, drew public attention to the 'wind of change' in Africa in terms which made Diefenbaker wonder if his own tactical freedom at the conference might be pre-empted.[2] He told me Macmillan would not have spoken as he did if he had not been tipped off about South Africa's intention to leave the Commonwealth.[3] Diefenbaker would frequently complain about 'the wind of change' speech, which he felt had brought the situation facing the Commonwealth to a crisis he had hoped to avoid.

As the conference came into focus, about three months before its opening, R.B. Bryce, secretary to the cabinet, confirmed his intention to be the prime minister's principal adviser in all policy issues relating to the meeting.[4] This was not a break with tradition, and indeed was logical enough, considering the diversity of agenda items, some of which were of concern to ministers and departments other than Green and External Affairs. Bryce was careful to clear his plans with Norman Robertson, who, while not objecting, could see the complications that would ensue. Bryce's presence in the chain of advice to the prime minister would mean that the views held on South Africa by Green, Robertson, and some others directly involved in External Affairs would inevitably be compared with those of Bryce when they reached the prime minister. Robertson correctly anticipated that Bryce would be much less concerned than External Affairs to find some respectable way of avoiding South Africa's exclusion from the Commonwealth.

The difference between the positions of Bryce and External Affairs did not, however, become exposed until early April, soon after the massacre of sixty-seven blacks by South African police at Sharpeville. On 8 April I reported to the department that the prime minister was showing anxiety in the face of criticisms that he had not been tougher in his public references to South Africa.[5] He was, I noted: 'strongly inclined to take a suitable opportunity to go further in public criticism of South African Government policies than he had done up to now in the House of Commons. He spoke in very critical terms of the South African decision to re-impose the pass laws.'[6] I also reported that the prime minister wanted to make it unequivocally clear that there should be 'informal discussions' on the South African problem at the London meeting. In this, Diefenbaker and other prime ministers were admitting that it would be totally unrealistic to meet without discussing apartheid in South Africa, even if it were not listed formally as an item on the meeting's agenda.

Diefenbaker's views would not have stirred things up except that Howard Green felt the government had already gone further than it needed in criticizing the South African government. Twice in the first week of April Diefenbaker expressed impatience with changes inscribed by the minister in draft passages sent forward for use in the House of Commons. Once Diefenbaker complained to me that I was too inhibited in my advice to him, and I was left to weigh his words against what the minister would have felt if, in my liaison role, I had tendered advice at variance with his.[7]

Sensing the tension, Bryce told me on 6 April that he intended to speak to the prime minister in the hope of establishing a clear course of policy. The line he was going to take may be summarized in three points:

1   that the future usefulness and reputation of the Commonwealth as such in world affairs depended on a common acceptance of certain basic social and political standards which South Africa did not accept;
2   that Canada should consider initiating South Africa's withdrawal from the Commonwealth so that its non-white members could hold up their heads; and
3   that though there would be a strain on relations with the United Kindom and Australia, Diefenbaker could be sure of a place in history if he had the courage to put a stop to our present hesitations.[8]

On that same day Bryce spoke to the prime minister and found him not unsympathetic, although not as far along in his thinking. Bryce then spoke to George Glazebrook, the assistant undersecretary responsible for Commonwealth matters in External Affairs. Glazebrook considered Bryce's position too radical and preferred to think of possible realignments in South African politics which might warrant waiting for an improving state of affairs. Bryce told me he thought we might not have time to wait. Later on the same day the prime minister showed signs of having absorbed Bryce's message. He mentioned that the time might have come to establish standards for Commonwealth membership. He also said, however, that if we were too outspoken against South Africa and brought about its exclusion, Canada would invite serious immigration problems – a larger flow of non-white applicants – and that had to be considered. I gathered that this point had been raised in cabinet meetings, and that the prevailing opinion among the ministers had been to continue with a cautious course.[9]

Meanwhile my own position was becoming more awkward by the hour, as some, though not all, of the responsible officials in External Affairs were bridling at Bryce's idea of precipitating South Africa's departure from the Common-wealth. Their argument was that Canada could be blamed for what might happen to the Africans and the whites in consequence of South Africa's isolation. The atmosphere was highly charged – earlier that day a Canadian newspaperman had been arrested in South Africa and news had come of an attempted assassination of Prime Minister Verwoerd.

Diefenbaker made a further statement in the House on 11 April in response to all these developments and to the opposition's request for a parliamentary debate. There had been a hectic weekend of preparation and, as usual, he left it to the last minute to decide what he would say. I was summoned an hour before the House opened and found him with a fistful of newspaper clippings and draft statements offered by Bryce and External Affairs, the two still at variance. Diefenbaker told me that personally he would prefer to be outspokenly critical of South Africa but that his colleagues were in favour of not going further than he had gone already. When he spoke, he surprised everyone by agreeing provisionally to a debate on South Africa after the Easter recess, in order to avoid agreeing to an immediate debate for which Pearson was pressing.

The idea of a full-scale debate on South Africa was anything but welcome to officials in External Affairs. They could not imagine how the difference between Green and Diefenbaker on this issue could possibly be concealed. But that was for another day. What seemed potentially more important at the time was the mention in the prime minister's statement of the idea of a declaration of Com-monwealth principles. When Diefenbaker returned to his office after making the statement, he called me on the phone. Well, was the statement good, bad, or indifferent? I said that two parts of it raised questions. Did he have in mind the drafting of a declaration for use at the prime ministers' meeting? He replied in the negative; it was the expression of a long-term hope, not intended to apply at the meeting nor for inclusion in the communiqué. He said that his words had been carefully chosen. I also asked whether he definitely intended to have a debate after the recess; he said that here too his words had been deliberately vague but that if the South African issue was still as difficult after the recess, he would not mind a debate.[10] He then took off for Easter in Saskatoon, carrying with him speech drafts and briefing notes for the visit of President de Gaulle and for his own impending visit to Mexico, both of which would take place in the following week.

Preparations for the Commonwealth meeting continued. Bryce was concentrating on finding a formula by which the Commonwealth would in some way pronounce against South Africa. Officials in External Affairs were thinking in terms of an appendix to the communiqué indicating that the prime ministers had listened to South Africa's case but had disapproved of what they had heard. Norman Robertson declared himself against any chastising action by Commonwealth countries. He saw the Commonwealth as a product of history, a family, some of whose members went to church, others to jail, but not susceptible as a group to discipline nor a court of morality. None of us could guess what the prime minister's final mood would be.

Parliament resumed on 25 April. The prime minister held a short meeting with some ministers before the House sat and came away still nervous about the London meeting but at least ready to agree to the South African problem's being discussed in the House on 27 April, the eve of his departure for London. Again the call went out for speech material, and again the different offerings conflicted. I attended him for an hour before the House met while he dictated his statement out of a mess of press clippings, diplomatic reports, and fragments of once pristine prose. The result went down the middle of the road, firmly anti-apartheid but carefully non-committal on the position he would take in London on South Africa's membership status. I noted in my diary that 'when the Prime Minister's speech came, after a very good one by L.B. Pearson, it set the stage satisfactorily for the Prime Ministers' conference.'

En route to London on 29 April, the prime minister told us that his tactics would be to test the South African reaction, to feel them out.[11] If their reaction was helpful, well and good; he would be able to point to the good sense of his (restrained) position. If not, he proposed to return home and say that restraint and tolerance would not work, that the South Africans were adamant against any change in their racial policy.

This plan served his purpose throughout the meeting. He played a quiet role, supporting informal discussion of the issue, seeking to explore every possibility of moderation in the South African position, resisting any tendency for the Commonwealth to exercise a judicial function, emphasizing the multiracial nature of the Commonwealth, and joining readily in the consensus that if, after its referendum, South Africa became a republic, it would have to apply for continuing membership in the Commonwealth. In a sense, the South African foreign minister, E.H. Louw, simplified Diefenbaker's position by the emphatic way in which, on two occasions, he rejected his overtures for small symbolic constitutional concessions which might justify, however tenuously, the argument that South Africa was not completely inflexible. Diefenbaker was quite content with the postponement of the issue until the next meeting, which would be held within one year.[12]

It was the first meeting of Commonwealth prime ministers I had attended, and it would be the last to be held in the Cabinet Room at No. 10 Downing Street. The Commonwealth was outgrowing its traditional place of meeting which, when crowded, had become as uncomfortable as it was drenched in history. I attended eleven of the thirteen meetings and several more informal ones. My impressions were mixed. I thought that Macmillan was a superb chairman, thoroughly on top of the issues, patient in often difficult circumstances, sensitive to every shade of opinion and personality around the table, and, with the shrewd and experienced counsel of Sir Norman Brook, secretary to the United Kingdom cabinet, flexible and resourceful in steering the meeting to a generally acceptable conclusion. Of the other prime ministers, R.G. Menzies of Australia, perhaps the least distant philosophically from the South African position, was helpful to Macmillan in bringing the South African Louw to accept the wording of the final communiqué. Nkrumah of Ghana was more restrained in tone and language than I had expected. Nehru, though seemingly withdrawn, was heard by all with evident attention and respect.

Of Diefenbaker, a letter I wrote after returning to Ottawa said: 'our man was not conspicuous and didn't do much to distinguish himself among his colleagues.' In private, he seemed mainly concerned to find a respectable formula for postponing the climax of the issue, a tactic he so often resorted to in time of crisis. But on this occasion postponement was the most practical course. By the time of the next meeting, South Africa would have held a referendum on the question of becoming a republic and would thus be in a position, if it so decided, to express a desire to remain a member of the Commonwealth. It would then be for the South African government to ask for the consent of the other members. The final communiqué of the 1960 meeting made these points clear. It went on to emphasize that 'the Commonwealth itself is a multi-racial association.'

On his return, Diefenbaker reported immediately to parliament. 'In Canada,' he said, 'there is no sympathy for policies of racial discrimination on whatever grounds they may be explained ... and such policies are incompatible with the multi-racial nature of the Commonwealth.'[13] In discussing the meeting with his cabinet colleagues, the prime minister again returned to the problems he saw as inherent in the changing make-up of the Commonwealth. He warned that if the Commonwealth prime ministers ever adopted a majority vote procedure, it might mean approval for free migration within the Commonwealth, a policy which had resulted in large-scale immigration into the United Kingdom and which he thought would not be acceptable to Canadian opinion.[14] How seriously he really took the possibility of the adoption of majority voting I was never quite sure, but his tactics certainly seemed influenced by it. In this regard, he told me he had derived some ironic comfort from observing what he took to be Nehru's preference for some solution other than a direct Commonwealth condemnation of South Africa. Diefenbaker attributed this to Nehru's fear that India's position would be at risk if the Commonwealth were to act as judge and jury in the case of the Indo-Pakistan dispute over Kashmir.

Less than a year later, the prime ministers would meet again to consider South Africa's request for continued membership as a republic. At that meeting the prejudice against 'interference' in domestic affairs would have greatly diminished in the face of South Africa's refusal to modify its racial policies. Diefenbaker, still worried that the Commonwealth might be damaged if it decided collectively to refuse consent to South Africa's continuing membership, would join in a course of action that put the onus for decision on South Africa.

Glimpsing the Summit – Before and After

DE GAULLE VISITS CANADA

Among the last items of business I had discussed with the prime minister before Christmas in 1959 was the prospective visit to Canada of President Charles de Gaulle. It was to take place in April, at a time when parliament might not be in session, and the question arose whether the dates should be adjusted to permit de Gaulle to be invited to address the Senate and the House of Commons. Diefenbaker showed no inclination to do this, and seemed rather lacking in enthusiasm for the visit. He was quite prepared to authorize a full-scale official program, including visits to Quebec City, Montreal, and Toronto as well as Ottawa, but I could see that he wanted to keep his own participation to the minimum.

Diefenbaker's sensitivity to his weakness in the French language was, I am sure, at the root of his reaction. He had felt awkward enough when he had visited de Gaulle in Paris in November 1958. But at least in Paris those within hearing range of him mostly voted in France and were not likely to go out of their way to cause him personal and political embarrassment in Canada. When the president of France came to Ottawa, it would be different. There were enough people in the national capital, including many in parliament and the French-language press, who would conspicuously deplore his unilingualism and, despite his disclaimers, make him feel inadequate. It was a great comfort to him to be able to rely on Governor General and Madame Georges Vanier to welcome their old friends, the de Gaulles, and to act as their hosts at Government House during their stay in Ottawa. Apart from naming ministers to accompany the visitors on the remaining parts of their program, the prime minister concerned himself only with what was required of him in Ottawa.

In the briefing material prepared by External Affairs, emphasis had been placed on international matters rather than on the intricacies of bilateral relations. Although the prime minister had not dictated this priority, the correct assumption was that he would not find it profitable to engage in discussion of France's relations with Quebec or of what de Gaulle later felt free to describe as 'the underlying realities which make the Canadian federation a state that is perpetually uneasy, ambivalent and artificial.'[1] Such delicate problems were not likely to be brought closer to solution in an encounter between these two men.

De Gaulle recalls in his account of the visit that he had told Diefenbaker, 'whose intentions were certainly highly estimable', that France was willing to enter into much closer relations with Canada. But if France were to do so wholeheartedly, Canada 'must have the will and the capacity to solve the problem posed by the existence within her borders of two peoples, one of which was French, and must, like any other, have the right to self-determination.' This was not language that John Diefenbaker would have warmed to, and in talking afterwards about his conversation with de Gaulle he did not dwell on this aspect of their private exchanges. His interest lay mainly in de Gaulle's views on the broad international outlook.

The French president's visit to Canada was a small part of an elaborate pattern of international consultations in preparation for the four-power East-West summit meeting, which was to begin in Paris on 16 May. Diefenbaker would not be a participant in that meeting, but he had been keeping himself as informed as possible, largely through reports on consultations in the NATO Council. Late in March when Macmillan had gone at short notice to see Eisenhower about the prospects for the summit, Diefenbaker had tried unsuccessfully to persuade him to come to Ottawa. De Gaulle had visited London earlier in April and would be going on from Canada to see President Eisenhower.

In the public statements he made in Canada, de Gaulle did not forget to take account of the traditional Canadian emphasis on the importance of consultation among the NATO allies. Perhaps he remembered how indignant Diefenbaker had been in 1958 when de Gaulle had floated the idea of an inner triumvirate (of the United States, United Kingdom, and France), to assume a kind of overall direction of the strategic affairs of the free world. Mr Diefenbaker, the French president would say in an address in Quebec City on 20 April, was a man of 'lucidité et fermeté,' a choice of words Diefenbaker told me later showed that he had made his point.

The Ottawa program had allowed for a private meeting with Diefenbaker and a separate session with members of the cabinet. With the exception of whatever discussions might be possible with Macmillan during the Commonwealth prime ministers' conference, the meetings with de Gaulle were the only opportunity for the prime minister and his colleagues to consult at length with a summit participant.

Having recently had discussions in Paris with Khrushchev, de Gaulle gave his impression of the Soviet leader. Khrushchev was aging and was impatient to achieve results. He had given every appearance of a determination to avoid war and of a deep preoccupation with raising living standards in the USSR. De Gaulle thought that Khrushchev would try to focus the discussion early in the summit conference on Germany and Berlin, since these related issues were his highest priority. He had many times emphasized his aims of recognizing the East German government and of giving Berlin the status of a free city. Because the Soviet and Western positions were so far apart, de Gaulle said it would be a mistake to expect progress on these issues. If they were to dominate the early proceedings, the atmosphere would be spoiled. Instead, he considered that the Western side should aim to make disarmament the first topic, possibly to be followed by an examination of East-West collaboration in the field of assistance to underdeveloped countries.

Diefenbaker, while accepting the point that Germany and Berlin should be relatively low on the agenda, nevertheless hoped that some progress could be made towards agreement on Berlin. He regarded it as essential to prevent West Berlin from coming under Communist control. He wondered if the United Nations might be given a role. De Gaulle made no comment on the possibility of a UN involvement, but agreed that some reduction of forces in Berlin might be an avenue of progress. On the question of German reunification de Gaulle said it was a problem for the long term. There would be opposition now on both sides to reunification but it would not be wise to declare that it would never come about. Almost the same observation had been made by Macmillan during his last visit to Ottawa a year before.

There was an exchange on possible approaches to disarmament and on the testing of nuclear weapons. Diefenbaker recalled that on several occasions he had offered to make available for inspection Canada's arctic and northern areas, provided that the Soviet government would allow Canada the right to inspection in comparable regions of the USSR. The prime minister also remarked on the tremendous significance attached by public opinion in Canada putting an end to nuclear tests. De Gaulle made it plain that France had no intention of giving up its nuclear testing program; he could see no alternative to continuing it unless there were a general international agreement to destroy nuclear weapons. On disarmament, de Gaulle thought that Khrushchev might be responsive to the idea of reciprocal control of rockets, missiles, launching sites, and strategic aircraft – the means of delivery rather than the nuclear weapons themselves. In the absence of agreements on disarmament, he thought it essential to maintain the nuclear deterrent.

Summing up the prospects for the summit meeting, de Gaulle said that it would be the first of many. In the time available, it would be difficult for the four leaders to do more than start work on the problems and to agree to study them together. The meeting would be a success if it were not a failure. These were the words that Diefenbaker thought of a month later when he received confirmation that the summit meeting had indeed collapsed.

On the day after de Gaulle had left Ottawa for Quebec City, the prime minister reminisced on their talks.[2] He was not as exuberant as he had been at the end of their meeting in Paris in November 1958. I noted: 'I would judge the P.M. as having learned quite a bit from de Gaulle, and as having realized, without openly admitting it, that de Gaulle is a giant ... It was clear that this was a performance by de Gaulle rather than a genuine exchange.'[3]

SUMMIT BREAKDOWN AND AFTERMATH

Both the prime minister and the minister were absent from Ottawa when the news broke of the shooting down of the American U-2 aircraft in the first week of May. Howard Green had been in Istanbul for a meeting of NATO foreign ministers, and the prime minister was in London for the conference of Commonwealth prime ministers. The minister returned to Ottawa after joining Diefenbaker briefly in London, and had to cope with anxious public reactions to the unconvincing early attempts of the US administration to explain the U-2 incident. In London the last days of the Commonwealth meeting were clouded by the prevailing uncertainty as the opening of the summit meeting approached.

Immediately after the prime minister's return from the conference, it became clear that the summit process was heading for a breakdown. The Soviet action in shooting down the American plane and Eisenhower's eventual acceptance of responsibility for the U-2's intelligence mission combined to make it impossible to salvage the meeting. When the inevitable cancellation was announced on 17 May, Diefenbaker's first private reaction was that Eisenhower was 'slipping' and that Khrushchev's behaviour indicated he had been thrown off course by a threat to his leadership in the USSR. Later I learned that this latter speculation had come from Macmillan. The disarray on the Western side was a worrying by-product of the whole episode.

On 17 May Diefenbaker asked for a statement for the House of Commons the next day and another for a CBC television broadcast, 'The Nation's Business.' He gave no instructions or guidance as to the line he wanted to take. I wrote in my diary that night: 'The P.M. is a negative thinker about these things – he waits for the news and has no apparent drive to do anything original or involving diplomatic initiative.' The key questions were how and where to place the responsibility for the breakdown of the summit, and what could usefully be said and done to limit damage and help get matters back on a constructive course.

The prevailing opinion in the Department of External Affairs favoured taking a moderate stand, with emphasis on shoring up the unity of the Western alliance but keeping open the channels of communication with the Soviet side. Important as these objectives were, I also knew that the prime minister's own inclination would be to respond to the popular demand for denunciation of Khrushchev. One of my concerns, therefore, was to see that whatever emerged from the debate within the department would have at least some bite in it. Otherwise he would brand it as statesmanlike and 'Pearsonian' and the department would have lost another skirmish. I was therefore a little apprehensive when Norman Robertson softened some of the tougher, anti-Soviet language which had been put into the original draft of the statement by assistant undersecretary Ed Ritchie and others. With Green away on a visit to Latin America, Robertson sent the text to me for direct delivery to the prime minister. When he had read it over he immediately put some of the bite back in, but the wording he settled for was not far from what the department had proposed, and it was well received by Pearson and the CCF leader, Hazen Argue.[4] An appreciative letter from President Eisenhower soon followed.[5] Diefenbaker was gratified by the reaction in the House and for once he was profuse in his thanks for the department's work, a message rare enough and pleasant to impart.

Our satisfaction was short-lived. In his television broadcast the next day, he followed his own political instincts and placed the blame squarely on Khrushchev, resisting all efforts to persuade him to stay with the line he had used before parliament. Later I realized that I might as well have saved my breath. I might have known that two 'moderate' statements in a row could not have served the prime minister's purpose. My diary for 20 May reads: 'Stayed out of close range today lest P.M. ask me what I thought of his broadcast last night. It would have required either dangerous honesty or degrading evasion and I didn't want to commit either.'

A considered analysis of the reasons for the summit breakdown had meanwhile been prepared in External Affairs for the use of Jules Léger, the Canadian representative in the NATO Council. The minister was still away and I was asked to secure the prime minister's approval or comments. One of the points stressed in the department's paper was that Khrushchev's rejection of the summit had been related to his earlier attempt to give Eisenhower the image of a man of peace, and that when this image was shattered by Eisenhower's acceptance of responsibility for the U-2, Khrushchev had been put in the position of having to disown Eisenhower in order to preserve his own self-respect at home.

To the prime minister this was interesting but wholly unconvincing. He said that he saw the summit breakdown as the product of (a) Khrushchev's realization that he would get nothing out of the meeting, and (b) the US mishandling of the U-2 incident which gave Khrushchev his good excuse to break it all up, while not damaging irrevocably the chances for preserving an atmosphere for eventual negotiation. Having given these views, he said, 'You fix it up; I don't want to see it again.' I have no record of how the instructions to Léger were 'fixed up.' By that time, however, I had become accustomed to marrying departmental prose with Diefenbaker thoughts, a kind of mental contortion that was necessary though disturbing to the peace of mind. I wrote, rather crossly, on 24 May: 'The P.M. has fallen comfortably back into the old easy superficial habit of blaming everything on the Russians, and nothing on God's earth will shake him. The fact that this is the politically popular thing to do makes it just that much harder to get him to do anything else. I suppose it was naive to expect that he would find the political courage and wisdom to see that the whole summit breakdown is more complicated than a simple insult by Khrushchev, or a simple retreat from the prospect of negotiation.'[6]

One weekend, after some difficult sessions about the summit collapse, Diefenbaker seemed to make a special effort with the healing process. It took the form of an invitation to bring my family for a visit to Harrington Lake, the prime minister's summer place. Watching him there, entertaining four children ranging in age from eight down to three, one saw a side of him that was seldom revealed. When it was over, he had four young disciples, and somehow the tension of the preceding week had miraculously cleared.

SEISMIC RESEARCH

Canada had played but a modest role in the approach to and descent from the Paris summit. Diefenbaker's eye was mainly on Berlin, but his occasional references to giving the United Nations a role in the city had not aroused much interest among the governments more directly concerned. Howard Green had worked on disarmament through the Ten-Nation Committee and the NATO Council.

A concrete proposal – that Canada should agree to the establishment of a number of monitoring stations on Canadian territory for the purpose of assisting in an international program of research in the detection of underground nuclear explosions – had been put to the prime minister in London by Macmillan during the Commonwealth meeting. On Diefenbaker's return, the cabinet discussed the proposal at length and produced a cautious response largely because of Green's reservations. The minister had been advocating a complete ban on nuclear testing, and argued that it would be inconsistent with this stand to take part in a research program whose purpose was to facilitate the detection of underground explosions.[7]

In a personal message to Macmillan on 17 May, the prime minister said that Canada would cooperate in the proposed seismic research program if agreement were reached among the nuclear powers. At the time of the cabinet discussions, the summit meeting had not been abandoned, and Macmillan had been hoping that an international seismic research network to assist in the control of nuclear tests might be acceptable to the Soviet authorities and thus be a positive element in the summit discussions. Diefenbaker's message to Macmillan added two conditions to Canadian readiness to participate in the program. First, the nuclear powers must have reached agreement among themselves on the institution of the research network. Second, 'in view of the definite stand which the Canadian Government has taken against further nuclear testing,' there should be no public reference to Canadian participation before agreement had been reached among the three nuclear powers.

This message caused difficulties for Macmillan, since it prevented him from informing the Soviet authorities of Canadian willingness to cooperate, and similarly would inhibit him from mentioning Canada's position in response to parliamentary probing in the British House. Macmillan explained these points in a message Diefenbaker received on 27 May. Diefenbaker was annoyed by two things in Macmillan's letter which he showed me but retained for his files. The following is quoted from a memorandum I wrote on 31 May, recording Diefenbaker's reaction: 'At one stage Mr. Macmillan had referred to the opportunity Canada would derive ... to play a 'leading role' in the effort to end nuclear testing. The Prime Minister said he was not concerned about playing a leading role. He was particularly irritated by the final sentence in Mr. Macmillan's letter, in which, as I recall, he had said that he would not like to be put in the position of having to admit to Parliament that the failure to achieve progress was attributable to Canada. I got the impression that if this had not been in the letter, the Prime Minister would have been prepared to go all out in working for Canadian participation. As it is his mind is still open to counter-argument.'[8]

Despite his irritation with Macmillan, Diefenbaker wanted to cooperate with the seismic research program and told me he intended to consult Pearson with a view to facilitating Canadian participation. Whether he did speak to Pearson I do not know, but early in June he told me that the cabinet had decided that Canada was prepared to cooperate but did not wish this to be announced for the time being. By then, however, the failure of the summit meeting had undermined the prospects of significant progress towards agreement on the control of nuclear testing. Howard Green kept up his single-minded crusade for the banning of all nuclear tests and the promotion of other forms of disarmament. The prime minister was more preoccupied with the outlook for unity among the Western countries and his forthcoming visit to President Eisenhower.

A TALK WITH IKE

The emphasis soon shifted to the Diefenbakers' visit to Washington, which was to take place on 3 June. It had a weird prelude. The invitation for a 'personal visit' had arrived on the morning of their departure for London late in April, and I had been alerted that Mrs Diefenbaker was wondering aloud whether such a 'personal' visit was not too informal in status, given the ceremony with which President and Mrs Eisenhower had been received in Ottawa in 1958. I spoke quickly to Arnold Heeney at the embassy in Washington and, fortified by his plea of alarm, I overcame the hesitations of the Diefenbakers. I did this by stressing that the 'personal' invitation was in fact a compliment. It would illustrate the friendly feeling of the Eisenhowers for the Diefenbakers and would give an opportunity which few other national leaders had for really informal conversations with the president. Mindful that a recipe for success with the prime minister was to avoid lengthy official programs, I also pointed out the advantages of a brief and concentrated visit such as the president had proposed, with a minimum of diplomatic icing on the cake.

As the visit grew nearer, I realized that with all his preoccupations in domestic affairs, Diefenbaker was not preparing himself for his meeting with the president. As the minister was not being included in the party, no support from that quarter could be expected. In Diefenbaker's briefcase was a meticulously prepared book of position papers for Washington which, on the day before the visit, he confessed he had not had time to look at. Even a summary of the main topics was unread, set aside no doubt for last-minute reference. For one blood-curdling moment on that day, word that Mrs Eisenhower was unwell caused him to contemplate postponement of the visit. Heeney, however, reported that there was no serious concern at the White House, and the prime minister gave up, though still protesting his anxiety over the First Lady's condition.

Despite its unpromising prelude from the planning point of view, the two principals made it a success in personal and political terms. Eisenhower, unlike so many other national leaders of that time, had the gift of making John Diefenbaker feel comfortable. If there was one thing Diefenbaker disliked, it was the strait-jacket of formal meetings, and the feeling of being surrounded by hordes of solemn-faced note-taking officials, whose expertise exposed the inadequacy of his own preparation and none of whom would have had the slightest hope of winning a seat in parliament even if they had had the guts to try. Eisenhower did not need to have this explained to him. And with the accomplished team of Arnold Heeney and Livie Merchant[9] stage-managing the affair, no detail was overlooked to provide an atmosphere that would sit well with Diefenbaker, who by this time was known in the trade as hard to handle.

The prime minister later gave me an account of his private conversation with the president. Eisenhower had reminisced about the sequence of events since the U-2 incident. He said he had had no alternative but to admit personal responsibility for the U-2 flight once Khrushchev had stated publicly that the president might not have been aware of it. Unless he had admitted responsibility, he would have been criticized for not being master in his own house. The decision to make the admission had been his own. The prime minister said there had been no implication whatever on the president's part that the United States had been wrong in the way it had handled the events leading to the collapse of the summit meeting. Since the Department of External Affairs had been propagating the subversive thesis that the USSR might not have been exclusively to blame for the failure of the summit, the prime minister was here in effect reasserting his earlier refusal to accept that view.[10]

In response to a remark by the prime minister that Khrushchev's conduct seemed to be becoming 'irrational' though not deliberately bent on provoking a war, Eisenhower had said that while the Soviet Union was inclined to trumpet its achievements in missile production, he did not think that the West need regard these boasts as a deliberate threat to peace. He might feel a sense of danger if the Soviet stockpile of missiles greatly increased. War by intercontinental missiles was 'a very uncertain thing.' There were all sorts of possibilities of unsuccessful firing. The president also mentioned that the US intercontinental missile had reached a range of 6000 miles and had landed 'within yards' of its target.

The most sensitive bilateral problems lay in the field of continental defence, and the prime minister took advantage of the private meeting to discuss some of these concerns with the president. The major issues – the acquisition of nuclear weapons by Canada, and the terms of a possible deal (the 'Swap Deal' for short) whereby Canada might acquire interceptor (F-101B) aircraft as replacements for the CF-100s in air defence and the United States would purchase CL-44 transport planes built in Canada – were not brought much closer to solution. The prime minister took occasion to emphasize the government's insistence on 'joint control' in the event of Canada's acquiring nuclear weapons for Canadian forces. The president did his best to encourage Diefenbaker to expedite decisions, and he secured a promise that Canada would shortly respond to a United States request for cooperation in 'Skyshield,' a continental air defence exercise.

When the few advisers – three on each side[11] – were invited to join in, the president made sure that the talk remained on a note of casual cordiality, never slipping onto a plane that might have discomfited his guest. The result was what one could have expected – a friendly, free-flowing exchange of impressions on the world scene and on the current agenda of bilateral issues. I wrote: 'Ike brimming over with goodwill and intermittent profanity, and seemed anxious to avoid any sharp differences.'

The program ended with a large sumptuous White House dinner at which it was clear that the Diefenbakers were being made to feel the guests of honour. The only other item I noted in my diary was that my dinner partner, a well-known and charming Washington hostess herself, introduced me to the elegant woman across the table from me by saying, slowly and with an establishment intonation: 'Mr Robinson, you are sitting opposite the most outstanding hostess in Washington and the biggest sapphire in the world.' Nothing in my training had prepared me for such a revelation. I was dazzled, and no doubt it showed.

THE STATE OF NATO

By the time of his visit to Washington, and largely because he realized that something more than castigating Khrushchev was politically advisable, the prime minister switched on to presciptions for the future. His meeting with Eisenhower and Herter was influential in this regard because he found them preoccupied with improving the international atmosphere as well as renewing the solidarity of the Western alliance. In a series of speeches – at Depauw University, Indiana, in the House of Commons, at Kingston to the Royal Society of Canada, and to the annual US Governors' Conference, held that year at Glacier National Park, Montana – he drew on a steady flow of advice and speech material from External Affairs and worked out a post-summit position which met his domestic political needs and gave him a more positive appearance internationally.

He wanted to be seen as a loyal supporter of Eisenhower, the leader of the Western nations, but also as the possessor of independent judgments on world affairs. The positive and the moderate would be accentuated to a degree which, I remember, surprised me at the time. At Depauw University, for example, he declared that 'The language of insults is best answered with restraint.' He reflected on methods by which the Western governments could keep the international temperature down. He supported Eisenhower's call for a maintenance of contacts and business-like relations with the USSR, and for an eventual renewal of contacts at the highest level. With encouragement from Howard Green, he urged a continuation of disarmament and nuclear-test negotiations and even a readiness to look objectively at yet another set of disarmament proposals advanced early in June by the Soviet government. He resurrected one of his old reliable themes – aerial inspection of Arctic regions if the Soviet government would reciprocate – relating this to the 'open skies' proposal which Eisenhower was planning to introduce before the United Nations. One thing would not change, however. Khrushchev was still cast as the arch-villain of the drama.

It will be recalled that, only a few months before, Diefenbaker and his ministers had been asking themselves whether the arguments for a Canadian military presence in Western Europe were still convincing. Now, with the United States calling for a reassessment of NATO's purposes, Diefenbaker had his own reasons to join in that task. How would the responsibilities of NATO develop over the next decade? What estimates could be made of changing military requirements? These questions were related in his mind to another project which he had first learned about at the time of the Commonwealth meeting in London. There, along with the prime ministers of Australia and New Zealand, he had been secretly informed of a special study which the United Kingdom government was undertaking, an attempt to forecast the defence responsibilities of the United Kingdom over the next ten years. The terms of reference of that study led to Diefenbaker's later approving a similar study on Canada's defence needs in the 1960s.[12] He asked Bryce, Norman Robertson, and Air Chief Marshal Frank Miller, Foulkes's successor at chairman of the Chiefs of Staff, to oversee personally the Canadian study, the drafting of which was undertaken by George Ignatieff on his return to Ottawa in November 1960 as an assistant undersecretary in External Affairs. Diefenbaker had found Ignatieff to be especially helpful earlier that year during a meeting of Commonwealth prime ministers in London, where Ignatieff had been serving as deputy to George Drew, the high commissioner. The study was duly prepared and submitted early in 1961 to the prime minister who, with enough problems on his agenda, read it and kept it under wraps but took no action on it.

Among the things which Diefenbaker deplored in the affairs of the Western alliance was the tendency for the United States, the United Kingdom, and France to work together in practice as a 'directorate' at the expense of full consultation with the other members of NATO. Perhaps because of their intensive preparations for the summit, Diefenbaker thought that the three governments were again acting as if they represented the Western alliance as a whole. It was no accident that he included in his address at Depauw University the following passage: 'It needs constantly to be recalled that NATO is an alliance of sovereign states each bearing its own responsibility for the safeguarding of peace, each with its own survival at stake. A special obligation falls on the larger, more powerful members to make a reality of consultation, and to reconcile the responsibilites of leadership with those of true partnership.'[13]

Soon after his return to Ottawa from that engagement, Diefenbaker was informed that the secretary-general of NATO, Paul-Henri Spaak, would shortly be visiting Washington and would also be available to visit Ottawa if this was the Canadian government's wish. Jules Léger, the Canadian ambassador to NATO, advised in favour of the visit, and Howard Green saw an opportunity to put a word in about the inadequacies of consultation in NATO on disarmament matters. Diefenbaker, with whom I discussed the visit a few days beforehand, was convinced that his words at Depauw had prompted Spaak's desire to come to Ottawa. In fact, Spaak had many other things on his mind. As Léger had been reporting from NATO headquarters, the problem before the alliance was to face up to the practicalities of its atomic policy. The current dilemma was how to reconcile the introduction of US medium range (Polaris) ballistic missiles into Europe with the difficulties raised by France's refusal to accept US nuclear weapons on French soil. If, as a result of US atomic weapons legislation and de Gaulle's atomic policies, France was driven further into military isolation, might not the effect be to upset the atomic equilibrium in Europe by concentrating large numbers of missiles in West Germany, albeit under US control? How the Americans could submit to de Gaulle's lack of cooperation on atomic policy and at the same time make concessions to his pretensions on global consultation was, Léger reported, not comprehensible to Spaak.

Spaak's visit to Ottawa was not as peaceable as he might have hoped. Two years before, on his last visit, he had unwittingly annoyed Diefenbaker by denying that NORAD was an integral part of NATO, a proposition that the prime minister had been trying for some time to nail down. Diefenbaker never forgot such history. Before the visit, the memory soured his mood, which darkened further when he heard that Green, on Robertson's advice, had authorized Léger to return to Ottawa to attend the meeting with Spaak. A waste of money, the prime minister said, and he also implied that bringing the ambassador back for a day or two of talks was making too much of the occasion. Furthermore, he went on, picking out a phrase from one of Léger's reports, Spaak was 'outspoken'. Therefore you couldn't talk frankly to him; he could not be trusted. I tried my best to remedy the situation without noticeable effect.

It was not a good omen, but the distinguished guest, unaware of what was being said of him, was received with the usual elaborate courtesies. That evening, at an informal dinner (the prime minister was not present), Spaak encountered a crossfire of argument which reflected the differing lines of thought about NATO in Ottawa. Europe, one high and influential official said, would not need Canada in the late 1960s. It would have its own deterrent, and its increasing prosperity should enable it to pay more for its own 'conventional' defence. Canada, with that situation in mind, should be preparing to withdraw its forces from Europe, and should be setting about making itself the leader of the middle, non-nuclear powers. The conversational fur was flying in all directions, and Spaak must have gone back unhappy to his hotel. His oddest comment in my hearing was 'After Tito, Diefenbaker,' by which I presume he meant that Canada under Diefenbaker would soon be joining the neutralist camp!

A program of four meetings with Canadian ministers, including the prime minister, had been arranged for the next day. Considering the shock he had been given the night before, the secretary-general was in good form and improved his standing with the prime minister particularly. He had been tipped off through Léger about Diefenbaker's strong views on the tendency towards a three-power directorate and he showed his awareness of the need to improve the quality of political consultation in the NATO Council. He also handled with a practised touch the prime minister's remark about the need for a study of the next ten years in NATO, while pointing at the same time to the difficulties of sketching a long-term plan when the alliance lacked a common policy both on atomic matters and on disarmament. A heads-of-government meeting, he agreed, might be worthwhile but not before 1961.

Spaak's most direct dissent was in response to views expressed by Howard Green and Norman Robertson. Robertson drew attention to the link between disarmament and nuclear policy. His preference was for a deferment of a NATO decision on Polaris missiles. There would be a risk in terms of defence capacity but it was a risk which had to be taken if the West seriously wanted an agreement on disarmament. Should the West not consider a reversal of its defence doctrine and make a declaration if its intention not to be the first to use nuclear weapons? Spaak disagreed. It was essential that the new missiles be introduced as a part of NATO's defence armoury. He displayed indignation over the tendency of some NATO governments, including Canada, to respond too readily to the latest Soviet disarmament plan. There should be much more emphasis on control and inspection and less on atomic disarmament. Green urged a more serious attempt to find common ground with the Soviet authorities on disarmament. If it sounds like a dialogue of the deaf, I suppose it was. Towards the end, George Pearkes weighed in with a question whether Canadian forces were really needed in Europe. 'Absolutely essential,' said the secretary-general, looking thunderstruck.

It had been anything but an orthodox series of meetings, but both Diefenbaker and Green told me later that they were very pleased with the visit. Trotting out one of his favourite accolades, the prime minister said that Spaak had been 'a hundred percent,' and, without referring to his earlier annoyance that Léger had been called back for the visit, he said it had been valuable to have the ambassador here.

15

Facing an Anxious Summer

In the last week of June, the prime minister and Mrs Diefenbaker attended the US Governors' Conference in Glacier National Park, Montana. He had been looking forward to the occasion, but it turned out to be a disappointment. The governors were much more fascinated by what New York governor Nelson Rockefeller was going to say about his political future than they were in meeting the Canadian prime minister. I wrote on 26 June: 'A bad day. P.M. disliked their room and he and Mrs. D. were insufficiently fussed over. We had to get a guard to stand outside the door because someone passed a bottle of bourbon in. Could not help hearing him scream: "I don't like it here." ' Gowan Guest, his executive assistant, Bunny Pound, his secretary, and the rest of us travelling with him did everything possible to calm things down. At one point I went for a walk with Mr and Mrs Diefenbaker but there were no sidewalks or paths around the hotel and too many Cadillacs. Too many governors too. Even the fishing was poor, despite the desperate efforts of a park warden, who finally coaxed an anaemic little trout on to the Master Angler's hook. And it did not help that an escorting official enquired of the prime minister how often he needed to go over to London to get instructions from the Queen. Thanks to resourceful staff work by Guest, a lunch was arranged at short notice with Governor Rockefeller, who kept the Diefenbakers waiting for twenty-five minutes but made up for it with gossip on the American political outlook, including his own undeclared but unmistakeable interest in the Republican nomination for the coming presidential campaign.

The prime minister's program called for a quick afternoon trip north from Many Glaciers, where the conference was taking place, to Beebe Flats, Alberta. There, in a ceremony of colourful dignity, he was initiated as an honorary member of the Blood (Kainai) band of the Blackfoot Indian Confederacy, under the name of Chief Many Spotted Horses. It was an honour bestowed on few non-Indians and it helped providentially to restore his spirits. On returning to Many Glaciers, he was astounded by the news that the Progressive Conservatives had been defeated in the New Brunswick election. He bounced back, however, and was in good form for his speech to the governors that evening, although the speech itself broke no new policy ground. He had originally intended to speak on dominion-provincial relations, an appropriate topic before a meeting of state governors. Why he set that text aside, I do not know. Increasingly, however, in speeches at home, or in the United States, broad international topics served as a safe diversion from issues that would be more likely to aggravate his political difficulties.

AT HOME

He returned to Ottawa and his gathering political worries. Apart from the unwelcome result in New Brunswick, the Liberal party had just won the right to form a government in Quebec. The government in Ottawa was beset with economic difficulties, and the rift between the external affairs and defence ministers threatened to become an open crisis. In international affairs, there were new anxieties brewing. The Soviet Union suddenly withdrew, with its four Eastern European partners, from the Ten-Nation Disarmament Committee in Geneva. The United States was becoming more and more restless about Cuba. The United Nations was facing a major crisis in the Congo.

Diefenbaker involved himself actively in the Canadian response to all these developments. A letter addressed to him from Khrushchev brought the formal Soviet notification of withdrawal from the disarmament negotiations. It was a serious setback. The message had come through the diplomatic channel and I took it immediately to the prime minister. In the normal way the minister saw a copy and gave directions as to the reply to be prepared. Before the reply was ready for the prime minister, he inquired about it and when I said that it would be coming to him from the minister very shortly, he went directly to the phone in his office and while I sat there he berated Howard Green for interfering in his correspondence with Khrushchev. A few minutes later he told me that he blamed the Department of External Affairs for trying to usurp his functions. When replies were being drafted to letters addressed to him, he wanted them to come directly to him and not through the minister or anyone else, a reference which I knew meant Norman Robertson, whose influence on the minister Diefenbaker suspected was contributing to the governments miseries in the defence-disarmament dilemma.

After this unpleasant contretemps I was asked to go to Green's office. I was doubly apprehensive because I had learned that the minister had been complaining that he was not being consulted on the prime minister's frequent speeches on foreign policy. But the minister was in a philosophical frame of mind. Ross Campbell and Geoff Murray, head of the UN Division, both of them well tuned to Green's wavelength, were helping him put together a reply to Khrushchev. The following morning I took it to the prime minister who promptly approved it, commenting that it was a good strong message. There was no sign of his mood of irritation of the day before – an example of his often rapid change of mood, usually, however, connected with the receipt of some good or bad political news.

At the end of June, the prime minister was feeling more pressure on nuclear weapons policy than he had experienced since the previous February. There was uncertainty about the future of the Bomarc program and about the need for interceptor aircraft for continental air defence. The Liberal opposition was pressing for a clear statement on the progress of negotiations on the whole question of nuclear weapons for Canadian and US forces. Pearkes and Green had made conflicting statements on the government's intentions in recent testimony to parliamentary committees.

Diefenbaker took the long 1 July weekend to reflect on how to reply to Pearson. It would be, he said, a holding statement, intended to patch over the differences between the two ministers and their departments. I spent most of Friday afternoon in the Privy Council Office and in External Affairs, where the officials were trying to find words to bridge the unbridgeable gap. As a result, the prime minister received two separate drafts, one from Bryce and one, reflecting Green's position, from External Affairs. Once again, he went on his own, somehow steering between the two positions. If anything, he came a shade closer to Green by implying somewhat greater hesitancy about accepting nuclear weapons for use by Canadian forces.[1]

It was at this time that I first became aware of the impact on him of correspondence from the public on nuclear matters. On 20 July he sent me a memorandum: 'I have a number of letters critical of any action being taken regarding the storage in Canada of nuclear weapons, and a number are strongly opposed to any defence alliance with the United States.' The Department of External Affairs was asked to draft a general letter which could be used in reply to letters of this kind. His mood seemed genuinely puzzled as to the relative strength of the pro and anti-nuclear arguments. His reliance on views expressed in public correspondence, even crackpot letters, to quote a member of his staff, was 'phenomenal.'[2]

CUBA

The month of July 1960 was marked by the addition of two new crises, Cuba and the Congo, to Canada's foreign affairs agenda. In Cuba, Fidel Castro had now been in power for eighteen months. It was already clear that US-Cuban relations were in a state of serious deterioration, and that Castro was becoming increasingly dependent on the Soviet Union for both economic and political support. The Canadian government, like the United States, had formally recognized the Castro regime in January 1959, but had not encountered difficulties over Canadian interests in Cuba.

The problem of worsening relations between the United States and Cuba, however, affected Canada directly. Like some other foreign policy issues, it contained elements which went to war inside Diefenbaker's mind. He had no sympathy for the Castro regime in Cuba. Yet he had to keep his anti-Castro emotions in check. There were Canadian business and other interests in Cuba; trade relations would have to be considered, diplomatic relations between Ottawa and Havana should be maintained, and he and Green both wanted to avoid any action that might prejudice Canada's capacity to ease the strain in US-Cuba relations. At the same time, the domestic political advantages of adopting a policy independent of the United States were not lost on the prime minister, battered as he felt the government to be by domestic misfortunes in the form of unemployment, labour troubles, and provincial electoral setbacks in Quebec, New Brunswick, and Nova Scotia. Within these pincers the government's Cuba policy would evolve, with Diefenbaker repeatedly expressing anxiety about its balance and its political merits.

On 11 July President Eisenhower sent a 'Dear John' message about Cuba to the prime minister.[3] The president said that despite the restraint he had used in the face of provocation, his hopes for a more reasonable attitude on the part of the Castro regime had not been borne out. A serious situation had arisen and he was worried about Soviet penetration of the Western hemisphere in Cuba. Secretary of State Herter and his counterpart, Howard Green, would be meeting in a few days (at a joint conference of US and Canadian ministers on defence matters at Montebello, Quebec), and the president asked that the two ministers discuss the Cuba problem.

The president's message arrived while the prime minister was attending the Stampede in Calgary and was telephoned to him by Green, who was just leaving for Montebello. Diefenbaker's reaction was ambivalent. On the one hand he was disturbed by what he took to be further evidence of the spread of communist influence; on the other, he was outspoken in his pessimism on the subject of US leadership. From his reaction it was difficult to detect whether he was aiming

145

his criticism at the United States for allowing the situation in Cuba to develop as it had in recent years, or whether he was more concerned at what might happen in the future, especially if Senator John F. Kennedy were to win the presidency. 'I'd be very worried if he became president,' the prime minister said on 12 July, probably because he thought Kennedy to be an opportunist and did not trust his judgment.

Although Herter was unable to attend the Montebello meeting, the United States sent a strong delegation. The agenda was heavy with defence policy issues, but a serious exchange on relations between the United States and Cuba took place. Merchant, representing Herter, first reviewed developments in Cuba from the US standpoint and gave the reasons for recent US decisions regarding Cuba. Measures had been taken against US interests – for example, sugar plantations and oil refineries – and Cuba was becoming increasingly reliant on the Soviet Union. Khrushchev had made threatening statements. The United States had tried restraint in its relations with Castro, but this had not worked.

Howard Green and Norman Robertson challenged the wisdom of US policy as it had recently developed. The Canadians spoke with such force and candour that the Americans present were shocked at the extent of the division between the Canadian analysis and their own. It was the formal start of a new and thorny issue which would rank with nuclear policy as a cause of friction between the two countries in the Diefenbaker years.

At the time of the Montebello meeting, the prime minister received a message from President Lopez Mateos of Mexico in which Canada was asked to join with Mexico and Brazil in an effort to ease relations between the United States and Cuba. Diefenbaker invited Green's views. Green sent forward a suggested reply, drafted in External Affairs by Ed Ritchie. It advanced a list of several questions which might be put to the US and Cuban governments in an effort to find common ground. Diefenbaker approved the letter but with two or three significant changes, all of them designed to make the operation more acceptable to the United States. In a letter to Green, the prime minister wrote: 'I believe that unless something along this line is set out in my letter, the contents ... would be regarded by the United States as unjust, unfair, if not completely undiplomatic ... I regard the establishment of a Communist bridge-head [sic] in North America [as] fraught with terrible consequences ... [it] would, I feel sure, lead to action being taken against the American control of the Panama Canal similar to that taken in 1956 against British and French control of the Suez Canal.'[4] The reply was altered accordingly. The head of the Latin American Division, Yvon Beaulne, who was well regarded by the prime minister, was assigned to pursue the three-power initiative in Havana, but after three months the effort was suspended.

A new phase in the Cuban problem arose in October when the United States clamped an embargo on the bulk of its exports to that country. Immediately the government was pressed for its reaction. I noted on 18 October that Diefenbaker 'was clear in his mind that there should be no embargo on Canadian exports but seemed to be open to some cooperation with the United States on re-exports.'[5] The extent of such cooperation would take some time to work out. In Ottawa, US policy towards Cuba was widely thought to be mistaken, and both Diefenbaker and Green certainly subscribed to that view. But it was something else to exploit the opportunity to expand trade with Cuba at the expense of the Americans. Diefenbaker was as keen to avoid being criticized for excessively cordial relations with Castro as for following the Washington line. After much reflection, he told the House of Commons on 12 December, that, apart from strategic goods, there could be 'no valid objection to trade with Cuba.' It was the government's wish:

to maintain the kind of relations with Cuba which are usual with the recognized government of another country.

It is, of course, not our purpose to exploit the situation arising from the United States embargo, and we have no intention of encouraging what would in fact be bootlegging of goods of United States origin.

The statement was well received by the opposition parties.

As 1960 ended, policy on Cuba had taken its place among Diefenbaker's major worries in foreign policy. It remained to be seen how the outlook would be affected by the imminent change of administration in Washington.

THE CONGO

On 12 July, the day after the Cuban issue had been raised, an urgent request came from the United Nations for Canadian assistance of various kinds in the Congo. The crisis in the Congo had exploded in the week after that country had been granted its independence by Belgium on 30 June. The details are beyond the scope of this account, but the decision of the Congo's prime minister, Patrice Lumumba, to appeal for assistance to the United Nations presented the organization with a peacekeeping and relief task of great urgency and massive proportions. The immediate centre of the danger lay in the presence of Belgian paratroops who had been sent in to protect and help evacuate Belgian nationals. The Soviet Union accused Belgium of 'imperialist aggression,' and the secretary general of the UN, Dag Hammarskjöld, considering that a threat to international peace existed, called the Security Council into immediate session. The problems facing the organization were not only military (to facilitate the withdrawal of Belgian troops); they also involved the provision of many types of technical aid to relieve the existing state of civil disorder and to enable the Congolese authorities to resume control. Canada was one of the countries actively involved in both the military and the non-military aspects of the UN operation in the Congo.

Howard Green was still in Montebello, and Diefenbaker took over the Congo file. Hammarskjöld at first asked for a military unit from Canada, describing his request in another context as having been made to a 'transatlantic French-speaking country.' On reading this, Diefenbaker shot out of his chair and told me to see that Hammarskjöld was told right away not to proceed with the idea of troops from Canada. At first I thought that in his anxiety to avoid the dispatch of French-Canadian troops, he was motivated entirely by traditional Canadian political reasons. It was, however, more than this. He was also worried about the difficulty of having white troops fighting or potentially fighting in an equivocal role in a black country, especially in view of Belgian involvement. His attitude, in general, was to avoid soliciting requests for help and to respond favourably to anything short of combat troops. We could, he privately said, always change our mind if a convincing case were made for fighting troops. On hearing Diefenbaker's reaction, Hammarskjöld settled for administrative and specialist personnel.

In the event, cabinet approved food aid, an airlift, and, after a delay, some 500 military communications and administrative personnel. It had not been as full-hearted a response to the United Nations from Canada as in the past and the government came under fire from the media for its hesitation. The requirement, however, had been more difficult to assess and the request for Canadian troops in particular had given rise to differences within the cabinet. It was, incidentally, one of the few issues on which Diefenbaker consulted Pearson, and Pearson supported the position taken by the government.

Partly because of the wide scope and difficulty of the Congo operation, and partly because the Soviet government took the opportunity to use it as a vehicle for bringing criticism to bear on the secretary-general, the Congo crisis raised 'the fundamental question of whether the United Nations would remain an effective organization for international action.' The prime minister recognized the danger and, in government decisions and speeches over the following few months, he did what he could to bring support to the secretary-general. He knew that in doing so, he was reflecting public opinion in Canada. The antagonism of the Soviet government towards the secretary-general, and Soviet efforts to rearrange the organization of the Secretariat, served to reinforce Diefenbaker's concern for the future of the United Nations, which up to that time had not been especially noteworthy.[6]

A DARK MOOD

In rereading my diary for June and July 1960, I am struck by the extraordinary pessimism which Diefenbaker expressed privately about world affairs in that period. At the root was his suspicion of Soviet intentions, as revived by the abortive summit meeting, Soviet withdrawal from the disarmament negotiations, and the situations in Cuba, the Congo, and Laos. He was constantly talking, too, about Communist China, wrestling still with the dilemma caused by the failure of an earlier Canadian government to recognize the Peking regime, and with the US refusal, recently reconfirmed in person by Eisenhower, to contemplate forward movement on that issue. Communist Chinese intentions, the prospect of Peking's acquiring or manufacturing the atomic bomb, the erratic elements in Soviet leadership, and, above all, the weakness he perceived in US leadership – all these were recurring themes. He looked upon Eisenhower as a man whom he admired, even revered, for his past achievements and whom he liked and trusted, but whose energies were now drained to the point where he could no longer give the leadership so badly needed by the non-communist world. Of course he would be quick to defend the president – when he saw Pearson about the Canadian troops for the Congo he objected to a public reference Pearson had recently made about the 'golfing president.' But in private moments he often compared the frantic pace demanded of him with the relaxed style which the president's health and advisers dictated in the final stages of the Eisenhower administration. Somehow it all seemed so out of proportion.

Diefenbaker's anxiety that something alarming might happen in the world was reflected in his reaction to a message from Macmillan in mid-July. Macmillan had sent a copy of a personal letter he was writing to Khrushchev. It was an effort to smoke out the real intentions of the Soviet leader in the aftermath of what appeared to be a series of deliberately provocative Soviet actions. Diefenbaker showed me a draft of what he was planning to send in reply to Macmillan. He had dictated it himself and it echoed very clearly his anxious mood. He felt no need for advice on this occasion. 'If Khrushchev is at all susceptible to reason,' he said, 'your letter is bound to make him think.' There had been, he went on, a marked increase in tension in recent weeks, and everywhere in the world communist activity was apparent. His reading of the *Peking Review* had brought home to him the 'overwhelming hatred' of the Communist Chinese leaders for the West. Developments in Cuba had 'dangerous potentialities,' and he would like to see something done which could lead to better relations between Cuba and the United States. Canada had not protested formally against recent Cuban policies because the Canadian government felt that protests would be ineffective and would inhibit Canada from acting to improve relations between the United States and Cuba.

16

Adventures of Autumn

ADDRESSING THE UNITED NATIONS

Prime Minister Diefenbaker spoke to the UN General Assembly on 26 September 1960.[1] He was to regard that speech as the most important he made on foreign affairs during his six years in office. He also said quite often in later years that the Department of External Affairs had obstructed his wishes in the drafting of the speech and that he had had to put his foot down before he got what he wanted. One remarkable thing about his speech was that Diefenbaker had only four days to prepare for it. He did not decide to go to the United Nations himself until 22 September, by which time it was clear that the opening days of the Assembly would take the form of a large gathering at the summit level with Eisenhower, Khrushchev, Macmillan, Nehru, Castro, and many other heads of government committed to attend.

At the time this decision was taken, it was not known what kind of a statement Khrushchev would make to the Assembly. There was much speculation on the subject, however. Diefenbaker was expecting that the Soviet leader would be provocative and even abusive, and I could tell that he was hoping to have good reason to retaliate. His own thoughts ran to themes he had frequently emphasized before: Arctic aerial inspection for arms control, the fate of the 'captive nations' in Eastern Europe, the expansion of the jurisdiction of the International Court of Justice, an international food bank under UN auspices, and an international peace force. He told me to consult the department and produce further thoughts. He also sought ideas and draft contributions from at least a dozen sources in and beyond the government. 'Moderate' approaches suggested by Norman Robertson and Donald Fleming were countered by a number of contributions cast in strong anti-Soviet terms. Some were from ministers, others were from friends in some ethnic communities, from academia, from the Parliamentary Press Gallery, or the Progressive Conservative caucus.

The soliciting of material for speeches was always more pronounced in cases which Diefenbaker regarded as important in the domestic political context. It signified a variety of characteristics – a persistent reluctance to be dependent on the civil service, a curiosity about the views of acknowledged specialists outside government, a feeling that somewhere there must be nuggets of wisdom or word-craft which could be used to advantage and which would not be forthcoming from the government's advisers, and a desire to make people who had a special interest in the speech feel that they were contributing to the making of policy. Most of these factors were present in the case of his address to the United Nations. The time available, however, was extremely short for contributors from outside the government service and he worked on the basis of the draft prepared in External Affairs for the minister.

Khrushchev's performance at the United Nations on 23 September had indeed confirmed Diefenbaker's retaliatory inclinations. The Soviet leader attacked the secretary-general of the United Nations over his role in the Congo crisis. That was bad enough, but what really got the prime minister's pulse racing was Khrushchev's assault on the colonial policies of the Western governments. All thought of restrained speech by Canada vanished. Diefenbaker was delighted. He would, as it happened, be the first Western leader to respond to Khrushchev, and in his mind there was no doubt of the kind of response it should be.

The speech which had been intended for Howard Green to deliver was by now in its sixth draft. Its tone was stern but sorrowful, as if Canada would have expected better behaviour but was still ready to give Khrushchev and his colleagues the benefit of the doubt. Green fully accepted that the speech must now be adapted to the prime minister's style and purpose but he was not ready to dissociate himself from its content. He would not take direct issue with Diefenbaker but showed himself to be more comfortable with a positive approach, stressing the importance of resuming negotiations on disarmament and recognizing the UN's role as a focus of support for the interests of the smaller nations. In these aims Green had the full support of the Department of External Affairs, where there was also strong scepticism that the domestic political payoffs of speaking out for the 'captive nations' in Eastern Europe would be matched by any practical international effects or benefits. Diefenbaker was impatient with such arguments. He wanted an open and vigorous denunciation of the Soviet Union. At last, in his mind, there was good reason to disregard the advice from External Affairs.

This was the atmosphere in which the production of the speech proceeded in Ottawa. At the same time, it was essential to relate the speech to current developments in the General Assembly. Hammarskjöld and President Eisenhower, in major speeches before that of Khrushchev, had sought to lay groundwork for an improvement in East-West relations and for a revival of efforts to resolve world problems, including disarmament, through the United Nations. It was therefore not unreasonable, despite Khrushchev's tough talk, to consider whether the prime minister of Canada would be better advised to back up Hammarskjöld and Eisenhower with the emphasis on moderation or, as Diefenbaker obviously preferred, to tackle Khrushchev head on.

There was considerable feeling among Canadian officials with experience at the United Nations that Diefenbaker's opportunities to exercise continuing influence with other heads of government would be strengthened if he avoided giving a straight Cold War speech. Nearly all the outstanding leaders were or would shortly be in New York. Some of them, such as Nasser of Egypt, Tito of Yugoslavia, and Castro of Cuba, he had not met. There was still, more than three years after the departure of L.B. Pearson, a yearning in External Affairs for a traditional Canadian 'constructive' role in the United Nations and in East-West relations. Howard Green was carrying on that tradition in the disarmament field, although he had been disillusioned by the recent Soviet exit from the Ten-Nation Committee. He would not let the opportunity pass to appeal for a revival of disarmament negotiations.

These arguments underlay the continuing preparation of the speech. In large part I suppose they account for the scathing criticism Diefenbaker later expressed of the part played in that episode by the Department of External Affairs. We gave what we judged to be the best advice in the circumstances. At the time he did not reject that advice out of hand. He simply insisted on our helping him to find dramatic language in which to attack Khrushchev, with particular reference to Soviet domination of Ukraine and the Baltic states. That was Diefenbaker's primary aim – along with references to a UN food bank and the International Court of Justice – and he was content to accept what Green thought advisable on other important subjects, such as disarmament, the Congo, and economic assistance to the developing world, including special aid to Africa.

For 24 September my diary reads: 'To N.Y. at 4 p.m. with P.M. after working through the day on the speech. After dinner at 8 he gave sufficient guidance for Ross Campbell, Geoff Murray and self to begin work on a single draft.[2] We worked in my room from 9.30 p.m. till 4.30 a.m. with Bunny Pound and Marion Wagner (the P.M.'s two principal secretaries) and at the end had a condensed single text which left lots to be done but was the framework of the speech. We took out some of the more fiery passages ... Our main problem was how much to put in about the Eastern European captive nations – we knew the P.M. wanted a hard line here.'

Continuing from diary notes, the following is a brief chronicle of events of 25 September, the day before the speech was given. It was Sunday:

Got only 2 hours sleep, being wound up. Checked in with P.M. at 9.30 by which time he was all over the floor of the bedroom with bits of paper. He gave me bits of the speech to polish and then later when Howard Green came with some sensible ideas, called me back for a further session. Ross Campbell and I worked from 2 p.m., stringing it together, re-writing some passages, and it was finally approved at 8.30 or 9. Putting it to bed took till 11 ...

On this day there was a low point around noon when it really looked as if P.M. was losing control but he came back very strong with Howard Green's help and a timely phone call from Grattan O'Leary with an eloquent concluding section. P.M. was very anxious for comment on speech as a whole. I said it was on the rough side and that he would please the U.S. but forfeit the role of peacemaker to the U.K. He took out the word 'arrogant' at one point but showed no special worry at being deprived of peacemaking role.

On the morning of 26 September the speech was duly given. He departed frequently but not fundamentally from his text, and his delivery was superb. Khrushchev himself was not in his seat. Apart from the Soviet bloc delegations, the reception in the hall was unusually warm, and there was much congratulation going on. The prime minister was elated too by the reaction in Canada to his speech. Telegrams and phone calls flooded in. He clearly felt that he had done something to boost the government's falling fortunes in political Canada.

Diefenbaker stayed at the United Nations for another day, soaking up plaudits. Despite his subsequent growling about External Affairs obstruction, he was embarrassingly appreciative of the help he had received from the department. On the trip to Ottawa that evening the minister of finance, Donald Fleming, was aboard and not overjoyed, it seemed to me, to spend half the flight admiring the prime minister's fan mail. Two days later, in order to hear Macmillan's speech and continue his program of meetings, Diefenbaker returned to New York. He was in a state of exhilaration.

It was notable that he did not much interest himself in broadening his international acquaintance. He did express a desire to see President Nasser of Egypt (then known as the United Arab Republic), who had come to the Assembly to hear him, but their exchange, though friendly, was stilted. Nasser offered no congratulations, and clearly no sparks of personal contact were kindled. Diefenbaker also saw President Nkrumah of Ghana with whom he discussed the Congo crisis and the best tactics for dealing with the South Africa question at the next Commonwealth meeting. He met Prime Minister Nehru of India for lunch. In my diary, I wrote that Nehru seemed 'mystic, patrician, and disdainful.' Certainly he was not caught up in the enthusiasm over the Canadian prime minister's speech.

It was quite different with Eisenhower and Macmillan. Diefenbaker was by this time on easy terms with them, and he was curious to have their reactions to his speech. Both were cordial and appreciative. Diefenbaker had taken on their chief adversary in terms which suited them both. Eisenhower, looking ruddy and relaxed, was happy to find Canada so unconditionally on his side. Macmillan, as amusing and sharp as ever, had his own reasons for applauding Diefenbaker. 'You stole my lines', he said in effect to Diefenbaker when they met on the 29th after Macmillan's carefully balanced address to the Assembly. But in a long talk the same night with some of Macmillan's advisers, Ross Campbell and I were told that Diefenbaker's hard line with the Soviet Union had made it easier for Macmillan to try to adopt a statesmanlike pose and thus preserve for himself some chance of exerting a mediatory influence on Moscow.

On that same day a small incident of some interest almost brought Diefenbaker and Khrushchev into direct contact. The Soviet leader had been in attendance when Macmillan was speaking in the General Assembly on 29 September and made his famous intervention by banging his shoe on the desk before him. This exhibition had been calmly handled by Macmillan but inevitably made Khrushchev even more the focus of attention. After the speech, Diefenbaker was in the delegates' lounge when Khrushchev hove into view, at the leading point of a phalanx of Soviet officials and security guards. For a moment it seemed as if he was making for Diefenbaker and the thought hit me that the prime minister should intercept the Soviet leader and at least engage him in a moment's conversation. At the last second, however, Diefenbaker turned away and the chance was lost. He said immediately afterwards that perhaps he had made a mistake in not taking advantage of the ricochet, but doubtless too he feared the consequences of a rebuff or of a Khrushchev victory in repartee. Another example of his shyness and insecurity.

The consequences of Diefenbaker's speech to the Assembly were much more significant in Canadian domestic terms than they were internationally. Canadian diplomatic missions in Eastern Europe reported some adverse comment, and some US ambassadors around the world commented on Diefenbaker's courage in directly challenging the Soviet leader. From the point of view of the Department of External Affairs, the speech disposed entirely of any surviving naïve hopes that Canada under Diefenbaker might still play a role of peacemaker in East-West or UN affairs. For Diefenbaker himself, however, the speech was the highlight of his international career. He never questioned the wisdom of the line he had taken. The domestic importance of his stance in foreign affairs had once more been dramatically underlined.

The effect of Diefenbaker's visits to New York was unmistakeable. He had been exhilarated by direct exposure to his foreign counterparts, and took almost childish pleasure in being privy to their secrets. His speech to the General Assembly had not placed him among the world's great peacemakers but it had yielded a harvest of applause from within Canada, where it counted. It would do him no harm politically to have demonstrated that Pearson was not the only Canadian who could move with success at the United Nations.

He returned to Ottawa with his appetite for international affairs further whetted. Something else was there too: the sense of uniqueness which he had always treasured, and too seldom experienced, in the office he held. It was John Diefenbaker and no one else who had held private talks with Eisenhower and Macmillan, Nehru, Nkrumah, and others. True, on some occasions Howard Green had been along, and sometimes anonymous officials, but no one else had had the *whole* experience. For the moment it made him feel stronger, better informed, better equipped to deal with parliament, his cabinet colleagues, the press, the public at large, foreign diplomats, and those all-knowing officials who, he suspected, were still comparing him, in their lofty way, with Pearson.

MORE PERSONAL DIPLOMACY?

The prime minister's experience at the United Nations had revived his interest in the prospect for more personal diplomacy. He knew from Macmillan and Eisenhower that an East-West summit meeting before the end of Eisenhower's term was out of the question, but he was still wondering about the possibility of high-level encounters among NATO leaders. On 31 October, one week before the US presidential election, he was thinking of a NATO heads of government meeting in Ottawa before the end of the outgoing president's term. This would provide Eisenhower with a last opportunity to give views based on his experience. Nothing came of it, or of a related idea that the heads of NATO governments should assemble to discuss the problems of the alliance sometime in the first half of 1961. Reasonably enough, the feeling was that plans for high-level meetings should be set aside until the new president had taken over in Washington.

One of the things that prompted poorly concealed cynicism in the Department of External Affairs was the prime minister's habit of asking for fresh ideas and then jettisoning them in favour of trusty stale ones. By late 1960 I was in no doubt as to the reluctance of some departmental colleagues to respond in a serious way to appeals for contributions to the prime minister's speeches. They had been disillusioned too often. There was at the same time a sizeable cluster of good soldiers who could be counted on to help, even though they knew well enough that their brain-children might never emerge in recognizable form.

Once, in October, when the prime minister asked for still another speech on relations with the communist world, I sat down with Peter Roberts, then the officer dealing with Soviet affairs, and one of a number in the department capable of writing speeches about foreign policy in language likely to be usable by ministers. I remember that he produced a good, thoughtful text which was approved by the department and sent on through the minister to the Prime Minister's office. Unfortunately, it contained the heretical thought that the Soviet Union's relations with the West should be treated separately from its relations with the underdeveloped world. The argument ran that the Western interest lay not in having the underdeveloped countries line up with one side or the other, but in supporting them in the way which would best enable them to resist Soviet encroachment themselves. As I might have foreseen, this was a point of emphasis that the prime minister was not ready to make his own. It cut across his conviction that the task of the Western nations was to attract the uncommitted countries into willing and fruitful membership of the free world. To suggest that they go their own way was to endorse the concept of non-alignment, and that would never do.

When the speech in question was made – to the Canadian Club in Ottawa on 24 November – it contained little that the prime minister had not said before on relations with Moscow. One new element in the speech was a reference to the need for a 'realistic review' of policy towards mainland China. The prime minister was still considerably alarmed by what he took to be the bellicose attitude of the Peking regime. His reaction, interestingly enough, was to wish that something could be done about the exclusion of Communist China from what he called, rather fuzzily, 'the areas of major political settlement.' If only Howard Green had been of the same mind, it is tempting to speculate that the Diefenbaker government might have taken action to recognize the Peking regime or at least to support its representation in the United Nations. But Green did not think that the time was ripe.

A similar attempt to inject new ideas also occurred in December 1960. It took the form of meetings with Escott Reid, the Canadian ambassador in Bonn and a distinguished veteran of the foreign service, who was on leave in Ottawa and had asked to see the prime minister. On his visit to Bonn in 1958 Diefenbaker had been impressed by Reid, and now again he found him 'a fine fellow – and a very able man.' At Diefenbaker's request Reid put his ideas together in a speech entitled 'The Free World's Approach to the Sixties.' It was a wise and persuasive speech, written with typical clarity and reflecting the breadth of Reid's understanding of the relationship between the Western world and the non-aligned nations. The burden of the speech was that the NATO alliance should stick to its vital function of maintaining a balance of military power with the Soviet Union, that its members must work together to enhance their internal unity and purpose, but that the alliance should not attempt to take on tasks which could be better done by some other agency or under some other auspices. Most of the critical political, economic, and social problems of the 1960s were not, the text continued, aspects of a contest with communism or with the Russo-Chinese bloc. NATO would of course be concerned with these problems but it should not seek to set itself up as a directorate of the whole non-communist world. The problems facing different regions or nations in the non-communist world would be better addressed by a functional and pragmatic approach, with different international agencies being chosen according to their suitability for dealing with the problem in question.

Diefenbaker paid Reid the compliment of carefully editing his text, and he kept it on his desk for some time, as if awaiting the moment to spring it. Unfortunately, the moment never came. Perhaps he felt in the end unable to endorse a thesis which made the struggle between democracy and communism almost irrelevant to the solution of so many of the world's central problems.

HARKNESS AT NATIONAL DEFENCE

By the fall of 1960, the prime minister felt the need for a change of leadership at National Defence. Devoted as Diefenbaker was to George Pearkes, the fact was that Howard Green had outplayed the defence minister in the cabinet infighting and was stimulating public opposition to the acquisition or use of nuclear weapons. Diefenbaker did not want to appear to be anti-disarmament but, at the same time, he was clearly uneasy with a state of affairs in which the arguments for defence preparedness were not clearly presented and heard. 'While disarmament was a laudable purpose,' he told the cabinet, he was afraid of 'the Conservative Party being dubbed the party of disarmament.' He wanted a minister who would provide a stronger voice for defence interests in cabinet and in the country.

His choice of Douglas Harkness, a distinguished Calgarian who had served as minister of agriculture since August 1957, was widely applauded. Harkness had what appeared to be virtually ideal qualifications for his new assignment. He had served overseas in the Royal Canadian Artillery for much of the Second World War, and he had the rare distinction of being awarded the George Cross for an act of great personal bravery. A capable minister and an effective parliamentarian with a reputation for speaking his mind, Harkness had maintained his interest in military affairs and seemed well suited to take over the defence portfolio from General Pearkes. If there was a question mark hanging over the appointment, it lay in the fact that Harkness had been a George Drew man in the past and had never had a close personal relationship with Diefenbaker. Yet, looking back, Harkness recalls no serious problem in his working relationship with the prime minister during the first eighteen months after he moved to National Defence.[3]

Harkness was soon in the thick of the government's debates on nuclear policy. The first issue of many that brought him and Howard Green into policy disagreement came from an unexpected initiative at the United Nations. It took the form of a resolution put forward by the Irish delegation, and calling on nations which did not possess nuclear weapons to refrain temporarily from manufacturing them or otherwise attempting to acquire them. It was a proposal certain to produce a division in the cabinet. At first, Diefenbaker himself dismissed the thought of Canada's voting in favour of such a resolution. He took this view in the belief that the wording of the resolution would limit the government's freedom of action on nuclear weapons policy.[4] He was far from ready, however, to make an irrevocable step towards acquiring nuclear weapons for Canadian use or permitting them to be stored in Canada for use by US forces. A passage in his speech to the Canadian Club of Ottawa on 24 November was typical of his ambivalence, and would be exploited to the full by Green in the weeks to come: 'No decision [on nuclear weapons] has been made ... While disarmament proceeds, it would be inconsistent ... When and if such decisions are required, then we shall have to take the responsibility.'

It is a point of some interest that the presence or absence of particular ministers often affected the outcome of cabinet discussions. If a minister wanted to be assured that an item of business dear to him did not go awry, he either had to be present to see it through, arrange for it not to be dealt with in his absence, or satisfy himself that it would not be torpedoed if it did come up for discussion. Sometimes a prior understanding with the prime minister was sufficient to avoid complications, but this was not always a sure bet, as the history of the decision taken on the Irish resolution shows.

Howard Green, having, as he thought, persuaded the prime minister that a vote in favour was the proper course, left Ottawa for an engagement in Seattle on the night before the item was to be discussed in cabinet. On the morning of the meeting, however, the prime minister showed by the questions he was asking me that he was not persuaded. Knowing the importance attached to the matter by the minister, I tried to bring the prime minister around again to Green's view.

But it didn't work. The cabinet decided to abstain from supporting the Irish resolution, along with the more powerful NATO allies, and we were left to wonder whether Green would make an issue of it.

On the following day, I had instructions to try to get Diefenbaker to reconsider the position taken by the cabinet. In reply to his question, I said that if we did not vote for the resolution, Green's position at the United Nations would be seriously undercut. To quote again from my diary: 'The P.M. said this was what Mr. Green had said ... If he [Green] could not prevail, there was only one thing he could do and that was to resign.'[5] In a note dictated that day, the prime minister wrote: 'On December 3rd Mr. Robinson saw me in regard to this question [the Irish resolution] and seemed to lean in favour of giving the resolution Canadian support. He also viewed with some fear the position which Mr. Green would be in and that if Canada abstained, Mr. Green, who has become known as the exponent of disarmament at the United Nations, would suffer severe loss of prestige ... I told Mr. Robinson that I did not give up hope of any disarmament discussions at this time and that the result of Green's disarmament campaign was already being felt in Canada, for with Macleans Magazine and other long hairs talking in favour of there being no nuclear defences, a weakening in Canada's defence effort would be an inevitable result.'[6]

Diefenbaker's skepticism did not, however, extend to his refusing to permit the reopening in cabinet of the decision on the Irish resolution. Green won on that point, after Diefenbaker had held a private meeting of the ministers concerned. The Canadian vote was reconsidered by the cabinet on 6 December and, under strong pressure from Green, the original decision was changed from an abstention to a vote in favour.

It was a tactical victory for Green, but the occasion had been seized effectively by Harkness to obtain a number of related decisions on future nuclear policy, the burden of which seemed to tilt the balance towards the eventual acquisition of nuclear weapons for Canadian forces both in Canada and Western Europe. In fact, the decision which had been made necessary by the Irish resolution produced a broad framework within which nuclear weapons policy would be pursued for the remaining Diefenbaker years. Thus, the earliest feasible discussions with the US government on the 'essential acquisition of nuclear weapons or warheads for use by Canadian forces' were authorized; the extent of the government's nuclear commitments to NATO in Europe dating from the 1957 heads of government meeting was drawn to the attention of the ministers (Green, Fleming, and Harkness) who would be attending the NATO meeting in Paris later in December; and preparations were to continue to enable Canadian forces to be ready to use nuclear weapons if and when these weapons were considered necessary.[7]

It was also decided at that time that no arrangement for the storage of defensive nuclear weapons for US forces in Canada should be made until after the discussions with the United States on other matters had been concluded. The purpose was to preserve all available bargaining power for use in future negotiations regarding weapons for Canadian forces. Henceforth, too, the prime minister insisted, only he would make statements regarding nuclear weapons. He was getting impatient with ministers making conflicting statements in public, he told the cabinet.[8]

On the day after those decisions, the prime minister was emphatic that the Irish resolution had only 'temporary' application. I put it this way: 'I am sure he is inclined to go ahead on the lines favoured by National Defence but that he has a sneaking fear that public opinion has formed up firmly against nuclear weapons and he is afraid of taking the big jump to nuclear. Meanwhile, Howard Green continues to fight a lone battle against accepting [nuclear] weapons ... The P.M. pretends not to be concerned about the delay but every day of indecision makes the government look worse.'[9]

The Eisenhower presidency would soon pass into history and Canada's prime minister would regret its going. He anticipated that the problems of highest concern to him would be even more difficult to solve once the new administration took office.

PART FOUR

Transition to Trouble

NOVEMBER 1960 TO
DECEMBER 1961

From Eisenhower to Kennedy

During their meeting in New York on 27 September 1960, Diefenbaker remarked to President Eisenhower that Vice-President Richard Nixon, the Republican presidential candidate, would have been wiser to decline the TV debates with Senator John Kennedy. On 18 October, three weeks before Kennedy's narrow victory over Nixon, Diefenbaker was speculating privately in Ottawa on the state of the election campaign. Nixon, he said, had got Kennedy in a box over Quemoy and Matsu, the two islands between Formosa and Mainland China which the United States had made certain commitments to defend. Diefenbaker thought that Kennedy, as a result of his statements in one of the TV debates, could be made to appear as a man who might back away from a commitment.

These remarks are significant for the light they throw on Diefenbaker's attitude towards the two candidates for the presidency. Without saying it directly, he was reflecting his uneasiness at the possibility of a Kennedy victory. Nixon he thought he could live with. He saw him as a known factor, a man of experience with predictable ideas on current issues, and as a non-threatening force on the Canadian political scene. Kennedy was another matter. His performance as a candidate for the presidency had become by that time a source of personal fascination and political anxiety for Diefenbaker. In Kennedy he perceived a difficult challenge, a man whose personal and political attributes – youth, wealth, connections, and charisma – contained much that was either alien or even threatening. If Kennedy were to win, Diefenbaker was asking himself, what new problems would arise? What would it mean for him personally, as prime minister and party leader? What effect, he was already wondering, would it have on Canadian-American relations, on the character of American leadership in world affairs, on the prospects for a more secure peace?

Diefenbaker's awareness of international tensions had been sharpened recently by the events in which he had taken a much publicized part at the UN General

Assembly in late September 1960. He was preoccupied by what he took to be a dangerous international outlook, and it was in this frame of mind that he followed the approaching climax of the presidential campaign. On election day, 8 November, I made a note in my diary after seeing Diefenbaker: 'The P.M. is not pro-Kennedy but in the past few days, as Kennedy has forged ahead as the likely winner, the P.M. has obviously been reconciling himself.' Yet, when I consulted him on the morning after the election about a message of congratulation to the president-elect, the prime minister again revealed his personal misgivings. With Kennedy in control, he said, we were closer to war than we had been before. When I expressed surprise, he went on to picture Kennedy as 'courageously rash.' My note of the prime minister's comments reads: '[Kennedy] had pushed himself to the top against all odds, had spoken of bringing world leadership back to Washington, and had given every indication of intending to pursue an active policy which the Prime Minister feared might prove dangerous.'[1] When I remarked that much would presumably depend on the people Kennedy had around him, Diefenbaker said that he doubted whether Kennedy would be deterred from adopting 'a policy of action.'

Diefenbaker's attitude towards Kennedy at that time might have been improved if someone on the US side had thought to generate a prompt and warm reply to his message of congratulations. Small things counted. When nothing had been received by 22 November, and Diefenbaker had started inquiring, the Canadian embassy in Washington was asked to give a gentle reminder in the right quarters, and the desired result was forthcoming in a matter of hours. It would be three months before Diefenbaker and Kennedy held their first meeting in Washington and a further three before the president's visit to Ottawa in May 1961. Meanwhile, however, Diefenbaker kept a critical watch as the president prepared to take office.

The Diefenbakers had been planning a few days in Florida in early January. As he was going to be in the United States, I phoned Arnold Heeney in Washington to let him know of the travel plans. One thing led to another and, after talking to the RCMP, I had to advise the prime minister that it would be unwise to go to Florida, on the ground that it was the hotbed of anti-Castro Cubans and therefore a potentially uncomfortable place for him to stay in view of the recent controversy over Canadian policy towards Cuba. Although somewhat surprised, he readily agreed. That evening, word came that the United States had broken off diplomatic relations in Cuba. By that time he had decided to try Jamaica. As he and Mrs Diefenbaker left, I noted in my diary: 'P.M. badly needs the rest he is going to have. He does nothing but work and worry and spends disproportionate amount of time simply on trivialities. He is coming to work, or beginning at home, at such an early hour that it lengthens the days for him and for the staff, almost to the point of diminishing returns. But he is strong and still comes back very quickly. His pettiness still asserts itself – latest is that the parliamentary restaurant is not to be opened for the Liberal Party convention next week, the House being in recess.'[2]

IKE'S LAST OFFICIAL ENGAGEMENT

The flow of government business continued, notwithstanding the imminent transition in Washington. While the prime minister was still on holiday on 12 January, President Eisenhower, in a gesture of goodwill, suggested that Diefenbaker join him later that week in the ceremony of signing the Columbia River treaty at the White House. The invitation gave Diefenbaker and Davie Fulton, the minister directly responsible for the treaty negotiations, an opportunity to participate with Eisenhower in the last official engagement of his presidency, in company with most of the cabinet members of the outgoing administration. During the signing ceremony itself and the lunch at the White House, Diefenbaker spoke about the US–Canada relationship in terms which must have been strikingly welcome to American ears. Some idea of the esteem which the president enjoyed in Canada, Diefenbaker said at lunch, could be gained from the answer given by a Canadian high school student who, on being asked to name the governor-general of Canada, promptly replied: 'General Eisenhower.' One had to hear it to be sure that he meant nothing but a friendly tribute to Ike.

It was a relaxed and nostalgic occasion, yet one made bittersweet for Diefenbaker by his conviction that with Eisenhower's departure he was losing a colleague of his own generation, a man he could trust and rely on to be understanding when problems arose which defied solutions at lower levels. With Eisenhower at the White House, too, Diefenbaker believed he had a source of information on the global game which would never be matched. All these things were true, and they sharpened Diefenbaker's sense of the loneliness of his own high office.

After his return to Ottawa, and before President Kennedy's inaugural address three days later, Diefenbaker referred frequently to the theme of the presidential transition. He harped on the candour and friendliness of Ike. He recounted unguarded confidences bestowed in their last private conversation – Ike's startling remark on the futility of limiting the spread of nuclear weapons; his disparaging comment about the 'gimme, gimme' demeanour of the developing nations; and his parting respect for Nikita Khrushchev, who had talked tough in order to retain leadership of the communist world over China, but who was nevertheless essential to the preservation of world peace. Not that Diefenbaker exaggerated the significance of these utterances. But to have the kind of relationship which permitted the blowing off of presidential steam – that was rare, and Diefenbaker knew it would not recur. Diefenbaker's sentiments are reflected in a 'Dear Ike' letter he sent to Eisenhower on 26 February:

It was kind of you to write me just before relinquishing the Presidency. The many evidences of your friendship to me will always be amongst the happiest of my memories. I felt that we were friends – and as friends could speak with frankness regarding the problems of our two countries. Indeed, whenever matters of disagreement, actual or potential, were brought to your attention they were acted upon by you to the last extent possible.

   Now that you are a private citizen you can look back with a sure knowledge that history will record your devotion to peace and to the raising of standards among people everywhere and that you discharged your responsibilities in the highest traditions of the Presidency, and in keeping with the magnificent leadership given by you as leader in wartime of the Allied Forces.

   Olive joins with me in wishing Mrs. Eisenhower and you many, many years of health and happiness.

THE NEW REGIME BEGINS

My diary entry on 18 January records that Diefenbaker 'has formed an irrational prejudice against Kennedy and Rusk which could be a serious portent.' There had been storm signals. Not only had they both failed to answer messages of goodwill but Rusk had remarked to Arnold Heeney, the Canadian ambassador in Washington, that he knew Canada quite well, having been on fishing trips there two or three times. Diefenbaker allowed this to infuriate him: 'Is that all he thinks we are good for?' He also bridled at Rusk's comment, again to Heeney, that the United States had to be careful about its special relationship with Canada so as not to let it affect relations with the other allies. In my diary on 19 January, I wrote: 'P.M. very conscious of this [the absence of a close relationship with the new administration] and apprehensive, and seems to be almost relishing the more pessimistic omens.' Canadian-American relations had been difficult enough in 1960. Were they going to get even worse in 1961?

   A sign of a possible shift in the prime minister's attitude came on 28 January. The occasion was Kennedy's order to US military leaders to keep quiet on policy matters. In Ottawa, Diefenbaker spoke approvingly of this, noting sardonically that his defence minister, Douglas Harkness, had publicly urged reserve officers to combat pacifism. Three days later the prime minister again remarked on Kennedy's 'muzzling of the generals,' but then found fault with Kennedy's State of the Union message which was being acclaimed by the press. He pointed to the president's reference to the Western Hemisphere without allusion to Canada, and he allowed himself an unseemly mutter that Prime Minister Nehru had been singled out for special tribute in the company of Churchill and de Gaulle.

It had not been Diefenbaker's intention to precipitate a meeting with Kennedy. He was facing a crowded calendar for the next three months and would have been content if his first meeting with the president had been delayed until May or even June. But on 2 February, a report from London caused him to change his mind: Macmillan would be visiting Kennedy early in April. On the spur of the moment, Diefenbaker told the House of Commons that Macmillan was always welcome in Canada. And although there had been no prior contact with Washington, he went on to say that he thought it would be beneficial to the Commonwealth Prime Ministers' Conference if it were possible for him to consult with the president before meetings began in early March. In this statement, he not only confirmed the report of Macmillan's visit to Washington before the news was confirmed by the White House, but he also invited himself to Washington. There was some tut-tutting among the bureaucrats, but Diefenbaker was unrepentant. He wanted External Affairs to explore the possibility of an informal meeting with the president. A meeting lasting two hours would be sufficient.

This unexpected instruction was telephoned by Ed Ritchie to Arnold Heeney, who also had news to convey. He told Ritchie that it had just been announced in Washington that Prime Minister Menzies of Australia would be visiting Kennedy from 22 to 24 February. The same evening, I took this news to the prime minister at 24 Sussex Drive. Diefenbaker at once said that this clinched it; it would not be right for Menzies to be Kennedy's first Commonwealth visitor. For purposes of the Commonwealth conference, in any event, he wanted to hear directly the president's thinking on major international issues. He said he wanted also to use the opportunity to sound out the president on Canada-US questions, especially NORAD and nuclear weapons policy.

For Heeney in Washington, it as one of those episodes designed to test an ambassador's influence and access. Hardly a head of government anywhere had not been trying for weeks to engineer a visit to the new president. It said a great deal for Heeney, and for the groundwork laid by Merchant, still undersecretary of state for political affairs in the State Department, that within three days of the first approach, Heeney was able to report that the president would be pleased to welcome the prime minister at an early date to be agreed. When it was confirmed for 20 February, Diefenbaker spoke admiringly of Heeney, managing at the same time to make it clear that the outcome was no more than was to be expected.

ENCOUNTER IN WASHINGTON

In the brief period available before the visit to Washington, preparations for the prime minister's conversation with Kennedy had to compete with a variety of other preoccupations. Diefenbaker was worried about the approaching meeting of Commonwealth prime ministers in London, where the issue of South Africa's membership would be coming to a head. Plans for official visits to Northern Ireland and to Ireland involved much consultation with individuals and organizations outside government circles, and Diefenbaker insisted on being consulted on every detail of the programs. Events in the Congo, Laos, and Cuba engaged his attention as well, and what was more immediately serious, a commitment to speak at Fort William on the weekend before the Washington visit prevented him from concentrating on his briefing papers until the last moment.

As was so often the case with Diefenbaker, the selection of those to travel and those to attend meetings had burned up much nervous energy before the final choices were made. At first the prime minister had proposed not to take Howard Green but to invite a minister without responsibilities or experience in foreign affairs. Eventually logic prevailed, after some discreet prompting. Green and Heeney attended the main meeting with the president, who had Rusk and Merchant with him. The talks began at noon in the Oval Room at the White House.

Considering all his other preoccupations, the prime minister made effective use of his time with the president. Bryce had supplied him with special notes on the Canadian economic outlook and on the current state of discussions on nuclear weapons policy. During the flight to Washington, Green spent twenty minutes making sure that the prime minister was fully briefed on disarmament issues, including the importance of avoiding nuclear commitments while Canada was actively involved in promoting disarmament measures at the United Nations. External Affairs had prepared notes on all the major international issues and on a list of bilateral problems which might arise.

Diefenbaker followed his normal course and concentrated on his political bread and butter. He saw the practical value of explaining to the president the economic measures the Canadian government had recently taken to help reverse Canada's adverse trade balance with the United States. These measures, he said, were not anti-American; the government had found them to be necessary for the protection of Canadian interests and independence of action. He spoke also of US investment which had been welcomed in Canada but had now grown, especially in the oil, gas, mining, and manufacturing sectors, to the point where it was causing a great deal of concern among Canadians. He commented approvingly on the emphasis which the president had been giving publicly to liberal commercial policies. Canada, like the United States, was subject to strong protectionist pressures. The government was hoping to bring about increases in industrial production and to alleviate the unemployment situation without having to take measures contrary to its international trade obligations.

To these statements of the Canadian government's approach, the president's response was sympathetic in tone. In dealing with one particular case – in which US Foreign Assets Control regulations were preventing Imperial Oil of Canada from supplying bunker oil for ships chartered to carry Canadian wheat from Vancouver to Mainland China – the president showed a desire to cooperate. The solutions he offered, however, did not satisfy Diefenbaker, who stuck to his refusal to agree to anything which might imply US control of a Canadian company. The issue was therefore not resolved on the spot but an atmosphere had been created which led to a mutually acceptable outcome of such problems.

Diefenbaker took occasion to test the waters on the new administration's attitude regarding the recognition of Mainland China and the representation of China in the United Nations. The president, while not as rigidly opposed as Eisenhower had been, seemed nevertheless convinced of the Peking government's 'deep belligerency.' Diefenbaker, while agreeing that Peking was in an intransigent mood, said that it was Canadian policy to trade with communist nations except in strategic goods. In the case of Cuba, Canada's trade had not increased since the imposition of the US embargo and was still below the value of US exports (medical supplies and the like), permitted under the terms of the embargo.

The prime minister was aware that Kennedy and his senior advisers would be expecting to have an authoritative explanation of Canadian policy on nuclear weapons. He began by assuring the president that 'Canada will not accept a policy which will lay upon the United States a responsibility which we should carry ourselves.' Canada did not intend to adopt a mere 'bird-watching' role, he said, in an obvious allusion to a recent Pearson statement on Canada's role in NORAD. As yet, he maintained, no final decision had been taken on the equipping of Canadian forces with nuclear weapons or on the storage of such weapons for the use of US forces at bases in Canada.[3] Having explained his view of the status quo, the prime minister went on to say that Canada's position would in part be dependent upon the actions of the United States in cooperation with Canada, for example, in the sharing of defence production. Decisions regarding the acquisition of nuclear weapons (for Canadian forces) or storage (for United States forces) would also depend on progress in disarmament.[4] Nevertheless, the Canadian government wished to be in a position to take action should conditions make it necessary. He proposed, therefore, that detailed arrangements be worked out on the various aspects of Canadian-American relations in the nuclear weapons field and embodied in agreements based on joint Canada-US control over custody and use of the weapons. President Kennedy, responding, agreed to the prime minister's approach and suggested that the formula employed in nuclear weapon arrangements with the United Kingdom (the 'double key') might provide a useful pattern.

This informal agreement, which was not recorded in detail at the meeting with Kennedy, suited Diefenbaker's purposes very well. It combined the course of action advocated by Bryce with the cautionary advice of Green, and it committed the Canadian government only to further negotiations with the Americans. The Canadian government's insistence on being a joint participant in nuclear affairs had been plainly stated. No agreements would be signed 'while disarmament was being pressed forward but all the preliminaries would be completed so that there would be no hold-up should the need arise'; and the Canadian government did 'not intend to enter into any of these agreements or arrangements piecemeal – the whole thing is a package.'[5]

The prime minister had won himself some time but the agreement was nevertheless a mixed blessing. Its significance as a step in Canada-US relations was to build up in American eyes the sense of a Canadian commitment to accept nuclear weapons. In this way, the meeting of 20 February contributed to the feelings of irritation and grievance which were accumulating in Washington.

No such thoughts, however, invaded the prime minister's satisfaction. He had been warmly received in the Kennedy White House and had had the satisfaction of an entirely private talk with the president. Afterwards, riding in Heeney's car to the airport, he said he thought he had established a 'very good' relationship with Kennedy. The president had clearly touched the political chord in Diefenbaker. 'Would I be right in thinking that the United States is not unhelpful to you for political purposes up in Canada?' the president inquired, to which Diefenbaker had said, 'That would be a not inaccurate conclusion.' He went on to describe him as having 'great capacity, a far-sighted judgment on international affairs, and an attractive human quality in private exchanges.' Rusk, too, he said, had 'very much impressed' him.

On the return flight to Ottawa, the prime minister was determined to arrive in time to report to the House of Commons before the end of the afternoon sitting at 6 PM. The notes for his statement were still being typed as we landed at Uplands Airport. He told an attentive House that he and the secretary of state for external affairs had found an 'attitude of the utmost friendliness' on the part of the president and Rusk. Kennedy had revealed a desire to preserve 'the distinctive quality of the Canada-US partnership, with each nation discharging its responsibility towards the attainment of the common purpose and without the sacrifice of sovereignty by either country.' Ending with a further tribute to the president, Diefenbaker confessed that their first meeting had been a 'revealing and exhilarating experience.' The president and Mrs Kennedy had accepted an invitation to visit Canada. A date would soon be set.

As this long day ended and he was leaving his office late that evening, the prime minister, in a moment of weary pride, said that he thought he had done a good day's work. It seemed a reasonable claim. Certainly the first encounter with President Kennedy had raised his hopes that a good working relationship would not be so hard to establish as he had feared.

18

South Africa Leaves
the Commonwealth

Let us turn now to examine Diefenbaker's role in the outcome of the issue of South African membership of the Commonwealth. In chapter 13 we left him returning from London, having played a modest role at the 1960 meeting of the Commonwealth prime ministers. He had been satisfied with the outcome, which had affirmed the multiracial character of the Commonwealth and left the door open, as he saw it, for South Africa to retain its membership if it chose to make even minor concessions to the unanimous opinion of its partners. Diefenbaker derived satisfaction from having kept his options open. His stand against apartheid was, after all, authenticated by his own record in matters of human rights. Yet he remained unwilling to be singly responsible for denying consent for South Africa's continued membership of the Commonwealth after its anticipated assumption of republican statehood. He knew very well that his position would be crucial at the next meeting. He correctly anticipated pressure from different quarters, both at home and in the Commonwealth. From the end of the 1960 meeting to the opening of the final round in London in March 1961, his consistent aim was to maintain his freedom of manoeuvre and decision. This proved to be a wise tactic, although it involved a lot of zig-zagging along the way.

By the end of 1960 Diefenbaker had taken a series of positions which at first reflected a hardening of his stand against South Africa's readmission. In August he had told the South African representative in Ottawa that his government's view that retaining Commonwealth membership was a mere formality was 'founded on blind optimism.' In September, reacting angrily to views expressed by Lord Home, the foreign secretary, that Britain would welcome South Africa as a republican member, Diefenbaker told me that if there were a vote in the next meeting of prime ministers, Canada would have no choice but to oppose South

Africa's membership after the referendum, which was to be held early in October.[1] On advice of the undersecretary, he addressed messages to Macmillan and other prime ministers suggesting that all should withhold public comment on the referendum's result, and this approach was generally accepted. British ministers were trying out various procedural gambits clearly designed to forestall a showdown. On 3 November Diefenbaker talked freely about the issue. I wrote to the undersecretary: 'He did not see how he could support South Africa's readmission if [the South African] government continued to refuse to pay even lip service to the idea of racial equality. He recognized that major concessions were not possible but said that public opinion in Canada was so strong ... that unless the South Africans made some move, e.g. in the direction of African representation in parliament, he could not possibly afford to adopt at the next meeting an attitude as tolerant of South Africa as he had before and during the last meeting.'[2] He wanted these views conveyed to the British and South African authorities and asked for a canvass of the positions of other Commonwealth governments.

These steps were on the point of being taken when the prime minister again intervened and asked for a personal message to be drafted for him to send to Macmillan. It was to follow the line he had given previously but more emphatically, so that Macmillan personally would be in no doubt of what to expect from Canada. Here Diefenbaker revealed more pointedly than before his sensitivity to supposed slights from Macmillan. It was distressingly clear that he felt ignored or in some way downgraded by the British prime minister and by Menzies of Australia whom, to quote my diary of 4 November, Diefenbaker 'dislikes intensely, as Menzies has created ... the impression that he is the old pro whose savvy puts him in the position of helping Harold Macmillan solve the thorniest problems.'

Diefenbaker said he wanted his message to go directly to Macmillan and not to pass through officials. I said that this would be next to impossible because Macmillan worked very closely with his officials. He resisted this suggestion and said he had secrets with Macmillan which 'you people' don't know about. Realizing that he wanted to bypass senior officials in External Affairs, I suggested that the message be sent through George Drew, the Canadian high commissioner in London, with explicit directions as to delivery. He agreed to this, and when the message had gone there was the usual problem of how to let Howard Green know what had transpired. It was not a small matter because Green had been objecting that he was not being kept fully in the picture on the prime minister's speeches and other activities in foreign policy. As usual Ross Campbell explained the situation to the minister, who knew better than to lose sleep over it.

Diefenbaker's annoyance with Macmillan and the British government spilled

175

over again on 16 November when he told the British high commissioner, Joe Garner, that he felt let down by Britain on South Africa. Macmillan himself appeared to be backing away from his 'wind of change' speech.[3] The British government had been shifting its ground from the agreed understanding at the last meeting of prime ministers that South Africa's request for continuing membership would be the occasion for a full debate on its qualifications for Commonwealth membership. They were now pretending that consent to South Africa's request should be a formality, on the ground that constitutional changes had previously been treated as an internal matter.

Garner was alarmed at Diefenbaker's mood and advised Macmillan to send a personal reply to Diefenbaker's message which by now would have reached 10 Downing Street. Within a day Diefenbaker received a telephone call and then a lengthy telegram from Macmillan who, as we know from his own memoirs, was disturbed by his understanding of Diefenbaker's position.[4] The Canadian prime minister was taking a 'holier than thou' attitude which could cause 'infinite trouble.' In his telegram Macmillan appealed in emotional terms to Diefenbaker's sentimental attachment to the Commonwealth, and pleaded with him not to take a definite position against South Africa's continued membership before the next meeting, which was now scheduled for early in March 1961. He made a strong argument for playing down the significance of the South African application for readmission.

It was a Sunday and I took the message to Diefenbaker at his residence. He was in a jovial, playful mood, and made a mini-performance of reading the message aloud to an audience of his wife and me. At the end of the rendition – he was not good at imitating an English accent – he switched to a serious tone and said that the message did not change his thinking. I knew, however, that he would read it again carefully and that while he would not be persuaded by Macmillan's argument, the message had served a purpose by forecasting what Diefenbaker would be up against at the meeting in March. He realized that the further the British government moved towards avoiding the issue of racial relations, the more exposed his position would be. He fretted about how to play his cards, his political instincts telling him to keep his own counsel until the moment for decision was at hand. It was a striking example of the difference between his approach and that of St Laurent and Pearson. They would have been scouting for common ground with other governments, perhaps New Zealand and India, searching for compromises that might become solutions. Diefenbaker was certainly interested in what others were thinking and planning, but the ambiguity in his own thinking and his concern to avoid political trouble at home deterred him from active consultation. Who knows whether the outcome would have been different if he had done otherwise?

As the year ended there was no sign that the prime minister was closer to deciding what his tactics should be. If anything he seemed particularly determined to avoid being responsible for South Africa's expulsion, and this tendency was reinforced by a meeting he held on 20 December with Sir de Villiers Graaff, the leader of the United party, the main opposition party in the South African parliament. 'A very thoughtful man,' was Diefenbaker's judgment, given in a memorandum in which he recorded the arguments de Villiers Graaff had raised against a failure by the Commonwealth to accept South Africa's application for continuing membership.[5]

My own concern at this time was that in the policy papers being prepared by External Affairs, public expectations were not being considered. In commenting on one paper on 27 December I wrote: 'The Canadian Government in particular is in an exposed position because of the publicity given to the Bill of Rights and because of the impression created by the Prime Minister's public statements that Canada is disinclined to be accommodating to an unrepentant South Africa ... South Africa's change of regime provides an opportunity ... for the members of the Commonwealth to rid themselves ... of one of their number whose policies represent, as you say, a divisive force within the association and invite discredit from without.' In giving these views, I probably went beyond my proper mandate. I felt justified in doing so because I was sure that the prime minister would want to have the department's frank views and advice on all sides of the issue. The paper was modified but it ended without making recommendations. The different levels in the department were having as much trouble in agreeing on what to submit to the prime minister as he was in deciding what to do.

I had hoped that he might be sufficiently moved by the paper to reach a definite view of his own, but it was an unrealistic thought. Instead, he retreated from the strong views he had been expressing for some months. He told me on 4 January, for the department's information, that his position was that he would not take the initiative in any attempt to force South Africa out. He said he was attracted by the idea of a further postponement with a view to placing the onus on South Africa either to make concessions or withdraw from the Commonwealth. Postponement, he thought, might help Sir de Villiers Graaff's United party to regain power at the next election and, at the same time, increase the pressure on South Africa to modify its racial policies. All his emotional reactions, except regarding racial policy, were favourable to keeping South Africa in the Commonwealth, he said, giving as examples South Africa's wartime record and its historical connection with other Commonwealth countries. If, however, after a further postponement, there was still no improvement as far as racial policy was concerned and if the United party were again defeated in the next election, the Nationalist government would have to pay the price for its obduracy.

177

In the same conversation the prime minister acknowledged that some of his previous statements, taken together with the Bill of Rights, might have led people in Canada and abroad to expect Canada to advocate or at least support a move to exclude South Africa from the Commonwealth. He did not, however, believe that comments along that line would be difficult to deal with. He said he was playing with the idea of having a resolution introduced in the House of Commons for the purpose of testing parliamentary opinion and, in particular, finding out how far the opposition parties were prepared to go.

Soon after Diefenbaker returned from his holiday in Jamaica in January, a new paper was sent forward from the department with Howard Green commenting that he found it 'excellent.'[6] It reviewed the arguments both ways and examined the implications of the various approaches that were thought to be feasible, bearing in mind the prime minister's latest views. The reasoning came down on the conservative side. It recommended that South Africa stay in the Commonwealth for the present; and it rejected the idea of a statement of Commonwealth principles, mainly on the ground that it might lead to complications with a number of members whose domestic policies might not pass the test. Instead, the paper favoured including a passage on racial equality in the communiqué to be issued by the prime ministers' meeting, even though it was recognized that to obtain unanimity on such a statement would be difficult in the extreme. It was thought possible that this process might cause South Africa to leave of its own accord, but it was also recognized that some member governments would not be satisfied with the kind of general statement which would be forthcoming. Nevertheless, 'the strength of opposition in the Commonwealth to racial discrimination' would be emphasized, and it would be made 'clear that tolerance alone could not be stretched indefinitely to bridge a wide gap in fundamental principles.'

The prime minister's reaction to the new paper was appreciative, but he was clearly drifting in response to the pressures of the moment. He said towards the end of January that he wished the Canadian newspapers would not press, as the *Toronto Telegram* and the *Globe and Mail* had done, for South Africa's exclusion.

At the beginning of February, Bryce re-entered the affair. In the summer of 1960 he had participated in a special meeting of senior Commonwealth officials held in the United Kingdom. The meeting had been called by Sir Norman Brook, the secretary to the United Kingdom cabinet, for the purpose of discussing the future of Commonwealth prime ministers' conferences as the number of member countries grew. Present with Brook and Bryce were a representative from each of India and Ghana as well as from Australia and New Zealand.

At this meeting Bryce had drawn out the views of the Ghanaian and Indian officials with regard to South Africa. They took the position that the presence of South Africa would deter other African and Asian countries from joining the

Commonwealth. They made it clear at the same time that existing members from Africa and Asia would seriously oppose South Africa's continuing membership. When Brook heard these remarks he was sufficiently disturbed to report them to Macmillan, who then dispatched a ministerial envoy around Africa and Asia to take soundings. Bryce's conclusion from this meeting was that the continued presence of South Africa would end the attractions and usefulness of the Commonwealth as an institution for its non-white members.[7]

On the basis of this experience, Bryce remained as convinced as ever that Canada should take the lead in denying readmission to South Africa. A refusal to admit South Africa would increase the value of the Commonwealth as a bridge between white and non-white nations, he argued, in a memorandum commenting on the External Affairs paper.[8] At the same time he gave his views to Diefenbaker, who did not commit himself but asked if Bryce thought it wise to have a parliamentary resolution. Bryce advised him against that step on the ground that the prime minister should go to London as free of prior commitments as possible. Diefenbaker would have to take most of the responsibility on himself for the government's position.

Throughout the month of February, Diefenbaker was the focus of increasing pressures from all parts of the spectrum. For the first time in many months he consulted his colleagues in the cabinet, where opinion was sharply divided. Howard Green was among those who argued against Canada's taking the lead to exclude South Africa.[9] To do so would not help the African population and would be contrary to the wishes of the English-speaking whites. He thought that the prime minister need go no further than to condemn apartheid and announce that Canada would not support South Africa in its recently declared candidacy for election to the UN Security Council. South Africa might well decide to leave of its own accord in the face of these statements, Green thought, with support from others. The opposite point of view – that South Africa's exclusion might in fact strengthen the Commonwealth as a multiracial association – was also strongly advocated. Both the prime minister's personal record as a proponent of civil rights and his sponsorship of the Bill of Rights were held to be important arguments against agreeing to South Africa's continued membership.

While the Department of External Affairs worked away to produce texts of statements for all conceivable contingencies at the meeting, George Drew maintained a steady flow of letters and telephone calls to the prime minister. Few of these were routed through the department, but Diefenbaker often passed them on to Bryce or me, and it was easy to see what direction Drew's advice was taking. Essentially, he was ensuring that the prime minister was fully aware of the British arguments against making an issue of the racial question. He was also promoting an idea that consideration of the racial issue could justifiably be postponed, on the ground that South Africa would not assume its republican status until 31 May and that its application for consent was therefore premature. Drew's persistence, combined with the superficial attractions of a procedural move that might avoid a showdown at the conference, had intermittent influence on Diefenbaker, as did signs, also conveyed by Drew, that some other non-white Commonwealth prime ministers would not force the basic issue and were looking for a lead from Canada.

The flow of advice from Drew, the consistent view of Bryce that Canada should instead take the lead against South Africa's continuing membership, the division of views in the cabinet, the continued striving of External Affairs to find a compromise position – these were the sounds he heard all through February. He was the recipient too of a plea, one might almost say a warning, from the chief minister of Tanganyika, Julius Nyerere: 'And how can Canada, or any other Commonwealth country which believes in justice and human rights, vote for the inclusion of South Africa ... as long as South Africa allows herself to be ruled by men whose policies are an outrage to such beliefs? A vote in favour of South Africa ... could logically be interpreted as a vote against the future membership of countries such as Tanganyika whose political philosophy condemns any form of racial discrimination as evil.'[10] Diefenbaker objected to the thought of 'votes' in the Commonwealth context, but he did not need to be advised on the significance of Nyerere's appeal. He was similarly impressed by a conversation with the distinguished economist, Barbara Ward, who warned him that the non-white members of the Commonwealth would shortly afterwards withdraw if South Africa were to continue as a member. She also favoured a declaration of principles.

THE MEETING AND THE OUTCOME

Before he left Ottawa on 3 March, a cabinet meeting gave him, in effect, freedom to follow the course he judged wisest at the conference. As he had in May 1960, he left for London without a clear sense of the best tactics to follow. His first aim, he told me late in February, would be to seek some concession from South Africa. If none were possible, he favoured postponement of the issue or some other way of avoiding an open break. He was not in a crusading mood, therefore, but at least he had contained and shielded his hesitations, and he arrived in London without having made specific commitments. He was not looking for the role of leader, but he was in a position to play an influential part.

Diefenbaker had brought with him two of his cabinet colleagues, Davie Fulton, the minister of justice, and Noel Dorion, the secretary of state. In the latter case, Diefenbaker had intended the experience to be educational, but Dorion, whose command of English was limited, found it uncomfortable and soon detached himself from the proceedings. Fulton was included only at the last moment because of his contribution, I understood, to the discussions in the cabinet.[12] He had an impressive grasp of the issues and he accompanied Diefenbaker to all the significant meetings on the South African item. Howard Green remained in Ottawa as acting prime minister and Diefenbaker kept in touch with him by phone during the conference, as he felt it necessary to monitor his colleagues' reaction to press reports and public opinion about the proceedings. In London, in addition to the ministers, George Drew was of course much in evidence, and the prime minister gave him full opportunity to offer advice. Bob Bryce was the senior official adviser, assisted by Geoff Murray of External Affairs and myself.

Bryce had preceded Diefenbaker to London and had sized up the situation by the time the prime minister reached London after brief visits to Belfast and Dublin. It was Bryce's view after talking to other delegations that the conference would be faced with a straight question of whether or not to consent to South Africa's continuing in the Commonwealth. It was also Bryce's view that unless something was done by Diefenbaker or others, Diefenbaker would have no choice but to refuse consent.

From Drew in London, however, directly opposite tactical advice had reached the prime minister in the week before the meeting. In a letter written on 24 February, the high commissioner argued strenuously for, as he described it, 'finding some device by which a clash with South Africa at this time may be avoided.'[13] Using arguments which would later be made by prime ministers Macmillan, Menzies, and Verwoerd, Drew urged that a clear distinction should be made between South Africa's status as a republic and the question of apartheid. The latter question had no bearing, he maintained, on whether South Africa continued as a Commonwealth member, so long as they expressed their desire to do so. South Africa should, therefore, be allowed to continue as a member for the time being and a committee of officials should be asked to formulate the conditions of membership, which could then be recommended to and considered by a later conference of prime ministers. At the time of Diefenbaker's arrival in London, he was undoubtedly much influenced by this view, and by Drew's further advice that since South Africa had not yet become a republic, it would be premature to make a decision on its status in the Commonwealth.

Diefenbaker's built-in tendency to favour postponement in contentious situations had been aroused by Drew's advice, but he was still not ready to declare his final position. I do not think that at that moment he even knew what it would be. He was still hoping for a miracle, in the form of a small but symbolic concession by Verwoerd, the South African prime minister. The first three days of the conference were devoted to other subjects, and, while Diefenbaker was taking part in those discussions, Bryce was to consider alternative solutions that might obviate the need for a straight refusal of consent to South Africa's request.

It was not a task that Bryce enjoyed, since he saw the exclusion of South Africa as the best outcome and believed that the 1960 communiqué had foreshadowed a clear-cut decision in response to South Africa's request. Moreover, Bryce, still convinced that the Commonwealth would be much more useful without South Africa, approached the senior South African official and told him so. He explained that he was not making moral judgments, but that the non-white countries regarded South Africa as poison and that it would be best from all points of view for South Africa to withdraw. But while the South Africans pondered this candid advice, Diefenbaker had to be provided with some alternative which he could consider and perhaps try out on Macmillan at Chequers, the British prime minister's country residence, on 10 and 11 March.

The several 'contingency' statements which had been prepared by External Affairs were now reviewed. They had been studied by the prime minister before departure from Ottawa, and one of them, which he had labelled as a 'Yes' version to South Africa's application, had then appealed to him. Now that he was looking for a formula that would postpone the South African issue, this version could be adapted and put forward as an alternative solution. Much against Bryce's and my personal inclination, the alternative we put forward combined consent to South Africa's continuing in the Commonwealth with an announcement that a statement of Commonwealth principles would be formulated at a subsequent meeting of prime ministers. Bryce's memorandum made clear his doubts about the wisdom of the formula, but added: 'It could be said, though perhaps not in the agreed statement, that the action in regard to South Africa made necessary a declaration of principles to ensure that the views of the members of the Commonwealth were not misinterpreted as an implication of their granting consent to the continued membership of South Africa.' Such a statement would apply mainly to the question of discrimination on the basis of race and colour, since to expand the terms might well make it unacceptable to various members.

Diefenbaker was quite taken with the new formula. All these ideas were discussed at length within the delegation before the prime minister took them with him to Chequers. Bryce had advised against trying to drum up support until the views of Macmillan, as chairman, were known. Exactly what Diefenbaker said to Macmillan was not entirely clear. On returning to London, however, Diefenbaker, again pressed by Drew and now Dorion, was still inclined to advance some variant of the new formula when the South Africa item was taken up on the Monday. Notes for a statement to this effect were prepared on the 12th. 'Not much disposition to face the issue,' I wrote in my diary.

A visit that afternoon from R.K. Nehru, secretary-general of the Indian Ministry of External Affairs, brought the first firm information on the position Prime Minister Nehru would take. It was immediately clear that India would take a strong stand against South Africa's remaining in the Commonwealth. For an unrealistic, fleeting moment as R.K. Nehru talked, it seemed as though Diefenbaker might be moved to join with India, but it was not to be. He asked several questions and promised to look at an *Economist* article which Nehru had said was close to Indian thinking. But he gave it as his personal view that it was not yet necessary to take a final decision on South Africa's membership. He mentioned the idea that a statement condemning apartheid might be made in the final communiqué of the meeting, and speculated that South Africa would probably withdraw from the meeting and also from the Commonwealth without direct action being necessary. Perhaps this would lead to increasing domestic pressure on the Verwoerd government and to its eventual downfall.

When R.K. Nehru had departed, there was another session in Diefenbaker's room. Bryce told him that he had three choices: to go along with Macmillan in agreeing to South Africa's continuing membership; to join Nehru in refusing consent; or to work for postponing the issue. Diefenbaker recounted a conversation with Green on opinion in the cabinet in Ottawa. The cabinet was 'foursquare against apartheid,' there was considerable support for postponement, but a negative reaction to the idea of a declaration of 'rights.' Diefenbaker thought that the cabinet had misunderstood the scope of the declaration he had in mind. It was focused mainly on equality of race and was not meant to be comparable, as some ministers might have imagined, to the Canadian Bill of Rights.

Diefenbaker chose to be accompanied by Davie Fulton to the three days of debate on the South African issue, each prime minister being allowed one colleague.[14] Macmillan had made it known that on the first day, 13th March, no decisions would be taken; there would simply be an exchange of views. The prime ministers all made opening statements, and at the end of the day, two points stood out. South Africa's Verwoerd was not in a conciliatory mood, and Macmillan's plans for the conduct and outcome of the debate were in need of amendment. The chances of mobilizing collective consent to South Africa's continuing membership, which the United Kingdom government had apparently thought might be achieved in conjunction with an assertion of the Commonwealth's belief in racial equality, had disappeared entirely by the end of the day. Having listened to the debate, Macmillan himself declared that the meeting could not avoid what he called the duty to declare principles on which the Commonwealth association was based. The remainder of the meeting was devoted to discussion of how such principles might be formulated, and, for Verwoerd, whether South Africa could accept a formulation in terms that would satisfy all the other prime ministers.

In his only major intervention of that first day, Diefenbaker, speaking second after Nehru, began with conciliatory references to South Africa's part in the history of the Commonwealth. He then denounced apartheid and declared that in matters of racial policy the Commonwealth could not accept a lesser commitment than the United Nations imposed on its membership. In present circumstances, the acceptance of South Africa's request 'would be construed as approval of, or at least acquiescence in, South Africa's racial policy. This could not but damage the future value of the Commonwealth association and assist communist propaganda in Africa and elsewhere.' He went on to argue, however, that it would be premature and unwise to decide at this meeting what reply should be given to South Africa's request. Action should be postponed until South Africa's course was finally determined by new legislation establishing a republic. Meanwhile, steps should be taken to draft a declaration of principles to which Commonwealth members should subscribe, for consideration at the next prime ministers' meeting.

This suggestion received very little support, no doubt because the likelihood of any change of heart on South Africa's part was considered remote and because, as Menzies of Australia said, the time for decision had surely arrived. But Diefenbaker had said enough at this conference and the last to establish himself as a champion of racial equality. Those prime ministers who followed him – Nkrumah of Ghana, Tunku Abdul Rahman of Malaya, Ayub Khan of Pakistan, Mrs Bandaranaike of Ceylon, and Abubakar of Nigeria – may have wondered why the Canadian wanted another postponement. They could hardly have doubted, however, that he was close to them on the essential points – that the Commonwealth must take an unmistakeable stand on the principle of racial equality, and that in the absence of a change in South Africa's racial policies, collective consent to its continuation as a member of the Commonwealth would be interpreted as condoning apartheid. Already, at the end of the first day, Diefenbaker, while not seeming or aspiring to form a coalition with his non-white colleagues, had drawn apart from Macmillan, Menzies, and Holyoake of New Zealand and, of course, Verwoerd.

On the second morning Macmillan tabled a draft communiqué which served as the focus of discussion through most of the day. It dealt separately with the constitutional aspect and the much more contentious issue of South Africa's racial policies. Verwoerd quickly objected to the wording on racial matters and was supported in part by Menzies of Australia, who found that the language amounted to an interference in South Africa's domestic jurisdiction. This provided the occasion for Diefenbaker's second of four main interventions. He disagreed with Menzies that the proposed declaration could be criticized as interference in domestic affairs. The racial policies of South Africa had such far-reaching effects that their impact was international rather than domestic. The draft declaration was not an invitation to South Africa to quit; it was merely a statement of principles.

Prime Minister Diefenbaker went on to state his belief in the necessity for the Commonwealth nations to declare and recognize the principle of non-discrimination on grounds of race or colour. All members of the Commonwealth, he emphasized, had subscribed to this in the UN Charter, and nothing less would be justified. There was no other principle which could unite the association. He appealed to Verwoerd to take some step towards alleviating a situation which was international in its consequences, perhaps by according some representation to disenfranchised people in South Africa.

In the afternoon of the second day, Macmillan brought forward further drafts – the first on racial and the second on constitutional matters – the burden of which was to say that while the Commonwealth leaders had no procedural objection to giving consent to South Africa's continuing membership, they could not refrain from expressing their own views on racial matters. Verwoerd again objected on the ground that the language went too far in prescribing rules to which member governments must subscribe. At this stage Diefenbaker read out the last paragraph of Macmillan's first draft which stated in effect that apartheid was inconsistent with the ideals of the Commonwealth and the United Nations. Verwoerd said he would not accept this statement in the communiqué. He was then invited to suggest his own wording. Again Diefenbaker, along with others, intervened to insist on the right of all the prime ministers to express their views on a matter of principle and to have this made public in the communiqué.

Although he stuck firmly to the right of the prime ministers to declare their support for the principle of racial equality, Diefenbaker was careful during these two days not to go too far. In telephone conversations with Green, he had been told that the cabinet was split about half and half on the advisablity of expelling South Africa, although unanimous in wanting apartheid condemned. On the second day, 14 March, he directed me to compile a quick survey of current Canadian editorial opinion. This I did by telephone with the aid of Ross Campbell in Green's office. Out of seventeen daily newspapers which had taken positions, nine favoured expulsion (assuming there would be no 'give' by South Africa), four advocated criticism of South Africa without expulsion, and four were broadly in favour of keeping South Africa in the Commonwealth.[15]

By this time, however, speculation about opinion back home had been overtaken by the momentum of the meeting. The second day ended without agreement, but I wrote in my diary that 'everyone is looking for a formula to prevent extreme action.' By this cryptic sentence, I must have meant that the mood did not favour an active measure to *expel* South Africa. I also wrote, however, that

'South Africa is being confronted with a take-it-or-leave-it proposition.' Day three would presumably produce South Africa's response.

On the third morning Macmillan reported to the meeting that Verwoerd had withdrawn his objections to the second of Macmillan's drafts on the understanding that he would have the right to state his own views in a more extended form. This compromise collapsed, however, when Diefenbaker, Nehru, and others felt that too much emphasis was being given to Verwoerd's views. Faced with these objections and with warnings from Nkrumah and Abubakar as to future trouble should South Africa remain in the Commonwealth, Verwoerd asked for a recess. Then, in the late afternoon of the third day, he withdrew South Africa's request for continued membership.

REFLECTIONS ON DIEFENBAKER'S ROLE

Although Diefenbaker was the most sympathetic of the white prime ministers to the positions of the non-white, he can hardly be said to have played the leading role in the drama of South Africa's withdrawal from the Commonwealth. The dominant figures were Nehru and Macmillan, the former because he knew his objectives and pursued them with clarity and conviction, the latter for his adroit chairmanship in a series of exceedingly delicate situations. Nehru's biographer shows how, in 1960 and 1961, the South African question was colouring his attitude to the Commonwealth.[16] One of his criteria for regarding Commonwealth membership as worthwhile had been the lack of racial discrimination. By the time of the 1960 prime ministers' meeting he was saying publicly that the racial policies of South Africa could not be ignored, notwithstanding the convention that the domestic policies of Commonwealth members were not discussed at these meetings. Nehru was largely responsible for the reference to South Africa in the final communiqué in May 1960. In 1961, despite Macmillan's efforts, supported by Menzies, to find a compromise that would avoid South Africa's withdrawal, Nehru once more led the way. To quote again his biographer, 'the members from Asia and Africa, under Nehru's guidance and with the support of Canada, were not prepared to temporize.' This describes rather strangely the credit due to Diefenbaker, since he advocated temporizing on the first day of the debate, but it is also true that when that avenue was blocked, Diefenbaker did take the same position as Nehru. In doing so, Diefenbaker put his distinctive stamp on the final resolution of the issue. By his insistence on a statement that would clearly express the Commonwealth's refusal to tolerate the apartheid policies of South Africa, he prevented a split on racial lines and helped to precipitate South Africa's decision to withdraw its application for continued membership. This was a substantial contribution to the outcome, if not quite as dramatic or determining as has sometimes been attributed to Diefenbaker. He cannot, of course, be blamed for making the most of his part in the affair.

Another significant outcome of the 1961 meeting concerned the relationship between Diefenbaker and Macmillan. For the United Kingdom government, the South African decision to withdraw was clearly a diplomatic setback. It had its roots in either a miscalculation of the strength of feeling in the Commonwealth against South Africa's policies or in a bold gamble that just did not come off. At the start of the South Africa debate, Macmillan was describing the problem as primarily constitutional. Later, in the face of the debate, and in suggesting drafts of the final statement, he was to describe the constitutional issue as of minor importance compared to the racial question. It was of course not only Diefenbaker who was responsible for this rapid evolution in Macmillan's views. Indeed Macmillan does not, in his own account of the affair, give much prominence to Diefenbaker.[17] The Canadian prime minister, however, had throughout stood apart from the other 'old Commonwealth' leaders, especially Macmillan and Menzies. If ever a compromise had been conceivable, which is highly doubtful, the position taken by Diefenbaker in the latter stages of the debate ensured that it would not have survived. Apart from the significance, therefore, of Diefenbaker's role in the context of the South African question, it marks a further stage in the decline of his relations with both Macmillan and Menzies.

Diefenbaker had not previously met Verwoerd of South Africa, and their respective roles in the meeting kept them from fraternizing. It was a paradox that nothing had been more constant in Diefenbaker's approach than his search for a tolerable way of averting South Africa's withdrawal. Moreover, despite his aversion to the racial policies that Verwoerd represented, Diefenbaker had been personally impressed with the South African, and later often commented on the calm and dignity he had shown in the closing stages of the drama. None of this, of course, prevented Verwoerd and his delegation from regarding Diefenbaker as the incarnation of evil and hypocrisy.

Among the Asian and African leaders, none had relished taking the initiative towards a full-dress, formal expulsion of South Africa. Nor was the prospect of a division along racial lines pleasant for them to contemplate. The part played by Diefenbaker, therefore, was undoubtedly helpful to them, even if they were at one stage puzzled by his interest in postponing the issue until legislative procedures in South Africa had been completed. His clear recognition that the question of Commonwealth membership could not be divorced from the international implications of apartheid, and his insistence that non-discrimination in race, colour, and creed must be an essential principle of the association, brought him into alignment with the non-white leaders. Yet, as Fulton, with his first-hand experience of the meeting, has pointed out, the positions that Diefenbaker took were taken for his own reasons and not consciously to gather support from around the table.[18] Characteristically, he preferred to keep his choices unfettered until the time came to speak. That method had always served him in the past and he was too set in his ways to learn the secrets of lobbying, or to ally himself in advance with one or more colleagues. As a result, while he was on friendly enough terms with all, he never came close to being an 'insider' or a leader of any grouping. As always, his tactics were influenced by his judgment of what he could defend and justify on the home front. He left it to others to play statesman.

An overnight flight brought him to Ottawa in time to report to the House of Commons on 17 March. The first draft of his speech was put together between London and Gander, with a short and stimulating fuel stop at Keflavik where those of us who were still awake, not including the Diefenbakers, attended a reception in their honour given by the Icelandic government. With that to animate us, Geoff Murray and I, cheerfully assisted by Annette Walls, Bryce's secretary, had the draft ready for the prime minister when he surfaced full of energy at Gander. He had been concerned about the speech because, although he had no doubt that he had followed the right course in London, he was sensitive to the divisions in the cabinet and in the party caucus, and to possible negative reactions in some sections of the press. He worked on the speech himself from Gander to Ottawa and made it his own. In the event, he had no reason to be anxious. Both Pearson, for the Liberals, and Argue, for the NDP, spoke approvingly and understandingly of the final outcome, and Diefenbaker received from them and generally from the press well-deserved credit for his part.

In a letter written on 26 April to Bruce Williams, Canadian high commissioner in Ghana, I wrote: 'The reaction in Canada has been generally good, although there is some controversy over whether the Government should follow up by supporting such things as economic sanctions against South Africa. There is no sign at all that the Government is willing to do this. The Prime Minister's attitude is that we have gone far enough in showing what we think of South Africa's racial policy, and that economic sanctions, apart from being ineffectual, would be harmful to Canada since the trade balance is strongly favourable to us.' In the aftermath of the Commonwealth conference, the cabinet was indeed disinclined to alter Canadian policies towards South Africa. Howard Green went so far as to deplore the thought of 'reprisals' against South Africa.[19] As that country approached its republican status at the end of May, it was decided that no change would be made in Canadian policies on the export of arms, the existing preferential trade arrangements, or on immigration.[20] While not resisting these decisions, Diefenbaker was embarrassed by the publicity given to the government's intention on trade preferences.[21] He also complained that insufficient thought had been given within the government to some of the possible consequences of South Africa's withdrawal from the Commonwealth. What would Canada do, for example, if the South African government decided to facilitate the passage to Canada of blacks and coloureds, as a means of embarrassing the Canadian government?[22]

By and large, however, his mood was that the practical problems must be left to sort themselves out. The Commonwealth he had grown up with had now backed into history. The new, multiracial Commonwealth was free to grow into an association where whites and non-whites could meet and help each other in a better atmosphere. He was reflecting on the implications of what he had helped to bring about. But in explaining his part in the transition, he did not want it thought that he had taken pleasure in the process. For the present, there were limits to the changes he was ready to make in Canada's continuing relationship with a former and old Commonwealth partner. The necessary had been done. He had plenty of other anxieties to cope with.

19

Planning the Kennedy Visit

In a brief meeting with his immediate staff after returning from Washington on 20 February, Diefenbaker made certain that we all understood the importance he attached to the visit of President and Mrs Kennedy. He naturally wanted to capitalize on the promising start he had made with the president in Washington, and he relished the thought of the domestic impact of a successful visit, with all that intense television and press coverage in which he and his wife would share. There had been a lot of bad news: it was only human for him to savour the prospect of a big political dividend.

In the meantime his mind would be on many other things. On the night of his return from Washington, he received word that his mother had died. It was not unexpected – she was eighty-six and her health had been frail – but her passing had its effect on his strength and spirits. Although she had long ceased to be a source of advice to him, the strong sense of indebtedness and filial obligation survived. Elmer, his brother, would look after things in Saskatoon, but as he was in the habit of consulting John on virtually everything, the burdens on Canada's prime minister were increased at a time when he had already enough political worries. Unemployment figures were rising, a rail strike was threatening and the government was in the midst of a damaging public dispute with the governor of the Bank of Canada, James Coyne. Abroad, too, there was little comfort. He was anxious about us-Cuban relations. Conditions in the Congo and Laos were worrying. A forthcoming series of official visits to Ottawa made him wince when he saw them on his calendar.

EARLIER VISITORS

One visit which stands out in my memory was that of the foreign minister of

Yugoslavia, Koca Popovic, who came to Canada at the end of March. Because of vehement protests by groups of Yugoslav Canadians, Diefenbaker became very nervous about the domestic political effects of the visit. For a week it was a regular subject of debate between Diefenbaker and Green, who had approved the idea of inviting his counterpart from Yugoslavia. Diefenbaker originally threatened to cancel the visit, then said that it if took place he would refuse to receive him. The Yugoslavs said that Popovic would not come unless he could be received by the prime minister. Green dug his heels in, and eventually a most ungracious compromise was reached: the visiting minister was escorted from a lunch table in the Parliament Buildings and brought face to face with Canada's prime minister for what must have been the most peremptory welcome in diplomatic history.[1] It lasted only long enough for a handshake and the briefest of welcomes.

I thought at the time that the prime minister had hoped that somehow he could deny having received Popovic. Eventually, however, he unwillingly signed a letter to the effect that visits to Canada by members of governments of communist countries did not indicate any change in his own thinking but could do much to increase cooperation in areas of mutual concern.[2] The whole affair had left the Yugoslavs baffled and offended. It had also aggravated once again the prime minister's suspicion of the Department of External Affairs which, he insisted, had been behind the minister's invitation to Popovic. It was all very hard on the patience.

Prime Minister Macmillan visited Ottawa early in April, after meeting with President Kennedy for the first time. I had been asked confidentially by the British high commissioner in February, when Macmillan's trip was being planned, whether Diefenbaker would take it amiss if Ottawa were not included in the itinerary on this occasion. I felt quite safe in saying that this was sure to cause annoyance, even though the two prime ministers would in the meantime have attended the meeting of Commonwealth heads of government in the first half of March. True to form, and in spite of an extremely heavy schedule of engagements, Diefenbaker invited Macmillan to come to Ottawa as soon as he knew the dates. There had already been one recent instance of Macmillan's passing up a visit to Canada, and Diefenbaker knew that two in a row would be noticed. Apart from that, he looked forward to the opportunity to trade impressions of Kennedy.

Macmillan had been very favourably impressed by Kennedy and his senior colleagues in the new administration.[3] He told Diefenbaker that he had found them more 'flexible in their approach to policy problems' than their predecessors. The president himself, Macmillan said, was 'more sensitive, more politically minded.' It was clearly the intention of the Macmillan government to do every-

thing possible to avoid causing difficulties for the president while his administration was finding its feet.

Macmillan spoke freely and interestingly, but I could not help feeling that
Diefenbaker failed to make the most of the occasion. For some perverse reason,
his old suspicion of Kennedy surfaced again. I noted in my diary that 'Macmillan
scarcely concealed his irritation at P.M.'s negative position.' The following day
Norman Robertson was told the same thing by a senior member of Macmillan's
staff. They too had been struck by Diefenbaker's negative attitude towards the
president.

THE BAY OF PIGS

Why Diefenbaker was moved to countervail Macmillan's admiring assessment
of the president, it is hard to say. But within a week, Diefenbaker's doubts about
Kennedy's judgment were revived with the collapse of the Bay of Pigs operation
in Cuba. It was not so much that he deplored the strike against the Castro regime,
but that he was concerned about the failure to carry it through efficiently. Never
was there a clearer example of the collision of his instincts: outright suspicion
of the (communist) regime in Cuba, the feeling that 'a stand' should be taken
against it, on the one hand; and on the other, an acute concern that Canadian
support for a risky American-sponsored enterprise should not be taken for granted.

In the days after the Bay of Pigs operation was mounted on 17 April, Cuba
was the prime political topic. Diefenbaker asked for a statement for use in the
House of Commons. He said he wanted to say publicly how disturbed the
Canadian government was about the growth of communism there. In the course
of discussing a text, he sharply criticized the Department of External Affairs for
being wishy-washy, soft, conciliatory, and concerned to find a way of doing
business with communism. At one stage, as if in a flashback to Chamberlain
and Munich, he said that the department's policy, if followed, would simply
postpone the destruction of the world. I said with rashness born of exasperation
that he would surely not wish us to advance it. He let this pass but went on to
say that the trouble was that we (this time he meant the Western nations) had
not put up a convincing enough front to the Russians, who thought we could be
pushed around. There was a tendency in External Affairs, he said, to play along
with those who were only half our friends.[4]

I tried to stem the tide and to explain the department's reasons for advising
a moderate attitude towards political developments in Cuba. I was bothered too
by the prime minister's habit of generalizing about the department, as if all its
members were of one view. He asked on what subjects there were conflicting

opinions, to which I gave a number of examples including four which I knew were on his mind: Cuba, nuclear weapons policy, South Africa and the relative importance of adopting a generous attitude towards the non-aligned nations.

All this took place as background to the production of the statement the prime minister intended to make on Cuba. Not surprisingly in the circumstances, the statement was considerably more anti-Cuban than the department had advised. There had been no time for me to obtain prior comment on the final text from either the minister or the undersecretary, and I was later told that both were unhappy. On the next day, Diefenbaker was being criticized by some newspapers for the slant of the statement. Howard Green told Norman Robertson that 'the Prime Minister had been speaking to the Cardinal,' as if this would explain the line he had taken.

On 27 April, ten days after the Bay of Pigs assault was launched, I was instructed to draw the prime minister's attention to assumptions apparently being made by US authorities in Washington and Ottawa that Canada was 'lined up' with the United States on policy towards Cuba. The statement made by the prime minister in the House of Commons a week previously was being interpreted by some US officials as a pledge of Canadian support of US policy in the wake of the Bay of Pigs operation. Diefenbaker reacted sharply to this information. He asked for a paper to be prepared explaining to the United States the essentials of the Canadian position. Concerned as the government was about Cuba and communist penetration, he now said, there were limits beyond which he would not go in endorsing US policies, especially if they involved the use of force.

An External Affairs debate was then taking place in the House of Commons and a statement was prepared for use by either the prime minister or the minister. Green decided this time to discuss the text personally with the prime minister, but Diefenbaker withheld his approval and the debate ended without a government statement on Cuba. The effect was that the government had been unable to make up its mind whether or not to demonstrate its reservations about US policy. To have done so would have pleased 'liberal' opinion in Canada but would have looked like appeasement of communism.

As I was leaving his House of Commons office that evening, Diefenbaker must have realized that I was puzzled – probably I seemed impatient – at the decision not to use the kind of statement on Cuba policy which had been prepared at his request. His way of responding was typical. 'This is a lousy job,' he said, going on to remark on one of the dilemmas of the day on the domestic front. Don't assume, he was implying, that your problems are the only ones the prime minister has to worry about. It was a reminder that might have been chosen for his epitaph.

PREPARATIONS

There were now fewer than three weeks in which to complete preparations for the presidential descent on Ottawa, scheduled for 16 May. As usual, the prime minister wished to be consulted on every aspect of the program: the arrival ceremony, security arrangements, invitation lists, the social calendar, the gifts to be exchanged, plans for briefing the media, the separate program for Mrs Kennedy (checked like so much else with Mrs Diefenbaker), and arrangements for the major items of the visit – the address to parliament, the meeting with members of the cabinet, and the private conversations between the president and the prime minister and their immediate advisers. In all the preparations, nothing so irritated the prime minister as having to accept the presence of American security personnel. That the RCMP was not trusted to look after the president, even in the Canadian parliament, caused Diefenbaker such waves of indignation and anger that it must have affected his concentration on his briefing papers and his attitude towards the visit as a whole. And who could blame him?

As the visit approached, the tempo of preparations mounted. Meetings among the most senior officials from the departments involved gave birth to agenda, briefing papers, talking points, speech drafts, and all the impedimenta associated with meetings between heads of government. As always, it was vowed that this time briefing material would be kept to a minimum. As always, the vow was impossible to keep. Heads of government do not often meet and when they do there is inevitably more business for them to transact than was at first imagined.

By 9 May, one week before the president's arrival, the main agenda items seemed likely to be Laos, Cuba, Berlin, NATO, foreign aid, Britain's relations with the Common Market, and, among numerous possible subjects of bilateral concern, nuclear weapons policy. Diefenbaker received a comprehensive advance briefing from Bryce and the results were fed into the final stage of the material being put together for the prime minister and other ministers concerned.

On two subjects in particular – nuclear weapons policy and foreign aid – the prime minister took firm positions in advance of the visit. In both cases he would be under pressure to make concessions which he judged politically unwise to make at that time. He told me that he intended to speak privately about these subjects to the president rather than have them discussed in the presence of others. In the event, both subjects were brought into the main official meeting, as we shall see.

It might have been expected that after the February meeting with President Kennedy, a new start would have been made on the various aspects of the negotiations on nuclear weapons. That no progress had been achieved was a matter of great frustration to the minister of national defence, Douglas Harkness, and his senior advisers, who considered, reasonably enough, that the government had accepted nuclear commitments to the United States and to NATO and who were exasperated by their failure to overcome the stalling tactics of Howard Green. It was the impatient hope of ministers and officials involved with defence matters that the presidential visit would cause the government to put an end to the uncertainty and delay.

Green was at this time deeply immersed in the promotion of ideas and tactics regarding the cessation of nuclear tests and disarmament negotiations. He was in no mood to yield to an arrangement which would involve the acceptance of nuclear weapons on Canadian territory, however strictly the custody, control, and use of the weapons might be guaranteed. Backed by the undersecretary and by many, though by no means all, of the senior officials in his department, he resisted any change from the position he and the prime minister had agreed on with Kennedy at the White House in February. He had no objection to the reopening of talks, but his tactics would be to block any progress towards the placing of nuclear weapons in Canada except in case of actual need. Green was to hold stubbornly to this position in the face of arguments that in a real emergency there would be less than enough warning time to transfer the nuclear ammunition from US to Canadian bases. With the Kennedy visit only a week away, Green made his position known to Diefenbaker on 9 May before leaving for a NATO meeting of ministers in Oslo and for a conference on Laos in Geneva.

Green had no sooner departed for Oslo than the US ambassador brought the nuclear issue to a head in a private meeting on 11 May with the prime minister.[5] The US government was prepared to work out an agreement on a triangular arrangement under which they would transfer sixty-six interceptors (F-101Bs) to Canada, the RCAF would assume maintenance of sixteen Pinetree Line radar stations, and the US government would place a $200 million order in Canada for F-104Gs to be assigned as Mutual Aid to NATO countries in Europe, one quarter of the cost of these being assumed by Canada.[6] There was just one catch, which Merchant knew would cause a problem. The deal would only be possible if the interceptors to be transferred to Canada were equipped with nuclear weapons. The US government could defend the contemplated procurement in Canada only if they could demonstrate that continental defence had been made more effective.

In his report to the State Department, Merchant said that the prime minister 'responded understandingly but with genuine concern.' The question of accepting nuclear weapons provoked strong opinions in Canada, and, Diefenbaker stressed, the opponents were not just 'communists and bums.' The Department of External Affairs was 'riddled with wishful thinkers who believed the Soviets would be propitiated and disarmament prospects improved if only Canada did nothing to provoke the Soviet Union such as accepting nuclear armaments.' This was 'ridiculous but a view strongly and widely held.' Cabinet must reach a decision soon and the prime minister said he would take the matter up within the next few days with his cabinet colleagues. Meanwhile, the ambassador was not to broach the subject in any way to External Affairs. 'I am certain we have a strong ally in Prime Minister as well as Harkness,' Merchant concluded, rather optimistically.

Despite what he had said to Merchant, the prime minister did not in Green's absence agree to have the issue debated in the cabinet before the president's visit. Instead, he went over the arguments on two occasions with Bryce. On the day before the president's arrival, Diefenbaker told me that he was not prepared to agree to begin negotiations on the basis suggested by Harkness and others who saw advantage in linking the acquisition of nuclear warheads with the conclusion of a 'Swap Deal.' The prime minister's position was that if he went ahead on this basis, he would in a sense be committing himself to taking the nuclear warheads onto Canadian soil.[7]

This decision meant that the nuclear weapons item in the impending talks would not give satisfaction to the United States. In domestic terms, moreover, Diefenbaker's decision showed that he was indeed impressed with the level of support which Green's campaign for disarmament was attracting in public opinion. It was a decision of high importance.

The second point on which the prime minister declared himself in advance of the Kennedy visit was foreign aid. It was a subject on which Diefenbaker had long professed scepticism. During the preparations for the visit, the prime minister agreed with the minister of finance, Donald Fleming, that the government should not approve a further increase in the aid flow. He also made it known, after considering a number of options put forward by Howard Green, that he was not prepared to give assurances about maintaining the level of Canadian aid over a period of years and that he did not favour increasing Canada's total aid appropriation. The idea that it might be possible to make a political virtue out of increases in foreign aid was enough to make him roll his eyes. 'I'm going to think of Canada for the next 14, 15, 16 or 18 months,' he said.

On the weekend before the president's arrival, the atmosphere was affected by a comment made by Green en route from Oslo to Geneva in response to questions about the Canadian position on Cuba. Press reports quoted him as saying that Canada would be ready to 'mediate' in the dispute between the United States and Cuba. Arnold Heeney was duly summoned to the State Department to hear an expression of US concern. Diefenbaker was taken aback by the sharpness of this reaction as reported by Heeney and, on being questioned in the House, gave full support to Green. He remarked privately, however, on the acute nervousness of the US administration on Cuba.

196

The Kennedy visit was to begin on Tuesday, 16 May. The previous Friday, Saturday, and Monday were spent in last-minute preparations – final insertions in the prime minister's briefing book, talking points for conversations, the drafting of paragraphs which might come in handy for the communiqué at the close of the visit, and continuing work on the various speeches.

Despite a substantial intake of speech material from a variety of contributors, Diefenbaker was still not satisfied with the draft of his speech introducing the president to parliament. He sent out a call for something 'exciting and brilliant' to weave into what he had. Most of those who had been contributing had by that time exhausted their brilliance if not their excitement. But Ed Ritchie, always steady and resourceful in a crisis, produced in thirty minutes a few pages of fresh material which Diefenbaker, mercifully, found to his liking. Lionel Gelber, at that time a special adviser in the Prime Minister's Office, was striving to edit and coordinate the various texts. Diefenbaker himself kept juggling the mixture, with the result that the sources of the pages and even the paragraphs were impossible to trace. In serving his speech-writing needs, it was best to have no proprietary interest in the fate of one's offspring.

Late in the afternoon before the visit was to begin, he left for home with his unfinished speech drafts and his loose-leaf briefing books. He still had plenty of homework to get through. My phone rang in the late evening. Were we quite sure that we had a comfortable rocking chair for the president to use at tomorrow's meeting? We were. Yes, prime minister, good night.

20

Taking Umbrage: Don't Push

The visit to Ottawa of President and Mrs Kennedy from 16 to 18 May 1961 began in an atmosphere of apparent goodwill, but seems bound to go down in history as the start of the breakdown of the Kennedy–Diefenbaker relationship. On the surface, no serious signs of trouble were evident. Admittedly there was one minor, though surprising, gaffe by the president. At the airport on arrival he mispronounced the Diefenbaker name – he gave it a long German 'a,' thereby touching his host on the raw. Nor was this offset by a good-natured allusion to the prime minister's command of French, which, the president said, had made him feel encouraged to use his. In French, let us face it, they were in the same class, but Diefenbaker's sense of humour was not aroused.

Ottawa is not noted for demonstrative behaviour, but the crowds gave the Kennedys a warm and eager welcome. The president's address to parliament, though later thought to have annoyed the prime minister, at first impressed him favourably. Perhaps on close reading he sensed an implied criticism of Canada's role in the sharing of international burdens in such regions as Latin America and, more generally, in aid to the developing world. But at the time, his one expressed regret was that members of parliament had not been given an opportunity to meet informally with the president, a suggestion made earlier by Davie Fulton and others but rejected by Diefenbaker.

No one but the president and those close to him could have known of the old back injury which had recurred while he was helping to plant the inevitable tree in the grounds at Government House. He gave no sign of discomfort. As he and his wife departed, and allowing for the euphoria of ceremonial farewells, things appeared to have gone off very well, at least from the Canadian point of view. In a letter written a few days later Mrs Diefenbaker confessed to being 'completely enchanted by Mrs. Kennedy.' And, 'it's quite a thing, isn't it, when two heads of state [sic] can be so comfortable and happy together,' she wrote.[1]

That was certainly not the way the prime minister or, presumably, the president would have put it. They had not quarrelled but between them there would never be the link of natural fellowship that had joined Diefenbaker and Eisenhower. Kennedy is said to have been bored by Diefenbaker. That strikes me as entirely possible. But how and why did matters go so badly awry? For some of the early clues to this riddle, let us look at the business they did together, keeping watch for signs of cooperation or disaffection.

The main formal conversation took place in the prime minister's office in the East Block of the Parliament Buildings on the morning of 17 May. The president was accompanied by Livingston Merchant, recently appointed to a second term as ambassador to Canada, W.W. (Walt) Rostow of the White House staff, and Ivan White of the State Department. Arnold Heeney, the Canadian ambassador to the United States, R.B. Bryce, and I were present on the Canadian side. The meeting lasted just under two and one-half hours.

As the president entered the room, the prime minister made a point of displaying the mounted marlin he had landed during his winter holiday in Jamaica, and, on a less recreational note, a painting of a British warship which had taken part in a victorious battle during the war of 1812. He had been determined to do this since visiting the White House in February, when President Kennedy had shown him a series of paintings depicting nothing but historic American victories on the Great Lakes.

Having been thus educated, the president, wearing a fading tan and looking a trifle tired, declared himself ready to go. I was struck by the care he took to introduce his advisers to the prime minister and, during the meeting, by the readiness with which he deferred to them. It gave me the impression that he took pride in giving them stature, a somewhat different feeling from that to which I had become accustomed.

The atmosphere of the conversation was informal and businesslike. The president was clearly well briefed and sensitive to the Canadian outlook and concerns. Alert and intelligent, he talked quietly and persuasively and often with a light touch. He proved to be adept at holding to the thread of an exchange, coming back more than once to a point if he felt it had not been covered to his satisfaction. The prime minister gave every appearance of enjoying the exchanges. I thought he spoke clearly, and he was certainly firm on issues which held the seeds of future domestic problems.

The principal subjects raised by the president were Latin America and Cuba, Southeast Asia, relations between the United Kingdom and the European Economic Community, foreign aid, and nuclear weapons for continental defence. Other items discussed were China, the Congo, NATO defence measures, Berlin,

relations with Western Europe, nuclear testing, and more generally US responsibilities and intentions on the world scale. Except for defence matters and some
trade issues arising from differences in policy on Cuba and China, bilateral
relations were not discussed in this meeting. The account that follows is focused
on the more contentious topics.[2]

LATIN AMERICA

It was only a month since the president had made his first mistake in foreign
policy – the decision to involve the United States directly in the Bay of Pigs
assault on Cuba. He seemed anxious to sketch the reasons for the decision, as
if in that way he might preclude an inquiry from the prime minister and clear
the way for a productive exchange on future problems in Latin America.

As the president explained it, the difficulty had been to decide what to do
with 1300 or so Cuban volunteers in Guatemala and Nicaragua. Either these
units would have had to be used in active operations or be disbanded. The
government had decided that they would be better in Cuba than out. At the same
time, it had placed itself under certain limitations in the hope that the role of
the United States would be covert and far removed from active involvement. As
it turned out, the limitations assumed did not prevent the operation from becoming
known or the United States from being engaged. Painful lessons had been learned,
the president confessed, with the air of one who wished to bury the subject. The
prime minister made no effort to keep it alive.

For the future, the president went on, Cuba presented a serious political
problem, not only because of its subservience to Soviet leadership but also
because it served as a rallying point for extreme leftist movements in other Latin
American countries. He hoped that Canada would use its influence more broadly
in the hemisphere. Canada had great prestige and was without the disadvantages
which attached to the United States in its dealings with other countries.

The prime minister began by assuring the president that, despite press reports
of remarks by Howard Green in Europe, Canada 'won't engage in mediation'
between Cuba and the United States. Acknowledging this, the president remarked
that, as he saw it, it was not a fight between Washington and Havana but rather
between Western and Soviet interests.

Although the president had not yet referred to the Organization of American
States (OAS), Diefenbaker volunteered that Canada was further from joining that
organization now than it had been a year ago. (He had been attracted by the
idea of OAS membership at the time of his visit to Mexico in April 1960). He
thought now that membership would create difficulties for Canada. We might
disagree with the United States and that would be awkward; or, if we agreed,

it would be said that Canada was being dictated to by the United States and we would be accused of subservience. Canada, he believed, might exert a better influence by remaining detached. The president countered that although the OAS had not fulfilled expectations, he hoped very much that Canada would join. Canadian influence could be profound. If a situation arose in which Canada disagreed with US policy, he said with a trace of a smile, the United States would probably be wrong. He again asked the prime minister to 'take a long look' at Latin America. Socially and politically it was 'more dangerous than any other place we are facing in the world.' He hoped that Canada would at least send an observer to the next meeting of the economic and social council of the OAS in Montevideo.

This was a modest enough proposal which the prime minister's advisers had thought could be accepted. But he had either not remembered the advice or been doubtful about even this small degree of commitment. All he would do was to promise to consider it. He was more interested in US intentions regarding Cuba, a subject of much greater concern in the Canadian press and in parliament than the OAS. Was there any change to be expected in the trade field? The US press had given a misleading picture of Canada's policy in trading with Cuba. Canada was following its normal course with communist nations. It would not, of course, export strategic or military items nor allow US goods to be bootlegged to Cuba through Canada. The president made no criticism or requests with regard to Canadian trade with Cuba. If further economic measures were required against Cuba, the United States would have to invoke the Trading with the Enemy Act, but he did not intend to take such measures unless 'we receive provocation.'

The prime minister asked about the military outlook in Cuba. Was there any suggestion of nuclear bases there? The president thought not, although Cuba had aircraft which could carry nuclear weapons. The United States did not plan to intervene again militarily in Cuba unless (a) there were serious provocation; (b) the administration thought it necessary to prevent the (communist) infection spreading throughout Latin America; or (c) the Soviet Union 'cut us seriously' in Berlin. The United States would 'talk with Canada before doing anything,' he added, without implying that he anticipated a situation of crisis.[3]

ASIA

The exchanges on Asian questions followed the pattern set with Latin America. The president explained US policy and then invited the Canadian government to improve on the role it was already playing. In Vietnam and Laos, the international commissions were failing to prevent frontier violations and guerilla warfare. As a result, the United States was contemplating an increase of 100 men in its military assistance group in Vietnam. He hoped for Canada's cooperation in the provision of this assistance, although he realized it was contrary to the Geneva agreements (which had brought an end in 1954 to France's war in Indochina). He recognized that it was necessary to approach India as chairman of the commission, but Canada's role was crucial.

Again the prime minister was cautiously negative. Taking the opportunity to explain the absence of Howard Green, he said that the minister had stayed longer than planned at the Geneva conference on Laos because of the importance the Canadian government attached to the problems in Indochina. He avoided comment on the strengthening of the American military presence in Vietnam but implied that there were strict limits to what Canada could do.

Almost as he had done in drawing the conversation from the OAS to Cuba, the prime minister slid from Indochina, a subject which in his mind belonged to Green's agenda, to the problems connected with China. He recalled that at their meeting in February he had gained the impression that the president did not contemplate any change in his China policy. He had said as much to the conference of Commonwealth prime ministers, which had taken place in London in March. Prime Minister Menzies of Australia, however, had given a quite different report. So far as the Canadian government was concerned, 'the mistake made before the Korean war of not recognizing the Communist Chinese government could not be rectified now without ill effects on all our friends in Asia.' What was the president's view?

Looking relieved for the first time, the president agreed that while it might once have been better to treat Peking's recognition as routine, the question had now acquired great symbolic importance. His administration had certainly not altered President Eisenhower's policy. Diefenbaker, always uneasy at the thought of Menzies, looked vindicated.

FOREIGN AID, THE EEC

The president next made a direct appeal for additional Canadian assistance in foreign aid, one of the subjects on which Diefenbaker had decided in advance that he could not make concessions and would have to discuss privately with the president. Confronted with the direct question whether Canada would join with the United States in increasing its aid level to approximately 1 per cent of Gross National Product, the prime minister said he could not see his way to increasing Canada's present aid contributions. Unemployment was growing to an alarming level and the government would have to turn a larger share of the budget into job creation. Again the president's hopes had been disappointed.

The president inquired about the effect in Canada if the United Kingdom were to join the European Economic Community. Canada's concern, Diefenbaker replied, was the loss of markets, particularly for agricultural products. He understood that the United States, however, was 'quite interested' in seeing the United Kingdom go into Europe. The president put stress on the international political effects. He favoured British entry because of the contribution it would make to the stability of Western Europe. The subject was not pursued but one could sense Diefenbaker's displeasure at having it confirmed that the president was so firmly in support of British entry.

NUCLEAR CHOICE

Although Diefenbaker had intended to broach the problem of nuclear weapons privately with the president, in the event he introduced it into the discussion. He had turned the conversation to the outlook for NATO and, after the president had talked for a few minutes on the dilemma of whether to help France with its nuclear program, Diefenbaker intervened to say that the Canadian government's position had been opposed to any 'extension' of nuclear power. This view had taken root among responsible groups – professors and the clergy, for instance – and a very active organization known as the Voice of Women. The government would have to face the problem with the Bomarcs. If they were to be used in Canada, it would have to be under some form of joint control. It would be impossible at the moment, however, to have Bomarcs with nuclear warheads.

The president asked if opinion would change, and Diefenbaker, acknowledging that negotiations on nuclear weapons had gone a long way, said that he was going to try to bring about a change in the late summer and fall when he would be undertaking a speaking tour across Canada.[4] Asked what the argument against nuclear weapons was, Diefenbaker replied that a ridiculous concept had developed that all would be well if we had no weapons of a provocative nature. Some professors took this view; there were even some at Harvard, he said, a remark made half in jest to which the president and Walt Rostow were quick to react. The group of professors in question, they assured the prime minister, were neither influential nor representative of university opinion.

The prime minister, recalling a recent visit to Philadelphia, agreed with the president that public opinion in the United States seemed more militant than the mood of the United States administration. When the president observed that the anti-nuclear weapons argument mentioned by the prime minister would take Canada into a neutralist position, Diefenbaker was stung. It was what he instinctively felt. He said that he might interpolate something about the dangers of neutralism in his speech introducing the president to parliament. In the event he did not tackle the theme head on, although he spoke of the need for Canada and the United States to maintain joint defences and for 'all freedom-loving nations' to pay the price of cooperation in defence and in economic matters.

When the prime minister later invited the president to raise any other matters of concern, the president referred the question to Livingston Merchant, who summarized the current position on defence cooperation. The prime minister said he understood that the triangular 'Swap' proposal as now formulated (ie, if it included F-104Gs built in Canada for use by European partners in NATO) was contingent on Canadian willingness to agree that the nuclear armament for the sixty-sixty F101B interceptors would be stored in Canada. His original understanding – or so he maintained – was that Canada would be required to have the necessary fittings and that the nuclear warheads could be held in storage in the United States. He made it sound as if the Canadian government would appear subservient to the United States if he agreed to what they wanted and the story were leaked.

The president and his advisers argued that in order to justify a large order of Canadian-built F-104G aircraft, the administration would have to be able to show that the transaction would result in a net increase, or at least no decrease, in continental air defence strength. The nuclear warheads for the interceptors would have to be stored at Canadian bases so that there would be no loss of time in arming.

The difference was not resolved. The president, looking somewhat puzzled, asked whether, apart from the triangular proposal, the prime minister thought it would be disadvantageous for Canada to have defensive nuclear weapons stored in Canada. The prime minister replied that in the present climate he could not stand up in the House of Commons and announce the acceptance of nuclear weapons. The strength of public opinion in Canada on disarmament had created a dilemma for the government. Personally he felt there was a need for Canada to be equipped with nuclear weapons. But it was necessary to have the support of the House of Commons and he could not be sure of that, given the state of public opinion and the position on nuclear policy taken by Lester Pearson, the leader of the opposition, and the New Democratic Party.[5] Perhaps after the next few months the government could move on storage rights for the United States at the bases in Newfoundland, but this possibility would be destroyed if he were to accept nuclear warheads for the F-101Bs as part of the triangular deal.[6]

A brief exchange on disarmament revealed once again Diefenbaker's scepticism on this subject. He spoke in terms which he would not have ventured to use if Howard Green had been sitting beside him. A major cause of the anti-nuclear feeling in Canada, he said, had been that some people had been fascinated by the hope of disarmament and had given it a disproportionate importance. The president, perceiving an opening, said that he was familiar with ideas such as the prime minister had mentioned, but was assuming that since Canada was not neutral it was obvious the country should be as well equipped as possible. The prime minister did not rise to this last fly. Instead he asked the president to give further consideration to the triangular deal, on the basis that nuclear weapons for the aircraft would be held in readiness in the United States and be sent to Canada only in an emergency.

Then, as if realizing that he had trespassed a little too far on his guest's patience and goodwill, Diefenbaker changed his tone and rather awkwardly complimented him on the powers of self-control he had shown after the Bay of Pigs operation in resisting public pressure for precipitate retaliation and in accepting full responsibility for the failure of the operation. I sensed that the compliment had missed its mark.

JFK's LAST TRY

The remaining part of the visit included the president's speech to parliament and various ceremonial and social engagements, including the unfortunate tree-planting episode. Before leaving Ottawa, however, in a private breakfast with Diefenbaker on 18 May, the president made one final effort to overcome the prime minister's reluctance to move on nuclear weapons and on involvement in hemispheric affairs. The president acknowledged that there was a political problem involved in anything connected with nuclear weapons. But since the weapons in question were entirely defensive and had to be ready for an emergency, it was difficult to see how they could be deprived of their nuclear capability. He told Diefenbaker that he hoped Canada would find it possible to accept arrangements similar to those already in existence with the United Kingdom and other NATO countries. On hemispheric affairs, Diefenbaker told the president he would inform him shortly about Canada's readiness to be represented at the meeting of the Economic and Social Council of the OAS but that membership of that organization would not be possible.

These leavings from the breakfast table were given to Heeney by the president and recorded in a letter from Heeney to the prime minister immediately after travelling back to Washington with the Kennedys on the 18th. On his return to Washington, Heeney was able to inform the White House and the State Department on the 19th that the Canadian government would send an observer to the Montevideo meeting. On the more substantial policy issues of nuclear weapons and OAS membership, Diefenbaker did not give final answers to Washington until the following Monday. By that time he had had the opportunity to talk with Green, who had returned from Geneva and who, Diefenbaker knew, would expect to be consulted on issues of such significance before final decisions were made known to the Americans.

After the discussion with Green, Diefenbaker dictated, on 21 May, a letter for Heeney's guidance on the two outstanding issues. In this letter, the contents of which he gave to Heeney by telephone, Diefenbaker confirmed his view that political opposition was too strong to permit the Canadian government to become a full member of the OAS. The prime minister's letter continued: 'As to the "Swap Deal," my views were made clear in the discussions with the President and I can see no possibility of change. I hope that in this regard the President will be prepared to recommend the "Swap Deal" without the qualification that the aircraft shall be armed with short-range atomic missiles.' Heeney's record of his telephone conversation with the prime minister on 22 May reads as follows: 'There was little possibility of any change in our position. If the United States insisted on attaching the qualification of our receiving the US fighters [re nuclear armament], we would be unable to accept. It would put us in a "false" position. He thought the President understood this and hoped an agreement could be worked out which would not involve this condition.'7

THE ROSTOW MEMO

Shortly after the president's meeting with the prime minister on 17 May, a member of the prime minister's staff, tidying the room, came upon a document left behind by the president's party. It was a single sheet of vellum paper containing a 'Memorandum for the President' from 'w.w.r.'' (W.W. Rostow) on the subject, 'What We Want from the Ottawa Trip.'

In Rostow's words, the objectives of the trip were 'to push the Canadians towards an increased commitment' to the Alliance for Progress in Latin America; to 'push them towards a decision to join the OAS'; and to 'push them towards a larger contribution for the India [aid] consortium and foreign aid generally.' Finally, 'We want their active support at Geneva [the Laos conference] and for a more effective monitoring of the borders of Laos and Vietnam.'8

I was shown this document in strictest confidence after it had been given to the prime minister. My first thought was that this was exactly the kind of last-minute reminder I had often given to Diefenbaker on the way to meetings. As it was obviously an internal American paper, I urged that it should be returned with an explanation to the US embassy. Two days later, however, in a post-mortem on the visit, the prime minister brought the paper out, remarking on its repeated use of the word 'push.' To him this personified the attitude of the Americans: they thought nothing of pushing Canada around. He seemed to be regarding the paper as a sort of trophy, and it was impossible to tell whether he would hold on to it for future display or return it as I had recommended. It was only later that I learned it had gone to the 'vault,' a filing cabinet in which all his special secrets were deposited. A year later he would find a use for it.

As Diefenbaker himself records in his description of the incident, there was in fact no handwritten notation of any kind in the margins or between the lines of this memorandum. (It had been rumoured that it carried the letters SOB.) In fact the only sign of handwriting was to be found alongside the typed letters 'W.W.R.,' where Rostow had initialled the memorandum. In more recent years I have again seen the original and two photocopies of the same paper. None had a marginal notation, although on one there was underlining, by Diefenbaker himself, of the word 'push' wherever it appeared.[9]

An interesting sidelight was that the document confined itself to broad international aims and was silent on continental defence, which was just as much an American objective of the talks as Latin America, Indochina, or foreign aid. The explanation for this probably lies in the fact that while Rostow was principally concerned with the world at large, the continental defence topics were left to Merchant because of his familiarity with the background and the bilateral relationship.

REFLECTIONS

At the end of the visit my own reaction included the following comments:

Most people think the visit was a great success. Personally I think it was a qualified one, our side having been so negative on things which, if we were less earthbound, we could usefully do without serious sacrifice ...

Considering the P.M.'s relative lack of preparation, he spoke clearly on most issues [but] was simply not ready to respond on such things as foreign aid which were important to the President ... His reluctance to commit himself on nuclear weapons was also striking, based as it was frankly on domestic factors ...

I was enormously impressed with Kennedy's performance – an intelligent and sensitive man with a sense of humour. I was surprised, though, to see how set he was in seeing foreign policy problems in straight Cold War terms.[10]

Norman Robertson, on reading the record of the main meeting, thought that the president's exposition must have been a measure of the low estimate in which the Canadian government was held by the new administration in Washington. Canada had to be jacked up. This might explain the black and white Cold War theme running through the president's remarks as well as Dean Rusk's statements to Howard Green in Oslo and Geneva, where he had virtually accused Canada of 'neutralism.'[11]

It takes two to build a disagreement, and, in attempting to account for this one, a starting point is to examine how these two quite different men approached their Ottawa meeting. Kennedy had set out to seek some measure of cooperation on a number of important current questions, especially the 'push' items on Rostow's agenda and the large issue of nuclear cooperation. The president was also prepared for a general discussion on the world situation, one of several he was holding with heads of allied governments before meeting the Soviet leader, Nikita Khrushchev, in Vienna in June.

Diefenbaker's approach was guarded. While interested in the president's review of the world scene, he had concentrated on explaining and defending the Canadian government's position and interests. He had given very little indication of flexibility on the main issues of concern to the president. Kennedy and his advisers, although equipped with some disparaging advice about Diefenbaker's character and political attitudes,[12] had doubtless hoped for a more obliging response, or at least for a somewhat more collaborative tone. They got very little. From the president's point of view, the results of the visit must have seemed an unpromising basis for future cooperation.

My impression of Diefenbaker's reaction at the time, however, was that he counted on being able to maintain a working relationship with the president. The impression he gave was one of relief that the most important of a punishing series of engagements was behind him, that public reaction had been favourable, that he had taken the measure of Kennedy and had held the line on issues of domestic political importance. It was, I think, only gradually that he allowed the abandoned memorandum, together with other imagined and later slights, to eat away like acid in the recesses of his mind. Looking back on that period, Green keenly regrets that Diefenbaker became so provoked by the contents of the memorandum and believes that if he had been present when it was found he might have convinced the prime minister not to take it so seriously.[13]

What was probably a more serious irritation – one that would fester and grow – arose from the dinner given by the President and Mrs Kennedy at the US ambassador's residence on the last evening of the visit. Americans present on that occasion watched apprehensively as the president so evidently enjoyed, and prolonged, his opportunity to talk with opposition leader Pearson. It was true that the president and the prime minister had been in each other's company most of the day. But Diefenbaker's anger at the president's insensitivity is not difficult to imagine. The Kennedy-Pearson relationship would henceforth be a constant source of resentment and anxiety for the prime minister.

It was an offstage factor in the developing drama that Kennedy and Macmillan had hit it off well and that they were evidently teaming up in the old Anglo-American special relationship. Diefenbaker allowed this to disturb him. Yet it was simply not in his make-up to develop with the younger man a bond that combined the roles of ally, counsellor, uncle, and friend, so successfully achieved by the British prime minister. John Diefenbaker was endowed with neither the subtlety of mind nor the generosity of spirit that would have been indispensable in such a relationship. He knew his limitations, and gallingly the knowledge reminded him that for all his strivings and for all his success and power, he was still the outsider.

But to persist further with these bleak reflections would be getting ahead of our time. Soon, the flow of events would again test the limits of Canadian-American cooperation and the relationship between the president and the prime minister.

21

Reshaping Old Patterns

Across the Atlantic, meanwhile, Prime Minister Macmillan, though determined
to maintain London's special link with Washington, was proposing to lead the
United Kingdom into a historic new relationship with Europe. In the spring of
1961 the United Kingdom's interest in joining the European Economic Community became a problem for the Diefenbaker government.

'SAY IT ISN'T SO'

Diefenbaker himself could never quite overcome a sense of mystified grievance
that Harold Macmillan, the personification of all that was admirable in the British
way of life and government, should have convinced himself that the United
Kingdom must, as it were, marry into Europe. It threatened Canada's 'British
connection,' traditionally important to the Conservative party in Canada and
sentimentally still full of meaning for Diefenbaker himself. Emotions apart, such
an aim was hard to square with 'an expanding Commonwealth in an expanding
world,' the watchword that he had adopted for the Commonwealth Conference
on Trade and Economic Affairs in 1958. More ominously still, if the United
Kingdom negotiated its way into Europe, not only would the Commonwealth
be weakened but, in both a political and an economic sense, Canada would be
thrown even more closely together with the United States. His recent talks with
both Macmillan and Kennedy had fed Diefenbaker's suspicion that the United
States was urging the United Kingdom into Europe in order to eliminate or
reduce the Commonwealth trade preferences. And amidst these broader considerations it was the impact on Western agriculture that seemed to interest him
the most.

The British government could not have failed to notice that Canada would be
difficult to convince. Diefenbaker's proclaimed attachment to the Commonwealth

and to the United Kingdom's role in it were well known to Macmillan, and the importance of the Commonwealth preferences was a factor taken for granted in Canada's trade relations with the United Kingdom and the many other countries directly affected by the British initiative. By its participation in the Organization for Economic Cooperation and Development (OECD), whose convention had been signed in December 1960, the Canadian government had reaffirmed its interest in trade and financial relations with Europe. But this did not increase Canadian influence on the issue of special concern: the United Kingdom government's desire to determine the conditions on which it could become associated with the European Economic Community.

George Drew was an outspoken and passionate critic of British entry into Europe. His appointment in 1957 as high commissioner had been Diefenbaker's first and most striking acknowledgment of the continuing significance in Canada of the 'British connection.' Now, hardly a day passed in Ottawa without the prime minister's receiving a telephone call or a personal telegram or letter from Drew warning of some impending British stratagem, or transmitting an editorial from the Beaverbrook press certain to stoke up the fires of Diefenbaker's disillusion. The *Daily Express* in particular had been conducting an all-out campaign against British entry into the Common Market, a fact which I confess inclined me instinctively to sympathize with what Macmillan was trying to achieve.

There were some hilarious episodes. Occasionally Drew, in an effort to keep some item of correspondence out of the hands of the Canadian bureaucracy, would ask me to see that it was routed directly to the prime minister. I presume he did this on the assumption that Diefenbaker would not object if he knew that the message was in my hands and had not otherwise gone astray. Unfortunately this was not always a safe assumption, even after my four years in Diefenbaker's service. Once, after I gave him a telegram that Drew had sent through External Affairs channels with a prefix asking me to give it personally to the prime minister, Diefenbaker told me that his correspondence with Drew on this subject was entirely private. On other days correspondence similarly addressed and on the same subject would be turned over to me to decide what needed to be done. One had to be flexible.

DUNCAN SANDYS'S VISIT

A typical mini-tempest occurred early in June over a proposal from Macmillan that Duncan Sandys, then secretary of state for commonwealth relations, should visit Ottawa and other Commonwealth capitals in the early summer of 1961 to talk about Britain's interest in joining the European Common Market.[1] Diefenbaker reacted impatiently to this. He told Howard Green to have a reply to

Macmillan prepared saying that the British government should have something specific to discuss if a visit by Sandys was to be worthwhile. From London Drew sent a special message to Diefenbaker expressing amazement at the choice of Sandys for this mission, and suggesting that the Canadian minister of finance, Donald Fleming, and of trade and commerce, George Hees, should instead go to London to see British ministers more directly concerned with economic matters.

Diefenbaker in this case decided not to act on Drew's suggestion, but in the final drafting of the reply to Macmillan he resisted efforts to soften the tone and would not agree to wording explicitly agreeing to Sandys's coming. Macmillan's reply two days later, in which he reiterated his hope that the Canadian government would agree to discussions with Sandys, again did not sit well with Diefenbaker. In fact it prompted him to think of the advantages of a special meeting of Commonwealth prime ministers to discuss Britain's interest in joining the Common Market. I discussed this idea with senior officials in External Affairs. They thought that Canada's special case would be diluted in a Commonwealth conference. On the following day, the prime minister spoke by telephone with Macmillan and asked me to prepare a further message to him. I dictated a note: 'He told me what he wanted to say. I drafted a message and checked it with External Affairs officials who prevailed on me to water down references to a possible meeting of Commonwealth ministers or prime ministers. Unwisely I changed the wording accordingly. When the Prime Minister saw the draft, he was very impatient and told Howard Green separately that he was very displeased with the External Affairs effort to divert him from saying what he wanted to say. It became clear to me that the Government has decided to try and kill U.K. participation in the Common Market and that efforts to point out the advantages of adjusting ourselves have no political appeal. Officials are of course also divided but all agree that collective Commonwealth consultation is not likely to advance Canadian negotiating interests. But the P.M. evidently thinks that if all the other Commonwealth members gang up, the U.K. may be dissuaded.'[2]

The problem was on my mind and I took an opportunity the next day to ask the prime minister about the government's real intention about Britain and the Common Market. Did they mean to scupper it? Diefenbaker denied wanting to prevent British entry but said he did not want to be hurried. He feared that in sending Sandys for bilateral talks, the British were pulling a fast one and might announce plans to enter Europe before there had been a full opportunity for consultation. The United Kingdom was free to enter Europe but his concern was to ensure that Canada would retain the trade benefits it possessed through Commonwealth preferences. He thought that there was a real risk involved to Canadian trade interests, especially as he felt sure that France would insist on Britain's joining the Common Market treaty without qualifications.[3]

Within two days a new message had come from Macmillan, this time delivered to the prime minister by the British high commissioner in Ottawa, Joe Garner. The upshot was that Garner obtained Diefenbaker's still reluctant agreement to a three-day visit from Sandys in mid-July. Garner told me afterwards that it had been agreed that Sandys would see the ministers concerned (Green, Fleming, and Hees) on the first two days and the prime minister later. Diefenbaker had made it clear, however, that he would not necessarily be bound by what took place in those meetings. Garner went away well enough pleased because, in addition to having the Sandys visit accepted, he had avoided the subject of a meeting of Commonwealth prime ministers. Diefenbaker was of course right in thinking that the British government would prefer to deal individually with Commonwealth governments.

On 13 June, Diefenbaker made a short statement in the House of Commons. He announced the impending visit of Sandys and spoke in terms somewhat more soothing to British ears. Before he went into the House he told me with an ingenuous look that Macmillan had somehow got the impression that the Canadian government wanted an immediate meeting of Commonwealth prime ministers; he had instructed Drew to assure Macmillan that this was not the case. I concluded that Diefenbaker was becoming worried about the level to which this controversy had risen.

In External Affairs, the undersecretary, Norman Robertson, was himself upset with the way things were going. A note in my diary for 13 June reads: NAR thinks that undignified public exhibitions between Canada and the U.K. are deplorable not only in Commonwealth terms but in the light of Berlin, Laos, etc. where we shall badly need to stay close to the U.K. whose position is sensible and close to our own. NAR spoke to Green today, blowing off steam. Green completely on the defensive ...' On the same day the issue of James Coyne's dispute with the government came into the open. Not a good time to tangle with the prime minister, and Howard Green knew it.

Robertson, however, felt so strongly about the barrenness of the government's tactics that just before Sandys's visit he took what was for him the unusual step of attending a meeting of the cabinet committee dealing with questions arising out of Britain's interest in joining the Common Market. He told me that he felt it his duty to speak out against the public line being followed by the government, and preferred to do this in a setting where it would not cause undue embarrassment. He said that he did not want to attend the meeting with Sandys for fear of feeling it necessary to disagree with Canadian ministers. I recorded what he said at that time because to me it reflected so poignantly the difficulty Robertson had in his role as head of the department during the Diefenbaker years and, at the same time, the spur of conscience which drove him to find a way to make his views known to the government.

Before reaching Ottawa on 12 July, Sandys had been to Australia and, through David Hay, the Australian high commissioner in Ottawa, Diefenbaker received a message from Prime Minister Menzies helpfully reporting the arguments the Australians had used in speaking to Sandys as well as the general atmosphere of their talks – polite but tough. Diefenbaker kept the message to himself but Terry MacDermot, the Canadian high commissioner in Australia, was well connected in Canberra and reported that a letter had been sent. Diefenbaker had not seen the contents but, on learning that the existence of Menzies's message was known to some other ministers and senior officials, he suspected that a conspiracy was afoot among the bureaucrats, Canadian and Australian alike. *Plus ça change!*

CONSULTATIONS

As planned, Diefenbaker left it to others to do most of the talking with Sandys but he stayed close to what was going on, instructing Green and Fleming to play it tough in the negotiations on the public statement to be issued at the close of the talks. The result was an unusually frank communiqué, in keeping with what the *Winnipeg Free Press* described as the 'icy reception' accorded Sandys. Most Canadian editorial comment was critical of the government, but Diefenbaker was not to be moved. He had hoped for a reference in the communiqué to an ultimate meeting of Commonwealth prime ministers. Sandys resisted this, but there would be many more exchanges with the British government on Common Market matters over the next year and, in the end, Diefenbaker's idea of a Commonwealth prime ministers' meeting would come to pass.

On the evidence of the Sandys visit, the calculation in Ottawa was that the United Kingdom government was determined to proceed towards negotiations with the European Economic Community. Macmillan, in a statement at the end of July, acknowledged the importance of full consultation with Commonwealth governments and said that the United Kingdom intended keeping in touch with them during the negotiating process. A month later the Canadian government accepted an invitation to take part in Commonwealth consultations – among officials rather than ministers – in London, the aim being to ensure that the interests of each Commonwealth government were fully understood by the United Kingdom before the negotiating process began. Diefenbaker realized that the time had not yet come to insist on a prime ministers' meeting but, under prodding from Drew, he kept a watchful eye on British tactics. At this stage he was putting considerable stock in the prospect that the United Kingdom's chances of joining the EEC would be diminished if not destroyed by de Gaulle's refusal to allow any derogations from the Treaty of Rome regarding trade preferences for Commonwealth countries. This, the prime minister hoped, might discourage the United Kingdom from pressing ahead and also obviate the need for Canada to take a firm stand against British entry into Europe.

In mid-September a conference of the Commonwealth Economic Consultative Council at Accra, the capital of Ghana, generated press reports to the effect that Donald Fleming and George Hees, the Canadian ministers attending, had warned the United Kingdom that it would have to choose between the Commonwealth and the European Economic Community. These reports gave rise to parliamentary questions. The prime minister, hoping that he would be borne out by the facts, replied that the ministers had been misreported. He then waited impatiently for the official reports of what actually had been said. Fleming had assured him by phone from Rome that he had not spoken as reported in the press. When the telegrams arrived, Diefenbaker was extremely relieved when he concluded that they could be interpreted to bear out what he had said to the House. Privately, however, I thought that Fleming and Hees had gone pretty far and that the press reports were not inaccurate.[4]

The Accra incident, aside from giving birth to a few memorable cartoons in the daily press, also prompted a lively debate in the cabinet over government policy and tactics. The minister of justice, Davie Fulton, was reported to have questioned whether Canada was justified in taking an obstructive attitude.[5] Canada had tried but failed to persuade the United Kingdom not to proceed with negotiations; now it should accept what was happening and put a stop to its opposition. The prime minister was absent from the cabinet on this occasion but the discussion was of course reported to him. Combined with critical press and parliamentary reaction to the reports from Accra, it was a reminder that the government would be wiser to avoid being seen as the scapegoat should the United Kingdom fail in its endeavour to negotiate its way into Europe. In some, though not all, future public utterances, he made the point that the United Kingdom was free to take its own decision, although Canada would expect the British authorities to protect the trade interests of Commonwealth countries and 'essentials' of the Commonwealth itself. A typical statement made on 10 November at Halifax included the following passages:

We said to the British Government that we had no objection to their entering the Common Market providing that as a Commonwealth member to enter would not interfere with the development of the Commonwealth and would not remove those preferences which are so important to us and to the maintenance of our national prosperity.

... the stand Canada has taken ... strengthens [the United Kingdom's] hand in dealing with the countries ... of Europe to ensure that if Britain enters the Common Market, she will preserve existing ties and preferences ...

... I know what Prime Minister Macmillan has said and I rely on his statement that if entry is made into the Common Market, there will be preserved and maintained those Commonwealth things without which this Commonwealth could not continue.

Meanwhile, in London, Drew did not conceal his utter distaste for the course of action being pursued so determinedly by the Macmillan government. A press report from London in November left the impression that Drew's failure to attend a meeting of Commonwealth high commissioners on the subject of United Kingdom negotiations with Europe was a deliberate snub to the British. Diefenbaker, worried at the public effect of the report, asked me to prepare a telegram to Drew instructing him to deny that his absence from the meeting had been deliberate. The message went off, and Diefenbaker followed it up with a phone call to make sure that the high commissioner acted on it promptly. The denial must have looked strange to those journalists who had been told by an official on the staff of the high commissioner that Drew's decision not to attend the meeting had indeed been intended as a snub. The incident was minor but, like the Accra affair, it illustrated the difficulty Diefenbaker had in coordinating the public statements of his senior colleagues on matters where his own feelings were mixed and his signal therefore muffled.

Towards the end of November, officials were asked to contribute material for a CBC 'Nation's Business' broadcast on the same issue. On 27 November:

'I spent an hour with Ed Ritchie, Gerry Stoner and Michel Dupuy working out the best way of approaching [the subject] without tying our hands in the negotiations or saying something unduly offensive to one or other of the parties ... The trouble is that we don't really know what attitude the government intends to adopt. This makes it hard to draft but at least officials have an opportunity to try to influence the public presentation for the first time in many months and it is therefore worth doing, especially if we can get away from the negative attitude the government has been criticized for ...

Bob Bryce is also in favour of saying something conciliatory to the U.K. after all this acrimony ... but P.M. may want to sustain a pose of injured apprehension.'[6]

A speech text was produced by the following day. It gave the factual background, examined what the British initiative meant for Canadian trade and industry, and reviewed the courses open to Canada. The prime minister did not object to its contents, but, as drafted, it did not serve his purpose. It turned out that a political approach was what he had in mind. Stung by opposition criticisms that the government had been needlessly negative, he mounted a partisan defence of its tactics. He quoted press reports of a recent statement by Edward Heath, the United Kingdom minister negotiating with the six European nations. Heath, he claimed, had made it clear to them that the terms of British entry must include special arrangements to ensure the continued agricultural exports of Canada, New Zealand, and Australia. This, he argued, showed that Canadian tactics were paying off. He gave no clues to future policy other than to reaffirm his faith in the Commonwealth and to register his reliance on the United Kingdom's pledge to protect the interests of Commonwealth countries.

It was, of course, for the prime minister to decide what needed to be said at that stage. To seek to protect Canadian trade interests was natural, but to stand in the way of UK policy seemed not only unrealistic but, from a Canadian point of view, self-defeating. It did not seem to occur to him that a total lack of understanding or conciliation towards the British position would tend to increase their indifference to Canada's problems and also obstruct the natural evolution of Canada's relationship with the United Kingdom. But as his political staff said, attempting to bring solace, the election in Canada was not far off and he was not looking for votes across the ocean.

As the year ended, the news did not improve. The British negotiator with the EEC informed Drew in early December that there would be no progress on the treatment to be accorded to manufactured goods by the Six so long as the United Kingdom insisted on the principle of maintaining existing arrangements for their entry into the United Kingdom.

More painful personally for the prime minister was the realization that he was not being invited to be in Bermuda on 21 December when President Kennedy and Prime Minister Macmillan were to meet. On 7 December 'He showed for the first time today his resentment at not being asked to go to Bermuda. "They could ask me to Bermuda," he said, when informed that Macmillan had implied that JGD had been invited to London to discuss the European common market.'[7] The following day, on being questioned by reporters, Diefenbaker said that no consideration had been given to his going to London for this purpose. He asked me, however, to 'remind' the new British high commissioner, Lord Amory, that Prime Minister St Laurent had gone to Bermuda at Macmillan's invitation in 1957, an indication of how wounded he was at not being invited. I noted in my diary that it was 'an impossible task to carry out in the present atmosphere,' and I am not sure how hard I tried.[8] In any event it had become known that Edward Heath would be free to visit Ottawa early in January to renew ministerial-level discussions, and Diefenbaker had no alternative but to accept this as a further stage in consultations with the United Kingdom.

217

22

Revisiting East-West Tensions

The Canadian government might have been well served if, after President Kennedy's visit, the prime minister had been able to devote himself more intensively to domestic problems. By the spring of 1961 the government was beset with economic anxieties, differences within the cabinet on defence policy, an increasingly unsympathetic press, and a bitter public quarrel over economic issues with the government of the Bank of Canada, James Coyne. The Liberal opposition was showing unmistakeable signs of recovery. The prime minister himself was showing evident strain, and there was much speculation about the timing of the next election.

Important as his domestic priorities were, he became as deeply involved in international affairs in the summer and fall of 1961 as he had ever been since taking office. Apart from nuclear policy and the European aims of the British, the government was concerned with numerous other issues, of which its policy towards Cuba, its responsibilities in the Congo and as a member of the International Commission in Laos, and its attempts to keep negotiations going on disarmament were only the most prominent. Although the minister handled most of these issues, he had frequently to be away from Ottawa and, rather than relying on an acting minister, it was Diefenbaker's normal practice to take over all important external affairs matters when the minister was absent. The fact that many of the international questions were sensitive in domestic political terms made the prime minister all the more inclined to become personally involved. It was obvious that the unofficial campaign for the next federal election was already under way. 'Most people,' I noted in my diary on 13 July, 'think that the Prime Minister cannot do otherwise than have an election this year.'

More threatening to world peace than any other of the current international issues was the sharp revival of East-West tensions in June. In two exacting days of argument and negotiation in Vienna, President Kennedy and Nikita Khrushchev, while apparently establishing a foundation of cautious respect for each other, failed to reach agreement on the two most vital specific issues – Berlin and nuclear bomb tests. Before the month of June was out, a new crisis over Berlin had erupted and, ominously, the Soviet government had withdrawn its delegates from the table in Geneva where for three years the nuclear powers (United States, USSR, United Kingdom, and France) had been negotiating for an end of, or at least limits to, the testing of nuclear weapons.

Since open disagreement between the superpowers preoccupies their allies as much as it does the powers themselves, there was for Canada no question of distancing itself from the crisis. What was clearly essential and urgent was to join in the process of containing its spread and of devising solutions. It was not an exaggeration to say that unless the emergency was handled with the finest judgment and the steadiest nerves, Washington and Moscow might become engaged in adventures from which neither would feel able to back down. Even if he had felt inclined, the prime minister of Canada could not have avoided becoming involved.

BERLIN: A CRISIS OF 'INEXPRESSIBLE GRAVITY'[1]

Twice before, in 1948 and in 1958–9, the Western allies had resisted Soviet attempts to reshape the agreements which the four allied powers (United States, USSR, United Kingdom, and France) had reached on Germany and Berlin. Now, Khrushchev had revived his 1958 proposal to conclude a peace treaty with East Germany, unless a 'peaceful solution' to the question of Berlin was agreed to by the end of the year. The Soviet chairman's initiative had been discussed at length with President Kennedy at Vienna and, having been rejected there, it soon became the focus of anxious discussion among governments and in the international press. If Soviet demands were acceded to, the rights of the Western powers in West Berlin and their access to the city might be seriously impaired, and so might the political and economic freedom which West Berlin had come to enjoy by reason of its links with the West German government in Bonn and the Western alliance. Among the Western governments, therefore, the conclusion was unanimous that the Soviet leader had thrown down a challenge which must be faced as a test of Western resolve. The leadership powers of President Kennedy were an important ingredient of this response. It was a challenge which he welcomed, particularly in light of the recent humiliation of the Bay of Pigs. On the president's instructions, American representatives in NATO and around the world made it clear that the preservation of Western rights and democratic freedoms in West Berlin were vital objectives for the United States. A great policy debate began in Washington, with the aim of deciding what steps the United States and its allies should take.

In Canada, a similar debate took shape. By the beginning of July, Diefenbaker was treating Berlin as a staple in the political dialogue. He had no personal doubts as to the gravity of the crisis that was developing or as to the basic justice of the Western case against Khrushchev's diplomatic offensive. Yet there was room for debate on how the Western countries should respond. It would be agreeable to be able to record that the prime minister entered this political debate with a solid confidence in Kennedy's capacity to give assured leadership to the Western alliance, but it would not reflect his mood. The Bay of Pigs blunder had revived his misgivings about the president's judgment. The reports from the Vienna meeting had not portrayed the president as having done more than hold his own in the rigorous exchanges with Khrushchev. When East-West tensions heightened after Vienna, therefore, Diefenbaker had not been surprised. There was an element of the doomsday philosopher about him, and this side of his restless mind often took command when he contemplated the vision of the inexperienced Kennedy coping with the Soviet leader. His pessimistic leanings had been reinforced late in June when the Soviet negotiators withdrew from the nuclear test-ban talks in Geneva.

Diefenbaker's continued personal reservations about Kennedy's leadership did not diminish the vigour of his own calls for allied solidarity or his public support for the president's position. The prime minister's first instinct was to take to the public platform, to denounce Khrushchev and all his works, and to campaign for Western unity in the face of Soviet pressures.[2] During the summer months he spoke frequently on this theme. He often advocated negotiation with the USSR but he was relatively slow in coming personally to grips with the intricacies of how the allies should respond to Soviet tactics. Thus, on 11 July I noted in my diary: 'He's much preoccupied with Berlin and seems to fear the worst. Shows very little interest in the positive side of looking for new formulas. Seems content to issue warnings of approaching trouble combined with homilies on the need for Western unity.'

This comment reflects my sympathy with the prevailing view at that time in External Affairs, where there was impatience with the absence of substance in the prime minister's speeches. The officials in External Affairs thought it was not enough, although it was necessary, to show firmness and unity; it was Canada's role to caution against bluster and to think of ways in which negotiated settlements could be reached without showing weakness. I suppose, in retrospect, that in External Affairs we were still not weaned from the Pearson method and outlook. One could equally say that the department had not fully adjusted itself to the realities of serving a prime minister whose priorities were so different – so much, as it were, closer to home.

On 13 July, the sensational affair of James Coyne, governor of the Bank of Canada, came to its climax on Parliament Hill. Coyne resigned, amid a tremendous political furore. In spite of the opposition's efforts to make capital of the affair, the prime minister had seldom appeared to be seriously discomfited by it, perhaps because he pushed the dirty work onto Donald Fleming. Yet it had been messy and time-consuming and he was relieved to have it removed at an extremely demanding stage. For one thing, he would have more time to devote to Berlin.

Consultations in NATO became purposeful late in July, after Kennedy's major speech on 25 July outlining the US approach to the Berlin situation, a speech which contained much that Diefenbaker approved. The question of how to react to Soviet tactics became even more critical with the closing in mid-August of some of the access gates to West Berlin and the decision of the Soviet and East German authorities that the Berlin Wall should be erected to seal off the escape routes to the West. On 14 August, referring to the interplay between the prime minister and External Affairs, I wrote: 'Much discussion of military, economic, psychological, and diplomatic counter-measures. General disposition as usual to appear firm, talk of unity, avoidance of nuclear war, hope for the best, and try like hell to think of something substantive for Canada to suggest. P.M. very interested-fascinated and somewhat awed by Khrushchev.'

Diefenbaker discussed Berlin in a speech to the Weekly Newspapers Association in Halifax on 15 August, stressing Western rights in the city and the determination of the Western allies not to be intimidated by Khrushchev. It was a solemn, tough speech, influenced by the news of the Berlin Wall and designed to condition public opinion for military preparedness measures that would come before the cabinet in the next week.

I suppose that during this period Diefenbaker had really been conducting his own brand of opinion poll. Statements and speeches drawing on the daily news and diplomatic traffic had naturally attracted press comment and correspondence from the public. Reactions, particularly on matters relating to Berlin, were discussed with his cabinet colleagues, with a view to determining what position the Canadian government should take in the NATO discussions of counter-measures. At least five meetings of the cabinet took place between 15 and 25 August, most of them touching on some aspect of the crisis.

Rather to the prime minister's surprise, he had to conclude from his soundings that Canadian opinion on the Berlin crisis was 'softer' than the line he had so far adopted. On 22 August he was, as I noted in my diary, 'evidently struck by the size of the correspondence from the public questioning the need for nailing down our commitments to Berlin. P.M. anxious to talk bravely but pretty shrewd about avoiding anything that could pin him down. Very anxious to say something publicly now about the substance.' The press in Canada, too, had been sceptical of the wisdom of provoking Khrushchev to further adventures. The prime minister knew that the moment had come to give a serious and comprehensive statement going beyond anti-Soviet rhetoric and exhortations to Western unity. The occasion was to be the meeting of the Canadian Bar Association in Winnipeg on 1 September. The Department of External Affairs, he said, was to produce its best effort.

The irreverent reaction in External Affairs was to inquire whether this time a serious speech was really needed. So many solid texts had been jettisoned in the cause of party politics. The moment of scepticism passed quickly but there was some question in Robertson's mind as to which of his senior colleagues might best be assigned to supervise the drafting. Robertson reckoned that a text emphasizing negotiations might not be strong enough for the prime minister's taste. It would have to be 'robust.' Partly for this reason he chose to give the job to Marcel Cadieux, a respected deputy undersecretary responsible for legal affairs whose strong anti-communist views were more likely to result in a speech acceptable to the prime minister. Cadieux was assisted by specialists in policy areas such as Soviet affairs, Germany, European security, defence, and disarmament. As the drafting proceeded, so did the crisis: US troops were reinforced in Berlin; cabinet was considering an increase in the strength of Canadian armed forces; another tough note on Berlin came from the Soviet government, followed a few days later by an announcement of the Soviet intention to resume nuclear testing; and contingency planning about the best tactics to follow politically and militarily was at a high pitch in the NATO Council.

For most of the next week Cadieux's draft ricocheted from one office to another in External Affairs. Everyone with the slightest excuse for contributing had a crack at it. There was disagreement on how much emphasis to put on negotiation and possible concessions. There were those who, like Cadieux himself, preferred to see the emphasis placed on a firm stand for Western rights in Berlin and solidarity in the NATO alliance, with the primary aim of deterring the Soviet government from further forcing its diplomatic offensive. Others thought it more important that Canada, while not breaking with its allies, should show itself ready to search out avenues for negotiation between the Western powers and the Soviet government. But with typical determination and concern for clarity, Cadieux held it together.

With members of his political staff and myself in attendance, Diefenbaker spent parts of 30 and 31 August working on the draft. A good deal of the language was changed but the substance remained. Reflecting his correspondence from the public, Diefenbaker spoke repeatedly, as the work went on, about the amount of anti-German feeling in the country, the need to say clearly why we must be prepared to fight if necessary over Berlin, and the importance of showing ourselves ready to negotiate. In the late stages of the drafting, word came that the Soviet government had decided to resume testing of nuclear bombs, an event which inevitably caused the tone of the speech to harden. And when, on the afternoon of the speech, it was announced that a Soviet bomb had in fact been test-exploded, further last-minute adjustments were needed to the text.

In the circumstances, as I read it over more than twenty-five years later, it strikes me as one of the best speeches Diefenbaker gave while in office.[3] Certainly, although he was facing a hypercritical audience, he gave a powerful and polished performance. He was pleased by the press reaction and went out of his way to be appreciative of the work which had been done by External Affairs. This kind of compliment popped up now and again and he obviously meant it to be passed on. He was much more reliant now on the department, though he would never have admitted it.

A few days later an unexpected tribute to the speech, and to the government's general handling of the Berlin crisis, came from L.B. Pearson. Diefenbaker had consulted Pearson on 6 September, a rare event but indicative of Diefenbaker's concern about the Berlin situation and his desire to obtain Pearson's support for the decisions the government would be bringing before the House on the strengthening of the armed forces. Pearson told Diefenbaker that his Winnipeg speech had 'struck the right note.' Diefenbaker was more sincerely gratified by Pearson's words than he liked to admit.

NUCLEAR TESTING

President Kennedy's decision to resume nuclear testing, in view of the recent Soviet resumption, also caused concern. To Diefenbaker this was, as he put it privately, 'a preposterous decision' which threw away the propaganda advantage the West had gained from the Soviet announcement. His disapproval was less explicit, but still manifest, in his speech in the House of Commons on 11 September. He implied that Howard Green's work for disarmament and against nuclear testing might have suffered a setback by reason of the Soviet and American decisions. Some press reports speculated that, in the ambiguous references Diefenbaker made to Green's idealism, he had been preparing the political execution of the minister. In fact, although his language was capable of different interpretations, I believe that in this case the prime minister was more concerned to show support for Green at an obviously difficult time. He had made notes to this effect beforehand.

What had also disturbed Diefenbaker about the US decision to resume nuclear testing was that the president had given him no previous notice. Afterwards, in the post-speech decompression period, he enquired how I had liked that part of his speech. I said I assumed he had considered speaking privately to the president first, rather than publicly and after the US administration had expressed regrets. (Heeney had conveyed the administration's regrets in explaining the Congressional pressures on the president to resume testing.) The view I had expressed was all very well, he replied, but the way to get attention was to say things so that people could hear. He had to maintain a balance, he went on, between the extremes of anti-Americanism and a readiness to do, or seem to do, as the Americans wanted. The United Kingdom could not be so independent. Macmillan had told him that they couldn't afford to ruffle the United States too much. But that, Diefenbaker said, did not apply to us.

EASING TENSIONS

The Canadian government's position in the Berlin crisis had now been established. After an uncertain start, it had become a balanced position, reflecting the recognized need for a blend of military preparedness and diplomatic exploration. Consultations in NATO continued, if only because, so long as there was a clear risk of interference with the access routes to West Berlin, it would have been imprudent not to have developed counter-measures.

For approximately a month after the parliamentary debate, Diefenbaker continued personally to supervise matters from day to day. Once he complained that a telegram of instructions which had been sent by External Affairs to Canadian representatives in NATO capitals had not reflected fully enough his speech to the House of Commons. Unfortunately for the department, he was right. In the last ten days of September he made several extensive speeches, justifying the steps taken by the government. He relied on well-tried themes, varying them according to the audience and the latest news. Significantly, too, as a speech by Kennedy on disarmament at the United Nations on 25 September found favour with Canadian public opinion, Diefenbaker dwelt on the vital importance of ending nuclear testing, preventing the spread of nuclear weaponry, and achieving progress towards general disarmament. Finally, among the recurring themes, was his yearning for a grand allied declaration, in which the governments of the Free World would proclaim the principles for which they stood. Again, though, there was no answering echo from abroad.

By late September the United States and the USSR began direct talks between their foreign ministers (Rusk and Gromyko) at the United Nations. At first there was no cause to assume that the danger was past, but as early as 4 October

Gromyko was said by the Americans to be showing greater flexibility than previously. Detailed ideas were being exchanged and the will to negotiate was maturing on both sides.

Further encouraging evidence that the crisis might be easing was given to Diefenbaker on 11 October by President Kekkonen of Finland, who was visiting Canada. Kekkonen quoted Leonid Brezhnev, who had recently spent several days in talks with the Finnish government, as saying that the Soviet authorities were 'not prisoners of the timetable.' If they found that useful negotiations with the West were possible, they would continue them regardless of the timetable.

In a speech to the Congress of the Soviet Communist party on 18 October, Khrushchev went an important step further. The Western powers were showing some understanding of the Berlin situation, he said, and were inclined to seek a solution. If this turned out to be the case, the Soviet government would not insist on signing a peace treaty with East Germany before 31 December 1961. This was the start of the winding down of the Berlin crisis and, although the international negotiations on the city's future continued for several months, Diefenbaker's personal involvement diminished after mid-October and, in effect, he handed the Berlin file back to the minister.

SOVIET COLONIALISM

In the anxious aftermath of the Vienna summit meeting in June, with the Berlin crisis brewing and Khrushchev at his most provocative, the prime minister had seen political gains in resuming his attacks on the Soviet government. He was particularly intent on exposing the hypocrisy of Soviet criticisms of the Western colonial powers. In one speech he denounced the Soviet Union as 'the leading agent of colonial subjugation in the modern world.' And with what, I confess, seemed to me a complete disregard for reality, he called on the Soviet leaders to give the Ukraine and 'the other subjugated countries' the right to free elections to determine the kind of government the people desired. Why did Khrushchev deny them their free choice, he would ask, in a tone that made his audience partners in the possession of an ugly secret.

Undoubtedly the benefits of these attacks on the Soviet government were calculated in terms of the vote in Winnipeg, Toronto, and other large concentrations of Eastern European ethnic groups. Diefenbaker was determined not to squander the dividends he had earned in September 1960 at the United Nations. He was being urged by some of his advisers and friends to return to the United Nations in the fall of 1961 and once again he had considered the idea of introducing a resolution on Soviet colonialism, and he had not failed to notice that in a foreign affairs debate early in September, Pearson had referred to 'the new colonialism,' a sign that the Liberal party recognized its political appeal. Diefenbaker asked late in September for an External Affairs memorandum on the prospects of success for a resolution on Soviet colonialism, including an estimate of the attitudes of other delegations at the United Nations.

Soundings had been taken at the General Assembly to assess the support that could be expected if Canada were to sponsor the kind of resolution the prime minister had in mind. The result was predictably discouraging. Diefenbaker did, however, retain for some weeks the idea of again addressing the General Assembly himself, but eventually decided against it. In preparing a speech for a Toronto audience he wanted to promise some action on Soviet colonialism at the 1962 session of the UN Assembly. With the aid of the department I advised him that it was by no means certain that sufficient international support could be secured to warrant tabling a resolution at the next session. He agreed to remove the promise and replace it with a hope, a small change which proved its worth a year later when a large majority of UN members again declined support.

Diefenbaker's insistence on keeping the 'Captive Nations' issue alive developed into the biggest single irritant between him and the Department of External Affairs. It was seen in the department as self-defeating, not because it was an invalid criticism of Soviet policy but because, if the issue had been taken up in the United Nations, it would certainly have been a defeat. Moreover, it had little, if any, chance of causing any change in Soviet policy, and might only engender baseless hopes in those whom it was designed to encourage. During the Berlin crisis, Howard Green, while no apologist for Khrushchev, thought it was the business of Canada to persuade its allies to be flexible and avoid threats, so that the atmosphere would be more conducive to negotiation. Khrushchev, for all his waywardness, was a communist leader you could at least talk to.

Diefenbaker, of course, could see the arguments for moderation. On occasions which he regarded as designed for international as well as domestic consumption, he observed a degree of restraint. When, however, the call of domestic politics was echoing, efforts to modify his message were often painful and generally unsuccessful. The gulf between External Affairs and the prime minister on this subject would widen noticeably in the months to come.

23

Growing Nuclear Debate

When Howard Green began in 1959 to have success in establishing a direct link between disarmament and defence policy, he had given a special character to the nuclear weapons controversy in Canada. Delay in moving forward on nuclear negotiations suited Green because it meant that he had more time to build public concern against the storage of nuclear weapons in Canada. For the new minister of national defence, Douglas Harkness, delay meant prolonged frustration, especially since the time was approaching when the delivery systems for the Bomarcs (in Canada) and the F-104Gs and the Honest Johns (in Europe) would become available. While Green was using every device to keep alive the vision of disarmament, Harkness was being forced to make the best possible justification for the government's failure to complete the negotiations with the United States and NATO authorities.

From the prime minister's standpoint, Green's campaign against nuclear weapons had afforded time and scope for continued improvisation, a phrase which offers a kindly description of Diefenbaker's conduct of the nuclear weapons issue. Improvisation had been a workable political tactic until matters took on a serious complexion with the Berlin crisis of 1961. During that crisis, circumstances nearly brought him to a point of decision, but when the moment passed without result he stepped back and seized what looked like a worthy opportunity to justify yet further delay. By late September, with the next election much in his mind, the prime minister had every reason to avoid bringing the nuclear issue to a head, no matter how exasperated his manoeuvres left Harkness and his advisers, not to speak of President Kennedy and his. Improvisation was 'in' again.

AT HOME

The discussions on nuclear weapons policy between Kennedy and Diefenbaker in May 1961 had added a new ingredient to the political drama that would eventually bring Diefenbaker's government down. Although Kennedy had not been able to talk Diefenbaker into accepting nuclear weapons, the president had himself heard the prime minister say that he personally favoured that course of action and intended to try to bring Canadian public opinion around. At the end of the Kennedy visit, Diefenbaker knew that while he had bought himself a few months' grace, his space for manoeuvre had been reduced. He was aware that Kennedy would expect him to 'produce' and this knowledge pestered him. It gave him the feeling, not unjustified, that he had an important obligation to the president. This feeling would be a factor, unwelcome and seldom mentioned, in the unfolding of the nuclear weapons controversy from that time forward. On 23 May, less than a week after the Diefenbaker-Kennedy meeting, the US ambassador called on the prime minister to confirm that the United States would not insist that the F-101BS be equipped with nuclear warheads. Pleasantly surprised, Diefenbaker took the news as a vindication of his tactics. He had avoided an immediate decision on the nuclear issue but, at the same time, had secured an additional large order for Canadair, the company that would manufacture the Canadian share of the F-104GS to be produced under the agreement. He had been under pressure from several ministers not to forgo the boost that the agreement would provide in the form of jobs in the Montreal area. As for the international effects, it was hard to tell whether the US concession would make it harder for Diefenbaker to refuse nuclear weapons in the longer run. At the time I thought it would, that the president might 'be better at poker than he looks.' In the light of later events I obviously underestimated Diefenbaker's powers of procrastination.

On 24 July, after delays reflecting the divisions between the responsible ministers and the readiness of the prime minister to temporize, the cabinet held the first of a series of important discussions on the position to be taken in negotiations with the United States on nuclear arms. These discussions were bound up, inevitably, with the continuing crisis over Berlin, although Canada was not, by direct consequence of that crisis, under NATO or US pressure to accelerate its decisions on nuclear arms. The atmosphere of the crisis nevertheless lent a certain compulsive emphasis to the strenuous exchanges in the cabinet on nuclear arms between 24 July and the last week of August.

Diefenbaker's role in these discussions was, of course, that of chairman, but he did not conceal his own inclinations. He agreed instinctively with what Harkness had to say in favour of going ahead with negotiations on nuclear arms, but he could not bring himself to disregard the force of the arguments made on the other side by Green. He knew the political appeal of disarmament and he sensed that Green was right in saying that public opinion was becoming steadily more concerned about the idea of accepting nuclear weapons. At the same time he did not wish to be accused of hindering the United States in its global defence responsibilities or of depriving Canadian forces of modern equipment, whether under NATO command in Europe or for the air defence of North America. He was stranded, alone, between his ministers of defence and external affairs and their supporters. It was an uncomfortable place to be. Harkness and Green were both strong characters, respected colleagues, and convinced advocates of totally opposite points of view. No wonder the prime minister, in the privacy of his office, would look out solemnly on Parliament Hill and remark on the loneliness of his job.

Diefenbaker's awareness of the opposition to nuclear weapons in the cabinet and in some segments of public opinion did not deter him from working towards an arrangement that would have partially satisfied Harkness and might not have been unacceptable to Green. And there was another powerful reason for edging forward. In a secret letter dated 3 August, President Kennedy, citing the importance of full defence preparedness in the Berlin situation, appealed to Diefenbaker to renew efforts to conclude negotiations on nuclear weapons for North American air defence.[1] This letter was a clear reminder of their discussion in Ottawa. Diefenbaker replied on 11 August with an undertaking to consider the decisions needed in order to initiate discussions with US representatives.[2]

Against this background, in his speech at Halifax on 15 August, Diefenbaker introduced a significant reference to the need for nuclear weapons in NATO. It read as follows in the notes he approved for the speech: 'Those who advocate that Canada should withdraw from NATO in the event that nuclear weapons are made available for the possession and control of NATO are advocating a course that would be dangerous to survival of the forces of NATO should war begin, and it would be dangerous for the survival of freedom itself ... Faced by the overwhelming power of Soviet might in East Germany close to West Berlin with large divisions fully armed, would you place in the hands of those who guard the portals of freedom nothing but bows and arrows? They would stand against overwhelming power – it is simple as that.'[3] He was disappointed by the absence of press reaction. Reports of his speech, he said the next day, had 'not taken the significance' of his reference to nuclear policy. He had been intending to prepare public opinion for the provision of nuclear warheads for Canadian ground and air forces in Western Europe. His private comments at the time, however, gave me the clear impression that he was contemplating, against the background of the Berlin crisis, a generally more tolerant stance towards nuclear weapons, not only for Canadian forces in Europe but also for North American defence. 'I just do not understand those who do not want to accept them,' he said, in puzzled frustration. In retrospect, I am reasonably certain that the part of the Halifax speech quoted above was intended to be the first real public step in fulfilling his

229

promise to Kennedy that he would try to move Canadian public opinion towards acceptance of nuclear weapons. He had made a promise to the president and did not like to to renege on it.

The end of August came and, in spite of rumours and press speculation, no announcement on nuclear policy was forthcoming. The government's decision on the strengthening of forces as part of the collective NATO effort on Berlin was announced by the prime minister on 7 September. It revealed nothing new on nuclear policy, but the speculation continued. After all, Diefenbaker had himself helped to stir it up, and when Harkness told the House on 12 September that it was only prudent to obtain the nuclear weapons systems 'now so that they will be available and our forces trained to use them,' the indications seemed to be clear enough. But once again, the prime minister was not ready: the hesitation waltz was played. Pearson, though helpful to the government on Berlin, was questioning whether Canada's air defence forces should be armed with nuclear weapons and whether they could be so armed without causing an expansion of the 'nuclear club.'⁴ Diefenbaker, scenting trouble, stalled, but the controversy continued.

A few days later there was more trouble. A *Newsweek* story reported that Kennedy had written recently to the prime minister on aspects of North American defence. Diefenbaker at first denied this and added that personal correspondence of this kind was in any case not revealed. Later it emerged that a White House press spokesman had admitted the existence of a letter, thus undermining Diefenbaker's position. Arnold Heeney, trying to restore peace, phoned from Washington with a message from the president offering to comment in a way helpful to the prime minister. But Diefenbaker was furious that the president's letter had been known to the White House press office. He instructed Heeney to tell Pierre Salinger, Kennedy's press secretary, that he was very disturbed and that the incident would have adverse effects on defence cooperation. On 19 September Diefenbaker told me that he had been intending to go 'quite far' on nuclear weapons policy in a CBC broadcast on 20 September. Now he could not take the position he had intended. He said that he had been bringing 'people' (he seemed to mean his cabinet colleagues and other political contacts) to a point of willingness to accept nuclear weapons, but that the leak and resultant appearance of pressure from Washington had set the whole process back. He was unusually agitated.

I am not sure what caused his sudden switch from a positive to a negative position at that time. Certainly he was extremely annoyed to have it known publicly that he had been chivvied by the president to get moving, at a time when he had been straining to find ways of bringing public opinion around to the acceptance of nuclear weapons.⁵ The CBC broadcast went ahead with no nuclear content, and it appeared that the leak from the White House had had the effect of discouraging the prime minister from doing what the president most wanted of him. It seemed ironic that this should have occurred just at the stage when he was bracing himself to move against the anti-nuclear advice he was getting from Green and also from opposition leader Pearson.[6]

What seems, again ironically, to have contributed to the outcome was a speech Kennedy made on 25 September at the United Nations to unveil a new US disarmament plan, with emphasis on the theme that there should be no extension of the 'nuclear club.' Canada had taken part in consultations that had led to the new plan, and the play given it by the press put the spotlight again on the relationship between disarmament and nuclear weapons policy in Canada. On 20 September the prime minister told the House of Commons that 'important proposals' on disarmament were to be expected shortly.[7] Clearly, he was now drifting away from a pro-nuclear stance. At the same time, the publicity was giving fresh impetus to the cause of Howard Green, whose political stock had seemed uncertain in recent weeks. A favourable commentary on the new plan was prepared in External Affairs. The department fully expected that it would be given by Green, as the recognized proponent of disarmament. Instead, by some dexterous manipulation, the prime minister gave the statement. He made the US disarmament plan sound as though he had written it.

It appeared that by whatever chain of reasoning, the prime minister had indeed decided to alter course. All of a sudden he was finding time to receive anti-nuclear delegations, a move which was not without its perils. At the end of one such meeting, on 6 October, the leader of the visiting delegation told the press that he had received assurances from the prime minister that Canada would not acquire nuclear weapons except in the event of war. Informed of this, the prime minister said it was 'not a correct quote.' But he went on to say that the government accepted the principle enunciated by President Kennedy that there should be no extension of the 'nuclear club.' Pressed as to how this policy would affect the Bomarc missiles, he would say only that they were equipped so that if nuclear weapons were needed in the event of war, the Bomarcs would have the necessary launching capacity. Green had captured the prime minister's interest in the theory that so long as the nuclear weapons systems were capable of being fitted with nuclear warheads, the actual decision to bring them into Canada for storage or installation could be postponed until they were needed in an emergency.

As this was so totally opposite to the line the prime minister had seemed convinced of only two weeks before, the department asked me if I could find out what was going on. I asked him about the change. His answer was that Kennedy's recent statement regarding the prohibition on transfer of control of nuclear weapons represented a 'pronounced change' as compared with the position the president had taken in their talks earlier in the year. The public position now taken by the president had 'killed' nuclear weapons in Canada unless there was war. I said it was the department's understanding that the disarmament plan put forward by the president had been drafted so as to provide that ownership of nuclear weapons would remain with the United States but that control of use would be joint between the United States and Canada. It was argued that since the weapons could not be released for use without the consent of the United States, an agreement such as this would not constitute an addition to the number of nations in the 'nuclear club.' The prime minister said that he was aware of this argument but considered it a play on words. He went on to say, however, that the same difficulty would not arise if there were a satisfactory form of collective control governing the use of nuclear weapons by Canadian forces under NATO command in Europe. The conversation was then interrupted, but as I left the prime minister volunteered that the information he had given me might be passed on. Later I showed him my record of the conversation which he returned to me without objection.

Realizing that the prime minister considered that he had taken and made known an important decision, I spoke immediately to Bryce and found that he had had similar, though not as explicit, indications that the prime minister was using Kennedy's UN speech as the excuse for declining to allow nuclear weapons into Canada except in the event of war. Bryce notified Harkness, who had heard nothing from Diefenbaker and was mystified. Green, however, was rejoicing. Kennedy's speech had given him a timely chance to underline the case for avoiding any further move towards nuclear commitments. Diefenbaker, apparently on the spur of the political moment, had decided to follow Green's advice, although I am sure he was perfectly well aware that the president's proposal at the United Nations could have been presented to Canadian opinion as not expanding the 'nuclear club.' For the Americans it must have been galling that Diefenbaker was giving to the president's words an interpretation exactly opposite to what was intended.

AT THE UNITED NATIONS

Despite reminders from the president and the impatience of the defence authorities in both countries, no progress was made on nuclear policy in the late months of 1961. A partial reason for this lay in the agenda of the UN General Assembly, where a series of resolutions aiming to end nuclear testing, prohibit the use or spread of nuclear weapons, and advance the prospects for disarmament required decisions with clear implications for Canada's defence policy. Like all such decisions at the General Assembly, these resolutions did not present themselves in orderly sequence. Often there was not enough time to place them before cabinet committees or the full cabinet. For the most part it fell to the minister of external affairs to decide how Canada would vote, and since Green was personally so devoted to the cause of peace through disarmament, it was to be expected that under his guidance the Canadian delegation would be instrumental in or associated with 'peaceful' initiatives. The minister took full advantage of this state of affairs.

Apart from being frustrating for Harkness and the Department of National Defence, the situation was also uncomfortable for the prime minister. It was Green's normal practice to seek Diefenbaker's approval for votes or tactical moves which had policy implications. Occasionally the two did not connect. Once, for example, there was a contretemps over a resolution urging a complete prohibition of the use of nuclear weapons. The resolution had been put forward by a group of non-nuclear countries and it was clearly at cross purposes with NATO defence policy, which depended for its effectiveness on the US nuclear deterrent. The obvious choice from the defence point of view would have been to cast a vote against it. But Green, strongly pressed by the government's disarmament adviser, General E.L.M. Burns, instructed the Canadian delegation to abstain in the vote, a middle course which placed Canada in the company of a group of political moderates but fell short of unswerving solidarity with the prevailing NATO line. Before the first vote was taken, an amendment had been brought forward and the minister felt it advisable to seek the prime minister's approval on the new wording.

As the minister was not available to speak personally to Diefenbaker, I was asked to show the documents to the prime minister and obtain his reaction. Unfortunately the minister had not consulted him before issuing the original instruction, an oversight which led Diefenbaker to say that he was not going to be drawn in on this one. He also made it clear that if he had been the one to take the first decision, he would have reached a different conclusion. I noted in my diary that 'the minister had been left to take the rap with the compensation, however, of not having been overridden.' Green held to the abstention when the first vote was taken.

On 23 November, before the final vote, I noted: 'P.M. called at 5:30 p.m. and I gave him the latest items including the current dilemma over whether we should change our vote in the General Assembly on resolutions dealing with the use and spread of nuclear weapons ... P.M. is obviously doubtful of the wisdom of voting in a way which throws doubt on our solidarity with NATO defence policy. The minister of national defence is not drawn into this and I think the P.M. hopes the U.N. votes can be left in a special compartment and not treated as creating an inherent contradiction in our foreign and defence policies.' At the time that note was written I was not aware of what, if anything, the prime minister would do. I presume (but cannot be certain) that he persuaded Green to alter the Canadian position because, when the final vote was taken, General Burns was obliged to explain the change in Canada's vote from an abstention to a vote against the resolution. It was a tactical defeat for Green which did not go unreported in the Canadian press.

Any satisfaction which the pro-nuclear champions may then have felt was quickly dispelled a couple of weeks later when Canada joined the three Scandinavian members of NATO in voting in favour of a Swedish resolution which called on the secretary-general to ascertain the conditions on which non-nuclear nations might be prepared to enter into 'specific undertakings to refrain from manufacturing or otherwise acquiring such weapons and to refuse to receive in the future nuclear weapons on their territories on behalf of any other country.' Although it was possible to argue that a vote in favour of this resolution did no more than express support for an enquiry, the fact was that this time the minister of external affairs had clearly come out on top. Twice in the early days of December, Diefenbaker talked about the implications of that vote for the government's nuclear policy. From his comments I formed the impression that our recent support for the Swedish proposal 'would prevent any Canadian decision to acquire nuclear warheads before the election.' It was not surprising that in a report to his cabinet colleagues after returning from a regular meeting of NATO ministers, the minister of external affairs acknowledged that 'Canada now amounted to very little in the NATO picture.'[8]

In the course of 1961, John Diefenbaker's ledger of personal achievement in international affairs had had its positive side. To mention only the strongest features, he could legitimately claim credit for his role in the South African question and for his shrewd, if cautious, leadership during the Berlin crisis. On the debit side, the decline of his relationship with President Kennedy and his failure to resolve the nuclear issue were the outstanding entries. True, he had tried once – how hard is another matter – in 1961 to carry out the undertaking he had given to the president. But as the new year began, he would, not surprisingly, stay away from a decision on which public opinion was by now so divided. Except as a source of domestic political dispute, the nuclear question would not arise again in a demanding light until after the next great international crisis over Soviet missiles in Cuba – in October 1962. Meanwhile, Diefenbaker would face new trials and strains, especially in relations with Canada's two closest allies, and, in personal terms, with their leaders, Harold Macmillan and John F. Kennedy.

PART FIVE

Trouble at Every Turn

JANUARY 1962 TO
APRIL 1963

24

Planning for the Election

Even more emphatically than before, and for quite understandable reasons, Diefenbaker's foreign policy in 1962 was electorally primed. When the year opened, it was clear that a federal election would be called before the summer. The House of Commons, which had not sat since late September 1961, was due to resume on 18 January. The opposition, scenting the recovery of office, was in full, taunting voice. In the Prime Minister's Office, the atmosphere was charged with political electricity. One had the sense of being in a battle headquarters, waiting for the climactic trial of strength to commence.

The prime minister himself had come through a rough year and it remained rough at the end. He had taken his cabinet to Quebec City in the week after Christmas and had contrived to give the impression that a major shuffle of ministers would take place. Instead, very little of significance occurred and the whole episode left him looking as Pearson and other opposition spokesmen were trying to paint him – a commander not in control of his troops.

When government business resumed after the holiday, and at a time when he needed to be at his strongest, Diefenbaker was showing signs of wear. Members of his staff said that he should have taken a holiday to refresh himself for the campaign that was looming. One of my colleagues from External Affairs who called on him at that time was surprised at his 'oldness and shakiness,' and also had an impression of his touchiness. In other words, wear and tear were setting in but were more noticeable to those with only occasional access.

Early in January there was no time for anything but politics. A cynic might say that this had been true ever since Diefenbaker came into office, but the priority he gave to electoral factors was overwhelming as 1962 began. In a sense this was not a new challenge for the department. Yet the fine line between offering non-partisan advice and providing material that would be politically useful to the government of the day had never seemed harder to draw or follow.

Most of the foreign policy problems that preoccupied Diefenbaker in the first half of 1962 had a direct connection with Canada-US relations. Outstanding among these issues were nuclear weapons and disarmament policy, trade relations with Cuba and China, and continuing difficulties over the Columbia River treaty. The other most worrying problem arose from the United Kingdom's negotiations with the European Economic Community. Every one of these topics had unmistakeable domestic political overtones.

NUCLEAR CHOICE

On 9 January the prime minister gave an indication of how he was thinking of handling the nuclear weapons issue. In explaining what he required from External Affairs for his speech in the forthcoming debate on the speech from the Throne, he said that he wanted to equip himself to deal with the question, 'Why Can't We Be More Decisive?' on nuclear weapons and other defence equipment. He wanted to do this in part by reference to difficulties other countries had had in being obliged to cancel or cut back weapons systems on which they had already made large expenditures. The United Kingdom's experience in cancelling the 'Bluestreak' missile was part of what he had in mind, but he hoped other examples could be found. It was clear that he wanted to improve his defence of the government's failure to reach a decision on the question of acquiring nuclear weapons.

A week later the responses to the requests began to arrive. National Defence provided case histories of weapons systems – one British and three American – which were cancelled after considerable development had taken place. External Affairs submitted a number of papers, including in particular a lengthy statement for possible use in the House of Commons. The explanatory note accompanying the statement informed the prime minister as follows: 'Also attached is a draft statement which approaches the question from the point of view that the difficulties in the way of making decisions on Canadian nuclear weapons policy are mainly attributable to the fact that our main allies have been reviewing their defence policies in the last year and that NATO as a whole has not yet completed its review. The draft also takes account of factors (e.g. disarmament, avoidance of expanding the nuclear club) which, even before the current review of allied strategy was undertaken, had militated against our taking premature decisions on weapons policy. The conclusion pointed to is that, apart from the difficulty of predicting the future utility of weapons systems, it might be imprudent to make major decisions at this time on some important defence problems.'

As is indicated by this explanation, Green's senior advisers took advantage of the opportunity to muster additional support for the minister in his determination to avoid a positive decision on the acquisition of nuclear weapons. The External Affairs paper went, in fact, a good deal further than the prime minister had asked. Not only did it address the limited tactical purpose which Diefenbaker had in mind; it offered him a detailed rationale for delaying the acceptance of nuclear weapons on Canadian soil except in case of an emergency.[1]

The argument began with the assumption that if there were nuclear war, Canada would be involved and would be attacked. Canada must therefore take a full share in the defence of the continent. War was not, however, imminent. Disarmament efforts were proceeding and Canada must be careful to avoid a nuclear policy which would diminish its influence in those efforts, add to the membership of the nuclear club, or increase in some other way the risks of nuclear war. In view, however, of Canada's proximity to the United States, it was necessary for Canada 'to attain the near maximum of nuclear defence potentiality in the event of nuclear aggression.' This could be done by working out an arrangement with the United States whereby nuclear warheads from nearby US bases could be delivered at very short notice to sites and bases in Canada which were equipped with Bomarc missile installations and interceptor aircraft 'positioned in readiness' to receive the warheads. In this way, the argument continued, somewhat tortuously, Canada, without joining the nuclear club, without accepting 'control' of nuclear explosives, could nevertheless discharge its responsibilities to its allies. And to those who objected that the transfer of nuclear weapons could not be achieved quickly enough in an emergency, it was said that the time lapse 'may well be reduced to a matter of minutes; at most to perhaps an hour. Canada would thus take its share in the defence of the continent in the very early stages of that defence.'

The External Affairs paper went forward to the prime minister but it was not unchallenged. On reading it, Bryce asked me to inform the department that he did not wish to be associated with it; that he disagreed with it on grounds of both policy and politics. Instead, he intended to speak to the prime minister and advise him against saying anything on nuclear weapons for the time being, until there had been full consultation with External Affairs and National Defence.

Advice from External Affairs to the prime minister for the first major debate of the new session on 22 and 23 January was affected not only by Green's adamant anti-nuclear stance but also by Diefenbaker's instinctive opposition to British entry into Europe. In the circumstances, there was not much that External Affairs could do on these two major issues but to serve up recycled material and put as good a face as possible on the attitude the government was taking. The prime minister carried off sheaves of paper for bedside shuffling, and it was impossible to know what he would decide to use, how he would express it, and what he would leave out. Occasionally he would phone to check a point, or to bewail the dearth of fresh ideas in the material he had received. Not a new thought in the carload was his familiar refrain.

The debate typified the rancorous encounters for which the Diefenbaker-Pearson years are remembered. While their wives exchanged glares at gallery level across the chamber, the two leaders, on the floor, abandoning all pretence of mutual regard, gave warning that this session would indeed be a stormy, malicious fight. The prime minister had not finished his speech by the end of the evening sitting and he resumed after question period on the following day. He made a blistering attack on the Liberal party, its leaders, and particularly its advisers who, he alleged, were publicly committed to state control of national affairs and were thus steering the party into socialism.[2] Pearson, he implied, was not a strong enough leader to control what his advisers and philosophers were saying. Elated by the cheers and desk-thumps of his followers, Diefenbaker emerged from the House with the air of a gladiator, exhilarated by success and professing to marvel at the openings he had been given by his opponent. I noted that night in my diary that on days like these, political leaders are not comfortable except with real, reliable partisans. I crept home, feeling apolitical.

Looking through the debate in the calm of retrospect, one can detect what the two leaders then saw as priorities in international affairs. After four months of parliamentary recess, there was much for the Liberals to question and criticize and for the government to explain and defend. Pearson began by chiding the government for its failure to make up its mind on nuclear weapons policy but his main fire was directed at its record in international economic affairs. He attacked its 'sterile, negative, and complaining' attitude towards Britain's interest in joining the EEC, and its indifference to the benefits to be sought in a freer trade area encompassing both Western Europe and North America. He touched a raw nerve on the government front bench by recalling the 'cool and qualified endorsement' given to new multilateral trade proposals presented by the American delegates to a recent joint meeting of economic ministers. Quoting liberally, as it were, from speeches by the prime minister and the minister of finance, Pearson reopened a file of incidents best forgotten from the government's standpoint – the Accra speeches, the Canadian high commissioner's absence from a meeting in London, and other examples of allegedly exaggerated anxiety over British aims and methods of consultation. The government, Pearson said, had gone out of its way to make things difficult for the British, and had overstated the political risks that British entry into Europe would pose for the Commonwealth.

In his response Diefenbaker avoided going into detail on nuclear policy. He was, I am sure, influenced by the advice he had received from Bryce as well as by his own judgment that he had nothing new to say that would not be politically damaging. But on economic matters, the prime minister felt it necessary to refute

240

at least some of Pearson's charges. He found a quotation from President Kennedy which helped deflate the notion that an Atlantic free trade area was a realistic aim. What had particularly stung him, however, was the allegation that the government had been needlessly obstructive in its dealings with the United Kingdom. To this charge, which of course he had heard before from some of his own cabinet colleagues, he replied in part:

What would they [the Liberal opposition] have said if we had not [placed Canada's position before the United Kingdom]?

We represent the people of Canada, and lest the result of what Britain was doing were to weaken the relationship within the Commonwealth, were to place us in a detrimental position together with Australia, New Zealand, and other countries of the Commonwealth, then it is our responsibility to place that view before the British government ...

We were concerned with the protection of our trade. We realized how much was at stake. We consider – and the British fully understood this and understand it now – that they should be provided with the fullest information on the implications for Canada, because only in that way could the British negotiators be aware of all the factors that have to be taken into account to safeguard those interests.

The prime minister completed his remarks on this topic by repeating his view that before a final decision was taken, a meeting of Commonwealth prime ministers should be held, if possible in Canada.

THE UNITED KINGDOM AND THE EEC

As if to remind the Canadian government that the United Kingdom's enthusiasm for joining the EEC would be as strong in 1962 as it had been in the previous year, Edward Heath was the first official visitor of the new year. He had asked for a private meeting with the prime minister in addition to lengthier sessions with ministers and senior officials involved in trade matters. Diefenbaker was pleased to oblige – he did not know Heath well, but the fact that Macmillan had appointed him as negotiator with the Six and had sent him to both Washington and Ottawa was enough. They met on 4 January with only the British high commissioner, Lord Amory, in attendance. Afterwards Diefenbaker told me that three points had emerged: France's attitude towards British entry was still undetermined but not likely to be favourable to Commonwealth interests; the United States favoured British entry, hoping that by this means there would be an end to Commonwealth preferences; and Diefenbaker had insisted that a Commonwealth prime ministers' conference was 'the only way in which proper consultation could take place.' 'Consultation,' he wrote in his own record of the conversation, 'was more than a briefing.' He thought that Heath 'seemed to agree,' but when Diefenbaker said that he was ready to attend a meeting of prime ministers in March, Amory pointed out that the United Kingdom's negotiations with the EEC would not be far enough advanced before July. Heath's officials said later that Heath had been puzzled by Diefenbaker's frequent speculation on the effect which the Common Market issue might have on Prime Minister Menzies's election prospects in Australia. It was a signal of Diefenbaker's own inner thoughts.

In the second week of January, Canadian ministers had been hosts to their US counterparts at a meeting of the joint committee of ministers on trade and economic affairs. Diefenbaker did not attend these meetings but kept a pipeline to Green, whom he could depend on as an admirer of R.B. Bennett and defender of the Commonwealth preferences. The American delegation was promoting the new multilateral trade proposals announced by President Kennedy, and they hoped that the meeting might produce, among other things, a declaration of the Canadian government's support. In his memoirs, Donald Fleming has described the circumstances in which Green, with the prime minister's concurrence, prevented him from declaring Canadian support.[3] My diary note about the same incident remarks on the open disagreement among ministers, especially Fleming and Green, with Green having the prime minister on his side. The impression I had at the time was that Diefenbaker and Green were reluctant to give public support to Kennedy's trade proposals because of the possible need for taking an anti-American line in the election campaign. A week later, however, Diefenbaker had swung around in response to criticism of his negative stand. In a speech in Montreal, he publicly welcomed the Kennedy proposals. I suspect that his earlier refusal to consent to Fleming's approach may have been based partly on a sudden anti-Kennedy impulse and partly on a desire to reserve to himself the opportunity to make the first announcement of Canada's support.

Diefenbaker seemed to be open to advice on how best to influence the United Kingdom. Green was taking a hard line against British entry to the EEC and Allister Grosart, Progressive Conservative party adviser, was also opposed. Bryce was more positive and conciliatory towards British aims but no less firm on Canadian and Commonwealth interests. Pearson's scathing criticisms in the recent debate hung in Diefenbaker's mind. The various cross-currents intersected when a public statement had to be made. An example was Diefenbaker's address to the Montreal Real Estate Board on 25 January. In a diary entry that evening, I wrote: 'The draft speech for Montreal was the usual frantic dog's breakfast, with bits from Grosart, Bryce, and External Affairs, patched together by the P.M. in great haste. The Bryce piece was unacceptable to Howard Green. Grosart's was opposite to that of Bryce. The final product full of glaring inconsistencies which I tried at the last minute to remove.' Why I attempted to remove inconsistencies after living with them for so long, I find it hard to imagine in retrospect. The prime minister went on his way, grumbling. Apart from a section on East-West relations, he had refused to authorize any advance notes for publication, a sure sign that he would improvise in the rest of the speech. Press reports the following day, later confirmed by the tape of his remarks,[4] indicated a tendency towards accepting British entry as a realistic possibility. This meant that Bryce's material had emerged more prominently than any other source. I heard (resignedly) from External Affairs that the minister was concerned at not having been properly consulted on the speech. In any case, Diefenbaker was by now concentrating less on aiming to prevent the United Kingdom from joining Europe and more on trying to ensure that Canadian and Commonwealth interests were safeguarded. After Macmillan had agreed to visit Ottawa in April, Diefenbaker felt that he had done all he could for the time being.

The first month of 1962 had shown that the government was going towards the election with a feeling of vulnerability, especially on the issues of nuclear weapons and British entry in to the European Common Market. The Progressive Conservatives had fallen behind in the polls in 1960 and had not recovered. Unfortunately for the prime minister, there was a strict limit to what he could do about British entry. And all that was needed on the nuclear weapons issue was a decisive act of political will of which he did not seem to be capable.

25

Politics and Foreign Policy

I had now entered my last six months in the Prime Minister's Office. Although my personal relations with Diefenbaker were on a solid footing, I had for some time been looking for an opportunity to escape back to the Department of External Affairs, preferably in a foreign post. The job had been in many ways fascinating but it had often been frustrating. My wife Elizabeth was extremely understanding but had her hands full with four children under ten years. We felt the need for a more regular pattern of life than had been possible since the summer of 1957. Obviously, however, it was not going to be easy to disengage. Several times over the previous two years the prime minister had asked me about my career, whether I was happy in External Affairs, and so on. Early in 1961 he had inquired if I would like to take charge of his office – a sort of chief of staff post. I had declined, with understanding help from R.B. Bryce and Norman Robertson, on the ground that I did not want to cross over into political as distinct from civil service work. Mr Diefenbaker had accepted this, and it was agreed that I would continue with the External Affairs liaison functions.

At various times in the late months of 1961 External Affairs, knowing of my interest in going abroad, told me informally of openings that were coming up in Canadian posts. There were three or four such possibilities and I discussed them from time to time with the prime minister. His first reaction was to wonder why I wanted to leave. Was this not one of the best jobs around? A hard one to answer. The problem did not really come to a head until late January 1962 when Charles Ritchie, then Canada's permanent representative at the United Nations in New York, was interviewed by Diefenbaker for appointment as ambassador to the United States. Ritchie asked me at that time if I would be interested in going to the embassy in Washington as his no. 2. Although Elizabeth and I had hoped for a posting in Europe, Washington was as interesting and active a mission as there was, and I knew that under Ritchie it would continue to be a happy and productive embassy. Schooling for the children would not be a problem. We decided to accept the job in Washington if it became available. There were still a number of bridges to cross, however, not the least of which was the prime minister's attitude. Whether he would 'cooperate' remained uncertain until some months later.

ONE THING AFTER ANOTHER

For most of the time between late January and the election in June, no single international issue was dominant and no major new departures in Canadian foreign policy occurred. The prime minister was preoccupied above all else with the forthcoming election, but international affairs were important in that context and he remained constantly attentive to them. The flow of events during this hectic period may be better portrayed with greater reliance on extracts from diary entries and other personal notes and letters. This will permit brief reference to a wider range of topics, and may convey more faithfully his mood and attitudes in coping with a chaotic, fragmented agenda. Chronological treatment, too, will show how the main international aspects of his task competed for his attention in the months leading to the 1962 election. Since much of the economic, financial, and other non-External Affairs background is not dealt with in this account, it does not pretend to provide a full context in which to view the troubles and disorganization into which the government was falling at this time.

Nearly all of the international issues that gave rise to difficulty in this period were extensions of well-established trends. In matters involving the communist world, for example, it was easy to foretell how he would react to events and advice. Speech material had to be in hard-hitting language. Conciliatory advice was sure to provoke disapproval or at least a sceptical look:

January 26, Friday

Saw PM several times for short periods. He was appreciative of East-West material for the Montreal speech last night but was preoccupied and distant.

I gave him the Department's request for approval of an expression of regret re recent demonstrations outside Soviet Embassy and suggestions on how to prevent them from happening in future. PM very impatient with Russians because they were not prepared to give evidence. Insisted they be told in writing that they couldn't expect us to bring demonstrators to justice if main witnesses not prepared to testify. He also refused Minister's idea of RCMP being asked to take over responsibility for protecting diplomatic premises, and objected to idea of special legislation. Altogether a frustrating day.

It was more difficult to anticipate his reaction to developments concerning the United States. Anything involving indifference to or disregard of Canadian interests was a sure bet to generate a defiant reaction. So was anything he could label as improper pressure by high-ranking officials in the United States, especially if they formed part of the circle of academics and intellectuals in the court of President Kennedy:

January 29, Monday

Saw PM at lunch: he was annoyed by indiscreet remark in Vancouver by Arthur Schlesinger, one of President Kennedy's special advisors, complaining about Canadian policy on trade with Cuba – it reminded him of Rostow's 'pushing' at time of Kennedy visit to Ottawa. He unloaded on Howard Green by phone.

But if some major misfortune occurred which might weaken the capacity of the United States to give effective leadership to the non-communist world, his resentment often turned to quite genuine concern: 'Afterwards he calmed down. Very conscious of US space disappointments this week [postponement of Glenn shot, first time right around] and the [unmanned] moon shot which missed.'

The continuing deterioration of US relations with Cuba, however, stimulated more strain than fellow feeling between the United States and Canada. When the OAS declared at its Punta del Este conference that the Cuban government was incompatible with the purposes and principles of the inter-American system, the prime minister lost no time in making his reaction clear:

January 31, Wednesday

Interesting firm statement by PM in the House of Commons that government would not change policy on Cuba in light of Cuba's exclusion from OAS. I think that Schlesinger's indiscretion a few days ago has solidified PM's views against moving any closer to the US on Cuba policy.

Sometimes he was caught out after indiscretions of his own:

February 1, Thursday

Cabinet met but not for long and PM went home for lunch, returning for question period, looking weary. He was questioned about a statement he allegedly made yesterday to a delegation from the Farmers' Union that he did not think President Kennedy's tariff cut proposals would get through the Congress. He more or less denied having said it but later admitted to me that he had, and called the farmers 'bastards' for having told on him. This could hurt him. He has said many times in private what he is reported to have said to the farmers.

Although he had been maintaining firmly that no policy changes on trade with Cuba were in prospect, Diefenbaker was sensitive to media reaction in Canada, some of which was reflecting US opinion:

February 5, Monday

PM steamed up about the bad press Canada is getting in US re trade with Cuba. Blames Embassy in Washington most unfairly and actually phoned Arnold Heeney today. Also blames Kennedy administration, again without justice, and relates it all back to the Rostow memo which will be with JGD until he dies.

Life was not all solemn. I went with Bill Neville, then with United Press International, to the Press Gallery dinner. In my diary I wrote that it was 'the best of the four I have attended. General Vanier was the star, taking a forward glance at his career after Rideau Hall.' I also attended a Rhodes Scholars' lunch for the British high commissioner, Lord Amory, at Carleton University. Amory made a wonderful speech. Rhodes Scholars were a sore point with the prime minister, one of whose great disappointments in life was not to have been selected for that scholarship. There were too many Rhodes Scholars around Ottawa for his taste.

Some days were more varied than others:

February 7, Wednesday

Strong rumours circulating about dissolution of parliament but seems most unlikely as PM does not appear to have made his mind up. Much behind-the-scenes activity re retirement of General McNaughton on his 75th birthday later this month, thus enabling Arnold Heeney to take over International Joint Commission from the General, and Charles Ritchie to go to Washington. Heeney naturally concerned that announcement covering all three be made soon. Bryce to the rescue.

Consulted PM today re policy on economic counter-measures for possible Soviet Union moves in Berlin. Canada has been holding out against a resolution now before NATO Council. PM doubtful about our position. Would rather be isolated on an issue like trade with Cuba than on economic countermeasures on Berlin.

PM said L.B. Pearson was being informed by someone of secret material. How did this old chestnut get revived? Told him I was sure this was not happening. He said it was. I was not to take it personally. If something was said which I was the only one he had said it to, he would know he had said it to someone else. Well ...

After being questioned by L.B. Pearson, PM asked for message to PM Macmillan requesting meeting of Commonwealth PM's before final decision is taken on British application to join European Common Market.

The next day brought a message from Macmillan informing Diefenbaker of the United Kingdom's decision to provide Christmas Island in the Indian Ocean as a site for US nuclear tests, but also stressing the importance of the new disarmament talks in the hope that new tests would not be necessary. Diefenbaker did not question the need to prepare for further nuclear tests, as Howard Green might have done, but he made a statement on disarmament following closely the External Affairs text and promising the minister's attendance if new disarmament talks were to be held at foreign minister level as then proposed.

Cuba continued to attract political lightning:

February 8, Thursday

Saw PM before and after lunch. He was irritable as he often is after Cabinet meetings ... Yet another US politician, Senator Keating, was cut down to size on trade with Cuba. I tried unsuccessfully to persuade the PM not to go after Keating who had made some unguarded remarks on CBC last night but PM obviously thinks anti-American statements are good and timely, and relished another opportunity. In the process he is getting more and more isolated as the dollar-hungry defender of commercial relations with Cuba and getting a lot of criticism for it in the US and Latin America.

The Soviet ambassador in Ottawa at that time, A.A. Aroutounian, was an exceptionally able diplomat who had made a considerable personal impression on Diefenbaker and, because of this, was always assured of ready access:

February 11, Sunday

Soviet Ambassador Aroutounian asked to see PM [in Toronto today], to present letter from Khrushchev proposing disarmament summit conference [heads of government instead of foreign ministers as earlier proposed by Kennedy and Macmillan]. I told PM by phone that US first reaction was not to fall in at once with Soviet idea but wait to see prospects of progress. PM did not like this. Obviously likes electoral benefits of attending a summit. PM to see Soviet Ambassador in the morning.

February 12, Monday

Just made it to the railway station at 7.30 a.m. to meet PM returning from Toronto. He read the message from Washington and at first repeated his doubt about US reaction, but I had the feeling that he was nonetheless affected by it. Aroutounian came with Khrushchev's message at 8 and PM simply undertook to reply soon. During morning he spoke to PM Macmillan who said a heads of government meeting should not be held until there had been preparation by foreign ministers. Howard Green spoke and PM agreed this made sense. Department to prepare text of reply.

Later the same day:

Charles Ritchie's appointment to Washington announced. PM very pleased at the surprise he had created and Department relieved no leak had occurred.

More rumours about early dissolution of parliament.

After considering the telegrams from Canadian offices abroad and talking it over with the Minister, Diefenbaker agreed rather reluctantly to take the same line as the United States and the United Kingdom in rejecting Khrushchev's proposal for a disarmament summit meeting at Geneva. I wrote that 'by now the PM had become cynical about the process of consultation ... He was right in saying that the US had laid down the line and had given the rest no chance to differ.' Green, however, was happy enough to have it left that foreign ministers would be in charge. It would be a month before the disarmament conference opened in Geneva.

The prime minister spoke again in Montreal on 14 February, concentrating once more on foreign affairs. He asked for some new material on the problems being faced by the United Nations but we ran into trouble with Howard Green, who found the text the department produced too critical. In the event the speech was a potpourri, full of the familiar ingredients – disarmament, nuclear testing, East-West relations, Soviet colonialism as against Commonwealth evolution, and so on. On the following day I wrote:

February 15, Thursday

PM very tired and frosty after a sleepless night returning from Montreal. I helped prepare statement for him to give in the House in tabling reply to Khrushchev message. PM accepted our draft, favouring meeting at foreign minister level, and got away without being questioned on a press report quoting him as saying last night that if there was a stalemate at Geneva, the heads of government should meet, quite different from the sense of his reply to Khrushchev. The press report was evidently accurate.

Diefenbaker simply could not admit that there was no foreseeable role for heads of government, whatever the Americans and British might have ordained.

In the midst of all this, there were miscellaneous developments. The prime minister had a talk with Sydney Pierce, Canadian ambassador to Belgium and also responsible for keeping an eye on UK negotiations with European Common Market governments. Pierce told Diefenbaker that the process of negotiations would take a long time and so would approval by each of the six parliaments should the negotiations succeed. This advice had a useful effect.

For some weeks the prime minister had been doing very little, if anything, to damp down rumours about the early dissolution of parliament. Working with him from day to day, it did not seem to me that he was temperamentally ready to make the decision to have an election, despite all the rumours. An interesting straw in the wind was his decision on 16 February to hold up the issuance of a press release giving the Queen Mother's program for her scheduled visit to Canada in the first half of June.

Meanwhile, Howard Green did not allow election prospects to distract him from his international pursuits. The prime minister was active when the minister was absent from the House:

February 19, Monday

Howard Green being away briefly, PM pulled usual trick of planting questions so that he could make statements on foreign affairs. One on US policy in Cuba, denying that it had been raised in NATO Council, awkward as Americans are expected to raise it in NATO tomorrow.

February 20, Tuesday

PM approved message to PM Macmillan proposing meeting of Commonwealth Prime Ministers 'before a final decision is reached' on UK's application to join EEC. Nothing said about holding meeting in Ottawa and PM did not raise it. No dates suggested either.

Policy toward Cuba continues to be the main headache. Confidential approach from US authorities on Cuba, trying to bring Canada into line following Punta del Este meeting. Contents of report from Embassy in Washington struck PM as 'a hell of a colossal nerve.' Reminded him of the Rostow memo and aroused spontaneous indignation. He said that closer to the election he might find use for the Rostow paper. I suggested taking advantage of US willingness to talk in private with us. PM did not entirely dismiss this but gave me the 'aren't you a dreamer' look. Separately I was surprised to learn that Howard Green is now impressed by political risk of continuing the present line on Cuba and inclined to be critical of PM's handling of it. This makes for real difficulty in recommending how to respond to US approach.

John Glenn flew three times around in Project Mercury. Day was alive with hope, fear and relief. PM signed a message to President Kennedy.

February 21, Wednesday

PM and Howard Green discussed Cuba policy privately. Green said to his staff later that he had argued for a somewhat less aggressive defence of existing government line.

February 22, Thursday

More indications that PM is in a resistant mood toward any change in trade policy with Cuba. The spectre of what he regards as US pressure overshadows all other factors. Ross Campbell reports Howard Green is concerned about effect of dispute over Cuba on Canadian-American relations and has asked for review of export criteria for 'border-line' items hitherto not included in prohibited list of strategic goods destined for Cuba. Bryce suggested that best course might to be have Ed Ritchie go to Washington for discussion.

The nuclear issue had been reasonably quiet for a month but suddenly late in February it flared up. I wrote:

February 25, Sunday

PM back from Party meetings in Edmonton. Bunny Pound [PM's secretary] phoned at night. PM had made a statement that our Voodoo (F-101B) aircraft could have nuclear warheads in one hour, and now wants an explanation drafted. I think it must have been a lapse.

The following day, before anything could be produced except copies of previous statements on nuclear policy, he answered questions in the House, maintaining that he had no new policy development in mind, evading questions on how nuclear warheads could be made available if no agreement had been reached with the United States, and asserting that 'joint control' of the warheads was 'impossible so long as the law of the United States is as it is at present.'

A very confused statement. I saw him in his office immediately after that. In a flash of apparent candour he blurted out: 'Did I go too far in saying that "joint control" was impossible?' Almost at once, however, and before I could reply,

251

he appeared to put the doubts out of his mind. He said he had intended to put the onus on the Americans to create the public impression that the degree or type of joint control which the Americans could offer under their existing legislation was not adequate for Canadian requirements. He said he knew that joint control arrangements satisfactory to the United Kingdom had been worked out on a 'two-key' system. Obviously he had chosen to take the position that that systems was either impossible for Canada to attain or incompatible with the degree of control Canada should have over the warheads. Since he had also said that Canada did not wish to add itself to the nuclear club, which it would do if it assumed sole control of nuclear warheads, it seemed quite clear that he was reverting to the rationale in which Canadian air defence forces would be equipped with nuclear weapons only by some stand-by procedure in an emergency. The US embassy staff, who had no prior notice, were baffled and annoyed; National Defence was exasperated; and External Affairs was surprised but resigned.

Arnold Heeney, in town about his next appointment, was dismayed at the government's lack of concern for the US relationship.

February 27, Tuesday

Charles Ritchie raised with PM the idea of my going to Washington and PM appeared to buy it. PM later asked me if I really wanted to go but he avoided final decision. PM very pleased with political reaction to his statement in the House on nuclear weapons.

February 28, Wednesday

More excitement in the House today on nuclear policy. PM admitted that no agreement with the US existed to enable us to obtain nuclear warheads in an emergency and that no discussions were going on. He has dug a hole for himself in the past few days: has spoken for a degree of control which will not allow us to say, if we decided we want the warheads, that we were doing so on terms which do not increase membership of the nuclear club. This could be a real embarrassment for him.

Spent much of today worrying about notes for PM's speech to US-Canadian parliamentary group meeting tomorrow. Main substance is on Cuba, designed to explain rationale for our policy. Some haggling among officials over emphasis to be given to differences with Americans, given Howard Green's recent anxieties.

March 1, Thursday

Nuclear weapons saga continued, with comment by Secretary of State Rusk, responding to PM's statement of February 26. Rusk quoted as saying that 'joint control' was quite possible and US was ready to negotiate. PM told me he thought Rusk's comment 'very fair.' I had a fleeting sense that in his statement on February 26 PM might not have really meant joint control in the sense others mean it, that he may have been confusing joint 'control' with 'custody,' which *would* be prohibited under US law. Could this be, or am I underestimating his deviousness?

More work on speech for interparliamentary meeting tonight. Started with a red-blooded defence of existing Cuba policy by Ed Ritchie, later watered a little to soften implied criticism of US policy, in view of Howard Green's views. Some parts of original draft were deleted but I was to give them to PM in case he wanted to develop reasoning why Canada thought it wise to avoid making Cuba an outcast. I gave it to PM at 1.30 p.m. but had no chance to explain background. Norman Robertson thought it best statement given to PM in some years.

PM upset by seating plan for interparliamentary dinner which he had been studying. After hearing from Mrs. Diefenbaker that she was to be below Mrs. Michener, PM phoned me at home at 7.20 p.m. and I was lucky to reach Murray Cook [US desk at External Affairs], who, God bless him, undertook to try to alter place cards before dinner began at 8.

March 2, Friday

Full speed ahead again all day. PM avoided questions on nuclear weapons policy, although Department of National Defence had given him a statement. I had the impression he had been through the storm and is now assessing the damage and realizing his position is not as healthy as he had thought. But he professes to be pleased with Rusk's comment of the other day. What is to be made of all this?

Some backwash from last night's dinner. PM said Ed Ritchie's speech had been excellent. 'We'll use it again.'' I wasn't sure if that meant he hadn't used it. [Later I found that he hadn't.]

We got word of President Kennedy's decision to resume nuclear testing. Began work on a statement in late afternoon but PM decided to withhold comment until morning.

PM said he did not want any commitment made concerning a government invitation to U Thant, new Secretary-General of the UN. Also approved the way in which Bob Ford, Ambassador in Cairo, had temporized when asked if PM would accept invitation to visit UAR this year. Too much going on at home but in principle would like to go.

March 3, Saturday

PM agreed to basic theme of draft comment on US resumption of nuclear tests – a combination of regret and realism – but wanted insertion of a reference to his traditional offer of inspection of northern areas, a point generally thought to be purely of propaganda value and irrelevant in this context. Somewhat to the pain of the experts, I put the required sentence in and we gave the statement out around midday.

March 5, Monday

Paul Martin had put down a written question in the House whether PM had met foreign minister Popovic of Yugoslavia when he visited Ottawa last year. PM was displeased with proposed reply put forward by External Affairs which acknowledged that PM had briefly met with Popovic. It looked as though PM had promised some members of Serbian community in Toronto that he would not receive Popovic, and that PM was hard put to it to justify circumstances in which they had shaken hands. We had a crisp exchange.

March 7, Wednesday

PM and Howard Green met in the Railway Committee Room in the Centre Block with a large group from the Voice of Women. One could not help being struck by the difference in the impact created by Diefenbaker and Green. PM produced standard clichés on disarmament, totally out of key with current state of affairs, while Green, on the point of leaving for the disarmament meeting in Geneva, brought them into the latest developments. The women listened politely with their children on their knees and gave perfunctory applause to the PM and a standing ovation to Green immediately afterwards.

The atmosphere was being polluted by speeches by Progressive Conservative politicians implying that civil servants were in league with the Liberal party. One implied that Pearson had won the Nobel Peace Prize by not standing out against the communists. Another called the Liberal party a cesspool of civil servants with Red friends. I noted, naïvely as it now looks, that 'it begins to look as though these speeches, if not coordinated, are at least not discouraged by the Government.' Members of the prime minister's staff, John Fisher and Bunny Pound, took him to task but he seemed unaffected by their advice.

Not all the villains were communists, however. I noted on 8 March: 'The PM had [US ambassador] Merchant in today, and may have taxed him with a story which Paul Martin had picked up to the effect that a US military officer had told him the essence of what the Prime Minister had said to President Kennedy about nuclear policy last May.' Nothing was more likely to annoy the prime minister than the thought that his undertakings to Kennedy would become public property. In the same interview, however, the prime minister gave Merchant the impression that the prospects for initialling an agreement on nuclear issues were bright. No doubt he was thinking in terms of a stand-by formula of the kind he had floated in his recent speech at Edmonton. Merchant was heartened, but was to wait in vain for the prime minister to act.

On 10 March Howard Green left Ottawa for the eighteen-power disarmament conference in Geneva which, as he later said, he considered his biggest assignment yet. In his absence, Diefenbaker took over all files flowing to the minister's office. Immediately, there was concern over the Common Market:

March 12, Monday

The PM blew fairly hot on the Common Market, having been alarmed by telegrams from George Drew over the weekend to the effect that the British are sliding away from their assurances re protection of Commonwealth interests, especially in agriculture. PM more suspicious than ever of British intentions. Bryce and Ed Ritchie went to work on a reply to the British.

A lesser but troublesome item had been in the news for several days. Some Canadians serving in Indochina were reported to have been smuggling drugs. This affair, involving External Affairs as well as National Defence personnel, combined with the speeches about the political loyalties of civil servants, were an unpleasant accompaniment to the working day. The next day was one of the worst:

March 13, Tuesday

First the PM showed impatience at failure of the Department to provide a considered reply on an hour's notice to a parliamentary question about diplomatic immunity in the Indochina smuggling case.

Later he exploded over being asked to approve a paper which had already been sent to Paris for a NATO meeting today. I should have known better than to have risked this reaction, which was to be expected in view of his nervous condition, the complexity of the subject, and the late afternoon hour. He made dark hints that the Department was deliberately delaying papers sent to him, and for a second I almost lost control. He sensed my irritation, put his hand over his face and said he did not want to argue.

After all this, a pleasant dinner with Bob Bryce, unwinding. Fortunately, on the following day a legal opinion came from Marcel Cadieux and other lawyers in External affairs on the Indochina smuggling business:

March 14, Wednesday

PM happy enough because he had said in the House yesterday that the smuggling case was not a question of diplomatic immunity, which was the burden of the legal opinion. The satisfaction one feels is tempered by the impression that the PM is really disposed to find some way to criticize External Affairs.

And later in the day, I noted: 'We had a frustrating time trying to get a reaction on how to reply to the UN Secretary General on the Swedish resolution about nuclear non-proliferation. PM has conflicting advice from Harkness and Green, and keeps promising to let us know his wishes.'

How to deal with the British in their negotiations with the Europeans continued to occupy much of the prime minister's attention in foreign policy during the last half of March. He put in many hours, always in close touch with Fleming, Drew, and Bryce, trying to hit on the right ingredients for advising the United Kingdom on how they should go about protecting Canadian interests and the Commonwealth's future. On 15 March, John McEwan, Australia's deputy prime minister and minister of trade and commerce, called on the prime minister for a talk about the outlook for the negotiations. McEwan had just been in Washington. He confirmed Diefenbaker's chronic fears by describing American officials as adamant in opposition to the continuance of Commonwealth trade preferences. Diefenbaker floated the idea of a Commonwealth prime ministers' meeting in Ottawa, and thought that McEwan's reaction was 'far from unfavourable.'

Later the same day, Lord Amory brought a letter from Macmillan with further thoughts on agriculture and the Common Market. Diefenbaker saw Amory alone. Afterwards he invited me to listen while he recorded what had happened:

March 15, Thursday

PM said he told Amory there had been no consultation on the problem of agriculture. Amory objected that officials had been meeting (but that is obviously not what PM means by consultation.) PM also told Amory he thought Britain was sliding away from the Commonwealth, and Amory denied it. Must have been a rough session.

March 16, Friday

More messages in from George Drew. Drew is maintaining, and urging PM to do so too, that no consultation has taken place yet on the Common Market question, this in spite of an explicit recognition of consultation in the communiqué issued after Heath's visit in January. Officials trying to work out a procedure for consultation, perhaps involving Howard Green, now in Geneva. PM reserved comment.

March 17, Saturday

Amory suggested to PM that Heath should return for further talks. PM agreed. He preferred this to involving Howard Green. 'This is not Mr. Green's field,' he said. PM approved a message to Macmillan on agriculture, to be sent to Drew for comment before delivery to Macmillan.

March 19, Monday

Much of the day spent with other officials trying to cope with amendments suggested by George Drew to PM's message to Macmillan. PM asked Donald Fleming to speak with Drew. Message sent off overnight.

March 20, Tuesday

PM away in Montreal for a speech to the Chambre de Commerce. Brief meeting of officials in External Affairs planning agenda for Macmillan visit in late April. A very academic air about these – a failure to grasp the limitations of the PM's interests and absorptive powers, or to appreciate the generality of talks he has with other top men and their disinclination to discuss things in the detail to which foreign ministers are accustomed.

March 23, Friday

Had a bit of a talk today, with PM re the Commonwealth and the Common Market, as a result of which I am sure he is still uncertain of his position. Seems to want to keep thumping the Commonwealth drum and hardly believes it can survive if UK enters the Common Market. Yet, having always put faith in the Commonwealth, he is most unwilling to admit its demise. Also said today that he thinks the UN is on the way to collapse or at least to total ineffectuality. He wants a speech on these themes for next week.

In a phone conversation with Green in Geneva, Diefenbaker encouraged him to stay as long as the minister thought it would be useful. A brief record of the conversation was sent to me. 'You stay where you are. You follow the cocktail circuit over there ... they haven't run out of tomato juice yet,' was his advice, offered good-humouredly but not without its edge. Then spontaneously he dictated a telegram to the minister: 'I am very proud of the superb contributions you have made to the cause of peace and disarmament ... and extend the congratulations of my colleagues and myself.'

26

From Majority to Minority

The chief milestones in the next three months would be the dissolution of parliament on 18 April, and the election itself, on 18 June. The single most demanding foreign policy item was the continuing debate over the conditions for the United Kingdom's proposed entry into the European Common Market. For the prime minister personally, however, it was also a period of more than usually resentful anti-American sentiments. Nuclear issues and Cuban-American relations were, of course, part of this picture, but neither they nor other aspects of foreign policy would become election issues in 1962. The campaign was fought against a background of financial turmoil, involving devaluation of the Canadian dollar and a major crisis over the exchange rate.

GEARING UP

When Edward Heath arrived in Ottawa on 24 March, further British proposals for safeguarding Canadian trade interests had just been received for study in Ottawa. The prime minister was in low spirits, and felt unprepared to talk on the Common Market. Heath did his best to reassure the prime minister on the new proposals. Negotiations would probably have to continue through the summer before Commonwealth governments could be consulted. No other prime minister had asked for a conference, but Macmillan was on the point of inviting comments from all concerned. Diefenbaker felt he had obtained a virtual assurance that a meeting of prime ministers would be held.[1]

March 28, Wednesday

I passed the day cleaning up loose ends of the speech for the Royal Commonwealth Society. It is an effort to look at today's Commonwealth, its promise and limitations. It is not pessimistic about the future of the Commonwealth should the UK decide to enter the EEC, but it emphasizes the importance of consultation with others whose interests might be affected. In remarking on the diversity of the association, it stresses the basic (multiracial) criterion of membership but refers to the flexibility which permits members to follow different foreign policies, including non-alignment between East and West. Commonwealth aid and trade are also discussed as basic instruments and benefits.

March 29, Thursday

Howard Green returned from Geneva, having been away for nearly three weeks. This relieves the pressure on the PM.

I gave the draft of the Commonwealth speech to the PM. Atmosphere very political. Not much time for foreign affairs, I gathered from his look.

A flurry today over General McNaughton's retirement due April 15 at the age of 75. PM nervous about saying too many complimentary things because he has heard that the General is planning to let loose a blast at the Government over the Columbia River treaty, and PM wants to avoid having his praise quoted back at him in the midst of a controversy at that time.

At night JGD phoned to say that he had found the Commonwealth speech 'excellent.' Is this genuine or placatory? Elizabeth thinks the call was to soften me up so the PM would feel free to change it.

March 30, Friday

All the satellites in the PMO were kept in orbit as he worked over his speech draft from 9 a.m. until 3.30 p.m. He was pretending to be interested in what External Affairs had given him but was mainly trying to discover something that would make headlines. Thus he wanted to make a big thing of bringing Ireland back into the Commonwealth and/or to criticize India for invading Goa last December. I advised against both these ideas, at least in the way he was thinking of presenting them. Meanwhile, just before leaving for Toronto, he approved for use by the press a text very close to the External Affairs draft. This signifies that he has no serious objection to its contents, but is not a guide to what he will actually say.[2]

March 31, Saturday

A message came in overnight from PM Macmillan suggesting September 10 for meeting of Commonwealth prime ministers. PM wanted an immediate yes which we got off in quick time, agreeing also to Macmillan's suggestion that the world situation as well as possible British entry into Europe should be discussed.

President Kennedy sent PM a message through US minister, Willis Armstrong, asking PM to appeal publicly for clemency for a group of US prisoners on trial in Cuba. PM reacted with great vigour in accordance with President's request. He clearly wants to make up for ground lost over Government's policy on trade with Cuba. US Embassy officials realize PM has his own reasons, but nonetheless this episode has been of some assistance in US-Canada context.

Reports from those present at the Prime Minister's speech to the Royal Commonwealth Society indicate that he put a lot of emphasis on the theme of what would happen to the Commonwealth if the United Kingdom were to join the EEC. However, I was glad to hear that he had responded to our influence on some of the points at issue. Thus, while common foreign and defence policies were out of the question, 'we have members ... that believe in non-alignment, that regard communism in a different light, while being opposed to it, than we do' he said in a rare acknowledgement that Commonwealth members did not react similarly to communism in the world balance. I was told too that he had in the end decided not to refer to India's takeover of Goa and had limited himself to an expression of hope that Ireland would some day decide to return to the Commonwealth.

April 1, Sunday

President Kennedy sent an appreciative thank you to the PM for the action taken on the prisoners in Cuba. I phoned it to the PM. A small thing but it pleased him.

More of George Drew's Sunday specials on the Common Market.

April 2, Monday

PM very relaxed today, full of a story about his dog, Happy, who swallowed some pigs' knuckles on the weekend and survived. Later in the day there was a small success in persuading the PM to permit the use of one or two warm phrases in the press release on General McNaughton. Most days progress arrives in very small slices.

April 3, Tuesday

Another speech in the gestation stage, this time to a Jewish labour audience in Montreal, where the PM will be receiving the *Histradut* humanitarian award, a distinction he greatly values. With help from colleagues in External Affairs, I gave him some material on relations with Israel, persecution of Jews in the USSR, immigration, and disarmament. Professor Max Cohen and others submitted contributions too.

April 4, Wednesday

Morning devoted to the customary pre-speech excitement with the various contributions being fed into the hopper.

PM was discussing with some old friends today the possibility of Howard Green's being awarded the Nobel Peace Prize. PM said he would not surprised.

Herb Moran, formerly High Commissioner to Pakistan and now Director General of the External Aid Office, has recently visited Pakistan. He told me that President Ayub Khan was concerned that our Prime MInister had gone sour on him. Perhaps that goes back to the collapse of arrangements to bring him to Canada at the time of his visit to the US last year. Or to the cautious letter the Prime Minister sent in January replying to Ayub's scorching attack on Nehru after the Indian invasion of Goa. I felt it was unlikely that the Prime Minister thinks any the less of Ayub, whose attitudes are much more comprehensible to him than those of Nehru. I arranged for Herb Moran to see the Prime Minister.

US Embassy phoned to ask that PM be informed of announcement to be made today that President Kennedy would be holding a dinner on April 29 for the US Nobel Peace Prize winners, and that other Nobel Prize winners in the Western hemisphere, including L.B. Pearson, will receive invitations. I sent a memo to the PM who will not see it until he gets back to Ottawa tomorrow night. He will not enjoy this news.

April 6, Friday

PM was back in Ottawa after a day of electioneering in Middlesex West, a constituency which made him feel relaxed and cheerful. I took the opportunity to discuss the program for PM Macmillan's visit. JGD does not want Macmillan to meet with the Cabinet as a whole; otherwise things will move more or less along expected lines. I also spoke to the PM about the flow of George Drew's letter and telegrams, and asked him if we could ask the High Commissioner to be a little less selective in his instructions for their distribution at this end. PM said not to send a message. Just see that the incoming messages are distributed here to those who need to see them. This is a procedural step forward which I thought we would never take.

April 9, Monday

As the political scene becomes more agitated, the PM's preoccupation with external affairs is diminishing, except today on the immediate problem of statements made by General McNaughton about the Columbia River treaty. A long and involved procedural wrangle in the House. The Speaker got himself in a box but wiggled out skilfully in the end.

Livie Merchant, the US Ambassador, outdid all the other newsmakers by announcing his retirement, which led to speculation that he is unhappy here, on policy grounds. We all denied this to the press but it is probably true.

April 10, Tuesday

Budget day. More fireworks in the House. PM quite relaxed as session draws to its end. If anything, though, he is harder to get decisions from than usual, e.g. plans for the Macmillan visit. We have a detailed program drawn up but all the PM will say is that he wants to have a meeting alone with Harold and so far he is refusing to agree to our arranging anything else. But he has lots else to worry about.

April 11, Wednesday

PM confessed that he was very tired – he was doing another Nation's Business broadcast today and he always sweats over these – and he wondered if it was advancing age.

I cleared with him the idea, received from the trade experts, of a speech on trade expansion for next Monday to the Canadian Club in Montreal. Assured him he would be given a good text.

April 12, Thursday

PM much preoccupied by a speech on senate reform which he is incubating but has found no opportunity to give yet.

I felt depressed today perhaps partly because of the difference between the Commonwealth speech as given and the prepared text as approved. He always goes back to the old clichés.

April 13, Friday

Speech for Montreal, written by Jake Warren in Trade and commerce, arrived in time to give to PM before he left for home. He asked for some notes on more general external affairs topics, like disarmament.

April 14, Saturday

With help from Max Yalden, an External Affairs disarmament expert, and Ross Campbell, I was able to give the PM a good note on disarmament which he thought was needed to balance the section on trade to the Canadian Club in Montreal.

At the suggestion of officials dealing with EEC questions in External Affairs, the PM signed a letter to the Australian, John McEwan, thanking him for his message on his talks with PM Macmillan, and summarizing the talks held here recently with Edward Heath.

April 16, Monday

PM to Montreal for luncheon speech to the Canadian Club. Began with disarmament and outerspace, but then a solid section on trade, close to Jake Warren's text.

April 17, Tuesday

After much manoeuvring, two talks with L.B. Pearson, and all sorts of other consultation, PM today at last announced June 18 as election day. Tumultuous scenes in the House, and a brief and quite effective speech by LBP. Now that the news is out, I have a feeling of relief but also, strangely, letdown. The politicians, of course, are spoiling for the campaign and we are not likely to see much of them for the next two months. PM remarked to Bunny Pound that it was a strange feeling to think that 60 days from now he could be out.

April 18, Wednesday

The last day of this parliament. I had some time with the PM while he ate his lunch (chicken sandwiches and milk). He was much more relaxed than for the past week and back in story-telling form in between phone calls and political ploys.

He is very proud of having forced the UK to hold a prime ministers' conference and takes credit for the apparent acceleration of arrangements. Very irritated by George Ball's repetition of US opposition to continuation of Commonwealth preferences.[3] Again insistent on having Macmillan all alone for their first talks. Wants to have a conversation in which they can say things to each other which they couldn't say with others present.

April 19, Thursday

The PM had a talk with Lord Amory, mainly about the Macmillan visit. Asked whether Macmillan should go through with his date with the Canadian Press in Toronto (where there is a picket line to cross at Royal York Hotel). PM said Macmillan should 'do what he thinks right.' Lord Amory said it was Macmillan's present intention not to stress the European Common Market but to deal with the Commonwealth. Amory was once again reminded that first meeting with Macmillan was to be 'just the PM and me.' The decision whether to attend the dinner given by Macmillan would be left to JGD at the last moment.[4]

April 24, Tuesday

PM had a meeting with all his ministers yesterday, planning strategy for the campaign. He is about to go on the road for four days. External Affairs had numerous queries about Macmillan visit but he shows virtually no interest, being completely preoccupied with election plans. I think he is now dreading Macmillan's visit and wants to make as little of it as possible. Not the same percentage in it now as there was when it was first floated.

PM approved reply put forward by Howard Green to message received yesterday from PM Macmillan giving warning of US-UK decision to go ahead with atmospheric nuclear tests at Christmas Island. It read in part: 'I cannot conceal from you my regret that it has not proved possible to find a solution at Geneva which would have enabled you and President Kennedy to dispense with further testing with a reasonable sense of security.'

As a result of PM's meeting with Herb Moran, who recently had seen Ayub Khan, the President of Pakistan, the PM signed a cordial letter to him. PM still regards Ayub Khan as a friend and would really like to have him visit Canada.

For the first time, PM referred to my impending posting to the Embassy in Washington, which has been discussed with him by the minister. He is evidently still doubtful but did not appear likely to resist. Timing remains to be decided.

April 25, Wednesday

PM left this morning for Port Arthur and a four-day absence westward. Before going he asked for a paper on the 'specific achievements of the government in external affairs.' This was to be for the campaign, obviously, but PM said all they wanted was a factual statement of the main points, so I reckoned it was a fair request. (I remembered that in 1949 as a very junior functionary in External Affairs, I had been assigned to draft material for campaign speeches for Prime Minister St-Laurent.)

Main divisions of the paper were (a) the Commonwealth (trade, aid, education, multi-racial association); (b) Disarmament; (c) the United Nations (peacekeeping, radiation and nuclear tests, world food program, and Soviet colonialism; (d) NATO; (e) the enlargement of Canadian representation abroad, especially in Latin America and French-speaking Africa.[5]

At lunch with a few colleagues from External Affairs, the talk was gloomy – the low regard in which the Department was held and the increasing tendency for experienced people to move elsewhere.

MACMILLAN'S VISIT

Among all the numerous visits of foreign dignitaries to Ottawa since the summer of 1957, none, with the exception of the Kennedy visit in 1961, had been so gingerly planned as that of Prime Minister Macmillan due to start on 30 April.

The uneasiness which had come to characterize relations between the two governments, and, I think the two prime ministers, permeated the planning. One could sense the British apprehensions as the visit approached. Diefenbaker, the recalcitrant Canadian cousin, had to be handled with extreme care or he might once again prove awkward. After all, he had not exactly been helpful over the South Africa issue, just over a year ago. And now the stakes were even higher as the United Kingdom sought to weave its way into the EEC.

Macmillan had come directly from Washington and, having had discussions with President Kennedy and his senior advisers, he was in a position to relay the latest trends in the president's thinking. This was always a subject of consuming interest to Diefenbaker, but what Macmillan had to say about American views on the prospect of British entry into Europe was anything but comforting. United States support for the course the Macmillan government was pursuing had been expressed largely in political terms – that the United Kingdom would be a stabilizing influence in Europe. Senior officials in the Kennedy administration had spoken in favour of eliminating the Commonwealth trade preferences, and thus had reinforced Canadian anxieties on this score. Now, Macmillan was warned by his Canadian host, if the Commonwealth preferences were ended the result would be to weaken Canada's resistance to US economic domination. This would 'create interesting possibilities in the next few weeks.' In a brief note in my diary I wrote: 'PM's performance full of overtones of anti-Americanism and thinly-veiled threats to use it in the campaign.'

The Canadian ministers, especially the prime minister, Green, and Fleming, also demonstrated concern over the political implications of British entry. Would Britain be able to resist being drawn into a federal Europe? Did Macmillan realize the special standing which Britain's position in the Commonwealth gave it in world affairs, and the danger its entry into Europe would pose for Britain's position as leader of the Commonwealth? What would happen if at the meeting of Commonwealth prime ministers, the general feeling, at least among the old members, were opposed to Britain's joining Europe?

Macmillan did his best to alleviate these and other concerns, but it was clear from his presentation that he was entirely convinced by the arguments in favour of British entry into Europe. He emphasized to Diefenbaker privately the degree to which his own political future was dependent on the outcome of the Common Market negotiations. Diefenbaker did not record *his* rejoinder but it is not difficult to imagine. At the close of the principal meeting he summarized the Canadian position in terms which underlined the depth of the government's concern. Macmillan acknowledged that there were great difficulties in any course, but asked that the matter be viewed 'in the light of the world as a whole.' It was necessary to 'adjust our minds to changing world conditions.'

A tranquillizing communiqué was prepared, in no way reflecting the differences between the two sides or the surviving anxieties of Diefenbaker and his ministers. The stage had been set for the prime ministers' conference in September:

May 1, Tuesday

I attended another meeting between the two prime ministers, this time covering a variety of international issues, including Southeast Asia, Cuba, Soviet colonialism, and the Congo. Both PM's were much more relaxed than yesterday and the air was clearer. PM Macmillan, drawing on talks with President Kennedy, remarked that the situation in Vietnam was worsening, and that the United States had found it necessary to increase the level of their military assistance, a decision for which he did not think they could be blamed in the circumstances they were faced with. PM Diefenbaker gave notice of his continued interest in proposing a resolution on Soviet colonialism at the next session of the UN General Assembly. PM Macmillan said that the Canadian Government was in a good position to do this, but went on to speak in terms which threw plenty of doubt on the prospects for support for an initiative of this kind.

BACK TO THE HUSTINGS

No sooner had Diefenbaker seen Macmillan than he left for a campaign visit to Newfoundland:

May 4, Friday

PM back from Newfoundland. I went to 24 Sussex Drive just after lunch. It was quiet for a while but as soon as he got on to the United States, there was an ungoverned rant about how they [the Americans] were out to get him. President Kennedy's invitation to Pearson to have three quarters of an hour with him before the Nobel Peace Prize dinner of April 29 has really hit home. PM talked about 1911 being repeated,[6] raved about Kennedy and Ball, and threatened to use the famous Rostow paper. PM had told Merchant how upset he was about all this. There is every sign that this will be an anti-American election. I reported this depressing news to Norman Robertson, Bob Bryce and Ed Ritchie, all very concerned.

I was told by a close friend in External Affairs of conversations with three foreign diplomats in Ottawa. The British man said that PM Macmillan had failed to communicate with Diefenbaker and had given up on him. The American said that Howard Green mistook Dean Rusk's courtesy for confidence in him. The Italian said he could not understand why Canada was isolating itself from its friends. A gloomy picture, and it will get worse as the election campaign proceeds.

May 6, Sunday

Saw members of PM's immediate staff who are very worried about his fatigue and extreme anti-American tendencies at the moment. They expect he will publicly blast the President for having that private talk with Pearson.

May 7, Monday

The PM left this morning for Quebec, creating a restful vacuum here. Howard Green back from NATO ministerial meetings in Paris.

May 8, Tuesday

Some excitement over instructions left by PM with Howard Green regarding 'recognition' of Baltic consular representatives in Canada, an idea which the minister agreed to pursue when he last talked to the PM. The experts in the European division of External Affairs prepared a statement as directed, but tacked on a fairly stiff memo emphasizing the disadvantages. Hard to say what the PM will do about this, but he has what he asked for.

May 9, Wednesday

PM away electioneering in Toronto and out West.

Norman Robertson had mentioned my Washington assignment to Livie Merchant and I went to call on him at the US Embassy today. Willis Armstrong was with him and we had a very candid talk. They are worried about the trend in US-Canada relations which Merchant thinks has been particularly bad in the last year and which PM seems to want to advance as a campaign issue. They listed defence, Cuba, wheat for China, Columbia River, disarmament, nuclear tests, and so on as examples. In general, they said, influential people in Washington were profoundly worried about the course which they think Canadian foreign policy has taken. They spoke of the difficulties of getting the United States and Canada to move in step on international problems. It was not simply that we found different ways of approaching mutually understood problems, but that we analysed the nature of the problems themselves in different ways. The US administration understood the Canadian desire to retain power of independent action and initiative. What they objected to was the tendency, which they found more and more prevalent, for Canada to take the initiatives without consultation on matters of direct concern to the United States.

Merchant said that he had a message from the President to the Prime Minister, arising out of PM's tirade last Friday over Pearson's private interview with Kennedy. The PM had been in a very overwrought state. Merchant was hoping that the message he had from the President would have a restraining effect. We discussed the best timing for Merchant's meeting with the PM to present the message.

Merchant and Armstrong gave me some helpful advice about contacts and methods in Washington. But I came away overwhelmed by the size of the problem of explaining Canadian policy in Washington, especially on defence.

Ambassador Merchant had clearly been staggered and angered by the vehemence of the prime minister's tirade against President Kennedy. There was little he could do about reports of the private meeting that Pearson had had with the president at the Nobel Peace Prize dinner. Diefenbaker had, after all, known in advance about the invitation to Pearson and it was not the fault of anyone on the US side if the Liberal party was exploiting the occasion in the heat of a bitter election campaign. The lost document was another matter. Diefenbaker had threatened to use it publicly against the president. Although the prime minister was in 'such an excited frame of mind,' Merchant succeeded in getting across the point that a private paper of the president's, a guest of the Canadian government in Canada, should have been immediately returned.'7 The prime minister, Merchant has recalled, calmed down, but gave no assurance that he would not reveal the document publicly.

Merchant reported at length to the State Department and soon received in reply the text of the Rostow memorandum and new instructions. He was to inform the prime minister that he was 'personally reluctant to report to Washington anything that could be construed as a threat by him to publish a private communication, and to warn him that this would cast a shadow over public attitudes between the two countries and create difficulties in the future in personal relations between the Prime Minister and the President.' He was to repeat what he had said to Diefenbaker in the earlier conversation that 'no friend of Canada in the United States could explain the publication of this document.'

On carrying out this delicate mission, the ambassador found the prime minister to be 'a different man ... charming and friendly ... [who] listened without interruption, calmly.' Diefenbaker went on to say that, in light of their earlier talk, he had now abandoned any intention of using the Rostow memorandum in the campaign. This was good news, but the effect was soon confused when Diefenbaker added that if developments caused him to change his mind, he would personally telephone Merchant in Washington 'as a friend' forty-eight hours in advance. The ambassador, who found the afterthought 'indeed in bad taste,' may have looked shocked, for Diefenbaker then reiterated that he had discarded the idea of using the Rostow paper.

Merchant, who was shortly to retire from the US foreign service after a long and most distinguished career, delayed his departure from Ottawa in order to deal with this extraordinary incident. On his return to Washington he discussed it with President Kennedy, and later recalled that the president had been 'understandably astounded and indignant' at what could only be described as 'a species of blackmail.' For Livie Merchant, who had understood Canada well but was baffled and finally appalled by Diefenbaker, it was a distressing end to a difficult mission, handled with professional poise and skill.

May 11, Friday

Announcement of several diplomatic appointments including ours to Washington. Hard to believe this phase is nearly over.

May 12, Saturday

The PM returned to Ottawa from Alberta amid talk that he is not recovering the touch of 1958. He warned of complacency in a recent speech and in general makes less confident noises and signs than usual. He also is said to have a cold. More and more the election looks as if it will be a real fight.

We told our children about Washington. Mixed feelings.

May 13, Sunday

I went to 24 Sussex Drive with a sheaf of papers. PM has a bad cold but was cheerful. Seemed very confident of Alberta, Saskatchewan, Nova Scotia and Newfoundland, doubtful about New Brunswick and Manitoba. Nothing said re Ontario and Quebec! He is off to Quebec again tomorrow morning.

He said he had not yet used the material we had sent him last week on Baltic consular representatives. I had the impression he was holding it in reserve against a possible move in that direction by the opposition.

We discussed timing of my departure from his office and he more or less agreed that it could be immediately after the election.

May 21, Monday

The PM was spending a day in Ottawa before going to Toronto for election rallies. He declared himself very confident, more so than some of the political staff travelling around with him.

Re Baltic representation, the PM said he was thinking of using the statement on June 14, which was 'the national day' of one of the groups involved. I could tell that he was fully conscious of the arguments against making the statement, and I did not try to rehearse them.

I had only occasional contacts with the prime minister, largely by telephone, in the last month of the election campaign.

May 23, Wednesday

The PM made an unexpected announcement in Winnipeg re the Government's readiness to help refugees now in Hong Kong. He had previously agreed to say nothing on this subject. Much agitation among officials and some concern that the British, responsible for Hong Kong, had not been notified in advance. On the phone from Winnipeg, PM quite unrepentant, wondering what all the fuss was about. Didn't we know there was an election on? Yessir.

May 29, Thursday

PM has been out West for several days, and not much phone contact. I had lunch with Rufus Smith of the US Embassy who told me that the Canadian record on defence policy would colour all the dealings with US officials in Washington – puzzlement and a feeling that they have not been squarely dealt with. This theme is too often repeated by US embassy officials to be a casual thought, but even if it is organized, it is what they genuinely feel. Cuba (trade policy) and China (wheat) are also irritants of lesser impact. Cooperation in Laos seems to be the one bright spot. We have been doing our best, through the International Commission, to work for an independent, neutral Laos.

May 31, Thursday

Papers are full of the PM's encounter with hecklers and demonstrators in the Forum in Vancouver last night. I spoke to the political staff by phone – all had praise for PM's behaviour in the face of severe provocation. Local press, however, suggests that the meeting was a disaster and that the PM, despite his best efforts, was bested.

June 12, Tuesday

A report from the Ambassador in Moscow reminded PM of ethnic group vote. He phoned PC candidate in Spadina, John Bassett, who promptly put in a word re the need for a statement to attract the Baltic community vote. PM assured him he had a statement but couldn't be sure of making it because Ukrainians might feel they were being discriminated against.

271

I told PM I planned to leave for Washington early in July. He took this easily and I feel all the uncertainly is now over. Mr. and Mrs. D. both friendly and kind.

June 14, Thursday

A note from the Soviet Embassy [protesting again the Government's alleged plans to accept nuclear weapons in Canada] was rejected by Howard Green on the ground that it was inadmissible interference in Canadian affairs. No one knows why the Russians sent it but everyone agrees that it helped the Government. PM was quick to pounce on it and said on the phone that he could not understand it, i.e. his good fortune.

PM made his statement to the Baltic community in Toronto, undertaking to 'give sympathetic consideration' to granting diplomatic status to acting Estonian, Latvian and Lithuanian consuls in Canada. To be expected.

June 15, Friday

Lunch with Willis Armstrong, US minister. More helpful advice about Washington. Intimated that US authorities would be approaching us on defence questions as soon as the election was history.

PERSONAL NOTES

The prime minister and the department had agreed that I would hand over my functions to my successor from External Affairs, Orme Dier, on the day after the election. So far as I know, there had been no thought of altering the role to be played by the External Affairs liaison officer or indeed of abolishing the position. Although on all important matters Howard Green dealt directly with the prime minister, it had long been the practice that all written communications on foreign policy matters were channelled through my office. The pace of events and the volume of paper were such that it would have been unrealistic to expect the minister or his office to provide the prime minister with the kind of detailed, day-to-day service which he had come to expect. Moreover, awkward as the prime minister's instructions, demands, and reactions often were, they might have been more difficult still for the department to interpret and cope with if they had been passed down through a non-External Affairs channel in the Prime Minister's Office.

I have heard it said that the presence in the Prime Minister's Office of a departmental liaison officer may have had the effect of restricting the access of the undersecretary of state for external affairs to the prime minister. In theory this may seem persuasive. In practice, it leaves at least two significant factors out of account. It ignores the fact that the undersecretary is regarded by the minister as being available and responsible to him and that the undersecretary would find it extremely difficult to satisfy the requirements of the prime minister as well as the minister, especially in emergency situations. The other factor is more a matter of the personal style of the main characters. Except in unusually urgent circumstances, neither Jules Léger nor Norman Robertson, the under-secretaries in the Diefenbaker years, was given to pressing for opportunities to call on the prime minister. Both tended to wait to be consulted. For his part, Diefenbaker was diffident about summoning senior officials, especially if, for one reason or another, he did not understand or feel comfortable with them. And so it was that, without deliberately setting out to create a small, exclusive circle of advisers, he came to use and trust those whose daily tasks required them to see him regularly in order to ensure that issues were brought forward for decision and that the business of government was carried forward. As I advised my successor in a memorandum:

It is sometimes said that the liaison job is what it is made by the incumbent, but it is more accurate to say that the job is what it is made by the Prime Minister.

Mr. Diefenbaker has certain habits of work which, together with the extreme pressure of his daily activities, determine the manner in which the liaison officer can perform his duties. Thus, it would be desirable if one could be sure of seeing the Prime Minister at definite times each day for an approximately equal number of minutes, or if one could be sure of seeing all, and not only part, of his correspondence on foreign policy matters, or if he followed the practice of noting his comments on Departmental papers, of if he would return all classified papers sent to him according to the normal security procedures. If all of these and many more conditions were fulfilled, it would be easier to define and regularize the functions of the liaison officer.

In fact, the only way the liaison officer can effectively represent the Department is by adapting himself to the Prime Minister's habits, interests, prejudices, and moods. Thus it is generally better to see Mr. Diefenbaker early rather than later in the day if one wishes to attract his undivided attention or if one has a particularly difficult subject to discuss. It is best to take soundings around the office before seeing him to get an indication of how much time or attention he is likely to give. In the same way, it is necessary to decide on each occasion, in the light of all his preoccupations at the moment, how much time one should take and whether one should try to complete the full agenda or retreat and cut one's losses. It is, of course, necessary to present each problem in a very brief time and in the most succinct manner possible. Normally, one can get a reliable reaction in this way but naturally if one requires a more comprehensive decision on a problem one should wait for a later, suitable opportunity.

On 18 June, as I watched the election results (Progressive Conservatives 116, Liberals 100, Social Credit 30, NDP 19), I realized how devastating they would be for the prime minister. Apart from the shock of the results themselves, he would not relish leading a minority government with the potentially unwelcome compromises it might entail, not to speak of the risks to the government's ability to hold the confidence of the House of Commons. I realized too that by leaving at such a time I might be adding to his burdens. I did not, however, have second thoughts. The decision to move had been taken and approved. I had confidence in my successor. And I was already making the practical and intellectual switch from Ottawa to the new life and job in Washington. I had no illusions that it would be easy there, but I was looking forward to the change.

27

Fresh Perspectives

The 1962 election had confirmed that the Diefenbaker government was on a downward slide which only a combination of decisive leadership and kindlier circumstance could hope to arrest. For, while the prime minister's past leadership could certainly be called in question, it was also true that the government was confronted by a number of inherently difficult problems not wholly of its own making.

By far the most urgent and serious problem after the election arose from the monetary crisis which had erupted during the election campaign. The prime minister's task of reconstructing the ministry (five ministers had lost their seats) had to be laid aside while the cabinet considered a set of emergency measures designed to bring the crisis under control. The emergency program was announced by Diefenbaker on 23 June, less than a week after the election. It included surcharges on a large proportion of Canada's imports, a reduction of $250 million in government expenditures, and substantial currency arrangements through the International Monetary Fund and institutions in the United States and the United Kingdom for the purpose of strengthening Canada's foreign exchange reserves.[1] The prime minister and others emphasized that the 'austerity program,' as it promptly came to be known, was intended as a short-term measure but that longer-term remedies would be introduced.

The strain of the election campaign, the shock of the results, and the critical urgency of the dollar crisis had together drained Diefenbaker's energies to a level lower than at any other stage in his terms of office. Exhausted and dispirited, yet reluctant to follow advice to take the rest he so badly needed, he could bring himself only to do the minimum necessary tasks once the emergency package had been agreed upon and revealed. Early in July he had hardly begun to wrestle with the shaping of the new cabinet when Senator William Brunt, a family friend of long standing and the mainstay at that time of his small circle of political confidants, was killed in an automobile accident. It was a cruel blow to both the prime minister and his wife.

FIRST IMPRESSIONS OF WASHINGTON

I had been in Washington on a house-hunting expedition in the last week of June. I spent as much time as possible at the Canadian embassy with the ambassador, Charles Ritchie, and his deputy, Saul Rae, whom I would shortly be succeeding. In those few days I formed two strong impressions. First was the sense of abundant confidence which seemed to permeate the atmosphere in Washington, so radically different from the uncertainty and disarray which prevailed in Ottawa. Second, I was struck by the spirit in which the US administration had responded to Ottawa's appeal for help in overcoming the dollar crisis. Obviously American assistance had not been entirely disinterested, but after what seemed like years of Canadian-American animosity, it was refreshing to see and feel that cooperation in important matters of mutual interest was still possible. It was too early to form conclusions but, on returning from that first brief visit, I felt encouraged. Despite policy disagreements between the governments and a growing personal rift between the leaders, it seemed that there was still a fund of goodwill for Canada in Washington.

I have included these first impressions to indicate how my mind was turning as I prepared to move with my family to Washington at the end of July. I called on the prime minister on 27 July. A few days before he had broken his ankle, and although he did not seem to be in severe discomfort, he was frustrated at being immobilized at a time when there was so much to be done. I remember having some apprehension that he might have resented my departing at that time. He was, however, very understanding and generous. He asked me about my visit to Washington, and I gave him my first impressions. Among the policy problems, the nuclear weapons issue had dwarfed everything else and I did my best to explain the importance of an early decision one way or the other on that issue. I also told him that American officials had noted a reference he had made, in announcing the economic emergency program, to 'positive long-term measures' that would be taken. As the conversation ended, he asked me to accompany him to London for the meeting of Commonwealth prime ministers in September. He also asked me to be sure to keep an eye out for developments in Washington which would be of particular interest to him. He gave me no reason to expect an early resolution of the nuclear issue or indeed of any of the other bilateral problems still on the agenda. I left for Washington in a sober frame of mind.

My role at the embassy was to act as the ambassador's deputy, to be in charge in his absence, and to supervise directly the political, defence, consular, and

276

administrative work of the embassy. Economic and trade matters were under the supervision of the minister for economic affairs, Maurice Schwarzmann. The Canadian Joint Staff, with its separate location, was the military link with the Pentagon, and the commander of the Joint Staff, Rear Admiral D.W. Piers, was the ambassador's military adviser. Close liaison was maintained between the Joint Staff and the embassy, especially on matters of defence policy, including the nuclear weapons issues, which were at that time as heavily political as they were military.

Despite the considerable volume and variety of my new functions, it seemed at first that a great weight had been lifted from my shoulders. I felt almost irresponsible in not being involved in the process which led to the words and decisions we were now to convey and explain to the State Department or the White House. This light-headed state did not long survive. One became bound up in the give and take of argument and interpretation between the embassy and the Americans, in reporting and analysing their reactions and intentions, and in developing contacts and sources across a seemingly unlimited range of possibilities.

Ottawa and Washington were physically not far removed, but at the highest levels of government they were worlds apart. How could one not be struck by the contrast between a president who seemed to feast on the intellectual distinction of those around him and a prime minister who relied so heavily on his own intuitive judgment; between a president unchallenged in his power and a prime minister vulnerable even within his cabinet and party; between a political regime which still bore the bloom of promise and one which would have to struggle to survive; between the world view and the parochial, the sophisticated and the old-fashioned?

Canadians working in Washington were not in danger of feeling self-important. Exposure to the Washington perspective was a great leveller. A superpower obsessively conscious of its world role must ration the time and attention it gives even to its neighbour. A small cluster of officials in the State Department spent their full time on Canadian-American affairs. But, with a few welcome exceptions, there was a considerable indifference to developments in Canada among government officials, the Congress, and the American press.

Canada's international role, however, was not as casually treated. And I was not surprised, as the steaming summer wore on, to find that to most of the American officials concerned with foreign and defence policy, the firm of Diefenbaker and Green was a gigantic enigma with which they found it impossible to come to terms. The business between Washington and Ottawa was varied and voluminous and the embassy's work could proceed without serious complication in some sectors. At the more senior levels of the Washington bureaucracy there existed attitudes ranging from curiosity to outright antagonism towards the policy positions adopted, and presumably to be continued, by Diefenbaker and his government in foreign affairs. Apart from defence matters, I was conscious of resentment over our trade with Cuba and mainland China; the delays in our approach towards ratification of the Columbia River Treaty; Howard Green's fixation, as they saw it, with disarmament; and an evident perplexity about our reliability as an ally and our readiness to cooperate in bilateral affairs.

Having been so closely associated with the prime minister, I was curious how that experience would affect my reception in Washington. Diefenbaker had few, if any, defenders in the Kennedy administration, and I wondered if his unpopularity would make it more difficult for me to gain the confidence of American officials. I had been favoured in Ottawa by the candid advice of Livie Merchant, Willis Armstrong, and Rufus Smith at the US embassy, and I was fortunate in that at about the time of my own appointment Armstrong was transferred from Ottawa to take over new responsibilities in the State Department, including Canadian affairs. In general I was not made to feel unwelcome but the experience was sobering. In a letter to my parents, I put it this way: 'Our man JGD is regarded with hostile suspicion here ... It is very hard to defend his position but we do of course do our best. It would be much easier if he would occasionally say something publicly which the US could regard as a friendly gesture. Unfortunately he is not given to this sort of thing and for Canadians in Washington it is very difficult to operate effectively when relations between the governments are cool. Some of the Americans I see are extremely blunt in what they say about Diefenbaker and one is constantly on the defensive.'

What helped immensely was to be able to share the day's adventures with Charles Ritchie. His sensitivity, shrewd judgment, and refusal to be dazzled by the glitter of the New Frontier kept the embassy family on a steady course; often, too, in fits of laughter. It was impossible to feel depressed in his company, in spite of the strained atmosphere in which our relations with the United States had to be conducted.

I had expected before leaving Ottawa that, before the summer was out, a new attempt would be made by the United States to persuade the Canadian government to proceed with the long-delayed negotiations on nuclear weapons. In the aftermath of the Canadian election, however, the Americans realized that Diefenbaker's new minority government might best not be confronted too soon with the nuclear issue. This was no doubt a sensible judgment, in view of the Canadian government's preoccupation with shaping the economic austerity program and its need to prepare for the new session of parliament in which the Progressive Conservatives would no longer have a majority. The prime minister, too, and three of his leading ministers, would be attending a Commonwealth meeting in London for a good part of September. Thus, in briefing Secretary of State Rusk for a visit to Ottawa late in August, the State Department advised him only to call the Canadian government's attention to continuing US interest in the nuclear weapons problem.

At the beginning of September I flew to Ottawa to join the prime minister's delegation to the Commonwealth prime ministers' meeting in London. I was away for almost the whole of that month.

LONDON INTERLUDE: THE UNITED KINGDOM AND THE EEC

When I reached Ottawa the black briefing books had been delivered to the prime minister and no one knew whether he would follow them or not. The basic advice reaching him from Howard Green's cabinet committee and Bryce's group of senior officials was cautious in tone, quite lacking in the decibels of indignation that Diefenbaker would have relished. Essentially, the advice was, first, that the decision on whether the United Kingdom should enter the EEC was for the UK government to make; second, that Canadian and other Commonwealth trade interests were not sufficiently protected by the results of the negotiations so far held between the United Kingdom and the EEC; third, that the occasion of the prime ministers' meeting should be taken to articulate the political and economic apprehensions of the Canadian government; and, fourth, that care should be taken to avoid a position in which Canada would be seen as leading the opposition to UK entry into Europe or of allowing Canada to be branded as the principal cause of the failure of the British application.[2]

While, intellectually, Diefenbaker could accept this advice, it did not measure up to his conception of the occasion presented by the London meeting. And it did not reflect the political message that he instinctively wanted to convey in Canada. To him, it seemed too compliant, too much of a surrender before the real battle had been joined. Here was a vital turning point in Commonwealth history, a moment he feared was about to pass without the great, collective debate that it deserved. He agonized over the part he should play in that debate, conceding that it was for the UK government ultimately to decide whether to enter Europe but determined somehow to ensure that the decision should not be rushed, or translated into a foregone conclusion as Macmillan, Heath, and Sandys were making it out to be.

Just before leaving for London on 6 September, at a meeting of the cabinet, this streak of defiance emerged. 'First consideration,' he is reported to have said, 'should be given not to the steps to be taken if Britain joined the Six, but to the position he should take on behalf of Canada at the Prime Ministers' Conference.' United Kingdom entry into Europe might be probable, but 'this should not be taken for granted.'[3] He told the cabinet that nine out of every eleven letters he received from the Canadian public were opposed to British entry. Opinion polls in the United Kingdom showed that only 28 per cent of the British population were in favour. He might have added that, at the London end, the Canadian high commissioner was straining every sinew to frustrate the aims of the Macmillan government.

Diefenbaker told me that he had decided to ask Howard Green to accompany him to London because Green had 'a better feel' for the Commonwealth than other ministers who were concerned with Commonwealth trade matters. Green was, in other words, more likely to be in tune with the prime minister's approach. Furthermore, Diefenbaker knew that with Bryce in charge of a highly capable group of officials (Jake Warren of Trade and Commerce, Simon Reisman of Finance, Gerry Stoner of External Affairs, and A.H. Turner of Agriculture), he and Green would be well equipped to handle the economic aspects of the conference. He was not going to be accused of failing to secure as much protection as possible for Canadian trade.

I found Diefenbaker in a very crotchety mood on the way to the conference. He would not disguise his resentment that the British themselves – there was no one else to blame – were undermining the faith he had placed in the Commonwealth and disturbing traditional patterns among nations in the non-communist world. That Macmillan was pursuing this course with the active encouragement of President Kennedy made the pill even more bitter, and also reminded Diefenbaker that the weakening of Commonwealth trade links would make it harder for Canada to resist US economic pressures.

With these thoughts infecting his judgment, it was not surprising that Diefenbaker's performance in London was erratic. Before the meeting had even begun, he made reference to 'alternatives' which might be presented if British entry in to the EEC seemed unlikely. This led to speculation in the British press that he intended to propose an alternative plan to the conference, as if to reverse or postpone the consensus of approval for which the UK government was hoping. Although he had in his briefing papers an outline of an 'alternative programme' – under which the trade problems arising out of the creation of the EEC should be tackled through a new round of multilateral tariff negotiations under the General Agreement on Tariffs and Trade [GATT] – Diefenbaker had not been expected to put the alternative forward unless there seemed to be some likelihood of the United Kingdom's deciding against pressing its application to enter the EEC. He let the press and the ministers wait and wonder. On 11 September, in his first statement to the conference, he referred only briefly to an alternative, implying that the moment for it had not arrived. Instead, he gave a stiffly questioning analysis of the reasons Macmillan had given in support of its application, stressed that it was impossible to tell what the final terms of British entry might be, exposed the inadequacy of the arrangements so far reached in the Brussels negotiations, and predicted that another meeting of prime ministers might be necessary when the negotiations had been completed. Several of his fellow prime ministers were clearly moved by Diefenbaker's words, and especially by his final, impassioned declaration of faith in the Commonwealth.

The British ministers were not among those applauding. Diefenbaker's speech had amounted to exactly the kind of performance they had hoped to head off. A more than usually hostile press-briefing operation was mounted in the London press, with the result that the Canadian prime minister was singled out as the principal obstacle to UK objectives – precisely the position which he had been advised to avoid.

As the conference ground on, Diefenbaker pondered the pros and cons of advancing the alternative plan despite the overwhelming evidence that the British would not be dissuaded from resuming their negotiations with the EEC. In the end, he decided against the plan, but instead proposed that the conference should issue invitations to an international conference, involving members of the Commonwealth, the EEC, the European Free Trade Association (EFTA), the United States, Japan, and other 'like-minded' nations, to consider problems of international trade. It was, as he phrased it, a Commonwealth initiative, with no reference to GATT. The idea got nowhere, not even a mention in the final communiqué.

The result of the meeting enabled the United Kingdom to resume negotiations with the EEC, but that endeavour, and all the endless consultations within the Commonwealth, were soon nullified. Diefenbaker had said that in the end de Gaulle would blow the whistle on the British, and, after a few weeks, he was proved right. On 29 January 1963 the French veto would be cast, and that would remove at least one troublesome item from Diefenbaker's agenda.

My impression of the 1962 meeting was that Diefenbaker was personally less effective than at the two previous meetings where the South African membership question had predominated. I think he would have been well advised not to advertise that he was thinking of an alternative plan unless he was intending to advance it. A more serious and puzzling question is why, if he believed that de Gaulle would in the end prevent the British from entering the EEC, he devoted such effort and emotion to opposing it. As it was, he was seen by the UK government as the one Commonwealth menace vis-à-vis British public opinion on the Common Market issue. The result was that he became the target of what appeared to be a deliberate smear campaign by the UK authorities, who knew they could not change Diefenbaker's policy or soften his public statements.

In the circumstances, press briefings became more than usually important and difficult. As he had done so often before at Commonwealth meetings, Bryce carried a heavy load in this regard. The nominal rules governing press briefings at these meetings limited each delegation to communicating information on its own part in the proceedings. Actual practice was something else, as a cursory glance at the morning press would confirm. Bryce had the necessary self-confidence to follow actual practice, and his grasp of the subject matter was always sufficiently comprehensive to provide briefings that would usefully supplement comments made by the prime minister or other ministers. That he could play this delicate role without giving offence to political leaders was a tribute to his command of the subject and sense of what the traffic would bear. Once at the 1962 meeting, however, he was inadvertently drawn into an awkward contretemps with Howard Green. Arriving in the course of a press conference given by the minister, who had felt it necessary to follow the nominal rules rather than actual practice, Bryce was unable to avoid being questioned in detail on matters already addressed by the minister. He gave more informative answers than Green had given, and the minister made known his concern on the ground that Bryce's answers might prove politically embarrassing to the government. Not even Bryce could win them all.

28

On the Brink: The Cuban Missile Crisis

When I returned to Washington from the London conference at the end of September, the talk was all of Cuba. The Kennedy administration and the Congress were becoming steadily more alarmed by intelligence reports of increasing Soviet shipments to Cuba, including military equipment. The media correctly assessed the depth of the official concern and helped to magnify it. The crisis took on an all-consuming, single-minded quality reminiscent of a capital at war. Having just spent some time in London and Ottawa, I was struck by the extraordinary force of Washington's preoccupation with Cuba and the arch-villain, Fidel Castro. On 7 October in a letter, I wrote: 'The current excitement is the Cuban situation and although it must look strange to people elsewhere, it is very real here. The Administration is doing its best to keep the temperature down but there is a very deep emotion stirring and it is to be devoutly hoped that extreme and stupid measures will be averted.' Some pre-emptive military action to prevent further penetration of Cuba by the Soviet Union was among the courses of action being floated in the press and by some political leaders. A senior administration spokesman described at length to a congressional committee the 'strategy of isolation' which was being conducted towards 'nullifying Cuba's usefulness as a source of infection for international communism.'[1] Armed with statistics, he listed the numbers and types of Soviet weapons and military personnel recently delivered to Cuba by the Soviet Union, including anti-aircraft and coastal missiles and sophisticated interceptor aircraft. President Kennedy had earlier warned that 'the gravest issues would arise' if, among other possible threats, the Soviet military build-up were to include missiles of an 'offensive' character.[2] Public opinion was being shaped to anticipate critical developments.

A TEST OF CO-OPERATION

On 15 October the embassy warned Ottawa that in the mid-term congressional election campaign which was then starting, Canada might come in for criticism over Cuba.[3] Concern about our general attitude lay not far below the surface and, although the administration understood the Canadian position, in Congress and the press we continued to be the targets of criticism, much of it admittedly uninformed. This would be less a matter of concern were it not for the depth of passions which had been aroused over Cuba. Unfortunately, the embassy's report continued, 'the sense of national humiliation is so pervading and the public feeling in favour of "doing something about Cuba" is so strong that it is almost impossible to exaggerate the inflammatory character of the issue. The President and his colleagues are making a creditable attempt to maintain a public sense of perspective and restraint and it is very much in the Canadian interest that this attempt should not fail.' The report concluded by suggesting that the government should adopt a helpful attitude towards measures recently proposed by the United States in the NATO Council on Soviet shipping and aviation bound for Cuba. To the extent that the allies of the United States could contribute to resisting domestic pressures, the trend towards irresponsible and even dangerous courses of action might be arrested. In the NATO Council, where the US representatives were doing their best to orchestrate allied cooperation, the Canadian response was generally positive and, accordingly, as the crisis drew to its peak, the embassy was not subject to last-minute pressures. There was a sense of calm before the storm.[4]

Although Ottawa had been generally well informed on US policy towards Cuba, the government was not privy to the Kennedy administration's planning as the missile crisis approached in September and October 1962. The crisis was developing rapidly, the source of danger was quite different from that envisaged in NORAD planning, and, most important of all, relations between the president and the prime minister were on nothing like the trusting, mutually respectful basis that would have inclined the president personally to initiate a special approach to Diefenbaker, as he had done by telephone with Macmillan. All the more reason, one might think, for taking advance precautions to bring the Canadian government onside. But if this thought had surfaced, it had not survived. Someone in Washington, however, had recognized that the Canadian government must be given some prior notification of US intentions. So it was that Livingston Merchant, recently retired from his post as ambassador to Canada, was selected as a special emissary to brief the Canadian government.[5]

On Monday, 22 October, in a memorable television address, President Kennedy disclosed the presence of Soviet offensive missiles in Cuba. He announced the US decision to establish a quarantine to prevent further Soviet shipping from reaching the island and made known his diplomatic strategy, which would be to use the Organization of American States (OAS) and the United Nations to chart a political way out of the military crisis. Merchant's mission called for him to see the prime minister in the afternoon of that day, some two hours in advance of the president's speech. Diefenbaker, however, had known since Sunday morning that a serious crisis over Cuba was imminent and that it involved the construction of large Soviet missile installations. Word of what was afoot had reached Norman Robertson and Bryce through an External Affairs official who had been attending a meeting of intelligence experts in Washington during the previous week. The meeting had not been related to the Cuban crisis but US officials attending it were being frequently called away and the Canadians were told confidentially what was going on. During the weekend, moreover, Bryce learned from Ivan White, then in charge of the US embassy, that Merchant was being sent to Ottawa, although at that time White was not aware of what the president would announce. Bryce kept the prime minister informed as the situation developed.

These details are related in order to explain that by the time he received Merchant on Monday, 22 October, at 5.15 PM, Diefenbaker was aware of the nature of the evidence available to the president and his advisers and of the general drift of the conclusions they were drawing from it. He did not know the extent of the evidence or in what way the United States would react. But he had had more than twenty-four hours to get steamed up about what he was to be told and perhaps also what he would be asked to do. Despite what he had learned in advance, it would have been completely out of character if he had not been upset at being presented with the evidence of the Soviet missiles and the outline of the president's plans, at a stage when he could do little more than acknowledge their receipt. It was, after all, a very important development for the defence of North America, and it had been he who had entered (hastily, it will be recalled) into the NORAD agreement five years before. That agreement had underlined the importance which the two governments attached to the 'fullest possible consultation on all matters affecting the joint defence of North America.' The prime minister's resentment at the absence of genuine advance consultation should have come as no surprise.

Merchant said sometime later that after a stiff beginning (he thought Diefenbaker's manner extremely cool towards him personally), the meeting had gone reasonably well.[6] The prime minister had shown some wounded pride at not having been genuinely consulted. He had, however, been clearly impressed by the photographic evidence Merchant had brought with him and said that the president had no choice but to take the measures he was about to announce. Harkness, the minister of national defence, was also fully in support of the president's action. Howard Green, the only other Canadian present, did not question the evidence. And the prime minister was to say in cabinet the following day that Green, as well as Harkness and himself, had been convinced there had been 'no exaggeration of the situation' by the president.[7]

As the meeting closed, the prime minister made a remark which indicated to Merchant that it would not be necessary for a statement to be made by the Canadian government until the following day. On returning to Washington that evening, he was therefore surprised to learn not only that the prime minister had made a statement to the House of Commons an hour or so after the president's address, but that the tenor of the statement seemed to question what the president had said about the missile sites on the basis of the evidence that Diefenbaker had been shown. Merchant thought that Diefenbaker had 'put a most unfortunate face' on what Kennedy had said.

Again the sequence of events seems worth tracing for it shows how accidents of circumstance can affect important policy declarations. For reasons no doubt connected with the rush of events, a memorandum from Howard Green to the prime minister, intended as the basis of a possible telephone conversation with President Kennedy before his 7 PM television broadcast, was not seen by Diefenbaker in advance of Merchant's arrival.[8] This memorandum, drafted in the Department of External Affairs in the course of the day on 22 October, was an attempt to anticipate the various possible courses that were estimated to be under consideration in Washington.[9] It speculated that there might turn out to be an analogy between 'the situation today' and the circumstances at the time of the Suez crisis in 1956, when urgent international action through the United Nations was taken to contain an outbreak of fighting. A similar move now to involve the United Nations might be as far as Diefenbaker and Green would be prepared to go in support of the United States, or so it was thought in External Affairs before the US position had been spelled out.

It was against this background that Green's memorandum advanced the idea of an on-site 'investigation' by a UN team. To be fully effective, the memorandum concluded, a proposal of this kind would have to be discussed with the president *before* (my underlining) his 7 PM broadcast. Indeed it would. In fact Bryce, on being shown a copy, told External Affairs that Green's proposal would just not do. And it seems unlikely that the idea would have survived in its original form, given the convincing evidence that Merchant had brought with him. In any event, Diefenbaker saw the original of the memorandum only when he opened his papers on reaching his residence after his meeting with Merchant. (Howard Green had shown him a copy of the memo in the course of Merchant's briefing.) Until later in the evening, however, when Pearson asked him by telephone for a statement in response to the president's speech, the prime minister thought he would have until the following day to give a first public reaction.

Pearson's request for a statement could not be ignored, all the less so after the External Affairs suggestion that in the affair of the Soviets missiles in Cuba there might be an analogy with the Suez crisis. It is not hard to imagine the lights that must have flashed on in Diefenbaker's mind at this reminder of an occasion on which Pearson himself had gilded his reputation and been rewarded with the Nobel Peace Prize. Moreover, the point had been made to Diefenbaker earlier in the day that the content of the president's speech could conceivably give rise to a real war scare in Canada. As a result of all this, the prime minister decided that a brief statement was needed without delay. On the resumption of the House of Commons' evening sitting at 8 PM, the proceedings were interrupted to enable him to report to the House and for other party leaders to respond. He called the president's speech 'sombre and challenging,' appealed for calm, and, in an attempt at peacemaking, advanced in foggy and tentative terms the suggestion for a UN inquiry. Not only had this idea been developed in ignorance of what the president would say, but it appeared to imply the need for 'an objective answer' to what was going on in Cuba. Hence the surprise and annoyance in Washington at what seemed to be a lack of confidence in their evidence and in their judgment of the most effective course of action.[10]

A second issue arose on that first hectic evening. Word was received at national defence headquarters in Ottawa that US forces were on an increased level of readiness (Defcon 3) and that NORAD headquarters expected Canadian air defence forces to be placed on the same alert level. Because he lacked the authority to issue a similar order for Canadian forces, and no doubt because he recognized the political importance of the decision, Harkness decided to consult the prime minister.[11] This he did immediately, being joined in Diefenbaker's office by Green. Harkness has recalled that Green did not on that occasion disagree that the necessary order should be issued, but Diefenbaker demurred, preferring to have the matter discussed in cabinet the following morning.

Diefenbaker had a number of worries in addition to the annoyance he felt at the president's failure to consult. What would the public reaction be to the announcement of an immediate military alert? How much solidarity with the United States should the government display? How would Macmillan be handling the crisis in London? These were typical of the thoughts that caused Canada's prime minister to take time to consider the implications of what he was being asked to do.

Diefenbaker's account of the crisis makes no mention of a telephone call or other message from Macmillan on 23 October, and the cabinet records confirm that UK views had not been received in time for the meeting on that day. After the meeting, however, Diefenbaker received a message from Macmillan through the UK high commissioner, Lord Amory.[12] The message reflected Macmillan's anxiety at the dangers inherent in the situation and counselled against any action that might disturb the balance at a critical time. Diefenbaker relayed a summary of Macmillan's message to the cabinet on the 24th. At least two of Diefenbaker's ministers are on record as having heard him refer to Macmillan's advice to avoid any provocative action.[13] It seems very likely that this advice reinforced his doubts about the wisdom of a declaration placing the Canadian forces in a state of readiness equal to that of US forces in NORAD and in the North Atlantic.

Against this background it is interesting to review Diefenbaker's account of his conversation with President Kennedy, which seems to have taken place on the late afternoon of the 23rd.[14] The prime minister's story is generally confirmed by his secretary, Bunny Pound, who took notes of his part in the conversation. It must have been a bad-tempered affair. When it was over Diefenbaker was annoyed, complaining at the president's attitude and particularly about being pressed to put the Canadian forces on an advanced state of alert. There seems little doubt that the message from Macmillan and the exchange with Kennedy helped to prolong Diefenbaker's refusal to agree to Harkness's recommendation.

All this was frustrating, of course, for Harkness and caused indignation in national defence circles in Ottawa, at NORAD headquarters, and also in Washington. Although cabinet meetings on the 23rd and 24th produced decisions on other aspects of policy in the crisis, no direction was forthcoming on the level of readiness of the forces. Only after Harkness had been informed in the late morning of the 24th that US Strategic Air Command (SAC) forces had been placed on the second highest level of alert (imminent enemy attack expected) was the nettle grasped. After the cabinet meeting on that morning, Harkness confronted Diefenbaker personally and Diefenbaker grudgingly gave the minister the authority he had been seeking. By that time Harkness and the chiefs of staff had long since taken informal measures to bring the forces to a state of maximum preparedness short of declaring the formal alert. Whether Diefenbaker knew that this was happening is a point of some interest. Harkness recalls that he did not tell the prime minister.[15] Bryce thinks that Diefenbaker had a pretty good idea of what was going on and preferred to let it happen in a less than formal way. Not much escaped the Diefenbaker antennae.

At the State Department on 23 October, senior officials had been anxiously monitoring the political responses of allied governments and at the same time had been trying to anticipate Soviet reactions to the president's speech. At the embassy we had no advance knowledge of the prime minister's decision to make a statement of his own immediately after the president had spoken. Obviously the proposal for a UN inquiry to ascertain the facts of the situation in Cuba would have to be explained very carefully. Before appearing at the State Department, we managed to obtain authority by telephone from External Affairs to give the assurance that the facts of the Cuban situation as outlined by the president were not questioned by the Canadian government. Even this modest assurance was welcomed with evident relief. Later in the day – there had been further cabinet discussion in Ottawa and the prime minister had asked for and received advice from opposition leader Pearson – the idea of a UN inquiry was being given a gloss more likely to appeal to the Americans.[16] That suggestion, the prime minister now told the House of Commons, was not intended to compete with the US proposal already before the United Nations. We were authorized to say that the prime minister's proposal had been inspired by the thought that a neutral inspection under UN auspices would be a good way of demonstrating that the president had been justified in the measures he had decided to take.

Before 23 October was out, the position of the government in Canada had developed further in the direction of practical cooperation with the United States. The embassy was told to inform the State Department that Soviet aircraft would not be permitted to fly over Canada except in agreed circumstances, and that Cuban, Czech, and other Soviet bloc aircraft would be subject to special regulations. It was put to us by the State Department that this decision, together with earlier measures taken to control Soviet transit stops and overflights, would be valuable for publicity purposes if it could be promptly announced. A statement had already been prepared and it was given on the 24th by the minister of external affairs.

Yet, in spite of these and other measures of cooperation, the degree of Canadian support for the US quarantine still seemed somewhat qualified. A television interview with Green on the 24th left the impression that Canada's position was based more on the obligations of an ally than on a conviction that appropriate and legally defensible action was being taken. One press report speculated that the government had 'strong reservations' about the quarantine. There was at the same time considerable public criticism of Green's statements in that interview.

In these circumstances, and with the aid of a discussion in the cabinet on the morning of the 25th, Diefenbaker became convinced that the government's position needed clarification. Both Bryce and officials in External Affairs had already begun work on what the prime minister might usefully say. Bryce concentrated on emphasizing the government's support for the United States and on a review of the variety of measures the government had taken in the face of the crisis, including information that the air defence forces had been formally alerted. The External Affairs draft, while reflecting Green's reluctance to endorse wholeheartedly the American action, nevertheless argued that it was the Soviet Union that had disturbed the balance and that they and their Cuban friends must restore it by dismantling the missile facilities. The legal debate over whether the quarantine was justified, the External Affairs draft said, was 'sterile and irrelevant' in the circumstances. The greatest hope for a solution lay in the United Nations. It was to be hoped that if the missiles were dismantled, under some form of international inspection, some good might come out of the crisis, some first steps towards disarmament.

Out of these offerings the prime minister composed, or one might say cobbled, his statement to the House on the 25th. Forthright in its support for the US position, it answered critics in Progressive Conservative ranks and was well received by Pearson.[17] It also gave rise to an appreciative editorial in the *Washington Post* which, whether or not echoing the administration's sentiments, concluded with the thought that, whatever the outcome of the Cuban crisis, it was 'deeply reassuring that no cool air is blowing from Canada.'

All this time, while the Canadian position had been evolving, the tension over the quarantine was rising. Would the Soviet vessels now heading for Cuba attempt to run the blockade or would they turn back? The climate was not altogether promising. On Friday, the 26th, I went with Charles Ritchie to see Dean Rusk, the secretary of state. If it had not been for the prime minister's most recent statement, I suppose that conversation with Rusk might have been more difficult in Canadian-American terms. But Rusk had his mind on the issues of the moment, especially on the urgency of eliminating the Soviet missile bases from Cuba. He talked of the importance of getting UN personnel onto the missile sites in the following few days, implying that further decisions of the administration would depend to a large extent on discussions with the secretary-general of the United Nations later that day.

After seeing Rusk and assessing other signs of mounting tension, Ritchie felt sufficiently concerned to warn Ottawa that, failing some significant concession by the Soviet Union and Cuba at the United Nations, the United States administration might

give early consideration to undertaking a further unilateral action to achieve their objectives ...

I do not want to base too much on indirect evidence but I cannot help feeling that ... a second and more critical phase of the crisis ... may develop.[18]

The administration was not in a mood to wait many days for the removal of the missiles from Cuba.

Ritchie's talk with Rusk took place at a moment when no one could foretell the outcome. Yet there were some signs of a break. Most of the Soviet cargo ships which had been tracked all week had stopped short of the American ring and some had turned around. This had given rise to great relief in Ottawa and had even caused the government's precautions for possible evacuation to emergency quarters to be relaxed. But the danger inherent in the continued assembly of the missiles in Cuba still existed. Should there be no move to dismantle and remove them, the various plans for counter-measures stood ready in Washington. So far as the Canadian embassy knew as that weekend approached, the possibility of the worst occurring in the next few days was stark and real. There was nothing exaggerated in a remark made later by Howard Green that on that Saturday night, 27 October, he thought there would be a nuclear war. A member of Diefenbaker's personal staff recalls being 'jumped on' by the prime minister for not believing that 'we would all be obliterated in a few days.' At the embassy in Washington, though there were rumours flying, we had no reliable knowledge of the negotiations and dramatic correspondence between Kennedy and Khrushchev which on Sunday the 28th brought the crisis onto a manageable plane. President Kennedy's executive committee had not only done its work well; it had done it with few, if any, unintended disclosures.

As for the atmosphere in the prime minister's presence at the height of the crisis, I am indebted to Orme Dier for the following lively account:[19]

As tension grew shortly before President Kennedy's speech, the P.M. readily agreed to a suggestion that he should receive all significant overnight traffic at breakfast time at his residence. Bill Olivier of External Affairs was co-opted to bring the latest intelligence reports and we would begin our day at 4:30 a.m. to collate the material to present at the breakfast table at 6:30.

Like most of us, Mr. D. was not his usual ebullient self at that time of day but the hour did seem to increase the power of his glower. His comments to us were at first infrequent but then he began to question us concerning the source and authenticity of some of the most highly classified material. He wanted to know how up to date the reports were, and most emphatically, whether or not the Canadian Government was receiving all the facts. Bill and I thought not but did our best to give reassurance on that score. Throughout this period, however, I do not recall that he expressed to us any direct criticism of President Kennedy or of American policies, although on numerous occasions he reiterated how serious he judged the crisis to be.

The hazards of trying to serve John Diefenbaker under pressure in accordance with official regulations are illustrated in this further extract from Dier's story:

One episode that I will never forget occurred just before the crisis reached its climax. Bill Olivier and I were at the breakfast table at the appointed hour but the P.M. was not waiting for us. He surfaced about 20 minutes later, in his bathrobe as usual, complaining that worry had kept him awake most of the night. Indeed, he did look pretty beat. Just as I was placing our material before him, the butler appeared with the breakfast. I immediately retrieved the papers and stood aside while the repast was laid. As soon as the butler closed the door, the Chief stood up at his choleric best and almost literally laying his finger aside of my nose, gave me the best of his House of Commons dressing-down. Pacing up and down, he made it excruciatingly clear that I was a guest in his house, that he would not stand being humiliated before his staff, and that he did not need a civil servant to point out what was right or wrong. When I managed to make reference to security classifications, I was immediately shot down for impugning his awareness of such matters as well as for my rudeness and lack of respect. The tirade ended abruptly, breakfast and the documents were quickly ingested and the meeting ended in silence.

Later in the day I met with him in his East Block office. As I was about to leave, he again voiced his concern over the Cuban problem which in his view threatened the whole world with destruction, while Canada had to stand by powerless to take any action to avert such a calamity. He again mentioned the loss of sleep the night before and said that this was the reason he had become upset at breakfast time. I was as much relieved as surprised at this explanation which could be construed as an oblique apology and certainly for the rest of my tenure with him, our relationship was correct if not cordial. I concluded that my boss was an extremely difficult but nevertheless human old curmudgeon.

LOOKING BACK

In the aftermath of the Cuban crisis, there was no use pretending that Canada had emerged with credit in Washington for the stand it had taken. At that time the old maxim that those who are not with you are against you – a favourite theme, ironically, of John Diefenbaker – governed all official, and much of the unofficial, dealing with the US administration. The fact was that despite the considerable range of practical assistance rendered the United States by the Canadian government, its embassy in Havana, and the Canadian armed forces, Ottawa's response to the crisis had appeared to be grudging and Canada's stock in Washington was low.

Looking back on the performance of the principal actors, and relating their actions to possible courses open to them during the crisis, what judgments can be reached? We can start with the fact that this was a major international crisis, a fundamental test of will between two superpowers. It was a crisis that did not suddenly erupt; it could be, and was, monitored as it developed. Although in its final stages it came rapidly to a head, there had been time for consultation with allies on what the American response should be in various contingencies. Yet, for reasons which doubtless seemed powerful to them, President Kennedy and his advisers preferred to act unilaterally, informing their allies at the eleventh hour of the chosen American response. The NATO Council was informed, and a very few allied governments, including the Canadian, were singled out to receive individual treatment in the form of special envoys or ambassadorial briefings.

As applied to Canada, these tactics had various consequences. From the stand-point of the prime minister, the issue on the night of the president's address was not so much *what* had been done as *how* it had been done. The president of the United States had confronted him with a *fait accompli*: he had obliged him at the shortest possible notice to face up to rapid decisions on questions of the gravest import on which Canadian opinion might well be divided. Diefenbaker did not like to be surprised, nor to be reminded in this way of the low esteem in which he was held by that young man in the White House. Without making a full confession of the 'wounded pride' that Merchant had acutely sensed, Diefenbaker revealed a part of his reaction in a speech on 5 November in Toronto:

It would not be too extreme to say that the world has been at the brink of war.

Canada and the United States are members of NORAD under which we are joined in the air defence of North America. As I look back on the Cuban crisis, I believe that it emphasized more than ever before the necessity of there being full consultation before any action is taken or policies executed that might lead to war.

Obviously stung by criticism of the government's position in the crisis, he continued: 'There was never any question as to where Canada stood on the Cuban situation and the establishment of missile bases by the USSR. We supported the stand of the United States clearly and unequivocally.' One might cavil at that interpretation, but a more pregnant sentence was to follow: 'In the light of this experience, it should be made clear that consultation is a prerequisite to joint and contemporaneous action ... for it could never have been intended that either of the nations [in NORAD] would automatically follow whatever stand the other might take.'[20]

This was 'of the essence,' as Diefenbaker himself put it. Alliances and re-lationships would not prosper if one powerful member took for granted the support of its partners. Many times previously he had remarked on what he thought was American insensitivity to Canadian interests and realities. Now, in a crisis of such magnitude and menace, when it could have taken its closest neighbour into its confidence, the United States was expecting a knee-jerk re-action. An emissary had been sent to give two hours notice of what had already been decided, confirming Diefenbaker's sense of exclusion and powerlessness. Asked in later years about the value of his mission, Merchant judged that it had been useful but not good enough to satisfy Diefenbaker in his frame of mind. Canadians had a particular sensitivity to situations in which the United States moved ahead, taking risks in defence 'not just of ourselves but of the whole free world.' The fact that Diefenbaker was 'informed, as he would put it, and not consulted,' Merchant continued, 'left him upset and annoyed,' but he would have been 'more so ... had the President not had the wisdom to send me or someone even that short period in advance.'[21]

It was self-evident that the Canadian government had been denied the opportunity to reach the timely political and military judgments which, as a party to the NORAD agreement, it had expected to be in a position to make. In the words of a memorandum prepared for Bryce: 'The Agreement did not foresee the circumstance in which one country would be aware of the impending need for an increased degree of air defence readiness but would not inform the other country of this need before the time for taking action had arrived, or would not consult with the other country about the implications of the developing situation and the kind of air defence measures that should be taken to meet it. These were in fact the circumstances that obtained in the developing Cuban crisis.'[22] All this was true, and could even be used to justify some measure of delay to permit the taking of decisions on what the government's position should be. But it had proved impossible to hide the conflicts within the government on what political and military responses would be appropriate. A justified delay had revealed disunity.

The confusion in Ottawa's response had no significant impact on the evolution of the crisis itself. In Washington at the time, it seemed a trivial side-show compared to the main drama. It did, however, have consequences of importance for Diefenbaker and his government. In Canada, it contributed to widely felt doubts about the prime minister's capacity to give steady leadership in critical times. His statements and decisions had lacked the stamp of certainty and conviction. By appearing to dither, he had called attention to his reputation for indecisiveness.

That was bad enough but, even more painful for him, his initial hesitations, aggravated as they had been by resentment at the absence of consultation, were challenged by public reaction in Canada. Kennedy, with his enormous prestige and his skilfully persuasive address on television, had reached and influenced Canadian as well as American opinion. And as the result filtered through the political process, Diefenbaker had been obliged to recognize how limited Canada's freedom of action was in a time of real crisis.[23]

In the context of Canadian-American relations, the consequences of the crisis were no less harmful. At the time, in Washington, one felt somewhat shielded from critical comment, perhaps because every day seemed to bring fresh instructions from Ottawa slightly more palatable to the United States. But once the larger picture could be assessed, the damage was clear. The rift between the prime minister and the president had deepened, and Diefenbaker's role at the height of the crisis had strengthened hopes in Washington that the final collapse of his regime would not be long delayed.

29

Meeting His Fate:
Nuclear Nemesis

Diefenbaker's part in the nuclear weapons controversy had reached a watershed in the early autumn of 1961. Up to that time his mind had remained open to the possibility of at least some advance towards the acquisition of nuclear weapons. His problem was how to do enough to fulfil his undertaking to President Kennedy without running an undue political risk in Canada. In the atmosphere of the Berlin crisis, a move towards equipping the Canadian air and land forces in Europe with nuclear warheads might just have served the purpose. Although only a partial step, it would have been welcomed by Harkness and by the Americans, and would probably not have provoked the resignation of Howard Green. But as the Berlin crisis eased, and the forthcoming Canadian election preoccupied him unceasingly, the arguments for avoiding a decision, even for the forces in Europe, became more and more attractive to Diefenbaker. It had become politically necessary – despite the cost – to back away from his commitment to Kennedy. The sense of obligation the prime minister had felt had been progressively diluted in response to a succession of disparate moves by Kennedy – his personal letter to Diefenbaker on 3 August (chivvying); the public confirmation of its existence (in bad taste); the US decision to resume nuclear testing within a few days of the similar Soviet decision (politically ill-timed); and the president's emphasis on non-proliferation of nuclear weapons in his speech to the UN General Assembly (a godsend to the anti-nuclear side of the debate in Canada).

Thus miraculously self-liberated from his obligation to the president, the prime minister had entered a new phase, which would carry him through to the 1962 election and, as it happened, the one after that in April 1963. Instead of being pressed, as he had been previously, to make a choice on the acceptance or not of nuclear weapons on Canadian soil, he would adopt what appeared to be a less vulnerable stance. It would be based on some variant – never fully defined

– of the 'stand-by formula,' whereby nuclear warheads or missing parts thereof would be held in the United States and made available on short notice to Canada in case of need. If the Americans could be persuaded to agree to something like this, Diefenbaker would claim to have made provision for emergencies. If the Americans would not agree, they could be made to look uncooperative, and he and Green could pose as champions of non-proliferation.

By adopting this new stance, the prime minister could also play Green against Harkness. Neither of them ever knew which way he would jump. But Green would rest content so long as an affirmative decision on the acquisition of nuclear warheads was avoided. And Harkness could always hope that some major new crisis or turn of events would have the effect of prompting Diefenbaker to accept an abandonment of the stand-by formula.

In the period from late September 1961 to the defeat of the government in February 1963, only two events caused him to consider seriously a positive move. The first event was the Cuban missile crisis in October 1962, and the second was Pearson's reversal of the Liberal party's previously anti-nuclear position in January 1963. Both events doubtless made the prime minister think of abandoning the stand-by formula in favour of the outright acquisition of nuclear warheads under a two-key system. Neither, however, was sufficient to alter his estimate that politically he had more to lose than to gain by accepting warheads into Canada, even under some form of joint control. And when, by the end of January, the Kennedy administration began openly to attack him, the chances of his making a last-minute change of tactics were finally gone.

NUCLEAR CHOICE

Even before the Cuban crisis erupted, Diefenbaker found himself under pressure once again on the nuclear question. Virtually nothing had happened since September 1961 to advance the acquisition of nuclear warheads for the various weapons systems for which the Canadian government had contracted. Harkness, who had been reappointed minister of national defence, and his military advisers were becoming increasingly frustrated. In recent months, the delivery systems had become available and it was impossible to find credible reasons to explain the lack of progress in negotiating agreements for the warheads with the US and NATO authorities. Harkness did his best, as did Bryce, to bring the prime minister to the point of decision. Green, however, having been reappointed to the External Affairs portfolio, was as determined as ever to avoid decisions that might run counter to his pursuit of arms control and nuclear restraint.

Early in October 1962 Harkness proposed to cabinet that negotiations should begin with the United States on the arrangements for nuclear warheads for the

Bomarcs and interceptors in Canada and for the F-104Gs and Honest Johns in Western Europe. Green did not oppose discussion, but before the subject came up in cabinet he ascertained that the prime minister would support the idea of stand-by arrangements. This idea had been canvassed before within the cabinet but, partly owing to the 1962 election, it had not been developed in detail for purposes of negotiation with the United States. In Washington, the embassy was warned in mid-October that the cabinet might soon decide to propose negotiations.

Just as the Berlin crisis had lent urgency to nuclear weapons issues in the summer of 1961, so now the Cuban missile crisis brought the issue to a head once more. Harkness's proposal was discussed in the cabinet on 30 October. In putting it forward, he emphasized that the government was in a vulnerable position because it was being asked in parliament and by the press what arrangements it was making to arm the weapons it had acquired.[1] Personally, he was highly sceptical of the feasibility of stand-by arrangements and did not expect that the Americans would buy the idea. He told the cabinet, however, that until negotiations had taken place, there would be no way of knowing whether some such procedure would be workable. Despite reservations, it was decided to propose negotiations on the basis that nuclear warheads for North American air defence 'would be held in the United States to be moved to Canada for use in Bomarc missiles and interceptor aircraft, on request by the Canadian Government when war appears imminent.' As for the forces in Western Europe, the decision foresaw that 'the nuclear warheads would be held in storage for and made available to the Canadian forces in Europe under NATO command for use in CF-104G aircraft and the Honest John rockets.'

The cabinet decision included a provision that the negotiations should be 'commenced forthwith' by Messrs Green, Harkness, and Gordon Churchill, then the minister of veterans affairs, with the US embassy in Ottawa. By including Churchill, the prime minister was seeking to install a balance between Green and Harkness, and also to assure himself of a trusted and neutral report on any discussion the committee of ministers might have with the Americans. Diefenbaker himself, worrying ceaselessly about public reaction, feared a leak from the American side. The United States should be warned that if a leak did occur the negotiations would stop.

The presentation of the government's approach was made immediately to Ivan White, the chargé d'affaires of the US embassy. Well tuned in to political realities in Ottawa, White was careful in sending his report to the State Department to warn against a hasty rejection of what might appear to be an impracticable scheme. One can surmise that with the Cuban missile crisis still in a dangerous phase, the Canadian initiative must have seemed strangely timed and even more strangely composed. It fell to the officials concerned with Canadian affairs at the State Department to explain the facts of current Canadian politics to the Pentagon in the hope that the idea of stand-by arrangements for Canada's air defence weapons could be examined constructively. Otherwise this new flicker of Ottawa's willingness to come to the bargaining table might quickly be extinguished.

The first response came quite rapidly. On 20 November a small team of American experts was to visit Ottawa. Before they left Washington, I reported on a meeting with the State Department.[2] No special problem was expected in reaching agreement regarding the nuclear weapons for the Canadian forces in Europe. They would be held under some form of NATO umbrella until the need arose for their transfer to Canadian formations in an emergency. My report continued: 'The question of the stand-by arrangements was, however, unique, and required much study by the Pentagon. The State Department's part ... was to emphasize that the readiness of the Canadian Government ... to discuss the possibility of such an arrangement was an important potential change in the Canadian position ... The principal concern of the US negotiators would be to explain ... what would be involved in implementing stand-by procedures.' I gave it as my opinion that 'the Pentagon's hope would be to demonstrate to Mr. Green the full extent of the practical difficulties foreseen ... and that having understood the nature of those difficulties, Canadian ministers might conclude on their own account that a stand-by arrangement might not be the most desirable solution.'

To the surprise of few, if any, of those involved, nothing came of this first encounter. The results of US studies showed that complete nuclear warheads for Bomarcs and F-101B interceptors could not be airlifted to Canadian air bases within the likely three-hour warning time of a Soviet bomber attack. The effort was not abandoned, however. The US side undertook to consider whether 'missing parts' of the weapons might be held in storage at nearby US bases, to be flown to Canada in case of emergency.

At a further meeting on 4 December the US studies indicated that the time required for airlifting 'missing parts' could be reduced to something close to two hours, depending on the parts selected. When Green and Harkness met their counterparts, Rusk and McNamara, in Paris on 14 December during a NATO meeting, the Canadian ministers came away without feeling that the 'missing part' proposal was considered impracticable by the US government. Soon afterwards, however, McNamara informed Harkness by telephone that the proposal was considered unworkable.[3] Through other channels it was made known to Ottawa that the lapse of time necessary for the transportation of the parts, and for their installation on arrival, posed technical problems challenging practical solution. Experience in the Cuban crisis, when the Canadian response in an emergency had been ambiguous, had weakened the theory that stand-by procedures for bringing nuclear equipment across the Canadian border could be relied on in a future crisis. Instead, the Americans suggested that missing parts might be stored separately in Canada and thus might be more quickly united in case of need. Not surprisingly, this idea had no appeal for Diefenbaker or Green. If the missing parts were already on Canadian soil, the government could hardly claim that nuclear weapons were not present in Canada.

Eager as the US authorities were to resolve the nuclear issue with Canada, the wider problems of East-West relations had become Washington's overwhelming concern in the months before and after the turn of the year. Although the immediate danger over Cuba was being defused, Soviet intentions were uncertain. The prevailing tendency in the administration was to say that time must be allowed to judge Soviet reactions to Cuban events. After a talk at the State Department on 27 November, Charles Ritchie reported to Ottawa: 'Reasonably or not, there is a sense of peril survived, and out of this has come a determined vigilance, which, just as much as the new spirit of self-confidence, is likely to underlie the US approach to the next stage.' At the same time, American officials dealing with NATO affairs were arguing that the outcome of the Cuban crisis should be followed by a greater effort to reinforce the unity of the Western alliance. There was a widespread feeling that the European members, and Canada, should be induced to carry a bigger share of the defence burden. Methods of making consultation in NATO more effective in times of crisis were also preoccupying some of the president's advisers. Yet another crusade in some parts of the administration was devoted to British entry into the European Common Market, where a decision was expected within a short time.

Canada had an interest in all these major issues, and when Diefenbaker learned, late in November, that Kennedy and Macmillan would soon be meeting in Nassau, he promptly invited Macmillan to visit Ottawa on the same journey. It would not do to be left out entirely. Macmillan countered with an invitation to Diefenbaker to join him in Nassau on 21 December, immediately following his meeting with Kennedy – an invitation which Diefenbaker accepted without knowing if it would include any time with the president.

NASSAU

When Diefenbaker reached Nassau, the Macmillan-Kennedy meeting was in its closing stages. It had been an exceedingly important meeting on all the major political and strategic issues of the post-Cuba world. Macmillan had achieved his prime objective of persuading the president to provide the United Kingdom with the Polaris nuclear defence system, on conditions which were announced in a joint communiqué on 21 December. The Nassau communiqué also contained a proposal for the establishment of a NATO nuclear force composed partly of tactical nuclear forces currently held in Europe. Although Canada's ground and air forces would be included if such a proposal were adopted, there was no implication that any such assignment would alter the role or the weapon systems already planned for those forces. Nonetheless, the communiqué as a whole did signify that the NATO alliance was entering a new phase of its defence strategy, and it was this fact that Diefenbaker would try to bend to his purpose a month later in Ottawa.

Diefenbaker's program in Nassau consisted of a luncheon on the 21st with both Macmillan and Kennedy and two subsequent meetings with Macmillan and Lord Home, the foreign secretary, on the 21st and 22nd. Some twenty years later Macmillan told Charles Ritchie that Kennedy had not wanted to attend the lunch, so he had promised him 'a good shellfish meal.' After some persuasion, the president finally agreed to stay, though protesting that he could get a fine shellfish meal at home in Hyannisport without having to sit down with Diefenbaker.

Before the luncheon began, Diefenbaker managed some brief private words with the president about North American nuclear weapons issues. As he later recorded: 'I informed the President when I first arrived that there were a number of matters I hoped we would have an opportunity to discuss soon in connection with the defence of North America and the provision of armed missiles for Canada. I did not go into the question of storage in the United States or the joint training there of Canadian and US squadrons[4] although on Saturday, December 22, in talking to PM Macmillan and Lord Amory, it was brought out that something along this line was planned for under the agreement now being considered by the US and the UK. I informed them that the plan I had in mind would provide the RCAF with the necessary defensive weapons but would not thereby be extending the nuclear family of nations which I believed should be kept strictly under control.'[5]

With the nuclear issues thus set aside, the luncheon talk could turn to less explosive topics. There had been signs that the US Treasury might be planning to take action against the parent company of Imperial Oil of Canada, for alleged violations of the US Trading with the Enemy Act. The prime minister recalled that the problem had arisen earlier and had been resolved as a result of conversations with the president. The administration was not giving consideration to any change in the present arrangements, the president said, and expressed no objection to Canada's trade with China. He took the same position concerning Canadian trade in non-strategic goods with Cuba, adding that the Canadian embassy had played an especially helpful role throughout the Cuban crisis.

In the subsequent meetings with Macmillan, Diefenbaker was given a comprehensive analysis of other current international problems – aid to India, India-

China relations, the Congo, South Africa (Diefenbaker declared himself opposed to sanctions and Macmillan agreed), and Latin America (on which Diefenbaker explained Canada's reluctance to join the Organization of American States and Macmillan and Home expressed understanding). Of great interest to Diefenbaker was Macmillan's estimate of the prospect for Britain's entry into the European Common Market. The odds on success were now less than 50-50, in Macmillan's judgment. He remained convinced of the reasons for joining, but de Gaulle's attitude had not changed and there was no indication of French willingness to make any concessions to facilitate a successful outcome of the negotiations. Macmillan expected that a decision would have been reached within two months. He and Diefenbaker would be able to discuss the outcome when Diefenbaker visited London late in February to receive the Freedom of the City of London.

The visit to Nassau had given Diefenbaker an immersion course in global defence considerations and in the new security arrangements NATO governments would be discussing in 1963. He had, of course, had no part in formulating the Macmillan-Kennedy communiqué. In speaking to the press at Nassau, he was careful to avoid any commitment to the idea of a multilateral nuclear force. Within a very few weeks, he would find it politically convenient to use the advent of these proposals as justification for yet further delay in reaching a decision on the nuclear issues facing his government.

The Diefenbakers remained in Nassau for the Christmas and New Year's holiday, knowing that there would be no rest or relaxation in the weeks and months ahead. The prime minister had agreed to speak to the local Kiwanis Club, and stirred up trouble by remarks he was reported to have made about the Cuban crisis and trade with communist countries. The press reports caused him concern because they put an anti-American cast on his remarks. Embarrassed by the construction that this might receive if it came to Kennedy's attention so soon after they had met, he sent me a hand-written note from Nassau, no doubt with the thought that the embassy might correct wrong impressions in the right places:

I am concerned over the complete distortion of my remarks here concerning Cuba. At no time did I say, directly or indirectly, that the United States action violated NORAD. What I did say was that consultation had not taken place and there was no information until the late afternoon of the day that President Kennedy made his speech.

I pointed out that consultation is necessary in the Commonwealth – even essential to its existence – and added that as [sic] Canada, having responsibility for joint air defence, had been consulted, we would have been in readiness to act forthwith.

My words were correctly quoted but whoever wrote the press articles interpreted them without any regard for what I had in fact said.

The text of his speech bore out the prime minister's complaint that the press interpretations were exaggerated, and in Washington we did what little we could to spread the remedial balm.

In a very short time, however, the president, the State Department, and the Defence Department would have much more demanding problems to face in their dealings with Canada. The month of January produced a string of surprises, each of them relating to nuclear weapons and each adding its own element of force to the Diefenbaker government's plunge to defeat in early February. These events all had repercussions in Washington.

Representing an unpopular Canadian government in Washington is one of the stranger experiences in a diplomatic career, if only because the treatment Canadians receive in normal times is so relaxed, generous, and candid. In this period the atmosphere was tense and personal relationships were inevitably affected. It was fortunate that we had in Charles Ritchie a seasoned ambassador who kept his lines open to the individuals who counted and did not take too tragic a view of things. We were fortunate too in our regular points of contact at the State Department, where Willis Armstrong put his first-hand knowledge of the Canadian political scene to intelligent effect.

The first surprise resulted from a farewell visit to Ottawa by General Lauris Norstad, the retiring NATO military commander, on 3 January. At a press conference held on his arrival, Norstad was drawn into an exchange on whether Canada had committed itself to provide its air division in Europe with tactical nuclear weapons. After remarking that this was a question for the Canadian government to answer, he replied that his answer was 'yes,' adding that as the air division was 're-equipped, it would continue to be committed to NATO and would continue to play an extremely important role.' 'With or without tactical weapons?' was the next question, to which Norstad said that he would hope 'with both.' He then appealed to Air Chief Marshal Frank Miller, the Canadian chairman of the Chiefs of Staff who was sitting at the back of the room, to say whether he was going beyond anything that had been 'released here.'

Miller is quoted in the official transcript of the press conference as having said, 'I think you're quite right on that; quite right on that.' Perhaps thinking that Miller's reply enabled him to answer questions in the same vein, Norstad soon got into deeper water when asked whether, if Canada did not accept nuclear weapons for these aircraft, 'she is not actually fulfilling her NATO commitments.' 'I believe that's right,' Norstad answered. The exchange continued at some length but the damage had been done. Although nothing he had said was inaccurate or inconsistent with NATO policy, the general had put a new head of steam into the political debate.

The assumption in Washington was that Norstad had spoken without any intention of adding to the Canadian government's discomfiture over nuclear policy. Certainly the incident came as a complete surprise to the State Department, and we received reports from Ottawa that Norstad was exceedingly concerned about allowing himself to be mouse-trapped in this way. Yet the fact remained that his comments gave timely ammunition to the government's political opponents, infuriated Diefenbaker, and helped to stoke up an increasingly anti-government press corps in Ottawa. The prime minister had been handed a stick with which to beat the Americans should he decide on an anti-American theme for the approaching election campaign.

The Norstad incident was soon succeeded by a development of far greater significance – Pearson's announcement on 12 January that a Liberal government would discharge the commitments regarding nuclear weapons accepted by Canada under NATO and NORAD.[6] Although Pearson qualified his change of position by declaring that subsequently he would negotiate Canada into more appropriate, non-nuclear roles, he had opened up for the United States, as for the political parties in Canada, a completely new perspective on future possibilities in nuclear weapons policy.

Indications of a change in American tactics began to appear almost immediately. The first solid sign came from the State Department on 22 January, when it was confirmed that McNamara was refusing to follow up on the meeting which he, Rusk, Green, and Harkness had held in Paris in December. The sticking point once again was the Canadian insistence on stand-by arrangements for nuclear warheads and the difficulty of finding effective procedures. Canadian interest in this endeavour was noticeably keener than American. In a letter to Ottawa on 23 January I reported on a feeling in Washington that 'they can afford to wait a little longer in the expectation that another election in Canada will result in a better prospect of a solution palatable to the United States.' A major debate on foreign and defence policy – the last such debate in the life of the Diefenbaker government – took place on 24 and 25 January. Pearson elaborated on the reasoning which led him to accept the necessity of acquiring nuclear warheads for Canadian forces. He also attacked the inconsistency and indecision which had marked the government's record in defence policy, particularly with regard to nuclear weapons.

Diefenbaker, starting out with notes prepared for him by Bryce, recalled in some detail the history of the government's decisions and statements on nuclear matters.[7] He made no attempt to deny that certain commitments had been entered into for Canadian forces both in Europe and North America, but sought to explain why it was that the decision to acquire the nuclear warheads had not been pressed forward. Partly this was because the government wished to exert influence on disarmament negotiations and on nuclear restraint. Other important factors, such as technological change and new strategic concepts, made decisions on defence equipment inherently difficult. He implied that Canada's contribution to NATO could be affected by the new concepts, one consequence of which might be the need to place greater emphasis on conventional weapons.

The prime minister then veered into more questionable arguments in an attempt to justify yet further delay. The premise was that since the Nassau agreement and the concepts it envisaged made it necessary for the NATO alliance to rethink its nuclear strategy and had cast doubt on the efficacy of some weapons systems previously thought necessary, Canada must re-examine its military commitments in Europe. In particular, he contended, in words that would soon be challenged, the role of the RCAF in Europe had been 'placed under doubt' by the Nassau communiqué. The NATO ministers, however, would conveniently be meeting in Ottawa in May, at which time the necessary clarification of Canada's role would be sought. If the result was to confirm Canada's obligation to acquire nuclear weapons for its role in Europe, the government would act accordingly. As for North American defence, he declared – without first notifying the American authorities – that negotiations on nuclear weapons had been going on in secret for two or three months and would be continued.

Although, summarized in so few words, the prime minister's line of argument may appear to have some superficial logic, the speech was, in the experienced opinion of Donald Fleming, 'without exception the most equivocal' he had ever heard in the House of Commons.[8] Diefenbaker had employed his normal technique of throwing together contributions from a variety of sources. In fairness to him it is important to point out that in concocting this speech he relied on something more than his own impressions. External Affairs had advised him that, as a result of the Nassau agreement, NATO would be reviewing the direction and shape of its military forces, including the question of how political and military control of nuclear forces would be exercised in future. These comments had not been intended to call in question the validity of Canada's existing ground and air commitments in Europe. But used out of context, they gave the prime minister the ammunition he wanted to support the case for additional delay.

Furthermore – although this was not publicly known at the time – he was also making use of the contents of a confidential report agreed upon by a committee of four ministers (Fleming, Green, Harkness, and Churchill) who had been meeting, with Diefenbaker's approval, in a desperate attempt to reach a solution to the crisis. As chairman of the group, Fleming had presented its hard-won points of agreement to Diefenbaker. Essentially, the paper acknowledged that the government had undertaken air and land nuclear roles in Western Europe, maintained (against Harkness's objections) that the Nassau agreement had placed the strike role in Europe of the RCAF's CF-104GS 'in some doubt,' anticipated that clarification of Canada's European role in NATO could be obtained at a NATO meeting in Ottawa in May, and affirmed that negotiations with the United States on continental air defence would be continued. Diefenbaker had summarily rejected the report when it was first presented to him by Fleming. But he resurrected it, in jumbled form, for his speech to the House. His habit of composing his speeches in cafetaria style had never before produced such an indigestible stew.

REACTION IN WASHINGTON

In Washington, the weekend passed and on Monday, the 28th, the impact of the prime minister's speech began to appear. We were told that 'a public reaction' was being considered at a high level. We did our best to warn against it and tried to dispel the confusion over the prime minister's references to the Nassau agreement. Our approach received a polite hearing but had no chance of survival against the wave of exasperated indignation which Diefenbaker's speech had unleashed.

On the 30th the expected happened, though in a form and with an intensity that went beyond our speculation. Having been called on short notice to see Willis Armstrong at the State Department at 5.45 PM, I was handed the text of a press release which was soon to be issued in Ottawa and Washington. It was obviously a frontal attack on the Canadian government for its nuclear policy, and particularly on the arguments advanced by the prime minister in his speech of 25 January. Armstrong, cool and business-like, waited until I had read it and then made supplementary comments. There had been, he said, four years of discussion. Every effort to solve the nuclear problem had been abortive and 'not really for technical reasons.' The possibilities of stand-by arrangements had been thoroughly examined, but this was a contrived solution which might also create added confusion in emergencies. As the press release said, 'the Canadian Government had not as yet proposed any arrangement sufficiently practical to contribute effectively to North American defence.' The prime minister's reference to the Nassau agreement was not understood, Armstrong continued, since if existing Canadian forces were to be assigned to a NATO nuclear force under the Nassau agreement, they would be effective only if equipped with nuclear weapons. As for the obsolescence of weapons systems, there was a difference between cancelling systems that were becoming obsolete and immobilizing modern weapons by not taking parts that were essential to their full effectiveness.

In making these comments, Armstrong made it quite clear that the US authorities knew that the statement would cause concern and controversy in Canada. They had, however, decided that, having studied Diefenbaker's speech, they could not withhold comment. He said that they had not referred in their release to the fact that the prime minister had disclosed the nuclear negotiations without advance notification, but he pointed out that the text was drafted so as not to preclude further negotiations.

I felt amazed and indignant at both the language and the method they had employed. But there was no point in arguing. After remarking that the press release would have grave consequences in Canada, I headed quickly back to the embassy. A few telephone calls later, Charles Ritchie was on his way to Ottawa, 'recalled for consultation' as the saying goes when things have gone awry.[9] There he found Diefenbaker relishing the prospect of an anti-American election campaign and not in the least interested in patching things up. Every day brought us a new intake of sensational political news from Ottawa. In Washington there was a considerable amount of disapproval of the State Department's press release. On 8 February I wrote to my parents: 'It has been quite notable that individual Americans – neighbours and some contacts at work – have gone out of their way to be friendly through this chilly period. It happened that we had a dinner party on January 31, the day after the crescendo. It was difficult because some of the people there were actors in the drama but it came out well enough ... The Ambassador was away in Ottawa for a few days – he saw the Prime Minister only once, and found him in right good form.'

In taking the course they had, the US administration had gambled heavily. I thought that if, after Pearson's reversal of the Liberal position, Diefenbaker had kept any lingering thought of accepting nuclear weapons, he would certainly abandon it now. It seemed as though the Americans had deliberately fostered an anti-American thrust in the tactics the prime minister would follow in parliament and in the coming election campaign. His speech had admittedly been provocative and in some ways irresponsible. But now he was able to charge the Kennedy administration with an 'unwarranted intrusion' into Canadian affairs. He would exploit this for all it was worth.

Exactly how the press release had been planned was not at first easy to discern. As the storm in Canada was reflected in headlines in the US press, various signs of anxiety appeared. Rusk made a conciliatory, if not contrite, apology; hearings by a Senate subcommittee were scheduled; and Max Freedman, a well-connected Canadian journalist, phoned the embassy to say that he had been asked by 'the White House' to inform us that the president 'had had no part' in the State Department's announcement. Not everyone at the embassy believed this disclaimer.

Piecing the story together in retrospect, one discovers elements that were then

307

unsuspected. For example, one of the factors that prompted the US authorities to 'set the record straight' was their worry that other allied nations might think, from Diefenbaker's public reference to the Nassau meeting, that some secret agreements had been reached at that meeting and that Diefenbaker had somehow become privy to them. Combined with this was a 'collegial' view among officials from the US embassy in Ottawa, the State Department, and the White House that Diefenbaker's speech would have to be answered and that the answer needed to be public, if only because numerous press inquiries were outstanding. Among White House officials, moreover, there appears to have been an assumption that, in the circumstances, the president would not object if Diefenbaker's speech were publicly challenged.

The result of the collegial consideration was to choose the press release as the instrument of response. This was in preference to a stiff diplomatic note which had been the original suggestion of US Ambassador Walton Butterworth in Ottawa. In the event George Ball, Rusk's senior deputy, approved the release for the State Department and McGeorge Bundy for the White House. Rusk, however, was called to account before the Senate subcommittee on Canadian affairs. There, under pointed questioning, he defended the course that had been decided on and, despite not having himself authorized the final text of the press release, insisted on taking full responsibility. Support from senior levels in the White House was, however, reported to be elusive after the release was published. My conclusion was that the president himself was not consulted. However, one senior and well-placed American source has firmly maintained that the press release was the product of a combined operation among senior officials in the Kennedy administration, sanctioned at the highest level in the White House, with the deliberate intent of unseating Diefenbaker.[10] In this connection Ed Ritchie recalls that at their Hyannisport meeting in May 1963, Kennedy asked Pearson whether the press release had had any effect in the recent Canadian election. 'It probably cost me 50 seats,' said Pearson, a reply which, whatever its factual basis, rather let the air out of the president's balloon.

It had been clear for many weeks that the government was in a precarious state. The Cuban missile crisis had tested again the prime minister's leadership and he had emerged looking hesitant under pressure. The sequence of dramatic events in January merely made matters worse. Harkness, increasingly frustrated by Diefenbaker's temporizing, told a meeting of ministers on 20 January that he could not remain in office if the nuclear issue remained unresolved.[11] Listening to the prime minister's confusing speech of 25 January, Harkness at first thought that his pro-nuclear position had been upheld. Only later, after studying the text in detail, did he decide that he must issue a statement 'interpreting' what the prime minister had said. In the process he precipitated a full-scale crisis within the government. Still hoping to influence Diefenbaker to accept his position on nuclear weapons, Harkness withheld his resignation until it was plain that the prime minister would not budge. Finally, on 3 February, after being at the centre of an extraordinary political drama for several days, Harkness concluded that he could no longer stay. On that day, at the end of yet another intense confrontation with the prime minister in cabinet, he submitted his letter of resignation. On the following day the crisis reached its peak. A motion of no confidence in the government led to its defeat on 5 February.

Diefenbaker pretended not to understand Harkness's decision, but probably he was in a sense relieved. For now he was free to campaign without having committed himself on the nuclear issue, and well placed to exploit public indignation about US interference. In any event, he was to stage a valiant campaign.

SLIDING DOWNHILL

As the campaign developed, there was not much to do in Washington except watch and hope that things would not get worse. Diefenbaker, with no other purpose in mind than to defeat Pearson and the Liberals, was in full anti-American cry. Those few Americans who took a close interest in relations with Canada could be forgiven for their anxiety. So apprehensive was the State Department of what the prime minister might do or say that in a meeting with Charles Ritchie on 21 February Rusk, a blunt-speaking man, made a point of saying that the administration wanted to feel free to clarify its position if it was misrepresented by anything said in the Canadian election campaign.

There were some who exaggerated the real significance of what Diefenbaker was saying to his election audiences. Butterworth thought that the election was 'about fundamentals' and about Canada's place both in the world and vis-à-vis the United States. This was a misreading of Diefenbaker's position and attitude. He had no serious thought of leading Canada to a different place in the world. Perhaps more importantly, anti-Americanism in a general sense was not a fundamental part of his thinking. What did characterize him was a kind of push-resistant nationalism, aimed at whatever the source of pressure might be. And this, like everything else, was related to the Canadian political scene – to be brought out when it seemed needed. Now, to be sure, was the time.

The Canadian political reaction to the State Department press release had been stronger and more lasting than its authors had expected. It had become woven into the election campaign, and one of the embassy's automatic priorities in Washington was to watch out for, and if possible head off, developments that would further enliven Canadian-American relations.

The negotiations on nuclear weapons – which Diefenbaker had made public on 25 January – were continued confidentially in February and March. The Canadian government continued to press for some way in which nuclear warheads or 'missing parts,' could be held at US bases close to Canada, in readiness to be transported to Canadian bases in case of need. To do them justice, the American officials involved took a serious look at the possibilities – they could not be sure that the election would turn Diefenbaker and Green out of office – but their heart was not in it and the talks were left in abeyance during the last stages of the election campaign.

Official Washington, or those parts of the vast machine that cared about Canada, prayed for Pearson and tried to avoid giving more ammunition to Diefenbaker than he already had. With just over a week to go until the election, publication of testimony to a congressional committee by McNamara gave the press a new sensation to exploit. In justifying the costs of the Bomarc program (in the United States as well as Canada), he had remarked that 'at the very least' these anti-missile weapons would increase Soviet missile requirements or draw onto Bomarc targets Soviet missiles that would otherwise be available for targets elsewhere.

Diefenbaker could not believe his good fortune at this political windfall.[12] He had never much liked the Bomarc – it had become a symbol of the trouble he had seen as a result of the painful Arrow decision. Now he had a fresh reason for holding back on nuclear weapons. The Bomarc was obviously of marginal value and would draw fire on Canadian targets. Not only that, but McNamara's words could be used against Pearson. After all, it was the Liberal leader who had come out in favour of acquiring nuclear warheads for the Bomarcs and other weapon systems. Pearson, he warned with mischievous glee, would make Canada 'a decoy duck in a nuclear war.'

At the State Department the officials coordinating the inter-agency effort to avoid further complicating Canadian-American relations were taken aback by this development and did not conceal their alarm. They had no desire to make any donation to the last stage of Diefenbaker's campaign. McNamara received a rebuke in a crisp personal memo from the president, who was not amused.[13]

The election results (Liberal 129, Progressive Conservative 95, Social Credit 24, NDP 17) were greeted with profound relief by the Kennedy administration. At the embassy, the news took a little time to sink in. The prospect of working under the leadership of Pearson and Paul Martin, who would become minister of external affairs, was good to contemplate. What it would mean in terms of new or altered policies could wait. For the moment, there was much sympathy expressed for Howard Green, who had surprisingly lost his parliamentary seat in the election. Green had inspired loyalty and affection, even among those in the department who had disagreed with his stand on nuclear issues. It was widely said then that he and his wife Donna had cared deeply about the department, and that they would be greatly missed. Many today who are old enough to remember his term as minister consider that the Canadian foreign service has never had a better ministerial friend.

My own reaction at the time was mixed. Diefenbaker's behaviour in recent months had been exasperating for those who were trying to represent his government in Washington. There was a lively sense of relief at the embassy that happier days were at hand in Canadian-American relations. The same was true for the Americans with whom we were in professional or social touch. At last, it was said, Canada would have a leader the United States could 'understand,' after the unspeakable Dief.

Although I welcomed the prospect of a government led by Mike Pearson, I did not exult in John Diefenbaker's fall. I felt a kind of private and sympathetic awareness of what he would be going through, as he came to terms with the consequences of his defeat. He would shudder at the thought of handing over to Pearson, and would not formally resign until he had completely satisfied himself that no other course was open. I remember thinking that I had seen him in better times, and that I knew enough of his performance to be sceptical of wholesale condemnations of his record. More than that I do not recall except that the time for such compassionate reflections quickly passed. It would be for history to decide the verdict on Diefenbaker's record in foreign affairs.

Conclusion

It is more than twenty-five years since I last worked for John Diefenbaker, and I confess that I find it exceedingly difficult to summarize my thoughts and feelings about him. What can one say about a man who embraced in his character so many conflicting qualities, who inspired such opposite sentiments in those who knew or watched him, and who seems today to be acquiring a persona magnified, even distorted, by retrospection? I am particularly aware that in this book I have concentrated on only one aspect of his responsibilities as prime minister – his conduct of foreign policy. His agenda in domestic affairs was frequently much more demanding, and, except at times of international crisis, it was my experience that domestic policies and politics generally took precedence over foreign policy problems, despite his keen interest and curiosity about world affairs. Looking back, I realize more clearly than I did at the time how deeply burdened he felt and how seriously and personally he took the responsibilities of office.

He was, of course, a difficult, egocentric man whose character defies simple definition. His faults have been more widely chronicled than his redeeming qualities. Attractive to an adviser were a number of underlying virtues. He was a hard worker, accessible, with an excellent memory, an intuitive intelligence, a desire to be well informed, and a determination to cope somehow with an all-consuming job. He was a generally considerate boss, given the pressures he was under. Often, even in the face of adversity, he was irresistibly amusing. At times he was disarmingly frank and trusting as if needing support. At other times he was suspicious, devious, and generally exasperating, yet there was a magnetic quality about him that made one want to know his next thought even if the last one had been outrageous.

He presided over national affairs at a time when international patterns that had seemed settled in the immediate postwar years were being shaken up and challenged in ways that could not fail to affect Canada. Europe and Japan were

312

quickly recovering power and influence; relations with the communist world were volatile in the age of Khrushchev; the Cold War seemed less perpetual in prospect and NATO's purpose more open to debate; the Commonwealth that Diefenbaker had idolized was in rapid transition, with no certainty of what would come after; the traditional Conservative party connection with Britain was being threatened by the British themselves in their anxiety to join up with Europe; and the developing countries, most of them emerging from colonial status, were posing new economic and political problems for the international community. Transcending all this were huge strategic, scientific, and political questions relating to the existence of nuclear weaponry. Even if the prime minister of Canada had wished to distance himself from these great tidal movements, it was not open to him to turn away. From the outset of his term, Diefenbaker was caught up in the exhausting, fascinating, addictive merry-go-round of top-level conferences, visits, correspondence, and telephone calls which heads of government cannot avoid.

He did not wish to avoid it. From his early days, international affairs had been of special interest to him and they remained so while he was prime minister. Though privately he held a modest estimate of what could be done to influence the sweep of world events, he knew it would never do to admit how powerless he felt his government to be in the face of external realities. He calculated that Canadians wanted their government to continue to be associated actively with the major institutions and alliances to which they had become accustomed in the years since the Second World War. This meant consistent support for NATO and the United Nations. It involved a warm response to the deep anti-Soviet emotions of Canadians of Eastern European origin. It required, because of his sentimental feeling for the Crown and the British connection, an attempt at making more of the Anglo-Canadian and Commonwealth links than his predecessors had done. And towards the United States, it meant solidarity in global affairs modified by a spirited nationalism in bilateral matters.

Although Diefenbaker spent very little time theorizing, he did periodically ponder the role that prime ministers in a parliamentary system should play in foreign affairs. He was influenced by precedents and, when faced with a problem, often asked himself how Mackenzie King or Louis St Laurent would have handled it. Conscious and proud of his place in the line of Canadian prime ministers, he looked also to London with romantic thoughts of Winston Churchill's years and somewhat envious admiration for Harold Macmillan's conduct of the prime ministerial role. He took comfort in belonging to a small circle of whom it could be said that only its members knew what it was really like to carry the burdens of national leadership. In September 1961, when the crisis over Berlin was cooling down, he spoke in the House of Commons of the special place he reserved for his role in foreign policy matters: 'As Prime Minister, I have always followed the course of not interfering with the ministers in the discharge of their responsibilities except that in regard to foreign policy, I have followed the tradition of the United Kingdom, that the prime minister must take a particular interest in that field of national activity on which the safety of the state so largely depends.'[1]

In practice, Diefenbaker's 'particular interest' in foreign policy amounted essentially to three elements. He kept himself conscientiously informed on current issues, spoke infrequently about them in public, and insisted on being consulted on any matter of political sensitivity. While this left considerable leeway to his external affairs ministers in matters of lesser importance, it also gave rise to a substantial number of situations in which the prime minister intervened.

His political priorities naturally influenced the process of decision-making in foreign affairs. The forces that would be influential in keeping his government in office, as he saw it, were basically domestic rather than international. When new situations arose in foreign affairs, his thoughts ran first to the tactics that should be used to handle them politically on the home front. His attention was easily attracted to issues that would have practical meaning for his 'fellow Canadians' – the sale of wheat, expanded export markets, benefits from the law of the sea, prudent ways of controlling foreign investment, and tough bargaining on border issues. National interest is, of course, the foundation for virtually all decisions in foreign policy, but the support he gave to the various traditional cornerstones – the Commonwealth, NATO, the United Nations, and disarmament – sometimes seemed to be of lesser weight because it had its roots so conspicuously grounded in domestic imperatives and because he often seemed unconcerned with the way in which his preoccupations affected other governments.

Prime Minister Macmillan, who knew Diefenbaker better than any of his non-Canadian counterparts, put it this way: 'He [Diefenbaker] seemed to me to be unduly influenced by internal political situations, which necessarily change from time to time, and to pay too little regard to the great underlying movements of world affairs.'[2] Perhaps it was not so much that he paid too little regard but that having come to office late in his political career, he had no history of personal involvement in the issues and lacked the adaptability that might have enabled him to assume an influential role. He had little feel for team play, the kind of sustained collective negotiation which is often essential to making the most of Canadian influence. He was always fearful of releasing forces that he might not be able personally to control.

Significantly, too, there were limits to the time and attention he felt it politically necessary to accord to international questions. A true populist, he concentrated on what had to be done to attract the general approval of the wider Canadian public. He could satisfy that need by conspicuous defence of Canadian interests in the face of external, especially US, pressures by asserting his responsibility at times of international crisis, and by judiciously chosen bouts of travel abroad. The foreign affairs experts at home and abroad might look upon him as an oddity, something of a stranger to the world, but that was of no concern to him. What they thought, he said a hundred times, was a long way down his list of priorities. It is perhaps not surprising that he left the foreign policy scene without having significantly altered the values, the priorities, or the continuing threads which he inherited from his predecessors. His impact on foreign policy was more in the method and the emphasis than in the substance.

Diefenbaker's ministers of external affairs – Sidney Smith and Howard Green – both totally inexperienced at first in foreign affairs, had to adapt themselves to their leader's style and interests. They were careful about trespassing on the turf he had marked out for himself. Much the more self-assured, Green sought out policy areas in which he was likely to be left relatively undisturbed, including the inviting field of arms control and disarmament, relations with the Third World, Canadian responsibilities in Indochina, and bread-and-butter issues such as the law of the sea and the conditions for the sale of Columbia River power. He was interested, too, in the new French-speaking nations of Africa, and promoted with enthusiasm not shared by Diefenbaker the introduction of a francophone dimension to Canada's foreign policies.

The division of labour between the prime minister and his external affairs ministers naturally affected the Department of External Affairs. Under St Laurent and Pearson, the department had somehow felt insulated from domestic politics. It was slow in adapting to the methods of the new regime. It had had the luxury of concentrating on the substance of foreign policy problems, often in close and trusting consultation with other governments taking similar approaches. Now there was less involvement in such informal consultations, and much more time and attention devoted to the presentation of government policy to the Canadian public. Difficult as the transition was, it exposed the department more directly to the realities of Canadian politics, and in this way laid a foundation for the future.

The Department of External Affairs had mixed success in adjusting to Diefenbaker's personal style and political priorities. Speech material was a chronic cause of misunderstanding, his determination to reach a wide popular audience in Canada almost always overriding the Department's concern for the international impact of a prime ministerial utterance. Intensely partisan himself, he was constantly on the lookout for any indication, however slight, that pro-Liberal sentiments might be infecting departmental attitudes. I spent a lot of time trying to interpret his idiosyncrasies to the department, and vice versa. On matters of substance, he frequently showed by his reaction to External Affairs advice that it had a 'soft' quality which he found unconvincing. He was especially uncomfortable with the department's approach to some aspects of relations between Western governments and the Soviet Union. In particular, it irritated him to be advised against outspoken public attacks on Soviet policy regarding the 'captive nations.' But on occasions when his audience seemed receptive to a more conciliatory stance in relations with, for example, the Soviet Union or Cuba, he did not hesitate to make use of External Affairs recommendations.

At times, the struggle to decipher and satisfy the needs of the prime minister conflicted with the effort to meet the needs and inclinations of his ministers of external affairs. Howard Green, while very much his own man, was close to departmental thinking on most issues and was sometimes thought by Diefenbaker to have been taken in by the department. Green's enthusiasms tended to stimulate the 'Pearsonalities' in External Affairs, while Diefenbaker often had fun at their expense. Not surprisingly, the hope in the department that its days of influence might return was not realized in the Diefenbaker years. At the end, however, it could safely be said that his criticism of the department as an institution was in a sense contradicted by his respect and liking for many of its individual members.

Since a leader's quality is put to the test in times of stress, it is worth asking how Diefenbaker performed in the major international challenges of his years in office. One must make a distinction here between the earlier and later periods. In the period 1957–61 he steered Canada through three serious world crises – one in the Middle East in 1958 and two centred on Berlin (in 1959 and 1961). True, these crises did not directly threaten Canadian interests but they might have, and he performed competently in these cases, if without special distinction. He emerged with substantial personal credit – and many admirers among the newer members of the Commonwealth – for his role in the crisis over South Africa. Closer to home, he weathered pressure from Washington over trade with Cuba, and broke important new ground with the sale of wheat to the People's Republic of China. In many other sensitive tests of will with the United States, especially in defence of Canadian economic or agricultural interests, Diefenbaker was practical, hard-headed, and generally successful. In all these situations, with the possible exception of the South African issue, he was able to act with reasonable certainty that he knew the state of Canadian opinion. Not only that, but he knew his own mind, and was confident and generally effective in explaining the government's position. That could not be said in 1962–3 with the Cuban missile crisis or with the nuclear weapons controversy, which together comprised the final and fatal test of his leadership.

Thus, although Diefenbaker's foreign policy record in the years from 1957 to 1961 had been marked by a considerable degree of success and no major setbacks, the remaining year and a half was a time of escalating breakdown. Late in 1961 it became evident that he was seriously worried about the outlook for the next federal election. The timing, of course, had not been fixed, but the signs were unmistakable. In international affairs a number of problems were causing his anxiety. His personal relations with President Kennedy were no more than coldly formal. British plans to negotiate entry into the European Common Market exposed his reluctance to recognize and adapt himself to the tides of change in European and Commonwealth affairs, as well as in Anglo-Canadian relations. And the nuclear weapons controversy, with its potential for trouble within the government as well as for worsening relations with Washington, was by now an open secret. Worst of all for Diefenbaker, the election in June 1962 deprived him of his majority in parliament and seriously undermined his confidence.

The nuclear weapons issue had not emerged as a major source of anxiety until early in 1960. By that time the government had undertaken to perform nuclear roles in both North America and Western Europe. At first, Diefenbaker had not been seriously troubled at the thought of cooperating with Canada's allies in nuclear defence and deterrence. Yet counter-pressures, some of them generated within the government rather than by the force of public opinion, were beginning to have their influence on his thinking. Green, ahead of his time, was calling attention to the dangers of nuclear fallout, and was campaigning at the United Nations and in Canada against nuclear testing and the spread of nuclear weapons.

Diefenbaker was impressed by the political response in Canada to Green's anti-nuclear crusade. Even before President Eisenhower left office in January 1961, Diefenbaker himself, caught up in spasms of anti-American feeling, had begun to hedge on how the government would in fact fulfil its nuclear commitments. Like Green, he worried in particular about weapon systems such as the Bomarc, the control and use of which would be subject to American decision and thus might be thought to impose limitations on Canadian sovereignty. The fact that integrated air defence required unavoidable sacrifices of sovereignty often got conveniently shunted aside. He latched gratefully onto the formula that nuclear warheads might be available on an 'if and when needed' basis. But the problems mounted. The Americans kept pressing, as did Douglas Harkness; Green's influence was always there; and Lester Pearson and Paul Martin were harassing the prime minister in parliament. For those who were serving up material in reply to questions or in speeches, it became a constant revelation to see how he tried day after day to escape from the dilemma. As the pressures grew, his capacity to overcome the stresses of the job noticeably diminished. Once commanding and confident, he became more often vulnerable and brooding, just when his authority needed to be asserted.

An individualist himself, Diefenbaker had little experience or talent for reconciling opposing viewpoints. When two strong and respected ministers, such as Green and Harkness, were going in different directions, the prime minister had no resources to resolve the conflict. He feared that if he chose between them, he would invite a resignation. That, with good reason as it turned out, he felt he could not afford.

He had a compulsive tendency to postpone decisions rather than to assert a position of his own, unless he was fully conscious of the political wisdom or futility of a particular course. After the Cuban crisis he was still undecided what to do about the nuclear issue, so it suited him to have Green and Harkness, and their American counterparts, working away for weeks at a complicated formula for nuclear cooperation. In the unlikely event that it could be agreed, Canada would be committed to accept nuclear warheads only in time of grave emergency. If it failed, he could easily divert the blame. In either event he would have borrowed some time.

Internationally, his greatest preoccupation had always been his relationship with the president of the United States. In his general attitude towards the United States he was, of course, ambivalent. He felt completely at home with Eisenhower, and he was more comfortable with the legislators on Capitol Hill in Washington than he was with their counterparts in London. He was a North American, not a mid-Atlantic man. Yet the personal link with Washington had become much less reassuring after Eisenhower's departure. While it would be simplistic to attribute this altogether to the change in American leadership, the fact was that with Kennedy in office, the supply of understanding and goodwill in the White House had quickly dwindled. And with Diefenbaker, so much was personal.

He felt slighted, for example, by the manner in which the Cuban missile crisis was presented to him and by the absence of consultation under NORAD. His reactions to events always included an intuitive response to personalities, quite apart from the policy issues involved. While he was not obsessively anti-American, there were situations which brought out his instinctive resistance to being pushed. There were people, like Kennedy, who made him feel that he was of little account, and who therefore could not in the end influence him against the temptation to make anti-Americanism an issue in the 1963 election campaign.

All along, too, there had been the Lester Pearson factor. Pearson was an obsession. Diefenbaker held him in envious admiration. He had always respected his experience in foreign affairs, but now Pearson had become a much more effective opposition leader. Diefenbaker was, at first, afraid to take the risk of acquiring nuclear warheads for fear that Pearson would gain politically. Only when the Liberal leader's change of position on nuclear policy was combined with interference from the Kennedy administration did Diefenbaker finally choose his course. He would not 'follow' Pearson, although to Harkness and others it seemed a providential chance to come down on the side of acquiring nuclear warheads. Neither would he 'oblige' the president, who, he was convinced, was presiding over a campaign to bring him down.

Towards the end, it became a question of deciding what Canadian public opinion would oppose or accept. He had let the decision go unmade for too long. It had been an extraordinarily difficult one, and he had agonized over it. Something visceral steered him away from the pro-nuclear choice but kept him short of openly endorsing Howard Green, despite the high regard he had for him. Perhaps he reasoned that the third option – avoiding a decision – was likely to find the most rewarding echo. Before long he paid the price for his preoccupation with short-term political tactics, for the distrust and dislike that had grown up between him and President Kennedy, and for the indecisiveness which had always sapped his powers of leadership.

From a prime minister's perspective, foreign policy, though only one part of government, is both important and treacherous. While external events can seldom be controlled, their impact can readily affect the political fortunes of national leaders. Until he had been in office for more than three quarters of his term, external pressures had not threatened Diefenbaker's position, although his domestic agenda had already taken on a worrying complexion. Had the balance sheet on his foreign policy been drawn up in 1961, it would have reflected credit on him. It was only later, when the strains associated with nuclear policy brought him into direct conflict with the administration in Washington, that his control of events unraveled and led to his undoing.

In a sense, therefore, he was a victim of circumstance. Yet the main fault lay with him, and especially with his failure to act decisively at critical times. The unfortunate fact is that, for all his efforts, his record in foreign policy will be clouded by the memory of his political collapse, largely self-inflicted and related to Canada's responsibilities in the world. At the end – torn, beleaguered, defiant, and grasping for the vestiges of receding power – he simply defeated himself. In his memoirs, describing an occasion in his youth when he lost his way while walking, he wrote this sentence: 'I don't like to admit that I don't know my way.'[3] Whether subconsciously he meant it in a more general sense is not entirely clear, but it is not misleading to give the words a wider application. They would go some way to explain his reluctance to seek expert advice. And they would testify to the presence of a lurking self-doubt which might contribute to indecisiveness and caution in situations where he did not feel thoroughly in control. A paradox indeed in a man capable of imagining far-reaching visions and with such an apparent faith in his own powers. The truth was that his powers were limited and his magic flawed. He had reached a sad milestone on his tumultuous journey.

It was not, of course, the end of the trail. On the day he stepped down, 22 April 1963, he sent a short note to his old friends in Prince Albert, thanking them for their support over the years.[4] 'In three hours,' he wrote, 'I shall be going to Government House to take leave of the Governor General but with the hope that I shall be able to do what Macdonald and King succeeded in doing after a term in opposition!' He was tasting defeat, but there was no doubt about his appetite for another spell in office.

Notes

CHAPTER 2 MEETING THE FAMILY

1 Much of the information in this and the succeeding paragraph is based on PCO Records, Cabinet Conclusions, 21–22 June 1957.
2 Mary Louise Hose Papers, Diefenbaker to Drs Lorne and Mabel Connell, 22 June 1957
3 The following account is based on a draft summary record of the meeting, then available in prime minister's office.
4 PCO Records, Cabinet Conclusions, 6 July 1957
5 Macmillan, *Riding the Storm*, 377
6 *Toronto Star*, 8 July 1957

CHAPTER 3 MEETING THE NEIGHBOURS

1 DEA, file 50399-A-40, J.W. Holmes to Jules Léger, 31 July 1957; NA, Robertson Papers, Holmes to N.A. Robertson, 1 Aug. 1957; Mudd Library, Princeton, Merchant Papers, box 13, Livingston T. Merchant interview for J.F. Dulles Oral History
2 Merchant interview. Donald Fleming mentions this meeting, but not the exchange on the government's intentions in trade policy. Fleming, *So Very Near*, vol. 1, 380–81
3 Merchant Papers, box 13, Merchant talk to US National War College, 30 Jan. 1959
4 See Jockel, *No Boundaries Upstairs*, for a detailed and well-informed commentary on the origins of the NORAD agreement, based on recently accessible Canadian and American primary sources. Pages 104–17 and 125–9 are especially interesting on the events of 1957–8.

5 See General Foulkes's testimony to the House of Commons special committee on defence, minutes of proceedings and evidence, no. 15, 22 Oct. 1963, 510, 526–7.

6 DEA, file 50309-40, vol. 2, minutes of Chiefs of Staff Committee, 15 Feb. 1957

7 PCO Records, minutes of Cabinet Defence Committee, 6–7 Feb. 1957

8 DEA, file 50309-40, vol. 2, memorandum to cabinet, 22 July 1957, enclosed with letter Foulkes to Holmes, 7 Aug. 1957

9 According to Foulkes, in an interview many years later, Pearkes said that he informed Léger immediately after the meeting with Diefenbaker. G.R. Pearkes Papers, R.H. Roy interview with Foulkes, 9 March 1967. I have encountered no direct evidence of what might have passed between them, but it is odd that other officials concerned with defence matters in External Affairs heard nothing. Although Léger was apparently called away on a family emergency that day, it would have been most unlike him not to have notified his department if he had received important information from the minister of national defence.

10 Diefenbaker, *One Canada*, vol. 3, 23

11 NA, Record Group 25, 1985–86/684, box 15; DEA, file 18-A-USA-1957-1, Diefenbaker-Dulles meeting-briefs, memorandum 'Canada-United States Defence'

12 Bryce himself had learned of Pearkes's 24 July meeting with Diefenbaker only as Pearkes left the prime minister. It was Bryce's understanding that Pearkes intended to notify Léger, and he therefore assumed that External Affairs knew about the decision.

13 DEA, file 50309-40, vol. 2, various letters

14 PCO Records, Cabinet Conclusions, 19 Oct. 1957

15 DEA, file 50309-40, vol. 2, Pearkes to Smith, 25 Oct. 1957, and Foulkes to Léger, 28 Oct. 1957, in reply to Léger's letter of 10 Sept. 1957

16 HBR Papers, Robinson to J.B.C. Watkins, 16 Dec. 1957

17 House of Commons, *Debates*, 21 Dec. 1957, 2719–24

18 *Canada Treaty Series 1958*, no. 9

CHAPTER 4 MEETING THE ALLIES

1 Macmillan, *Riding the Storm*, 756–9

2 Ibid., 323

3 PCO Records, Cabinet Conclusions, 26 Oct. 1957

4 Dulles made these points at a background press briefing at the State Department in Washington, 28 Oct. 1957. DEA, file 50359-A-40, A.E. Ritchie to Léger, 8 Nov. 1957

5 DEA, file 50030-K-40, Dec. 1957

6 DEA, file 50102-S-40, Holmes memo to USSEA, 8 Nov. 1957

7 HBR Diary, 28 Nov. 1957

8 DEA, file 50102-S-40, brief for Canadian delegation to NATO heads of government meeting, Dec. 1957
9 DEA, file 50030-K-40, vol. 5, 30 Nov. 1957
10 HBR Papers, HBR to J.B.C. Watkins, 16 Dec. 1957
11 Diefenbaker, *One Canada*, vol. 2, 129–31
12 House of Commons, *Debates*, Dec. 1957, 2719–24

CHAPTER 6 SURVEYING THE WORLD SCENE

1 This summary of parts of the Macmillan-Diefenbaker meeting is based on my notes taken during the conversation and afterwards when Diefenbaker was checking over the official record.
2 DEA, file 1415-E-40, May–June 1958
3 One frequently encounters questions about what John Diefenbaker was like to work for (one did not speak of working *with* him or at least I did not). Time blurs memories, and just as well, because there were many rough and discouraging passages. As the bearer of information or advice which he sometimes found unwelcome or inadequate, I not infrequently felt the lash of his irritation or disapproval. Now and then he was warm and appreciative. One seldom knew what to expect. On the whole, I found him a considerate chief, especially in situations affecting my health and family responsibilities. On this occasion, both Diefenbakers went out of their way to be kind, although it was not in their style to compete with Sidney Smith's inspired delivery of a large bottle of scotch as an incentive to recovery.
4 DEA, file 50162-A-40, vols. 2–7, is informative on the build-up and conduct of Canadian policy in the Lebanese crisis.
5 PCO Records, Cabinet Conclusions, 25 June 1958
6 House of Commons, *Debates*, 29 Nov. 1956, 140

CHAPTER 7 WORLD TOUR: EUROPE

1 For Donald Fleming's account of the conference, see *So Very Near*, vol. 1, 509–20.
2 Accounts of the prime minister's conversations during the tour are principally based on my notes taken at the official meetings. I have also made use of the telegraphic reports sent to Ottawa by the heads of our mission at each main port of call. See DEA, file 12687-M-1-40.
3 HBR Papers, Memo to Far Eastern Division, 5 Sept. 1957
4 Despite the prime minister's professed suspicion that information was passed to Lester Pearson by External Affairs officials, I have never seen a shred of evidence

that this took place. Pearson himself was always very correct in any contacts with his friends and former colleagues.

5 Diefenbaker Centre, Saskatoon, Family series correspondence, John Diefenbaker to Mary Diefenbaker, 21 Dec. 1958

6 The term 'free world' was in regular use at the time. It was used, as a rule, to group nations with democratic systems of government, but Diefenbaker often extended it to include non-democratic regimes as long as they were outside the communist orbit.

7 Based on a brief account given me by the prime minister immediately after the meeting.

8 The term 'official meeting' denotes the main occasion for formal discussion during a visit of this kind. Normally it is attended by a small number of others on each side. Diefenbaker's pattern on this trip was to be accompanied by the Canadian high commissioner or ambassador in the host country and myself. George Drew, the Canadian high commissioner, and I attended the meeting on 3 November.

9 The British government had for well over a year been negotiating with the six member governments of the European Common Market for the establishment of a free trade area between the six and the other European members of the Organization for European Economic Cooperation. The negotiations were now at a critical stage. The Treaty of Rome, by which the six members of the Common Market were bound, was to come into effect on 1 January 1959. Since de Gaulle's return to power in May 1958, France's attitude towards the free trade area had quickly hardened. Macmillan's memoirs show how agitated he was on this issue during the days of Diefenbaker's visit to London. *Riding the Storm*, 455

10 De Gaulle was not yet the president. This would not come until 9 January 1959, with the installation of the Fifth Republic.

CHAPTER 8 WORLD TOUR: ASIA AND THE PACIFIC

1 He was to visit Pakistan, India, Ceylon (now Sri Lanka), Malaya, Singapore, and, very briefly, Indonesia. He had visited Australia and New Zealand in 1950 for meetings of the Commonwealth Parliamentary Association.

2 Diefenbaker, *One Canada*, vol. 2, 104–5

3 This point is discussed in ibid., 115.

4 This was a summary of the administrative lessons learned from the tour. HBR Papers, 29 Jan. 1959

CHAPTER 9 NO REST FOR THE LEADER

1 PCO Records, Memorandum to cabinet, 13 Aug. 1958

2 Press release from Prime Minister's Office, 23 Sept. 1958
3 House of Commons, *Debates*, 20 Feb. 1959, 1221–4
4 PCO Records, Minutes of Cabinet Defence Committee, 28 April 1958
5 DEA, file 50234–40, vol. 12, especially 28 Jan. 1959
6 *Globe and Mail*, 30 Jan. 1959
7 DEA, file 50234–40, vol. 12, 11 Feb. 1959
8 Ibid.
9 I was in the Official Gallery of the House of Commons at about 2:30 PM on 17 March when Ross Campbell phoned with the first news of the minister's death. I sent a note to the prime minister on the floor of the House, and he came behind the curtains immediately. I gave him the news and said that the undersecretary was on his way to notify him officially. The prime minister was stunned and profoundly upset. After the undersecretary had had a brief discussion with him, the prime minister went immediately back into the House and made the announcement with the greatest emotion. The House adjourned.
10 For a full account of Macmillan's visit see *Riding the Storm*, 582–656.
11 The Air Division had been flying F-86s and CF-100s, which were close to being obsolete.
12 PCO Records, Minutes of meeting of ministers with General Norstad, 18 May 1959
13 In January 1959 Arnold Heeney had succeeded N.A. Robertson as Canadian ambassador in Washington. It was Heeney's second tour of duty there, the first having been from 1953 to 1957.

CHAPTER 10 TEAMING UP WITH HOWARD GREEN

1 Vancouver City Archives, Howard Green Papers
2 HBR Papers, personal correspondence, 19 June 1959
3 PCO Records, Cabinet Conclusions, 19 June 1959
4 HBR Diary, 8 July 1959

CHAPTER 11 TWO SIDES OF THE DEFENCE COIN

1 The prime minister informed the House of Commons of the agreement on 25 May 1959. House of Commons, *Debates*, 3965-6
2 PCO Records, Cabinet Conclusions
3 Fleming, *So Very Near*, vol. 2, 18
4 At a more junior level the intricacies of nuclear strategy were more deeply and sympathetically explored by officials who were in working contact with National Defence and other departments. Advice rising to the top levels in External Affairs at this stage was thus not normally cast in anti-nuclear terms. For the most

part both Léger and Robertson were pragmatic enough to let such advice pass upward, although both found means of making their personal views known.

5 Conversation with John Holmes, a close friend of Robertson.

6 DEA, file 50309-40, Vol. 7, 16 March 1959

7 *The Spectator*, 1 May 1959

8 Chairman, Chiefs of Staff Records, file 'The Development of Nuclear Weapons for Canadian Forces in Europe,' Exchange of letters, Norstad-Diefenbaker, 23 and 30 July, 1959. Diefenbaker's letter reads as if dictated personally.

9 DEA, file 50219-AL-2-40, vol. I

10 HBR Papers. The paper was drafted in the defence liaison division of External Affairs, but in circulating it, Robertson said that it represented his personal views.

11 Heeney Papers, Heeney memo, 4 Sept. 1959, with attachment, 'Lessons from Skyhawk'

12 Speech to Canadian Club, Halifax, 14 Nov. 1959

13 Formerly commander of the UN Emergency Force in the Middle East

14 PCO Records, Cabinet Conclusions, 25 Jan. 1960

15 The five-power talks were the forum for Western consultations on disarmament in preparation for the intended summit meeting. The Ten-Nation Committee, set up by the UN General Assembly in 1959, began its operations on 15 March. It continued to meet until 27 June, when the Soviet Union and its four Eastern European allies walked out.

16 HBR, Diary, 25 Jan. 1960

17 Ibid., 12–13 Jan. 1960

18 Ibid., 17 Jan. 1960

19 HBR Diary, 24 Feb. and 1 March 1960, based on second-hand information said to have originated with Canadian representative on the NATO Council in Paris. No independent confirmation of this report has come my way.

20 Ibid., 1 and 5 March 1960

CHAPTER 13 TESTING THE COMMONWEALTH: SOUTH AFRICA

1 HBR Papers, HBR memo to USSEA, 28 Jan. 1960, and excerpts from prime minister's remarks to the CLC

2 Macmillan, *Pointing the Way*, 155–9

3 HBR Diary, 2 March 1960

4 The tradition had been that Commonwealth prime ministers' meetings were not *foreign* affairs. Prime ministers were usually advised by secretaries to cabinet plus other officials as appropriate. The United Kingdom encouraged this view and practice. Ministers of external affairs were normally not present at these meetings,

and even when they did attend, as in 1962, the secretary to the cabinet was still the senior official there.

5 DEA, file 11827-40, HBR memo to Commonwealth Division, 8 April 1960
6 Laws limiting the freedom of movement of blacks in South Africa.
7 HBR Diary, 5 April 1960
8 Based on diary notes, 5–11 April 1960
9 Ibid.
10 The substance of the paragraphs on the statement of 11 April is based on a memo I dictated that evening after receiving clarification from the prime minister.
11 South Africa's foreign minister, E.H. Louw, represented Prime Minister Verwoerd, still recovering from the attack on his life.
12 The prime minister's own account of the meeting is given in *One Canada*, vol. 2, 209–13.
13 House of Commons, *Debates*, 16 May 1960, 3898–903
14 Confidential source

CHAPTER 14 GLIMPSING THE SUMMIT – BEFORE AND AFTER

1 De Gaulle, *Memoirs of Hope*, 238–42 and 268–9
2 The foregoing account of Diefenbaker's talks with de Gaulle is based on a report I sent to the USSEA on 25 April 1960. DEA, file 6956-A-40
3 HBR Diary, 20 April 1960
4 House of Commons, *Debates*, 18 May 1960, 3994–6
5 HBR Papers, HBR memo to USSEA, 31 May 1960
6 HBR Papers, personal correspondence
7 PCO Records, Cabinet Conclusions, 14 May 1960
8 HBR Papers
9 Merchant had been US ambassador in Ottawa, 1957–9, and was now the no. 3 official in the State Department. He was not a favourite of Diefenbaker's, although Diefenbaker often acknowledged his diplomatic skill.
10 Based on comments by the prime minister after the meeting. HBR Papers, HBR memo of 9 June 1960
11 On the US side were Messrs Herter, secretary of state, Wigglesworth, ambassador to Canada, and Merchant; on the Canadian side, Bryce, Heeney, and Robinson.
12 An undated, unsigned memo records in some detail how the prime minister learned of the British study. HBR Papers
13 Diefenbaker Centre, Notes for speech at Depauw University, June 1960

CHAPTER 15 FACING AN ANXIOUS SUMMER

1 House of Commons, *Debates*, 4 July 1960, 5653–4
2 HBR Diary, 4 July 1960
3 HBR Papers
4 Ibid., draft dated 17 July 1960
5 HBR Diary
6 Department of External Affairs, *Canada and the United Nations, 1960*, 3. See also 20–5 for further detail on Canadian policy in the Congo operation.

CHAPTER 16 ADVENTURES OF AUTUMN

1 DEA, *Statements and Speeches*, no. 60/32
2 Geoff Murray, head of the UN Division in External Affairs, was a key adviser on the delegation.
3 Interviews with D.S. Harkness, 26 April 1986
4 HBR Papers, HBR memo to USSEA, 9 Nov. 1960
5 HBR Diary, 3 Dec. 1960
6 HBR Papers
7 PCO Records, Cabinet Conclusions, 6 Dec. 1960
8 Ibid.
9 HBR Diary, 7 Dec. 1960

CHAPTER 17 FROM EISENHOWER TO KENNEDY

1 HBR Papers, Memo for file, 9 Nov. 1960
2 HBR Diary, 5 Jan. 1961
3 Diefenbaker was by this time so anxious about the political risks of accepting nuclear weapons on Canadian territory that in this, his first talk with the new president, he allowed himself to disregard the uncomfortable truth – of which he had been reminded at the cabinet meeting of 6 December – that the version of the Bomarc which the government had undertaken to purchase was effective only with nuclear warheads. See PCO Records, Cabinet Conclusions, 6 Dec. 1960. He and Green were both much less worried about Canada's nuclear commitments in Europe, since they could be wrapped in a NATO cloak. As for the arrangements for storing nuclear weapons for US forces in Canada, the Canadian government was deliberately holding back until the issues involved in the different weapons systems for Canadian forces had been resolved.
4 Howard Green has recalled that President Kennedy took him aside during an interval and assured the minister that the United States would shortly be putting

forward new disarmament proposals. This gave great satisfaction to Green, who took it as a signal of the president's understanding of the priority Green had been advocating in the arms control field. Green interview, 2 May 1986

5 The quotations in this paragraph are from notes dictated by the prime minister on the morning after the meeting. HBR Papers, HBR memo to USSEA, 21 Feb. 1961

CHAPTER 18 SOUTH AFRICA LEAVES THE COMMONWEALTH

1 DEA, file 50386-40, vol. 8, Robinson memo to USSEA, 21 Sept. 1960

2 DEA, file 50085-J-40, vol. 1, Robinson memo to USSEA, 3 Nov. 1960

3 A speech made at Cape Town in February 1960 during Macmillan's tour of South Africa

4 Macmillan, *Pointing the Way*, 293–6

5 HBR Papers, note for Prime Minister's Office file on South Africa, 20 Dec. 1960

6 DEA, file 50085-J-40, vol. 1

7 Based on notes by R.B. Bryce

8 DEA, file 50085-J-40, vol. 1

9 PCO Records, Cabinet Conclusions, 11 Feb. 1961

10 Confidential source

11 Any account of a commonwealth prime ministers' meeting by someone other than a prime minister is bound to be incomplete. Diefenbaker reported to the House of Commons after his return, and he has provided a further account in his memoirs. Diefenbaker, *One Canada*, vol. 2, 217–21. What follows here is an adviser's view only. It is limited to what I either saw or have learned reliably about the role played by Diefenbaker. A full account will have to await a complete release of the official records.

12 But Davie Fulton to whom I sent a draft of this chapter writes: 'However, a reading of this chapter confirms in me what I felt for some time was actually the case: that is, that JGD took me to London for that conference purely as a precaution, so that he would have his Minister of Justice there in case the South African problem appeared to raise a question on which a constitutional or legal opinion in the formal sense might be required. He would then be protected and/or reinforced by having his Minister of Justice there. He certainly did not have me there in any sense as a confidant or advisor. I was not informed as to the background, nor kept advised as to his views, nor consulted as to what stand he should take or what reaction he should express, at any stage while those meetings were in progress, at his hotel in London, or on the way over. And at no time was I informed, or called into consultation, as to the information and comments that he received from George Drew. I realize that this is not a very flattering view of the reasons for having me there, but the fact is that I felt something of a "passenger" at

329

the time, and your research and description of the developments have confirmed this impression, unflattering though it may be.'

13 DEA, file 50085-J-40, vol. 3

14 This account is based on handwritten notes by E. Davie Fulton, now in the Fulton Papers, vol. 67; my notes recording instructions or comments by the prime minister at breaks during the meeting; DEA files, especially 50085-J-40; and a helpful research paper by F.J. McEvoy, historical section, DEA.

15 HBR Papers

16 S. Gopal, *Jawaharlal Nehru: A Biography, 1956–64*, vol. 3, 51

17 Macmillan, *Pointing the Way*, 297–300

18 Interview, 5 May 1986

19 House of Commons, *Debates*, 16 and 17 March 1961, 3033 and 3088

20 PCO Records, Cabinet Conclusions, 9 and 30 May 1961

21 HBR Diary, 8 May 1961

22 Ibid., 29 May 1961

CHAPTER 19 PLANNING THE KENNEDY VISIT

1 A very good first-hand account of this episode is given in Ignatieff, *The Making of a Peacemonger*, 195–7.

2 HBR Papers, 14 April 1961

3 Macmillan, *Pointing the Way*, 335–9 and 353

4 HBR Diary, 19 April 1961

5 Merchant reported on this meeting in a telegram to the secretary of state, 11 May 1961. See Kennedy Papers, POF, box 113: Canada Security, JFK Trip to Ottawa, 5/16–18/61, folder B.

6 Not to be confused with the F-104Gs already on order for the RCAF in Europe.

7 HBR Diary, 15 May 1961

CHAPTER 20 TAKING UMBRAGE: DON'T PUSH

1 Merchant Papers, Mrs Diefenbaker to Mrs Livingston Merchant, 22 May 1961

2 This account is based on notes taken at the meeting.

3 This exchange was doubtless in Diefenbaker's mind when he wrote in his memoirs about the Cuban missile crisis in October 1962. There was no advance 'talk' on that occasion, but this may well have been because personal relations between the president and the prime minister had been steadily deteriorating since the president had been in Ottawa. Diefenbaker, *One Canada*, vol. 3, 77–80

4 Merchant's account coincides with this report. He refers to Diefenbaker as saying that he was not 'unwilling to face the issue,' but that the timing was wrong.

The prime minister had said he needed more time to educate the public, but undertook to start the process in the months immediately ahead 'with the hopeful result that it would be politically feasible.' Merchant Papers, box 13, Merchant interview for J.F. Kennedy Oral History

5 See Kent, *A Public Purpose*, 92, 187, on the evolution of the Liberal party's nuclear policy at and after the National Liberal Rally in January 1961.

6 In editing the draft record, the prime minister excised this sentence. HBR Papers

7 HBR Papers

8 The full text of the document is as given in Diefenbaker, *One Canada*, vol. 2, 183.

9 As a footnote to this bizarre episode, it may be added that on the occasion of Prime Minister Pearson's meeting with President Kennedy at Hyannisport almost exactly two years later, the president enquired about the same document. Had somebody written something on it? He had not remembered doing so himself. The question was referred to me – I happened again to be taking the notes on this occasion – and I gave it as my clear recollection that the Rostow paper was indeed free of marginal notations.

10 HBR Diary, 17 and 18 May 1961

11 Ibid., 24 May 1961

12 Kennedy Papers, POF, box 113, Canada Security (C) File, Biographical Material, May 1961

13 Interview, 2 May 1986

CHAPTER 21 RESHAPING OLD PATTERNS

1 HBR Diary, 2–3 June 1961

2 Ibid., 9 June 1961

3 Ibid., 10 June 1961

4 Ibid., 16 Sept. 1961

5 PCO Records, Cabinet Conclusions, 14 Sept. 1961

6 HBR Diary, 27 Nov. 1961

7 Ibid., 7 Dec. 1961

8 Ibid., 8 Dec. 1961

CHAPTER 22 REVISITING EAST-WEST TENSIONS

1 These words were used by the Hon. J.M. Macdonnell, a respected senior Progressive Conservative member of parliament and former minister, in the House of Commons debate on the Berlin crisis. House of Commons, *Debates*, 8 Sept. 1961, 8132

2 He worked particularly hard at his speech in Toronto to the Kiwanis International Convention on 3 July 1961 and later regarded this as one of his best statements on US-Canadian and East-West relations. *Statements and Speeches*, DEA, 61/7

3 See ibid., 61/9

CHAPTER 23 GROWING NUCLEAR DEBATE

1 HBR Papers

2 Ibid.

3 Diefenbaker Centre

4 Normally the phrase 'nuclear club' was taken to refer to the small number of nations possessing the independent capacity to manufacture and use nuclear weapons, at that time the United States, USSR, United Kingdom, and France.

5 Merchant told me later that President Kennedy felt that he had indeed been let down on a personal commitment.

6 For Pearson's position at that time see, for example, House of Commons, *Debates*, 14 Sept. 1961, 8342–54.

7 Ibid., 8596

8 PCO Records, Cabinet Conclusions, 18 Dec. 1961

CHAPTER 24 PLANNING FOR THE ELECTION

1 HBR Papers, copy of draft speech notes, 21 Jan. 1962

2 He had in mind Tom Kent, Allan MacEachen, and Maurice Lamontagne, particularly Kent. See Kent, *A Public Purpose*, 128.

3 Fleming, *So Very Near*, vol. 2, 444–5

4 Available from the Diefenbaker Centre, Saskatoon

CHAPTER 26 FROM MAJORITY TO MINORITY

1 DEA, file 12447-40/41, 26 March 1962. See also Fleming, *So Very Near*, vol. 2, 456.

2 DEA, *Statements and Speeches*, no. 62/8. See diary entry for 4 May 1962.

3 Then undersecretary of state in the State Department

4 HBR Papers, note by prime minister, 19 April

5 Ibid.

6 A reference to the reciprocity issue as a factor in the defeat of the Liberals under Laurier.

7 Merchant Papers, box 13, Merchant interview for J.F. Kennedy Oral History

CHAPTER 27 FRESH PERSPECTIVES

1 For first-hand accounts of the action taken by the government on the exchange crisis in June 1962 see Diefenbaker, *One Canada*, vol. 3, 132–6, and Fleming, *So Very Near*, vol. 2, 516–24.
2 Howard Green Papers, vol. 9, 13 Aug. 1962; also PCO Records, Cabinet Conclusions, 30 and 31 Aug., 3 and 5 Sept. 1962
3 PCO Records, Cabinet Conclusions, 30 Aug. 1962

CHAPTER 28 ON THE BRINK: THE CUBAN MISSILE CRISIS

1 Undersecretary of state George Ball to the select committee of the House of Representatives on export control, 3 Oct. 1962. HBR Papers, Canadian embassy, Washington, telegram #2883 to Ottawa, 4 Oct. 1962
2 White House press release, 4 Sept. 1962
3 DEA, file 2444-40, vol. 9, Canadian embassy, Washington, to DEA, 15 Oct. 1962
4 Much of the chronology of the Cuban missile crisis, as it involved Canada, has become public knowledge. Because, however, it is my purpose to try to interpret the prime minister's attitudes and actions in international affairs, I venture to recount the story as I understand it, based partly on direct knowledge of what transpired and partly on evidence obtained through interviews and official documentation.
5 Dean Acheson, a former US secretary of state, acted as special envoy to President de Gaulle. Prime Minister Macmillan had already been in telephone contact with President Kennedy. He and Chancellor Adenauer were also briefed and shown in advance the photographic evidence of the Soviet missile installations in Cuba.
6 Personal conversation with author
7 PCO Records, Cabinet Conclusions, 23 Oct. 1962
8 Confidential information
9 DEA, file 2444-40, 22 Oct. 1962
10 See Lyon, *Canada in World Affairs, 1961–63*, 34, especially note 45.
11 Harkness Papers contain the minister's careful personal account of the Cuban crisis, followed by the nuclear weapons crisis, which was published in part in the Ottawa *Citizen*, 22, 24 and 25 Oct. 1977.
12 Macmillan mentions having sent a message to Diefenbaker at this time. *At the End of the Day*, 194
13 Stursberg, *Leadership Lost, 1962–67*, 16 and 17
14 Diefenbaker, *One Canada*, vol. 3, 82
15 Harkness interview, 26 April 1986

16 Mary Macdonald, Pearson's executive assistant, remembers that the prime minister came to Pearson's office and sought his advice on the stand Canada should take in the crisis. As this was one of the rare occasions on which he had been consulted by Diefenbaker, Pearson responded in some detail. It was arranged between them that he would ask the pertinent questions when orders-of-the-day were called in the House that afternoon. Diefenbaker, however, did not allow Pearson the opportunity to put the question. Instead, he launched into a statement at the start of parliamentary business, making use of Pearson's advice without acknowledging the source or without giving the Liberal leader an opportunity to speak. Pearson was angry about being double-crossed and his regard for Diefenbaker sank even further.

17 At Diefenbaker's invitation, Pearson had that morning attended an intelligence briefing given to the cabinet defence committee. Conversation with J.J. McCardle, DEA, who took part in the briefing as head of the department's intelligence and security division.

18 DEA, file 2444-40, 26 Oct. 1962

19 HBR Papers, Orme Dier to HBR, 25 Jan. 1987

20 To the Zionist Organization of Canada

21 Merchant Papers, box 13, Merchant interview for J.F. Kennedy Oral History

22 PCO Records, file F-2-8(a), 9 Jan. 1963

23 This point is well made in an excellent memorandum entitled 'Lessons of the Cuban Crisis' from D.B. Dewar to Bryce, 20 Nov. 1962. PCO Records, file F-2-8(a)

CHAPTER 29 MEETING HIS FATE: NUCLEAR NEMESIS

1 PCO Records, Cabinet Conclusions, 30 Oct. 1962

2 HBR Papers, Robinson letter to Ross Campbell, 20 Nov. 1962

3 Ibid., memo for file, Canadian embassy, Washington, quoting Willis Armstrong of State Department, 25 Jan. 1963

4 Presumably under the stand-by or 'missing parts' arrangement.

5 The prime minister authorized his office to send copies of summary records of his Nassau discussions to the Canadian embassy in Washington for confidential use. It is not clear from the context if he gave this information to Macmillan and Amory only, or if he had also given it to the president, although the latter seems more likely.

6 See Pearson, *Mike*, vol. 3, 69–76; also Pearson Papers, 1957–63, vol. 50, Pearson to Bruce Hutchison, Dec. 1962, for insights into Pearson's dilemma at this time on the nuclear weapons issue. See also Kent, *A Public Purpose*, 187–93.

7 House of Commons, *Debates*, 25 Jan. 1963, 3125–37

8 See Fleming, *So Very Near*, vol. 2, 581–3, for a very interesting account of this episode. Harkness's record of events is also valuable for its detailed coverage of the crisis. Ottawa *Citizen*, 22, 24 and 25 Oct. 1977
9 See Ritchie, *Storm Signals*, 32–4.
10 Confidential source
11 Ottawa *Citizen*, 24 Oct. 1977. See also Diefenbaker's account in *One Canada*, vol. 3, 90–4, 158–69.
12 *Canadian Annual Review, 1963*, 311–12
13 Kennedy Papers, POF, Departments and Agencies: Defence 1/63–6/63, memorandum from the president to the secretary of defence, 2 April 1963

CONCLUSION

1 House of Commons, *Debates*, 11 Sept. 1961, 8174
2 Macmillan, *At the End of the Day*, 29
3 Diefenbaker, *One Canada*, vol. 1, 88
4 Mary Louise Hose Papers, Diefenbaker to Drs Lorne and Mabel Connell, 22 April 1963

Select Bibliography

PRIMARY SOURCES

CANADA

Department of External Affairs, Ottawa (DEA)
Department Records*
Oral History Interviews*
Department of National Defence,
Directorate of History, Ottawa (DND, DHist)
Chairman, Chiefs of Staff Committee Records
General Charles Foulkes Papers*
Office of Chief of the Defence Staff Records*
Rt. Hon. John G. Diefenbaker Centre, Saskatoon
John G. Diefenbaker Papers*
National Archives of Canada (NA)
Marcel Cadieux Papers,* MG 31, E 31
E.D. Fulton Papers,* MG 32, B 11
H.C. Green Papers,* MG 32, B 13
D.S. Harkness Papers,* MG 32, B 19
A.D.P. Heeney Papers, MG 30, E 144
Jules Léger Papers,* MG 32, A 3
L.B. Pearson Papers, Leader of the Opposition Series, 1957–63, MG 26 N
N.A. Robertson Papers,* MG 30, E 163
Private Papers
Mary Louise Hose Papers, Toronto
H.B. Robinson (HBR) Papers and Diary*

* Indicates records are restricted

337

Privy Council Office, Ottawa (PCO)
Cabinet Conclusions*
Privy Council Office Records*
University of Victoria Archives
G.R. Pearkes Papers*
Vancouver City Archives
Howard C. Green Papers*

UNITED STATES

J.F. Kennedy Library, Boston, MA
Presidential Papers*
White House Central Files*
Oral History Transcripts*
Seeley G. Mudd Library, Princeton University, Princeton, NJ
Livingston T. Merchant Papers*

SECONDARY SOURCES

Blanchette, Arthur E. *Canadian Foreign Policy 1955–1965: Selected Speeches and Documents*. Toronto 1977

Bothwell, Robert, Ian Drummond, and John English. *Canada since 1945: Power, Politics, and Provincialism*. Toronto 1981

Corbett, E.A. *Sidney Earle Smith*. Toronto, 1961

Cox, David. *Canada and NORAD, 1958–1978: A Cautionary Retrospective*. Ottawa 1985

Diefenbaker, John G. *One Canada: Memoirs of the Right Honourable John G. Diefenbaker*. 3 vols. Toronto 1975–7

Fleming, Donald M. *The Political Memoirs of the Honourable Donald M. Fleming: So Very Near*. 2 vols. Toronto 1985

Foulkes, Charles. *Canadian Defence Policy in a Nuclear Age*. Toronto 1961

Ghent, Jocelyn Maynard. 'Did He Fall or Was He Pushed? The Kennedy Administration and the Collapse of the Diefenbaker Government.' *International History Review* 1(2)(April 1979): 246–70

– 'Canada, the United States and the Cuban Missile Crisis.' *Pacific Historical Review* 18 (May 1979): 159–83

– 'Canadian-American Relations and the Nuclear Weapons Controversy, 1958–1963.' PH D thesis, University of Illinois, 1976

Granatstein, J.L. *Canada 1957–1967: The Years of Uncertainty and Innovation*. Toronto 1986

– *Man of Influence: Norman A. Robertson and Canadian Statecraft 1929–68*. Ottawa 1981

Harkness, Douglas. Three articles on the Nuclear Weapons Crisis, 1962 *Ottawa Citizen*, 22, 24, 25 Oct. 1977

Heeney, Arnold. *The Things That Are Caesar's: The Memoirs of a Canadian Public Servant*. Toronto 1972

Hilliker, John F. 'The Politicians and the "Pearsonalities." ' Canadian Historical Association, *Historical Papers*, 1984

– Draft chapter on 1957–63 period for volume 2 of forthcoming history of the Department of External Affairs

Holt, Simma. *The Other Mrs. Diefenbaker: A Biography of Edna May Brower*. Markham, Ont. 1982

Hutchison, Bruce. *The Far Side of the Street*. Toronto 1976

Ignatieff, George. *The Making of a Peacemonger*. Toronto 1985

Jockel, Joseph T. *No Boundaries Upstairs: Canada, the United States, and the Origins of North American Air Defence, 1945–1958*. Vancouver 1987

– 'The Military Establishments and the Creation of NORAD.' *American Review of Canadian Studies* 12 (3) (fall 1982), 1–16

Kennedy, Robert F. *Thirteen Days: A Memoir of the Cuban Missile Crisis*. New York 1968

Kent, Tom. *A Public Purpose: An Experience of Liberal Opposition and Canadian Government*. Kingston and Montreal 1988

Lloyd, Trevor. *Canada in World Affairs, 1957–1959*. Toronto 1968

Lyon, Peyton, V. *Canada in World Affairs, 1961–1963*. Toronto 1968

Macmillan, Harold. *Riding the Storm, 1956–1959*. London and New York 1970, 1974

– *Pointing the Way, 1959–1961*. London and New York 1970, 1974

– *At the End of the Day, 1961–1963*. London and New York 1970, 1974

Martin, Lawrence, *The Presidents and the Prime Ministers*. Toronto and New York 1982

Martin, Paul. *A Very Public Life: So Many Worlds*. Toronto 1985

McEvoy, F.J. 'Canada, South Africa, and the Commonwealth – 1960–61,' unpublished research paper for Historical Section of DEA

McIlroy, Thad. *Personal Letters of a Public Man*. Toronto 1985

McIntosh, Dave. *Ottawa Unbuttoned*. Toronto 1987

McLin, Jon B. *Canada's Changing Defence Policy, 1957–1963*. Baltimore 1967

Newman, Peter C. *Renegade in Power: The Diefenbaker Years*. Toronto/Montreal 1963

Nicholson, Patrick. *Vision and Indecision: Diefenbaker and Pearson*. Toronto 1968

Pearson, Lester B. *Mike: The Memoirs of the Right Honourable Lester B. Pearson*. 3 vols. Toronto 1972, 1974, 1975

Pickersgill, J.W. *The Road Back: By a Liberal in Opposition*. Toronto 1986

Preston, Richard A. *Canada in World Affairs, 1959–1961*. Toronto 1965

Reford, Robert W. *Canada and Three Crises*. Toronto 1968

Ritchie, Charles. *Diplomatic Passport*. Toronto 1981

– *Storm Signals*. Toronto 1983

Robinson, H. Basil, 'Diefenbaker and the Nuclear Weapons Controversy,' paper given at conference 'Canada, the United States, and the Atlantic Alliance' organized by Centre on Foreign Policy and Federalism, University of Waterloo, and other sponsors, 20–23 May 1987, Toronto

Roy, Reginald, H. *For Most Conspicuous Gallantry: A Biography of Major-General George R. Pearkes, VC, through Two World Wars*. Vancouver 1977

Saywell, John T., ed. *The Canadian Annual Review*. Toronto 1960, 1961, 1962, 1963

Sévigny, Pierre. *This Game of Politics*. Toronto 1965

Sorenson, Theodore, C. *Kennedy*. New York 1965

Stursberg, Peter. *Diefenbaker: Leadership Gained, 1956–1962*. Toronto 1975

– *Leadership Lost, 1962–1967*. Toronto 1976

Index

Picture Credits

Every reasonable precaution has been taken to trace the owners of copyright material to secure permission and to make due acknowledgment; any error or omission will be gladly rectified in future editions.

In his element: Canada Pictures Ltd; a cordial moment: NA/PA-115202, Duncan Cameron photograph; with Léger and Bryce: Diefenbaker Centre 3966; Sidney Smith: National Film Board, NA/C-37751; Norman Robertson: Eric Coop, courtesy Mrs N.A. Robertson; with Macmillan: Diefenbaker Centre; with de Gaulle: NA/PA-117500; with Adenauer: Diefenbaker Centre; with Ayub Khan, with Nehru, with Menzies: Dominion Wide Photographs Ltd, Jim Thomson photographs, courtesy Diefenbaker Centre; 'Explorer' in Orbit: *London Free Press*, 29 Oct. 1958; P.M. Rides His First Elephant: *Saskatoon Star-Phoenix*, 27 Nov. 1958; Mr. Diefenbaker – I Presume? and Any Comments, Gentlemen? *Halifax Chronicle-Herald*, 3 and 13 Dec. 1958; with Massey and Green: NA/PA-114895, Duncan Cameron photograph; Chief Many Spotted Horses: Sir Alexander Galt Museum Archives, Lethbridge; with Kennedy: NA/PA-154665, Duncan Cameron photograph; with Robinson: author's collection